Analysing Academic Writing

Open Linguistics Series

Series Editor
Robin Fawcett, University of Wales, Cardiff

This series is 'open' in two senses. First, it provides a forum for works associated with any school of linguistics or with none. Most practising linguists have long since outgrown the unhealthy assumption that theorizing about language should be left to those working in the generativist–formalist paradigm. Today large and increasing numbers of scholars are seeking to understand the nature of language by exploring one or other of various cognitive models of language, or in terms of the communicative use of language, or both. This series is playing a valuable part in re-establishing the traditional 'openness' of the study of language. The series includes many studies that are in, or on the borders of, various functional theories of language, and especially (because it has been the most widely used of these) Systemic Functional Linguistics. The general trend of the series has been towards a functional view of language, but this simply reflects the works that have been offered to date. The series continues to be open to all approaches, including works in the generativist–formalist tradition.

The second way in which the series is 'open' is that it encourages studies that open out 'core' linguistics in various ways: to encompass discourse and the description of natural texts; to explore the relationships between linguistics and its neighbouring disciplines – psychology, sociology, philosophy, cultural and literary studies – and to apply it in fields such as education, language pathology and law.

Recent titles in this series

Classroom Discourse Analysis: A Functional Perspective, Frances Christie
Construing Experience through Meaning: A Language-based Approach to Cognition, M.A.K. Halliday and Christian M.I.M. Matthiessen
Cognition, M.A.K. Halliday and Christian M.I.M. Matthiessen
Culturally Speaking: Managing Rapport through Talk across Cultures, Helen Spencer-Oatey (ed.)
Development of Language, Geoff Williams and Annabelle Lukin (eds)
Educating Eve: The 'Language Instinct' Debate, Geoffrey Sampson
Empirical Linguistics, Geoffrey Sampson
Genre and Institutions: Social Processes in the Workplace and School, Frances Christie and J.R. Martin (eds)
The Intonations Systems of English, Paul Trench
Language, Education and Discourse, Joseph A. Foley (ed.)
Language Policy in Britain and France: The Processes of Policy, Dennis Ager
Multifactorial Analysis in Corpus Linguistics: A Study of Particle Placement, Stefan Thomas Gries
Pedagogy and the Shaping of Consciousness: Linguistic and Social Processes, Frances Christie (ed.)
Register Analysis: Theory and Practice, Mohsen Ghadessy (ed.)
Relations and Functions within and around Language, Peter H. Fries, Michael Cummings, David G. Lockwood and William Spruiell (eds)
Researching Language in Schools and Communities: Functional Linguistic Perspectives, Len Unsworth (ed.)
Summary Justice: Judges Address Juries, Paul Robertshaw
Syntactic Analysis and Description: A Constructional Approach, David G. Lockwood
Words, Meaning and Vocabulary: An Introduction to Modern English Lexicology, Howard Jackson and Etienne Zé Amvela
Working with Discourse: Meaning beyond the Clause, J.R. Martin and David Rose

Analysing Academic Writing:

Contextualized Frameworks

Edited by Louise J. Ravelli and Robert A. Ellis

continuum

Continuum
The Tower Building   15 East 26th Street
11 York Road   New York
London SE1 7NX   NY 10010

First published 2004 by Continuum
This paperback published in 2005

British Library Cataloguing-in-Publication Data
A catalogue record for this book is available from the British Library.

ISBN 0-8264-6107-7 (HB)
    0-8264-8802-1 (PB)

Library of Congress Cataloging-in-Publication Data
A catalog record for this book is available from the Library of Congress.

Typeset by BookEns Ltd, Royston, Herts
Printed and bound in Great Britain by MPG Books Ltd, Bodmin, Cornwall

To our parents,
Nancy and Dolf, Betty and Rex,
for bringing us to the door of Higher Education.

Contents

List of tables — ix

List of figures — xi

Contributors — xiii

Acknowledgements — xvi

1 Introduction — 1

2 Patterns of engagement: dialogic features and L2 undergraduate
  writing — 5
  Ken Hyland

3 Managing attitude in undergraduate academic writing: a focus
  on the introductions to research reports — 24
  Susan Hood

4 Scholar or consultant? Author-roles of student writers in
  German business writing — 45
  Helmut Gruber

5 Word power: negotiating success in a first-year sociology essay — 66
  Sue Starfield

6 The exegesis as a genre: an ethnographic examination — 84
  Brian Paltridge

7 Signalling the organization of written texts: hyper-Themes in
  management and history essays — 104
  Louise J. Ravelli

8 Developing discipline-specific writing: an analysis of
  undergraduate geography essays — 131
  Ann Hewings

 9 IELTS as preparation for tertiary writing: distinctive
interpersonal and textual strategies 153
Caroline Coffin and Ann Hewings

10 Technical writing in a second language: the role of grammatical
metaphor 172
Mary J. Schleppegrell

11 Problems with the metaphorical reconstrual of meaning in
Chinese EFL learners' expositions 190
Youping Chen and Joseph A. Foley

12 Supporting genre-based literacy pedagogy with technology – the
implications for the framing and classification of the pedagogy 210
Robert A. Ellis

13 Teaching academic writing on screen: a search for best practice 233
Helen Drury

14 Learning to write in the disciplines: the application of systemic
functional linguistic theory to the teaching and research of
student writing 254
Janet Jones

 Index 275

List of tables

2.1 Frequency of engagement features in articles and student reports (per 10,000 words)   10
2.2 Frequency of engagement features in student reports (per 10,000 words)   11
2.3 Overall functions of directives by genre (per cent)   17

3.1 Categories and examples of attitude   27
3.2 Examples of instances of evaluation oriented to either FD or FR   29

4.1 Epistemic and deontic modality in the students' texts   50
4.2 Overall frequencies of epistemic and deontic modals in different parts of the texts   51
4.3 Occupational wishes of the seminar students (N=20)   61

6.1 Titles of the exegeses and their visual projects   91

8.1 Summary of Theme choices analysed and coding system used   138
8.2 Theme choice analysis I   139
8.3 Theme choice analysis II: textual and interpersonal thematic elements within the multiple Theme category   140

9.1 Theme patterning in student test essays   158

10.1 Expectations for the laboratory report   175
10.2 Roles of grammatical metaphor   186

11.1 Sampling of texts across genre and university   194
11.2 Grammatical problems with 'favourite clause type' construction across genre   204

12.1 The double classification and framing potential of genre-based literacy pedagogy   214
12.2 The assessment framework of plant science and physiology   215
12.3 Examples of the writing tasks in the scientific writing portfolio   216

12.4 Records of postings made by students on the topic of plant
     growth regulators   223
12.5 A framework indicating the potential impact of technology on
     genre-based literacy pedagogy   227
12.6 Distribution of the classroom level discourse region of PSP over
     three tutorials – substantive and technical discourses   229

List of figures

2.1 Categories of directives   17

3.1 Model of Appraisal   26
3.2 The system of graduation with examples of graduation evoking
     attitude   28

7.1 Synoptic view of the first management essay (M1)   106
7.2 Dynamic view of the first management essay (M1):
     logico-semantic relations   108
7.3 Dynamic view of the second management essay (M2
     partial)   109
7.4 Dynamic view of the first history essay (H1)   110
7.5 Extracts from H2   111
7.6 Extracts from H3   112
7.7 Organizing Vocabulary   117
7.8 Retrospective and prospective connections   119
7.9 Colligational patterns   119
7.10 Colligational patterns: lexically specific post-modification
     (Elaborating)   120
7.11 Colligational patterns: textual markers
     (Extending)   121
7.12 Colligational patterns: pre-modification and textual markers
     (Extending)   121
7.13 Colligational patterns: grammatical metaphor (Enhancing)   122

9.1 An outline of APPRAISAL resources in English   160

11.1 Congruent and metaphorical realization of meaning in
     lexicogrammar   191
11.2 Generic structures   193
11.3 Taxonomy of the types of things   195
11.4 Identifying relational process (elaboration)   198
11.5 Attributive relational process   199
11.6 Construing words as thing or as the quality of a thing   200

11.7 The ambiguity of the grammatical functions of some elements
     in Chinese   202
11.8 Different ways of construing meaning in Chinese   203

12.1 A genre-based teaching and learning model   212
12.2 A continuum of weak and strong framing   213
12.3 The structure of the scientific writing database   218
12.4 Database item 06ex.02: structure of a paragraph on the topic of
     genetics   219
12.5 Database item 06ex.03: focus in paragraphs under the topic
     of genetics   219
12.6 Plant science and physiology web site – history of use by
     student X   220
12.7 Plant science and physiology web site – history of use by
     student Y   221
12.8 Database item 06.01: passive constructions under the topic of
     'genetics'   225
12.9 Database item 02.27: passive voice use under the topic of 'plant
     nutrition'   226

13.1 Continuum of contexts for teaching academic writing at
     university   235
13.2 The teaching/learning cycle in first-year biology at Sydney
     University   236
13.3 Flow-chart illustrating the teaching/learning cycle behind the
     on-screen writing reports at university program   237
13.4 Navigation design for the laboratory report writing program in
     biological sciences and biochemistry   241
13.5 Part of the screen display, making explicit the information
     structure of the conclusion of the chemical engineering
     laboratory report. The feedback is in the lower half of the screen. 243
13.6 Adaptive hyperlink prototype design for laboratory report for
     chemistry   247

14.1 Teaching students to write a literature review: the role of SFL
     and collaboration with staff in the disciplines   264
14.2 Extract from Part 2 of the LC course *Writing a Literature Review* 265
14.3 Criteria and sub-criteria for Area C (MASUS)   267

Contributors

Youping Chen is Associate Professor in the Management School, Shanghai Jiaotong University, teaching Business English and Business Communication. He has over 15 years' experience teaching English as a foreign language (EFL) in China, and his current research interest is the application of systemic functional theories to EFL teaching and research.

Caroline Coffin is Lecturer at the Centre for Language and Communications at the Open University, UK. Her area of specialization is educational linguistics and the role that language plays in the teaching and learning of disciplinary knowledge. Currently she is carrying out research into the affordances of electronic conferencing in the context of distance and higher education. Her most recent publication is *Teaching Academic Writing: A Toolkit for Higher Education* (co-authored with M.J. Curry, S. Goodman, A. Hewings, T. Lillis and J. Swann (Routledge 2003).

Helen Drury is Lecturer in the Learning Centre at the University of Sydney. She has taught academic literacy for more than 15 years in Australia, the UK and Indonesia. She is currently involved in developing and evaluating online learning programs for report writing in the disciplines. Her main research interests are scientific and technical writing, genre and multimodal analysis and online learning of academic literacy.

Robert Ellis is Senior Lecturer at the Institute of Teaching and Learning, University of Sydney. His research interests are learning, linguistics and technology, particularly how a linguistic approach to researching learning can complement other research methodologies such as Student Learning Research. He previously taught and researched English for Academic Purposes and Information and Communication Technologies in Learning at the University of NSW and the University of Western Sydney.

Joseph Foley is currently a language specialist with the Southeast Asian Ministry of Education Organization, Regional Language Centre based in Singapore. Prior to this he taught at the National University of Singapore for 20 years, mainly in the areas of systemic functional linguistics and socio-psycholinguistics. He is editor of the *RELC Journal* and has published extensively in the field of applied linguistics.

Helmut Gruber is Associate Professor of Applied Linguistics at the Linguistics Department of Vienna University. He has undertaken research on prejudice and racism in language, conflict communication and mass media communication and published widely on these topics. His current research interests include German academic writing and language use in the New Media. He teaches academic writing for young scholars at the Viennese Business University.

Ann Hewings is Lecturer in Language and Communications at the Open University, UK. Her research interests are in the area of discourse analysis and particularly academic literacy and disciplinary variation at tertiary level. Recently she has begun researching the relationship between students' writing in online electronic conferences and their ultimate essay sub-missions. Before lecturing she taught English in Britain and around the world and worked for some years at COBUILD developing corpus-based English language reference materials.

Susan Hood is Senior Lecturer in the Faculty of Education at the University of Technology, Sydney, and her current research brings together her inter-ests in discourse analysis, systemic functional linguistics and TESOL teacher education. Previously, Susan was Principal Lecturer in the Department of English at the Hong Kong Polytechnic University. She recently co-authored a preparatory textbook on academic reading, *Academic Encounters: Life in Society* for Cambridge University Press.

Ken Hyland is Professor at the School of Culture, Language and Communi-cation, Institute of Education, University of London. He has taught EFL and Applied Linguistics for 25 years in Africa, Asia, the Middle East and the Pacific. He has published over 90 articles and chapters on language teaching and academic writing. His books include *Hedging in Scientific Research Articles* (Benjamins 1998), *Disciplinary Discourses* (Longman 2000), *Teaching and Researching Writing* (Longman 2002), and *Second Language Writing* (Cambridge University Press 2003). He is co-editor of the *Journal of English for Academic Purposes* (with Liz Hamp-Lyons) and reviews editor of *English for Specific Purposes*.

Janet Jones is Lecturer in the Learning Centre at the University of Sydney, and was previously Head of the Centre. She has had over 20 years' experi-ence teaching and researching academic writing. She has contributed to research and practice in the fields of accounting and pharmacy education, generic attributes and English for academic purposes. For a number of years she has been actively engaged in researching the application of systemic functional linguistics (SFL) to academic literacies. Her current research interest is multimodality and hypertextuality in computer-based resources in science at university.

Brian Paltridge is Director of Graduate Studies and Associate Professor in TESOL in the Faculty of Education and Social Work at the University of

Sydney. He is author of *Genre, Frames and Writing in Research Settings* (John Benjamins 1997), *Making Sense of Discourse Analysis* (AEE Publishers 2000), and *Genre and the Language Learning Classroom* (University of Michigan Press 2001). His main areas of research are academic literacies, thesis and dissertation writing, and genre-based language teaching.

Louise Ravelli is Senior Lecturer in Linguistics at the University of New South Wales. Her research interests include systemic functional linguistics and multimodal discourse analysis, and she is primarily interested in the communication demands of specialized language contexts, such as academic writing and museum communication.

Mary Schleppegrell is Associate Professor of Linguistics at the University of California, Davis, USA. Her research interests include functional grammar, educational linguistics, and the challenges of academic language for second language students, especially the linguistic challenges of science and history discourse. She is co-editor, with M. Cecilia Colombi, of *Developing Advanced Literacy in First and Second Languages: Meaning with Power* (Erlbaum 2002), and is the author of a forthcoming volume from Erlbaum, *The Language of Schooling: A Functional Linguistics Perspective.*

Sue Starfield is Director of the Learning Centre at the University of New South Wales and an adjunct Senior Lecturer in the Department of Linguistics. Prior to moving to Australia, she taught for over 15 years in South Africa, mainly at the University of the Witwatersrand in Johannesburg. She currently teaches thesis writing to PhD students and is involved in programme development to enhance students' successful access to academic skills. Her current research interests include academic writing, issues of identity in academic writing and language learning, and thesis writing.

Acknowledgements

We would like to extend our thanks to Emeritus Professor Frances Christie, who provided impetus for the idea of this volume, and to those colleagues who acted as anonymous referees for papers.

1 Introduction

In the context of ongoing and focused attention on the processes and practices of academic writing, this volume reflects in particular on the writing of novices, that is students, rather than experts. The analysis of student writing is used as a point of departure for reflecting on the particular demands of this context, highlighting some of the ways in which students negotiate identity, construct roles and develop argumentative positions, engage in technologically supported writing processes, and deal with the demands of specialized disciplines and of a language which may not be their own.

The research in this volume is contextualized in a variety of ways. First, the complex phenomenon of language is contextualized in relation to a theoretical framework which views texts as intimately related to their contexts. Context is theorized in a number of complementary ways in this volume, focusing largely on systemic functional linguistics, but including related social-constructivist frameworks and more generalized perspectives on ethnography. These approaches are consistent in their concern for a rich account of text-context relations, one which can account for meanings across a wide range of dimensions, from the overall purpose of a text to its various inflections for ideational, interpersonal, and textual meanings.

The second way in which the research is contextualized is in terms of the particular type of student writing which is examined in each chapter. The chapters demonstrate a broad range of writing contexts, in terms of level, discipline, task and language background. In terms of level, both pre-tertiary, undergraduate and postgraduate writings are examined, although there is particular emphasis on undergraduate writing, and some of the changing demands of different levels within that, such as first versus final year. A wide range of disciplines are examined, from plant science, to business, to history, geography, art and design, and biology, each problematizing the ways in which these specific disciplines shape students' potential for making meaning appropriately. As well as variation in discipline, there is also variation in the overall task, or genre, demanded of students, from expository and report writing, to exegesis, to contributions to online discussions. And importantly, the chapters demonstrate a wide range of language contexts within which learning takes place, from the experience of first language speakers, such as

English speakers in Australia, or German speakers in Austria, to that of second and foreign language speakers, such as immigrant students in the USA, or Chinese students learning English in Hong Kong. These first and second/foreign language contexts are drawn from a wide geographical domain, including Australia, Austria, China and Hong Kong, South Africa, the UK and the USA.

A third interpretation of context in this volume is the overall focus of the chapter, in terms of a relative emphasis on theory and practice. For each chapters, and in the context of their relevant frameworks, these two perspectives cannot be separated. A theory only has purpose when it can be used to illuminate analysis, and analysis only has validity when it relates to broader issues accounting for a variety of texts, not just one. Even so, each chapter emphasizes these aspects to different degrees: some focus on descriptions of particular lexicogrammatical and discursive resources, enhancing our theoretical knowledge in these areas; others focus on accounting for what students are doing in the process of writing, enhancing our knowledge of actual texts and their relevant discursive practices. It is hoped that both emphases will enable reflection on what it is that we do as teachers, and provide both theoretical and practical insights to enhance processes of teaching and learning in academic contexts.

Specifically, the chapters take up the following issues. The first group of chapters has a particular focus on interpersonal meanings, in terms of issues of identity and the construction of writer roles. They take up complementary theoretical perspectives on interpersonal meaning, including systemic functional linguistics, social-constructivist frameworks, and ethnography. Hyland examines how undergraduates in Hong Kong choose to play out writer/reader relations in the genre of their final-year reports, in terms of their engagement with their audience in an ongoing dialogue which crafts agreement with their argumentative position. Hyland provides evidence that the students' meaning potential is strongly constrained by the genre and by their awareness of the assessment constraints and their role as novices within their disciplines. Hood focuses in particular on the system of APPRAISAL[1] as a resource for managing attitude and constructing an evaluative stance in an otherwise 'objective' text. As well as examining the general system of APPRAISAL, the chapter extends our understanding of the ways in which APPRAISAL choices intersect with aspects of Field, and how they unfold dynamically in a text, creating a particular prosody which may colour whole segments of a text. In an examination of German speakers in an Austrian University, Gruber focuses on the lexicogrammatical resource of *modality*, demonstrating the particular patterns which are distinctive to a business-writing context, and arguing that students' use of this resource demonstrates a tension between their potential roles as scholar or as consultant. A deep perspective on the context of identity is demonstrated by Starfield, who complements textual analysis with an ethnographic perspective, revealing some aspects of the complex socio-political positioning of a black student in a South African University. Writing in first-year sociology, this ESL student is seen to successfully negotiate potentially contradictory aspects of his positioning as a student and as a participant in South African society. Ethnography is also drawn upon by Paltridge, who undertakes a 'textography' of the exegesis in art and design Masters degrees. While closely related to the thesis genre, Paltridge demonstrates the significant ways in which the exegesis is also different, in terms of its academic setting, its contextualization of research, and its disciplinary boundaries.

The next group of chapters has a primarily textual focus, examining the various ways in which the management of textual resources is an issue in academic writing. Ravelli explores the textual resource of hyper-Themes[2] in first-year management and history essays, extending the lexicogrammatical description of this resource in relation to their intersection with particular argumentative and disciplinary frameworks. Hewings also investigates Theme as a textual resource, focusing on the discipline of Geography and contrasting the ways in which novice first-year and more experienced third-year students make use of the resource, reflecting their relative appropriation of disciplinary discourse practices and gradual development of an appropriately evaluative voice. The textual and the interpersonal metafunctions are brought together by Coffin and Hewings, who examine the intersection of Theme and APPRAISAL resources in IELTS University entrance tests, revealing an interpersonal positioning which is somewhat different to that expected in actual academic contexts, but which nevertheless has value and relevance within its institutional context. Both Schleppegrell and Chen and Foley focus on grammatical metaphor as a textual resource. Schleppegrell examines lab reports written in upper-level chemical engineering by second language speakers in the USA, who may not have had the chance to develop first language literacy skills. She shows that, even after several years of academic experience, some linguistic resources remain a challenge, especially grammatical metaphor as a resource for developing technicality and constructing an appropriate voice. Chen and Foley demonstrate how the expository writing of EFL students in China is affected by L1 interference. While the students make an appropriate attempt to use grammatical metaphor, and so achieve a more academic style of writing, they still have problems in selecting effective lexicogrammatical resources to realize the complex meanings at stake.

While all the chapters in this volume have pedagogic implications, the last group focus explicitly on this dimension. Ellis and Drury each examine some of the pedagogic implications of supporting writing with technology. Ellis uses Bernstein's tools of framing and classification as a way of understanding the impact of technology within a genre-based literacy pedagogy, in a first-year plant science course. He shows the potential for student control over learning to increase with the use of well-designed technologically supported writing experiences. Drury uses Laurillard's conversational framework as a way of reflecting on the design of technologically supported writing experiences in biology, focusing on the special challenges of this context for issues of multiliteracy, and identifying key principles for designing technologically supported writing experiences. Jones provides an overview of how the theoretical framework of systemic functional linguistics has shaped the research and pedagogical practice in one student learning centre in Australia, providing resources to enable students to engage with many of the complex linguistic challenges dealt with elsewhere in the volume.

Together, these studies provide new insights into our developing understanding of academic writing and its importance in the academic lives of students, teachers and researchers. We trust that this volume will make a useful contribution to the theory, teaching and practice of academic writing, and ultimately help students better negotiate the complex demands of this context, in its many inflections.

Louise J. Ravelli
Robert A. Ellis

Notes

1 Small caps are used to distinguish APPRAISAL systems as semantic systems.
2 Functional elements, such as Theme, are labelled with an initial capital letter.

2 Patterns of engagement: dialogic features and L2 undergraduate writing

Ken Hyland

1 Introduction

In recent years there has been a growing interest in the interactive and rhetorical character of academic writing, expanding the focus of study beyond the ideational dimension of texts to the ways they function at the interpersonal level. Such a view argues that academic writers do not simply produce texts that plausibly represent an external reality, but use language to acknowledge, construct and negotiate social relations. The ability of writers to offer a credible representation of themselves and their work, by claiming solidarity with readers, evaluating their material and acknowledging alternative views, is a defining feature of successful academic writing. Controlling the level of personality in a text is central to maintaining interaction with readers and building a convincing argument. Put succinctly, every successful text must display the writer's awareness of both its readers and its consequences. This concern with the interpersonal has always been central to both systemic functional and social-constructionist frameworks, which share the view that all language use is related to specific social, cultural and educational contexts. These approaches have sought to elaborate the ways by which interpersonal meanings are expressed, describing such linguistic resources as *evaluation* (Hunston and Thompson 2000), *appraisal* (Martin 2000; White forthcoming), *stance* (Biber and Finegan 1989; Hyland 1999) and *interpersonal metadiscourse* (Crismore 1989; Hyland 1998).

Because this work is still relatively new, much of it has tended to concentrate on mass audience genres such as literary, journalistic and broadcast texts which are likely to yield the richest crop of explicitly interactive features. But while an understanding of these resources can be invaluable to novice writers, students writing in a foreign language need to know what features are typical, rather than which are possible, as the texts they are expected to read and write at university offer them far less freedom to position themselves interpersonally than these public genres. In this chapter I will therefore explore how some interpersonal resources are used by final-year undergraduates in a Hong Kong university, attending mainly to features of engagement: the ways writers explicitly bring readers into a dialogue.

2 Interactional resources in academic writing

Although academic writing is often distinguished by its apparent absence of explicit appraisal and attitude, it is nevertheless clearly structured to evoke affinity and engagement (Hyland 2000; Swales 1990). In presenting informational content, writers must also adopt interactional and evaluative positions, anticipating readers' expectations and responses to participate in a virtual dialogue with them. To view writing as interactive, then, means examining discourse features in terms of the writer's projection of the perceptions, interests, and needs of a potential audience.

While the idea of audience is elusive, it represents the writer's awareness of the circumstances which define a rhetorical context and the ways that the current text is multiply aligned with other texts. Writers construct an audience by drawing on their knowledge of earlier texts and relying on readers' abilities to recognize intertextuality between texts (Bakhtin 1986). Because readers can always refute claims, this gives them an active and consti-tutive role in how writers construct such claims, ensuring that arguments incorporate viewpoints from prior texts. Arguments and interpretations thus need to be presented in ways that readers are likely to find both credible and persuasive, and so writers must draw on recognizably appropriate means of expressing their views, representing themselves, and engaging their audiences. By anticipating readers' background knowledge, interests, and interpersonal expectations, a writer can seek to monitor their response to a text and manage their impression of the writer. At the risk of oversimplifying, we can see writers occupied with two broad areas of interaction management, corresponding to the categories of *stance* and *engagement,* oriented to the writer and the reader respectively and represented by overlapping clusters of rhetorical and linguistic strategies.

Stance concerns the ways writers explicitly intrude into the discourse to stamp their personal authority or beliefs onto their arguments. It refers to the features writers use to annotate their propositions to convey epistemic and affective judgements, opinions and degrees of commitment to what they say, boosting or toning down claims and criticisms, expressing surprise or importance, intruding though self-mention, and commenting on their pre-sentations. Stance thus refers to *writer*-oriented features of the dialogue and highlights how authors construct a credible academic identity (Hyland 1999, 2000).

Engagement is the other side of the coin, where writers intervene to actively pull readers along or position them, focusing their attention, recognizing their uncertainties, including them as discourse participants and guiding them to interpretations. Here writers explicitly mark the presence of what Thompson (2001) calls the 'reader-in-the-text'. While this can also be achieved by stance features, which necessarily presuppose readers' know-ledge and beliefs if they are to be effective, the most obvious indication of writers' dialogic awareness occurs where they overtly refer to readers, asking questions, making suggestions and addressing them directly (Hyland 2001).

Here writers introduce readers as real players in the discourse rather than merely as implied observers of the discussion.

This conception of engagement differs somewhat from that discussed in systemic functional language literature, particularly by Martin (2000) and White (2002), who use the term to refer to the options for indicating writers' commitment to their expressions of emotions, judgements and evaluations in a semantic system called APPRAISAL. Appraisal is thus more closely related to what I have here called stance, and engagement to the metadiscoursal resources for conceding, averring, attributing, hedging, boosting and otherwise modalizing the status of their utterances to negotiate arguability. While there is a great deal of overlap between this view and my own, Martin and White are largely concerned with representing the writers' attitude or opinion towards the propositions they are setting out, rather than with exploring the ways that language is used to anticipate possible reader objections, acknowledge their interpersonal concerns, and explicitly mark and bring readers into their texts.

Obviously this distinction between stance and engagement is often a fine one as interactional devices often have the potential to both elaborate the writer's positions and position the reader. However, it does seem to be a distinction worth making as it tends to involve different resources and has generally received less attention from teachers and applied linguists. As a result, establishing an appropriate relationship with one's readers can pose a considerable challenge to non-native English speaking undergraduates. On the periphery of their academic communities and frequently taught to keep their writing impersonal and objective, students often find themselves at a rhetorical disadvantage, unable to communicate appropriate engagement in their assignments. English for Academic Purpose (EAP) teachers' efforts to create greater 'reader awareness' among L2 writers typically involve tasks which stress exemplification and organization, ideational and textual strategies rather than interpersonal ones, and the situation is not helped by the fact that we know little about how writer–reader relationships are typically managed in academic texts. In what follows I outline some features of engagement, and go on to discuss how a group of Hong Kong students use these dialogic resources.

3 Some features of engagement

The literature, particularly previous research into interactive features of academic writing (e.g. Hyland 2000, 2001) and grammars (Biber *et al.* 1999; Halliday 1994), suggests a range of forms that signal reader engagement. Illustrated below by examples from a large corpus of research articles, these features are: (1) interrogatives; (2) inclusive first person pronouns, second person pronouns and items referring to readers; (3) directives, including imperatives, obligation modals referring to actions of the reader (*must, ought, should, have to, need to*), and adjectival predicate controlling a complement *to-* clause directing readers to a particular action; (4) references to shared knowledge; and (5) asides addressed to the reader, marked off from the ongoing flow of text:

(1) Well, can pictures represent the absurd?   (Philosophy)
     Do you agree with me?   (Sociology)

(2) Unless your application requires all or   (Mechanical Engineering)
     most of these advantages you should
     consider natural gas-fired infrared
     heating.
     As we can see, their algorithm is practical   (Electronic Engineering)
     for solving the problems with up to 35
     jobs.
     Some readers will want to argue that this   (Sociology)
     is a comparative analysis of
     neighborhood associations more than
     social movements.

(3) We must take into account the finite time   (Physics)
     W shown in Figure 2b.
     Note that xylem pressure (tension)   (Biology)
     values are quoted as absolute pressures.
     However, it is important to note that our   (Business Studies)
     discussion is not intended to reflect how
     strongly these feelings are held.

(4) The obviously correct relation between   (Physics)
     these two lengths is a=b.

(5) And – as I believe many TESOL   (Applied Linguistics)
     professionals will readily acknowledge –
     critical thinking has now begun to make
     its mark, particularly in the area of L2
     composition.

In these expert texts, there are two main rhetorical purposes of these appeals to the reader.

1 The first is interpersonal and acknowledges the need to meet readers'
   expectations of inclusion. Here, we find readers addressed as participants
   in an argument with inclusive or second person pronouns and interjections to effect interpersonal solidarity and joint disciplinary
   membership.
2 The second purpose seems more to do with rhetorically positioning the
   audience. This recognizes the reader's role as a potential negater of
   claims by predicting and responding to possible objections and alternative
   interpretations. Here the writer captures the audience's attention and
   selectively focuses them on key issues, pulling them into the discourse at

critical points to guide them to particular interpretations with questions, directives and references to shared knowledge.

These broad functions are not clearly distinct, of course, as writers invariably use language to solicit reader collusion on more than one front simultaneously, arousing interest, establishing solidarity and credibility, anticipating objections, and so on. However, these two overarching purposes allow us to see some of the ways writers project readers into their texts and to compare the rhetorical patterns of such engagement in different genres and contexts.

4 Methods and corpora

The study reported here is based on an analysis of dialogic features in a corpus of 64 project reports written by final-year (third-year) Hong Kong undergraduates and interviews with students in eight fields.

The final-year report is a major assessment genre in most Hong Kong universities. It is the product of a directed research project spanning an entire year with credit for two courses. Students are assisted by a supervisor who, through regular individual consultations, approves their proposal, guides their research, and monitors their progress. The purposes of the projects are to enable students to apply theories and methods learned in their courses and demonstrate ability to effectively review literature, conduct research, analyse results and present findings. Reports are typically between 8,000 and 13,000 words long and follow guidelines based on the research paper formats of the discipline. The reports are assessed by two examiners in terms of how well students meet the objectives of the project and on the quality of the written work. This, then, is a high-stakes genre for students and is by far the most substantial and sustained piece of writing that they will do in their undergraduate careers.

Reports were collected from a broad cross-section of disciplines: biology (Bio), mechanical engineering (ME), information systems (IS), business studies (Bus), TESL, economics (Econ), public administration (PA), and social sciences (SS). These reports were scanned to produce an electronic corpus of 630,000 words. A much larger parallel corpus of published academic writing was also collected, comprising 240 research articles from ten leading journals in each of eight related disciplines, a total of 1.3 million words. The disciplines were selected to relate to the student disciplines as closely as possible and the journals themselves were familiar to faculty and students alike, being regularly recommended to students in reading lists and by project supervisors.

The purpose of this second corpus was not to evaluate learner performance. Novice and professional writers differ considerably in their understandings of academic conventions and practices, making direct comparisons unhelpful. The study of parallel corpora, however, can provide information about what different groups of language users actually *do*. They are useful because of what they tell us of different writers' linguistic and interactive schemata, in this case helping to throw light on student perceptions of academic conventions and how these reflect and construct a particular context. Not only are the patterns of use in 'expert' texts likely to contribute to supervisors' understandings of appropriacy and conventions of good disciplinary writing, they also provide the background by which we can understand learner practices. So, by using a corpus twice as large as the student database it was possible to identify expert academic practices while commenting on their use by a specific student population.

The two corpora were searched for over 100 items seen as potentially productive of initiating writer–reader dialogues using *WordPilot 2000*, a commercially available concordancer. All examples were then examined to ensure they addressed readers. All instances that referred to other participants or expressed the writer's stance were eliminated. The corpus data were supplemented with focus group interviews with final-year students from these disciplines using a semi-structured format of open-ended prompts to explore subjects' practices and their impressions of disciplinary conventions. The results are discussed below.

5 Patterns of engagement

Frequency counts reveal the extent of dialogic interactions in the two corpora, suggesting that academic writing is not the impersonal monologue it is often depicted to be. The target features occurred about 24 times in each report, about one every two pages or so, with inclusive first person pronouns and directives amounting to about two-thirds of all devices.[1] As Table 2.1 shows, however, this is considerably less than in the research articles, which contained well over twice as many devices overall.

The results also show some interesting cross-discipline comparisons. Few student writers made personal asides to readers or addressed them using second person pronouns, for instance, and directives were the most common device in almost all fields. More obvious, however, are the disciplinary variations with, for instance, students in Information Systems and

Table 2.1 Frequency of engagement features in articles and student reports (per 10,000 words)

Corpus	Questions	Inclusive Pronouns	2nd person Pronouns	Directives	Shared Knowledge	Asides	Totals
Student reports	4.3	5.6	0.5	10.6	2.5	0.3	23.9
Published articles	5.0	21.5	2.0	19.0	4.9	1.1	53.5

Mechanical Engineering employing almost twice as many devices than those in economics and Marketing (see Table 2.2). Questions and inclusive pronouns were most frequent in the more discursive soft fields, while over 60 per cent of directives were used by science and engineering students.

These distributions broadly reflect those in the professional genre (see Hyland 2001), although with far lower frequencies, revealing something of how different disciplinary and genre contexts influence argument and interaction. Academic disciplines differ along a variety of dimensions, but one principled means of characterizing their textual practices is to associate discourse features with the domains of hard and soft knowledge fields (sciences/engineering and social sciences/humanities). Admittedly, this distinction is not without problems, and runs the risk of reductionism, but it is a tangible categorization which represents actors' own perceptions (Becher 1989; Hyland 2000). As we shall see below, it also provides a means of understanding writing behaviours in academic contexts.

6 Features soliciting reader solidarity

As noted above, while expert writers often employ personal pronouns and interjections to acknowledge and claim affinity with an active audience, these students significantly underused such features. In particular, they rarely addressed their readers directly by interrupting the ongoing discussion to initiate a brief interpersonal dialogue or offer a meta-comment on what they had said. For students this is a rather risky interactional strategy and, because it was generally avoided, I will focus on the use of pronouns in this section.

Table 2.2 Frequency of engagement features in student reports (per 10,000 words)

Discipline	Questions	Pronouns inclusive	Pronouns 2nd Person	Directives	Shared knowledge	Asides	Totals
Info Systems	2.2	3.7	2.0	24.5	3.5	0.0	35.9
Mechanical Eng	3.0	2.6	1.0	23.7	4.7	0.0	35.0
Social Sciences	8.8	6.3	0.0	7.7	0.3	0.2	23.3
Public Admin	6.0	10.0	0.9	3.3	2.0	0.7	22.9
TESL	6.7	3.3	0.0	9.2	2.8	0.0	22.0
Biology	1.0	5.3	0.0	11.9	1.7	0.3	20.2
Economics	1.5	3.1	0.0	8.9	3.8	1.0	18.3
Marketing	1.1	5.7	0.3	3.7	2.2	0.2	13.2
Overall	4.3	5.6	0.5	10.6	2.5	0.3	23.9

6.1 Second person pronouns

Perhaps the clearest textual acknowledgement of the reader, second person *you* and *your*, occur only rarely in the student corpus. On the face of it, *you* is the most interactive device in the writer's repertoire as it explicitly acknowledges the reader's presence. In (6), for example, we see readers addressed directly concerning how they might participate in the text:

(6)   Lastly, you will have a clear understanding on how the   (IS)
         application helps the children to learn in a more interested
         and interactive way in this report.
         This list is extensive but I am sure you can extend it.   (Bus)

The widespread avoidance of this use, however, suggests students' clear reluctance to engage readers in this way. In part, this may be because *you* implies a stark separation of writer and reader, implying a detachment which could sound offensive and which does little to draw readers into a collusive association. Perhaps, more importantly, the second person is largely a feature of familiar registers such as casual conversation, where it is 25 times more common than in academic writing, for instance (Biber *et al.* 1999: 334), and students are traditionally taught to avoid such informal features (Chang and Swales 1999). Students, in fact, often have firm views about what is actually appropriate:

> Science writing is neutral. I know my supervisor will read my project but I cannot talk to him like in the tutorial. I must just put down the facts without personal idea, just show that I understand the books and that I follow the method. (Bio student)

> In school we learn not to say 'I' or 'you' in our essays. I can use these when I write to my friend, but you don't see them in the formal essays I think. (Econ student)

You, then, conjures up informal or personal relationships for students. As a result, when it does occur, it is used with a different semantic reference, similar to the indefinite pronoun *one*, referring to people in general rather than specific discourse participants:

(7)   Whenever you run Windows or any Windows application,   (ME)
         you see the API in action.
         Thanks for the advancement in information technology,   (IS)
         today, you can get online and find the information you want
         and communicate with friends who live in foreign
         countries.

Here, *you* carries an interactive and encompassing meaning which shows writers seeking to engage with readers by recruiting them into a world of shared experiences.

6.2 Inclusive pronouns

The pronouns *we, us, our,* and *ours,* on the other hand, are far more frequent, comprising the most frequent engagement feature in the articles and representing almost a quarter of all devices in the student corpus. As noted above, inclusive pronouns were particularly common in the soft fields with over 70 per cent occurring in the social science and business reports. This is comparable to patterns in the professional corpus (Hyland 2001) and largely reflects the rhetorical conventions of different communities.

One important element of this distinction is that science students learn to see knowledge as emerging from relatively steady cumulative growth while soft-knowledge fields are typically more interpretative and less abstract. Science textbooks and lectures are shaped by disciplinary schemata which regard knowledge as the emergence of solutions to prior problems, with fairly clear-cut criteria of what is true and confidence in the procedures used to determine this. In contrast, social sciences students discover that truth is beset by contextual vagaries and that their disciplines offer less control of variables, more diversity of research outcomes and fewer unequivocal bases for accepting claims. Interpretation replaces truth, and the acceptance of claims depends on the elaboration of a discursive framework.

In other words, there are generally fewer unequivocal bases for accepting claims in the soft fields and so writers cannot generally rely with the same confidence on shared assumptions of tested procedures and proofs. Instead they must also appeal to the reader's willingness to follow their reasoning and must rely far more on focusing readers on the negotiation of the arguments themselves, rather than how they have processed and understood natural phenomena. Writers therefore generally work harder to engage their audience: readers must be drawn in and persuaded of the plausibility of the writer as well as the views they express, and inclusive pronouns work to accomplish this by inviting readers to pursue the argument with them.

Like their professional counterparts, some students sought to signal communality, textually constructing both the writer and the reader as participants with similar understandings which bound them in a single discipline:

(8)   As Psychologists we know that no matter which approach we   (SS)
       use to assess intelligence, we just focus on one aspect only:
       mental, biological or anthropological.
       Over time, we might expect that good grammar teaching   (TESL)
       will facilitate self-error correction of the learners.
       Customary, our understanding of the Japanese business   (Bus)
       mind as collectivism and vertical hierarchy and this is
       well-illustrated in their ringi-system of decision
       making.

More often, however, inclusive pronouns were employed to guide readers through an argument and towards a preferred interpretation, a practice which shades into explicit positioning of the reader:

(9)   Many people think that we should control scientific   (PA)
       progress and prohibit its application to new human
       problems. But if we do that, we are choosing to have all the
       misery and suffering that we could prevent by further
       scientific progress.
       Before we take a close look on the project, we may slow   (IS)
       down and think what impacts has been made to us by the
       fast developing Internet.
       However, from Fig. 6, we can see that the protective effect of (Bio)
       chorion was more effective at lower concentration of
       cadmium chloride solutions.
       If effective learning is dependent upon emotional growth,   (SS)
       then we need to understand the relationship between affect
       and learning.

Here writers seem to be engaging in a genuine dialogue with their imaginary readers, taking their position to suggest what any reasonable, thinking person might conclude or do, weaving the potential point of view of the audience into the argument to predict its thoughts and head off objections. This is, of course, a persuasive strategy as the writers are trying to secure agreement to their argument. It is also clear that this kind of appeal addresses the reader from a position of confidence, since there is a claiming of authority: the writer is inviting the reader into a shared journey of exploration, but taking responsibility for leading the expedition.

Many students were, however, reluctant to assert this kind of writer control, with the project reports containing only a quarter of the inclusive pronouns found in the published papers. Inclusive *we* appears to be inconsistent with the kinds of social relationships seen as having legitimacy in this context. All interpersonal choices are underpinned by institutional and intertextual constraints. Whether writers decide to establish an equal or hierarchical affiliation, adopt an involved or remote stance, or choose a convivial or indifferent interpersonal tenor, they will be influenced by the dominant ideologies of the genre they are employing. In this respect, the undergraduate project report has a clear audience and straightforward writer–reader relations, it is regarded as an assessment genre as much as a research one and so lacks the cultivated illusion of equality we find in peer-oriented research papers. These projects therefore pose students the problem of demonstrating an appropriate degree of rhetorical sophistication while recognizing readers' greater experience and knowledge of the field. As some students noted:

> I cannot tell my supervisor that he must think this or that. My idea may be wrong and not what my supervisor believes. He might have a different idea. (IS student)

> I must be careful when I write. I don't want to make myself important. Of course it is my project and my result, but I am just ordinary student. Not an academic scholar with lots of knowledge and confident for myself. (TESOL student)

As a result, we find that there was not only a large difference in overall frequencies, but also in the ways students chose to use inclusive pronouns in their texts. Rather than claim an uncertain equality, students largely withdrew from a role which guided or directed their reader–assessors, to one which simply shortened the distance between them. Writers simply chose to claim shared acceptance of a body of general knowledge with readers, drawing on common values and principles of reasonableness:

(10)   As our society needs literate and mathematical people who   (IS)
       are literate and educated, a multimedia educational system
       on Mathematics is proposed.
       By knowing the demand for private cars, government is able   (Econ)
       to make the above decisions that best fit our economy.
       With friends, we can talk about everything because we   (PA)
       already understand each other very well.

In sum, in this section I have shown that these Hong Kong undergraduates considerably underused the features found in professional writing to establish or maintain solidarity with readers. While there are broadly similar disciplinary distributions of dialogic features, the constraints of the genre are greater than those of the academic discipline, and students seem uncertain of the part they should play in such a dialogue. In the next section I turn to more explicitly persuasive features of engagement.

7 Crafting agreement

I turn now to strategies of explicit persuasion. Obviously the use of solidarity and inclusion discussed above are clearly not innocent of rhetorical intention, since writers often emphasize inclusion for explicitly persuasive ends, encouraging readers to see what they see and to draw the same conclusions. More overtly rhetorical strategies, however, draw on directives, interrogatives, and appeals to shared knowledge as a means of directly positioning readers, leading them to acceptance of the writer's claim.

7.1 Directives

The most frequent devices used to initiate reader participation in the student texts, comprising 45 per cent of all features, were directives. These are utterances which instruct the reader to perform an action or to see things in a way determined by the writer (Hyland 2002). As noted earlier, directive force is typically realized by the presence of an imperative, by a modal of obligation addressed to the reader, or by a predicative adjective expressing the writer's judgement of necessity/importance controlling a complement *to-* clause. What distinguishes these features is a clear reader-oriented focus and an explicit recognition of the dialogic dimension of argument as writers intervene to direct the reader to some action or understanding:

(11)   Firstly, assume that people with higher creative efficacy   (SS)
        score equivalent to people of high creativity.
        (See Appendix II for details of this).   (PA)
        Since a large amount of investment has been attracted, it is   (Econ)
        necessary to understand its impact on the economy.
        It is important to note that those explanation are limited to   (IS)
        their coatings tested.

Once again, the frequencies suggest something of the rhetorical purposes of writers and their sensitivity to readers, a point underlined by the fact that the student reports contained only about half the number of directives found in the articles (per 10,000 words). Since reports are written primarily to gain credit for a research project, an overuse of directives to impress one's examiner to act or see matters in a certain way might seem a perilous strategy. Directives convey a very definite attitude to the reader and so have the potential to seriously affect the writer–reader relationship, claiming an authority which these L2 students did not wish to display:

> I never use 'must' or tell to 'notice' or 'consider'. These words are too strong. It is like a demand and I cannot demand my supervisor to agree with me. (L2 student)

However, while directives are often seen as a way of constructing status differences in interaction along dimensions of social distance and relative power, it is clear just from the above examples that these forms exhibit considerable functional variety which can mitigate any threat to readers. In fact, we can classify directives according to three main forms of activity they direct readers to engage in: textual, physical and cognitive (Hyland 2002). First, directives allow academic writers to guide readers to some *textual act*, referring them to another part of the text or to another text. They can also be used to instruct readers to perform a *physical act*, either involving a research process or real-world action. Third, directives can steer readers to certain *cognitive acts*, where they are initiated into a new domain of argument, led through a line of reasoning, or directed to understand a point in a certain way. Figure 2.1 summarizes this scheme and gives some example realizations.

So despite their apparently threatening quality, directives are better seen as complex rhetorical strategies that writers can use to modify a relationship

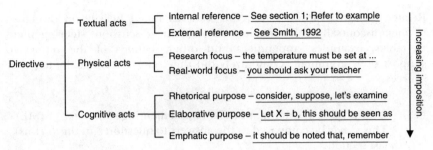

Figure 2.1 Categories of directives

with readers and indicate the ways they should follow the text. An imperative deployed to guide a reader through a text is radically different from an instruction to undertake a real-world action, and different again from an injunction to understand a point in a particular way. This lack of rhetorical equivalence is clearly reflected in the degree to which directives may imply a threat to the reader's face, roughly indicated by the direction of the arrow in Figure 2.1. These different functions suggest that the distribution of directives is unlikely to be uniform across contexts and Table 2.3 shows how uses reflect the conventional relationships implied by participation in the two genres.

The most imposing use of directives involves positioning readers, directing them to some cognitive action by requiring them to *note, concede* or *consider* some aspect of an argument. Typically these directives lead readers towards the writer's conclusions by emphasizing what they should attend to in the argument. But while about half the directives in the research papers expressed cognitive actions, the students tended to avoid the more imposing forms, preferring to simply lead readers through an exposition:

(12)   When a traveller proposes, *let's say*, to purchase a tour   (Econ)
        package, it may be very difficult for her/him to determine
        whether to purchase from a tour operator.
        Suppose there are two students with identical ability in   (TESL)
        language learning but come from two different families.

Table 2.3 Overall functions of directives by genre (per cent)

Genre	Textual		Physical		Cognitive			Total
	internal	external	research	real world	rhetorical	elaboration	emphasis	
Reports	19.4	1.7	54.3	4.0	5.6	11.3	3.5	100
Articles	14.3	22.0	13.2	2.2	13.9	19.5	14.9	100

Related to this expository use, the students relied heavily on directives to metadiscoursally guide readers through the discussion, steering them to tables, examples, appendices and other sections of the report to support their argument. Only rarely did they refer intertextually to other sources.

(13)   *Look at* Table 2 which summarizes implementing situations.   (ME)
        This *should* be compared to the answers to question 3 in the   (Bus)
        last section.
        . . . which was listed in the questionnaire (*refer* Appendix 5).   (PA)
        . . . (*see*, for example, Bredemeler and Greenblat, 1981).   (TESL)

Overall, the student reports were dominated by directives which steered readers through research procedures. Some 90 per cent of all research-focus directives occurred in the hard sciences, perhaps influenced by the traditions of precision, tight space constraints, and highly formalized argument structures in these fields:

(14)   Nonetheless, a radioiodinated probe has to be utilized in   (Bio)
        the test at the same time.
        Test results should be recorded and reported using the   (IS)
        standard test report format.
        However, it is important to ensure that the surface   (ME)
        roughness of the disc of the same material is the same.
        Otherwise, it will affect the result.
        Mount the specimen on the lower grip of the machine first,   (ME)
        then mount the upper end of the specimen on the upper
        grip carefully.

Once again, this is an extremely cautious use. Telling someone how they should navigate a text or carry out an experimental procedure is far less likely to impede their freedom of action and decision-making than directing the way they should follow a line of argument or the significance they should give to a claim. Several student respondents saw this research use as a conventional means of describing procedures with no potentially face-threatening implications:

In engineering we must be clear in describing our method so it can be easily followed. If we are direct then it can be done by another person without problems. I am only reporting what I did and how the method needs to be. It is a general procedure. (ME interview)

Yes, I use 'should' here to show how I tested the programme. It is like this in the textbook, I think. This is how we have to describe our work in the report. It is just normal, saying how anyone can do this not just us. (IS interview)

In sum, the reports contained a much smaller proportion of the relatively more imposing uses of directives. While their commitments and authority are important ways by which professional academics negotiate their ideas, these students seemed reluctant to direct their supervisors to particular views.

7.2 Direct questions

Style guides and academic textbooks tend to be largely silent on the use of interrogatives. The only study of questions in academic writing is Webber's (1994) paper on medical journals, for instance, and the pedagogic literature tends to refer to them as strategies to be avoided (e.g. Swales and Feak 1994: 74). They are, however, a central strategy of dialogic involvement, inviting direct collusion because the reader is addressed as someone with an interest in the problem posed by the question, the ability to recognize the value of asking it, and the good sense to follow the writer's response to it. Largely confined to the soft disciplines, questions serve up an invitation for readers to respond, to orientate themselves in a certain way to the argument presented and to enter a discourse arena where they can be led to the writer's viewpoint.

Once again, there were broad similarities in the overall frequencies of the feature and its distribution in the two corpora, but considerable differences in the ways it was used. Questions in the articles sought collaboration and served to express the writer's confidence and intimacy with the discipline's current understandings and ways of establishing truth. The experts used them to arouse interest, to establish a research niche, to convey a claim forcefully, to express an evaluation, to counter-claim and to suggest further research. The students seemed less certain about the effects of questions and tended to follow conversational patterns in employing more yes/no forms and using questions far more to organize their discourse. Many students employed interrogatives to recycle their research questions as section headings, for example (15), although others used them with expert competence (16):

(15) Chapter 2: How metal fatigue?   (ME)
      Why choose zebrafish as model in this study?   (Bio)
      Introduction: What is Pornography?   (PA)

(16) Is this pattern more obvious in Chinese dating couples? Do   (SS)
      men and women behave differently in handling conflicts?
      How does Chinese culture influence this sex differences in
      handling the conflicts? Will the high-context society, like
      Chinese, with well-defined gender roles in dating and
      marriage, affect the conflict-management skills of couples?
      Would the women still use accommodation in handling the
      conflicts?

> If this is the case, why did the students in the traditional　　(TESL)
> group possessed a high level of relaxation? What can be said
> is that the relaxation of the students did not come from the
> teaching method but from something else. The students'
> responses in the interviews did shed light on what
> 'something' referred to.

In both corpora, the overwhelming majority of the questions posed were rhetorical in that while they appeared to invite readers into the discourse and insert their words into the argument, they actually anticipated the writer's own response. This kind of rhetorical positioning of readers is most obvious when the writer poses a question only to reply immediately, simultaneously initiating and closing the dialogue:

(17)　However, in such a short period as one year, Sony's　　(Bus)
　　　　Playstation has won world sales of over 10 million units.
　　　　Why? Because Sony can catch up with the customers
　　　　demands.
　　　　If one does think that pornography implies woman as a　　(PSA)
　　　　class enjoys being degraded, is it appropriate for us to
　　　　say that this thought is derived from the misinterpretation
　　　　of the readers? The answer is YES! The readers
　　　　exaggerate the notion of degradation existing in
　　　　pornography.

Questions can therefore be an important resource as they bring readers into the argument as participants, introducing an interactive dimension which acknowledges readers' concerns, helps guide them though a text, and works to position them in relation to the writer's claims. However, the students generally failed to exploit the full range of engagement functions which questions offer.

7.3 Appeals to shared knowledge

A less imposing involvement strategy than directives or direct questions is to position readers within the apparently naturalized and unproblematic boundaries of disciplinary understandings through appeals to shared knowledge. Obviously readers can only be brought to agreement with the writer by building on some kind of implicit contract concerning what is relatively incontrovertible. In explicitly asking them to identify with particular beliefs or knowledge, however, writers are actually constructing readers by presupposing that they hold such beliefs. Typically, the students were again reluctant to employ such direct and explicit calls for the reader to recognize some acknowledged perception, with less than half the frequencies of the research article corpus. Some students used the strategy effectively, however:

(18)   Coating is known to have enhanced surface properties of   (ME)
       engineering materials.
       Effects of lead on the nervous system, both central and   (Bio)
       peripheral, are well known.
       It is commonly known that in Hong Kong secondary   (TESL)
       schools a 'core' textbook would be chosen for students' use
       throughout the whole academic year.

The most common ways of signalling the reader's presupposed understandings involved using *of course* and *obviously*. Both forms are often
regarded as markers of epistemic stance, indicating the writer's certainty
of a proposition. They can, however, move the focus of the discourse away
from the writer to shape the understandings of the reader:

(19)   From this issue, it is obvious that most of Fuji Xerox and   (Bus)
       Rank Xerox' energy was focused on each other, not on
       Canon.
       One of the main sources of economies of scale is that they   (Econ)
       can provide large variety of travel services. This, of course,
       will attract more consumers and hence travel agents can
       lower the average cost by increasing the numbers of
       consumers.
       The question of 'who comes next' is obviously not a   (PA)
       concern in the ADPL.

Here then we see students using a sophisticated rhetorical strategy to imply
that the audience already knows, or will readily accept, the accompanying
statement, recruiting them as partners in the argument.

Taken together, then, these different features are important ways of
situating academic arguments in the social interactions of writers and
readers. Through the use of directives, personal pronouns, interjections,
questions, and so on, we can recover something of how writers construct
their readers by drawing them into both a dialogue and a relationship.

8 Conclusions

Engagement is a crucial element of most types of argument as we need to
encourage our audience to at least continue reading, if not accept what we
have to say. This means that any act of writing is embedded in wider social
and discursive practices which carry assumptions about how participant
relationships should be structured and negotiated. Writers, of course, always
have choices concerning the kinds of relationship they want to establish
with readers, but in practice these choices are relatively limited, constrained
by interactions acknowledged by participants as having cultural and institutional legitimacy in particular disciplines and genres. We communicate
effectively only when we have correctly assessed the readers' likely response,

both to our message and to the interpersonal tone in which it is presented. Because texts carry the imprint of their contexts in this way, the analysis of interpersonal features such as those discussed here can help show how perceptions of audience in different genres influence rhetorical choices, and how writers both respond to the constraints of their contexts and construct them through patterns of engagement. For teachers, helping students to understand written texts as the acting out of a dialogue offers a means of demystifying academic discourse for students and of helping learners gain control over their writing to more confidently meet the challenges of participating in their disciplines.

Note

1 Since these signals cue much longer stretches of text where writers seek to involve readers, the totals obviously under-represent the extent of dialogic interaction in the corpus.

References

Bakhtin, M. (1986) *Speech Genres and Other Late Essays*. Austin: University of Texas Press.

Becher, T. (1989) *Academic Tribes and Territories: Intellectual Inquiry and the Cultures of Disciplines*. Milton Keynes: SRHE/OUP.

Biber, D., Johansson, S., Leech, G., Conrad, S. and Finegan, E. (1999) *Longman Grammar of Spoken and Written English*. Harlow: Pearson.

Biber, D. and Finegan, E. (1989) 'Styles of stance in English: lexical and grammatical marking of evidentiality and affect', *Text*, 9(1), 93–124.

Chang, Y.-Y. and Swales, J. (1999) 'Informal elements in English academic writing: threats or opportunities for advanced non-native speakers?', in C. Candlin and K. Hyland (eds), *Writing: Texts, Processes and Practices*. London: Longman.

Crismore, A. (1989) *Talking with Readers: Metadiscourse as Rhetorical Act*. New York: Peter Lang.

Halliday, M.A.K. (1994) *An Introduction to Functional Grammar* (2nd edn). London: Edward Arnold.

Hunston, S. and Thompson, G. (eds) (2000) *Evaluation in Text: Authorial Stance and the Construction of Discourse*. Oxford: OUP.

Hyland, K. (1998) 'Persuasion and context: the pragmatics of academic metadiscourse', *Journal of Pragmatics*, 30, 437–55.

Hyland, K. (1999) 'Disciplinary discourses: writer stance in research articles', in C. Candlin and K. Hyland (eds), *Writing: Texts, Processes and Practices*. London: Longman, pp. 99–121.

Hyland, K. (2000) *Disciplinary Discourses: Social Interactions in Academic Writing*. London: Longman.

Hyland, K. (2001) 'Bringing in the reader: addressee features in academic writing', *Written Communication*, 18(4), 549–74.

Hyland, K. (2002) 'Directives: power and engagement in academic writing', *Applied Linguistics*, 23(2), 215–39.

Martin, J.R. (2000) 'Beyond exchange: appraisal systems in English', in S. Hunston and G. Thompson (eds), *Evaluation in Text: Authorial Stance and the Construction of Discourse.* Oxford: Oxford University Press, pp. 142–75.

Swales, J. (1990) *Genre Analysis: English in Academic and Research Settings.* Cambridge: Cambridge University Press.

Swales, J. and Feak, C. (1994) *Academic Writing for Graduate Students: Essential Tasks and Skills.* Ann Arbor, MI: University of Michigan Press.

Thompson, G. (2001) 'Interaction in academic writing: learning to argue with the reader', *Applied Linguistics,* 22(1), 58–78.

Webber, P. (1994) 'The function of questions in different medical journal genres', *English for Specific Purposes,* 13, 257–68.

White, P. (2002) 'Attitude and arguability: appraisal and the linguistics of solidarity'. *Text.* Special Edition on Appraisal, vol 22.

3 Managing attitude in undergraduate academic writing: a focus on the introductions to research reports

Susan Hood

1 Introduction

The management of an evaluative stance is frequently cited as a challenge to novice academic writers. This is particularly so in the context of the introductory sections of research papers or theses where there is most often an expectation that the writer will evaluate the field of research in the process of arguing for, and positioning their own study (Swales and Lindemann 2002; Hart 1998). In this context evaluative stance is taken to refer to the ways writers position their own research in relation to other knowledge and other knowers. Evaluative stance is understood not as a fixed writer viewpoint that characterizes a whole text, but as a dynamic process of positioning throughout the text, realized through the strategic deployment of resources of interpersonal meaning.

An understanding of the difficulties faced by novice academic writers in representing an evaluative position can be approached from a number of perspectives. There is, for example, the issue of whether students are adequately inducted into the expectations of their academic community, as well as questions of access to various discourses dependent on one's relative status in the community (Ivanič 1998; Geisler 1994; Bizzell 1992). In the case of students' writing in English as a second or foreign language, there are also arguments that cultural expectations associated with academic English may be at odds with expectations based on the students' socio-cultural heritage (Taylor and Chen 1991; Bloch and Chi 1995). In this chapter I want to consider the question from a linguistic perspective, to explore linguistic choices in the construction of an evaluative stance in a way that can inform other approaches to addressing the issue. Linguistic considerations are an essential contribution to debates and discussions on expected outcomes, allowing us as EAP teachers to negotiate those expectations with students on the basis of an understanding of how they are articulated in texts.

From a linguistic perspective, an understanding of evaluation in academic writing has been well informed by studies focusing on genre or move structure pointing to the underlying argument function of academic texts (Swales 1990; Samraj 2002; Dudley-Evans 1997; Paltridge 1997). There is also a rapidly growing body of research into the functioning of specific grammatical resources for interpersonal meaning (Swales 1990; Thompson and Ye 1991; Hyland 1998; Hunston 1994, 1995; Thetala 1997; Groom 2000; Thompson and Zhou 2002). However, there has, as yet, been little attention paid to the semantics of interpersonal meaning in academic discourse, that is, to how meanings are realized through the positioning and co-articulation of interpersonal resources across phases of text. This chapter aims to explore the task facing undergraduate ESL students from such a perspective. The chapter focuses on the construal of evaluative stance in the introductory sections of the texts, and examines in particular how attitude is constructed dynamically in the discourse.

2 Research design

The research is designed as a discourse analytic study of data from two sources: the introductory sections from a set of four published research articles (coded P) read and discussed by a group of six students in an EAP class, and the introductory sections of the six undergraduate dissertations (coded S) produced by the same students. Analyses provide both a synoptic picture of the kinds of evaluative choices that writers make, individually and collectively, and a dynamic picture of the patterns of interrelatedness among those choices in the construction of evaluative stance in particular texts. It is hoped that a better understanding of how academic texts do and do not work evaluatively can inform EAP support programmes for novice writers, and assist teaching staff and supervisors in deconstructing model texts, and articulating more clearly their expectations to their students.

The introductory section is taken to be the initial section of the longer text (research article or dissertation) that follows any abstract and precedes any description of methodology. The rationale for this selection is twofold. First, regardless of the final forms of the research reports, that is, whether they are published articles, chapters or dissertations, the introductory sections share a common set of general purposes. In these sections the writers contextualize their own research by positioning it within a topic and in relation to a body of theory or research. In the process the writers construct an argument for the their own study. Second, the nature of the texts as argument means that they provide a relevant site for an investigation of evaluative strategies in academic writing.

3 Theoretical framework and methodology

While many recent studies attend to aspects of evaluative language, including much recent corpus-based work, for example Hunston (2000), as well as a number of very comprehensive studies of positioning under the description of hedging (notably Hyland 1998), there has been until recently no integrated theory of interpersonal meaning in discourse that would enable a comprehensive study of the construction of evaluative stance in texts. However, recent developments in systemic functional theory at a discourse semantic level, namely the work on APPRAISAL[1] theory by Martin and colleagues (Martin 1992b, 1997, 2000; Martin and Rose 2003; Martin and Macken-Horarik 2003; Martin and White in press), provide such a theoretical framework. The theory is a multidimensional one incorporating the expression of values (as categories of ATTITUDE), the manipulation of the strength of values (as GRADUATION), and the introduction and management of voices to whom values are attributed (as options for ENGAGEMENT). A diagrammatic outline of the model is provided in Figure 3.1. Kinds of ATTITUDE include AFFECT (valuing as emotions or feelings), APPRECIATION (as the valuing of the aesthetic qualities of things), and JUDGEMENT (the valuing of people's behaviour). The theory also accounts for further distinctions between kinds of AFFECT, APPRECIATION, and JUDGEMENT. Subsystems of APPRECIATION, for example, include APPRECIATION as REACTION, COMPOSITION or VALUATION (see Martin 1997 for a detailed account). ATTITUDE can be realized explicitly in overtly attitudinal lexis, as in 'a *favourable* choice', or it can be evoked through indirect means. The dominant means for evoking ATTITUDE in the data in this study is the use of GRADUATION, examples of which are provided later in the chapter. As a model at the level of discourse, the system of APPRAISAL enables a consideration of resources across a range of grammatical categories. So, for example, ATTITUDE could be expressed as an adjective in 'a *useful* alternative' or as a noun in 'the *benefits* of peer review'. While all three dimensions of APPRAISAL, that is, ATTITUDE, GRADUATION, and ENGAGEMENT, are implicated in the construction of an evaluative stance in academic writing, for reasons of space, the focus in this chapter will

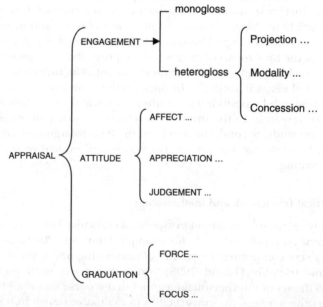

Figure 3.1 Model of Appraisal as in Martin and Rose (2003)

be on the role of ATTITUDE with resources of GRADUATION implicated in evoking ATTITUDE. In the extracts presented in the chapter, inscribed ATTITUDE will be indicated in bold, and instances of GRADUATION evoking ATTITUDE are underlined. Where relevant to the discussion, instances of conjunction are boxed.

The theory acknowledges that in any interpretation of attitudinal meaning in texts, there is always a need to account for reading positions, and the reading position taken up in this analysis of the texts is one of a native English speaking academic involved in supervision and marking of under-graduate dissertations such as those analysed in this study. As a member of the academic discourse community, the analyst is inclined, for example, to read references to the size, depth, breadth, or quantity in research studies as implying some kind of evaluative position with respect to that research.

The first phase of the analysis involves the identification of expressions of ATTITUDE that are explicitly encoded in texts. Explicit ATTITUDE is identified as resources that carry a meaning of either positive or negative value, and which can, in their adjectival form, be graded up or down – as in '(*very*) *important*', '(*quite*) *successful*'. Attitudinal meanings are categorized as representing either AFFECT, JUDGEMENT, or APPRECIATION. The canonical realization of ATTITUDE is adjectival (Martin and Rose 2003), but attitudinal meanings can be encoded through a wide range of grammatical resources as indicated in the examples in Table 3.1.

Important to this model is also the recognition that ATTITUDE can be implied as well as explicitly expressed. Martin and Rose (2003) identify resources for implying or 'evoking' ATTITUDE as including lexical metaphor and also GRADUATION. The resources for evoking ATTITUDE in this data are predominantly those of GRADUATION. In Figure 3.2 the system of GRADUATION as represented in Martin (2000) and Rothery and Stenglin (2000) has been extended to accommodate the extensive range of resources deployed in the data. In particular I have elaborated options in quantity as well as the system of focus. GRADUATION, as noted above, functions in con-junction with inscribed ATTITUDE to intensify or downgrade a given value. In

Table 3.1 Categories and examples of attitude

Kinds of ATTITUDE	Examples from the data
APPRECIATION (aesthetic qualities of things)	His methodology showed certain other **refinements** (P1)
	Peer review is a **useful** technique (P2)
	the issues are **clouded** to some extent (P3)
AFFECT (feelings and emotions)	They usually feel . . . **depressed** (S3)
	(they) may **suffer** from **stress** (S3)
JUDGEMENT (people's behaviour)	(they) **neglect** to observe . . . (S2)
	(it) was **rude, intrusive** and **impolite** (S2)

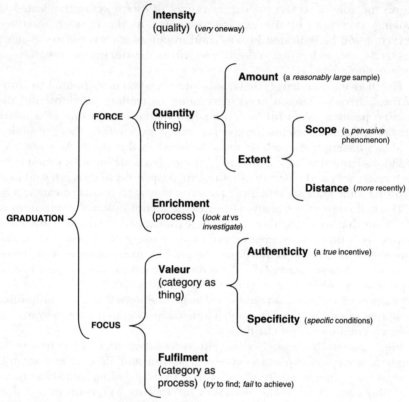

Figure 3.2 The system of GRADUATION with examples of GRADUATION evoking ATTITUDE

this data, however, GRADUATION is very frequently employed in relation to resources of ideational meaning, that is, non-attitudinal meanings. In such instances the GRADUATION retains some of its evaluative potential. It functions to give a subjective orientation to the ideational meaning, and, as such, has the potential to evoke ATTITUDE. So, for example, when a writer refers to '*a large amount of studies*' or '*relatively little attention*' in support of ideas, this suggests that the writer attributes different values to those ideas. The quantitative grading evokes a graded APPRECIATION. There are other examples that I have also taken to be instances of GRADUATION evoking attitude, such as '*very oneway*' or '*more direct*' that are borderline with field-specific ATTITUDE. That is, while a term such as 'direct' is not intrinsically attitudinal, it could be interpreted as having shifted over into explicit ATTITUDE in relation to specific fields of activity. (For more detailed explanations of the theoretical model see Martin and Rose 2003; Martin and White in press; Hood 2004).

The remaining step in an analysis of ATTITUDE is the identification of what is being appraised. In most published accounts of APPRAISAL analyses to date (e.g. Martin 1997; Eggins and Slade 1997; Rothery and Stenglin 2000), that which is being appraised is identified at a micro-level within the text as a specific entity or phenomenon. For example, in 'a large sample', that which is being appraised is the sample. In this study, however, the appraised is considered at a more macro-level as related to a specific field of discourse (see also Thetala 1997; Hunston 2000). An analysis of the data in respect of field reveals two broad fields to which the evaluation is oriented. The first field is the *domain* or the subject matter that is the focus of research by the writer and by other sources. This is coded as FD. The second field is that of *research* itself as an activity. This is coded as FR. The field of the domain (FD) will vary in specific content from text to text. The domains of study include, for example, issues of age and performance at universities, or problems experienced by returnee children in Hong Kong. The field of research (FR) constitutes a set of activities that are referred to in all the texts, and include identifying research issues, processing data, identifying findings and claiming and disseminating outcomes. Examples of ATTITUDE oriented to one or other field are provided in the extracts in Table 3.2. Coding instances of evaluation in terms of the field that is being evaluated facilitates the identification of patterns in the orientation of ATTITUDE across the texts.

4 A summary of findings from a synoptic perspective

A synoptic perspective on patterns and preferences points to a number of features in the choice and distribution of expressions of ATTITUDE that are typical in the discourse of the data as a whole. In the first instance, both the published writers and the student writers show a similar willingness to evaluate explicitly. All texts include multiple instances of explicit attitudinal choices. However, when field is taken into account, some interesting patterns of distribution emerge. In all the texts studied, most of the explicit ATTITUDE is directed to the domain (FD). Very few instances are directed to aspects of research activity (FR). It was also found that instances of explicit ATTITUDE in the texts are far outnumbered by instances of implicit

Table 3.2 Examples of instances of evaluation oriented to either FD or FR

FD – Domain oriented ATTITUDE	FR – Research oriented ATTITUDE
The interruption was **successful** (S2)	the correlation . . . was **too straightforward** (S2)
students . . . obtained **better** degrees	(the study) represents the **best** British attempt to (P1)
a **key** feature of process writing (P2)	It is necessary to focus in certain **key** features (P4)

ATTITUDE, evoked through resources of GRADUATION, and that these instances of GRADUATION-evoking ATTITUDE are most often associated with the field of research activity (FR). In other words, research is typically construed as a graduated activity, and by such means evaluated indirectly rather than in explicit ways, as illustrated in Extracts 1 and 2.

Extract 1
Research findings (. . .) have been reported for at least 30 years [grad:scope], from the work of Stiff (1967), Marzano and Arthur (1977) [grad:amount] to [grad:scope]findings reported by Hendrickson (1981), Sommers (1982), Hillocks (1982) and Graham (1983) [grad:amount] in the early 1980s. Further studies [grad:amount]carried out in the late 1980s and more recently [grad:distance] (e.g. Cohen 1987; Robb et al. 1988; Anson 1989; Hyland 1990; Lockhart and Ng, 1993) [grad:amount]all [grad:amount] report similar findings. (P4)

Extract 2
Over the past decade, [grad:scope + distance] many [grad:amount] scholars have studied the features of language (Leech 1966; Tannen 1982, 1985; Vestergaard & Schroder 1985) [grad:amount] and the cross-cultural differences of language in print advertisements (Tse. D., Belk R. W., & Zhou. N. 1989; Snow 1993) [grad:amount], there are few [grad:amount] diachronic studies on the language variation of print advertisements. (S2)

In both Extracts 1 and 2 a positive APPRECIATION of the research findings as significant is implied through the amplified quantity of references, as well as scope in time. The consequence of such evaluative encodings is not to objectify a subjective stance, as we sometimes advise our students to do, but, in fact, to subjectify the objective. Ideational ('objective') meanings are interpersonalized through the grading of those meanings (lots of researchers; a long time), and as such are given a subjective orientation.

Analyses of ATTITUDE also indicate a strong preference across all the texts for ATTITUDE expressed as APPRECIATION, rather than JUDGEMENT or AFFECT. Again such a choice can be interpreted as contributing to the overall merging of the ideational and the interpersonal in construing ATTITUDE. While the overt expression of ATTITUDE functions to personalize the discourse, the preference for APPRECIATION, as the valuing of phenomena (Martin 1997), functions to objectify the evaluation to some extent, or at least reflects the nominalized, objectified nature of the discourse. This is further explained in the discussion below.

One interesting difference that emerges in patterns of use in the published and student texts is in the degree of dominance of APPRECIATION. Where the published writers evaluate the domain very dominantly through APPRECIATION, the student writers also include evaluations as emotional responses (AFFECT) and as ethical concerns (JUDGEMENT). An example is provided in Extract 3. The student writer is evaluating aspects of the research topic, namely problems experienced by Chinese children returning to Hong Kong from overseas. In this example the writer evaluates the physical and human environment in terms of APPRECIATION (largely negative), but this is interspersed with expressions of the negative emotions felt by the people concerned.

Extract 3
When someone has left a **familiar** [app:reaction+] place for *a certain years* or even just *a month* and then return, he/she will feel **uncomfortable** [aff:satisfaction−] because of the **strangeness** [app:reaction−] of the city. So it is **not surprising** [app:reaction+] that *many* Chinese people who went overseas may **suffer** [aff:happiness−] from **stress** [aff:security−] and **disorientation** [aff:security−] when they come back to Hong Kong. Even children are usually under pressure facing this '**strangeness**' [app:reaction−]. These Chinese returnee children sometimes may have the **unpleasant** [app:reaction−] experiences in interacting with peers in Hong Kong. (. . .) They find **difficulties** [app:reaction−] in sharing the values and the subcultures with peers and also they behave in different ways. These returnee children cannot build up a close relationship with peers in Hong Kong and hence they usually feel **isolated** [aff:security−] and **depressed** [aff:happiness−]. (S3)

By including more expressions of ATTITUDE encoded as AFFECT, the writer constructs a more personalized expression of evaluation when she writes, for example, '*they usually feel **isolated*** [AFFECT]' than would have been the case had she written '*their social networks are **inadequate*** [APPRECIATION]'.

Further, while APPRECIATION is still the dominant kind of ATTITUDE used overall in the student texts, as it is in the published texts, there are some differences in the kind of APPRECIATION that is expressed. In the published texts the writers in most cases encode APPRECIATION as *valuation* (construing meanings of significance, usefulness or worth), as illustrated in Extract 4.

Extract 4
Peer review is a technique that reverses such a **traditional** [app:valuation−] approach to writing. Students may still start off by writing on their own; however, once the first draft is done, they get their peers to read it and comment on it. Then they revise it, taking into account their peers' remarks. Writing becomes more **purposeful** [app:valuation+] and **meaningful** [app:valuation+] as it is read by an **authentic** [app:valuation+] audience. (P2)

Valuation, Martin (2000: 160) explains, 'has to do with our assessment of the social significance of the text/process'. In the student texts, there are more frequent encodings of APPRECIATION as reaction, as in Extract 5.

Extract 5
Attention value refers to the use of **surprising** and **unexpected** [app:reaction+] language to provoke audiences' attention and **curiosity** [aff:security−]. (. . .) Selling power is the crucial and most **mysterious** [app:reaction+] part of the advertising process because it is an indicator (. . .). (S4)

Reaction 'has to do with the degree to which the text/process in question captures our attention (. . .) and the emotional impact it has on us' (Martin

2000: 160). While not coded as AFFECT, a connection to an emotional response is evident in this kind of APPRECIATION used by the student writers.

Insights into overall patterns and preferences in the choices and distribution of expressions of ATTITUDE that are typical of the discourse of research paper introductions contribute to our understanding of how writers meet the challenge in academic writing of constructing a persuasive argument on the one hand, while refraining from being seen as too 'personal' on the other; how they maintain the 'appearance of objectivity' (Johns 1997: 60). The findings also reveal some areas of difference in the choices made by published and student writers that need to be further considered in the light of their different writing contexts.

5 A dynamic perspective on attitude and grading

At this point, I want to shift the perspective from the characteristics of the discourse to the processes of strategically managing evaluative stance in individual texts. My purpose here is to show how attitudinal resources are positioned in texts and interact with each other with a view to providing further insights into the challenges faced by novice writers.

6 Prosodies of attitude in published texts

The discussion of a synoptic perspective drew attention to the interaction of ATTITUDE with field. The resources constructing field (in metafunctional terms, experiential meaning) construe the world categorically (Martin 1992a: 10). So as attitude associates with field, it takes on a categorical distribution.

An analysis of ATTITUDE according to field results in categorical preferences or patterns. In this study, those patterns were reflected in the means for expressing ATTITUDE, that is, as either inscribed or evoked. Inscribed ATTITUDE is associated with FD and evoked ATTITUDE with FR. Interpersonal meanings, on the other hand, are realized prosodically, that is, they are not bounded by neat categorical boundaries, but flow across stretches or phases of discourse (Halliday 1985/1994; Martin 1992a). The co-articulation of attitudinal meanings results in a 'colouring' of phases of discourse in prosodies of interpersonal meaning. Any explicit attitudinal choice in the discourse can contribute to a prosody of meaning that extends over accompanying text. In the following, for example, the choice of the evaluative attribute '*useful*' sets up a positive prosody that enables the reader to interpret '*encouraging revision in writing*' as a positive consequence.

'peer review is a **useful** technique for encouraging revision in writing' (P2)

In this case the term 'encouraging', while not explicitly attitudinal, seems to take up the positive value encoded in 'useful'.

The example above represents a prosodic flow of meaning within a clause. But a prosody set up through an evaluative lexical choice can extend beyond the clause, as in Extract 6.

Extract 6
His methodology showed certain other **refinements**. First, he excluded overseas students. Such students tend to be older than average and also to fare worse academically (Woodley 1979), thus influencing any age/performance relationship. Secondly, he used two measures of performance; the proportion leaving without obtaining a degree and the degree results of those taking final examinations. Finally he weighted the degree class obtained according to its rarity value in each faculty. (P1)

The APPRECIATION of the research methodology as showing '*refinements*', sets up a positive prosody that extends over several subsequent clauses, extending a positive meaning, without any further explicit encoding of ATTITUDE, and apparently giving a positive colouring to '*excluded*', '*used two measures*' and '*weighted*' (cf. Francis 1986 on anaphoric nouns, and also Hewings and Coffin, and Ravelli this volume on hyper-Theme).

In prosodies of meaning, 'the prosody is realized continuously, amplifying ATTITUDE wherever the potential for expressing attitudinal meaning is made available' (Martin 1992a: 11). An obvious resource with potential for extending the prosody would include another attitudinally loaded term. However, in the example above, there are no other instances of inscribed ATTITUDE. There are, however, some resources of GRADUATION in '*First, . . . Secondly, . . . Finally*' that function to maintain the positive association with 'refinement'. There is also the numerative 'two' which, in taking up the positive prosody, functions here as amplification, in the sense of 'more than one'. The terms to '*exclude*', to '*use . . . measures*' and to '*weight*' are also attitudinally coloured within the prosodic domain of '*refinements*'. Reading from within the discourse community of academic researchers, these terms also offer the potential to be interpreted attitudinally. Each could be read on a cline of graded meanings of enrichment, to do with effort, care, or precision in methodology. Yet a reading of the underlined terms as evoking positive ATTITUDE relies on the prosody of strong positive value initiated with the description of '*refinements*'.

This can be seen in a rewording of the text, where the initial coding of explicit ATTITUDE is eliminated, as in Extract 7.

Extract 7
The methodology he used was as follows. First, he excluded overseas students. Such students tend to be older than average and also to fare worse academically (Woodley 1979), thus influencing any age/performance relationship. Secondly, he used two measures of performance; the proportion leaving without obtaining a degree and the degree results of those taking final examinations. Finally he weighted the degree class obtained according to its rarity value in each faculty.

The values evoked could even be reversed in polarity by the inclusion initially of negatively encoded ATTITUDE, as in Extract 8.

Extract 8
There were certain **problems** with the methodology he used. First, he excluded overseas students. . . . Secondly, he used two measures of performance; . . . Finally he weighted the degree class obtained according to its rarity value.

In the case of terms such as '*excluded*', '*used . . . measures*' and '*weighted*', as in Extract 7, there is no apparent grading of experiential meaning. The only implication for an attitudinal reading is through a prosodic association with explicitly encoded ATTITUDE. In such cases the terms are not coded as evoked ATTITUDE in the analyses. There are instances, however, where apparently ungraded experiential terms can be seen to enter into graded sets in the data. This condition applies, for example, to the lexical set that refers to the process of inquiry as '*look at*' in contrast to '*examine*' or '*explore*'. These terms are interpreted as encoding degrees of enrichment, and are analysed as evoking ATTITUDE.

The robustness of a prosody seems to be influenced by the intensity of the original choice as well as the frequency, explicitness, or amplification of subsequent choices. A robust prosody has the power to colour more resources and draw them into its domain of influence. In Extract 9, a phase of text is introduced with strongly amplified APPRECIATION as '*the best*'.

Extract 9
Walker's (1975) study of mature students at Warwick University represents **the best** British attempt to unravel the relationship between age and performance. He took 240 mature undergraduates who were admitted to the university between 1965 and 1971 and compared their progress with that of all undergraduates. This gave him a reasonably large sample to work with and the timing meant that the results were not distorted by any 'returning servicemen factor'. (P1)

A prosodic domain can be broken by the use of a counter-expectancy marker. Common in the discourse are the use of concessive conjunctions (Nwogu 1997) such as *however, but, although*. It also seems that paragraph boundaries can be assumed to indicate the completion of a prosodic domain – although the explicit coding of conjunctions, such as *similarly*, or *another*, may function to signal maintenance of the stance across such paragraph boundaries. The functioning of such resources is illustrated in Extract 10, although this does not constitute a link across a paragraph break. Conjunctive links are boxed in the analysis.

Extract 10
Harris (1940) in the United States found evidence to suggest [graduation: fulfilment] that younger students tended to obtain better degree results. Similar findings have been made in Britain by Malleson. (P1)

The discussion to this point has focused on prosodies that function prospectively over subsequent text, but prosodies of value can also function retrospectively. At clause level this is evident in the final clause of the extract above from P1, namely

the timing meant that the results were **not distorted** by any 'returning servicemen factor'

The evaluative colouring of '*timing*' is retrospectively enhanced by the explicit positive APPRECIATION encoded in '*not distorted*'. Extract 11 illustrates this prosodic patterning over a longer phase of text.

Extract 11
In the **traditional** classroom, writing is often done in isolation – the students write on their own, hand in the product to the teacher, get written feedback from him or her, and finally put aside the writing. This is followed by another cycle and the pattern persists. Peer review is a technique that reverses such a **traditional** approach to writing. Students may still start off by writing on their own; however , once the first draft is done, they get their peers to read it and comment on it. Then they revise it, taking into account their peers' remarks. Writing becomes **more purposeful** and **meaningful** as it is read by an **authentic** audience (Mittan, 1989). Peer reviews reflect writing as a truly communicative process rather than an **artificial, lonely** exercise where students write for a **pseudo**-reader, the teacher, who reads students' essays predominantly for assessment purposes rather than for real communication. (P2)

The term '*traditional*' is interpreted here as inscribed negative APPRECIATION. However, such an interpretation assumes a reading position that recognizes the pedagogic debate of traditional versus progressive, and recognizes, too, the positioning of process writing as within the domain of progressive pedagogy. The evaluative impact of '*traditional*' is left pending to some extent, although it is then weakly reinforced in the term '*isolation*', which could be read as a token of negative APPRECIATION, and further in the negative implication in '*persists*'. The contrast between '*traditional*' and '*peer review*' is then established experientially in the process '*reverses*' and textually in the use of the concessive conjunction '*however*'. Peer review is then evaluated with a flurry of explicit positive APPRECIATION in '*more purposeful and meaningful*' and '*authentic*'. This contrastive evaluation of pedagogies is then reiterated and extended in the final clause of the phase, with '*truly*' and '*real*' versus '*artificial*', '*lonely*' and '*pseudo*'. The attitudinal loading comes at the end of the phase of text, and operates retrospectively to clarify or reinforce a negative reading of '*traditional*' assumed at the beginning of the phase.

This strategy of building the intensity of ATTITUDE over a phase of discourse is also evident elsewhere in the same text, in fact in each phase of text that elaborates on a benefit of peer review. In Extract 12 the same writer builds on the non-amplified APPRECIATION encoded initially in '*useful*', culminating in the amplified APPRECIATION of '*the best*' at the conclusion of the phase.

Extract 12
Peer review is a **useful** technique for encouraging revision in writing. It provides a <u>true</u> incentive for students to revise their work. What is <u>more direct</u> and **relevant** than a peer saying, 'This sentence is not clear to me,' or 'I don't understand this part?' <u>Exposing</u> student writers to readers who are their fellow students not only <u>broadens</u> the audience, but helps **develop** their critical thinking skills – both as readers and writers. As readers, students read their classmates' drafts **carefully**, make judgements, and <u>attempt</u> to put across their messages clearly so as to help their peers. As writers, they have to listen to their peers, judge the **usefulness** and **relevance** of their comments, and respond accordingly. The process enables the writers to reflect on their own writing, **clarify** their thoughts, and come to a **better** understanding of the needs and expectations of the readers. Peer review provides the **best** means for writers to turn 'writer-based prose' to 'reader-based prose' (Flower, 1979). (P2)

In Extract 13 from the same text the intensity of ATTITUDE towards the end of the phase is also evident

Extract 13
Peer reviews also provide **opportunities** for collaborative learning. Students in pairs or small groups can pool ideas, and it is through interacting with others that students learn and **develop** (Vygotsky, 1978). Students learn to become <u>more</u> **autonomous** writers as they are prepared to write without the help of a teacher (Jacobs, 1989). Through collaborative learning, students can gain a **better** understanding of their peers' **difficulties** in writing, and as a result they may gain <u>more</u> **confidence** in themselves (Mittan, 1989). Peer reviews can <u>boost</u> **confidence**, make writing a <u>more</u> **positive** learning activity, and help students develop <u>greater</u> **independence** in writing. (P2)

The variations in the ways prosodies are developed in texts P1 and P2 represent two distinct strategies for construing evaluative stance. In the example from P1 in Extract 9, the attitudinal stance is foregrounded and amplified in '*the best*' at the beginning of the phase, and is then reinforced and maintained over a subsequent phase of text. In the examples from P2, the writer accumulates attitudinal resources throughout the phase, culminating in an amplified stance at the end of the phase. (The coding of ATTITUDE at the beginning and/or end of a phase of text can also be addressed though an analysis of periodicity patterns, associated with hyper-Theme and hyper-New, although this perspective is not explored in this chapter. For discussion of the relationship of APPRAISAL to periodicity see Martin 2003.)

The examples above illustrate the interactive constructions of attitudinal meanings at a discourse semantic level that result from the co-articulation of attitudinal meanings in texts. The interpersonal meanings encoded by the writers are not constrained to the instance, but spread dynamically across phases of text, in prosodies of attitudinal meaning that function both prospectively and retrospectively in the discourse. The construction of an attitudinal stance in texts involves not just a particulate orientation of kind of ATTITUDE or means of expression with a particular field, as indicated in the synoptic perspective, but the management of the co-articulation of attitudinal resources, construing prosodies of ATTITUDE that spread across phases of text, drawing non-attitudinal resources into their sphere of influence.

7 Prosodies of attitude in student texts

Managing the co-articulation of attitudinal choices in discourse, as seen in the published texts above, is contingent on the placement of explicit ATTITUDE within phases of text, the strategic amplification of attitudinal meanings, the accumulation of attitudinal resources across a phase of text, and the exploitation of resources with attitudinal potential including graded non-attitudinal lexis. It is not surprising to find that such a complex process can present a challenge to novice writers of academic discourse. The extracts discussed below highlight some of the discourse management issues that confront the student writers.

8 Ambiguities in stance arising from a lack of evaluative coding

Extract 14 represents a separate paragraph in a student text. It introduces for the first time the source '*Roger, Bull and Smith (1988)*'. There are no instances of inscribed ATTITUDE that evaluate the study itself in this phase of text, although there are multiple expressions of ATTITUDE that relate to the domain being studied – '*unsuccessful*', '*complex*', etc. In this extract I focus only on ATTITUDE in relation to research (FR). The underlined expressions can be interpreted as GRADUATION evoking ATTITUDE.

Extract 14
Roger, Bull and Smith (1988) studied interruption in another angle. They formed the Interruption Coding System (ICS) for the classifications of interruptions. The subjects chosen for their two experiments were instructed to interrupt as often as possible and to monopolize the conversation as long as possible. Based on the results, Roger, Bull and Smith organized the coding system into a flow chart. They divided interruptions into single and complex ones according to the number of interruption attempts. For more than one attempt, the interruption was regarded as complex. If the interruptor could prevent the other from completing and ultimately completed his own utterance, the interruption was successful. Otherwise it was unsuccessful. If the interruption followed a clear offer of the floor by the interruptor, it was called snatch-back. The completion of an utterance by the interruptors and the occurrence of overlapping were also considered in the whole system. At last there were 14 categories of interruptions in total. They were successful complex/single interruption, unsuccessful complex/single interrupted interruption, unsuccessful complex/single interruption with completion, unsuccessful complex/single interruption, unsuccessful complex/ single snatch-back, unsuccessful complex/single overlapping interruption, snatch-back and interjection. These classifications were based on the structure of turn-taking. Compared with the work of West of Zimmerman, Roger, Bull and Smith did not relate interruptions with any social issue. (S2)

The length of the paragraph and the detail of description devoted to one study is likely to lead the reader to anticipate an evaluative stance on the part of the writer towards the study itself. It is assumed that the writer has included such detail because she considers the study worthy of an extended reference. Yet no explicit attitudinal stance is apparent towards the contribution of the research in the passage. A closer analysis of the text reveals a lack of explicit ATTITUDE and weak GRADUATION. The initial reference in this phase of text to '*another*' may suggest the maintenance of an evaluative stance established in the preceding paragraph. But the immediately preceding passage of text does not in fact set up such a prosody. There is some weak support for an interpretation of positive writer stance in the reference to '*at last*'. However, the meaning is ambiguous. It could be taken as GRADUATION:extent, giving emphasis to the extent of the process of analysis and supporting the detailed account given in the passage, in which case it would be read as evoking APPRECIATION:composition. Alternatively it could be interpreted as GRADUATION:fulfilment, giving emphasis to the achievement of the outcome, in which case it would be read as evoking APPRECIATION: valuation. There is further weak support for an interpretation of a positive stance in the expressions of GRADUATION:amount in '*14*' and in '*in total*' also potentially evoking APPRECIATION as valuation. The weakly and somewhat ambiguously encoded positive APPRECIATION could be made more apparent through a stronger or more explicit encoding of positive values in the opening of the phase, as in the following rewording:

> Roger, Bull and Smith (1988) studied interruption in another angle. They formed the Interruption Coding System (ICS) for the **detailed** classification of interruptions. . . . (*detailed description of methodology omitted*) . . . At last there were 14 categories of interruptions in total. They were . . . (list of categories) . . . These classifications were based on the structure of turn-taking.

This would set up a positive prosody allowing the subsequent resources of GRADUATION to take up this clearly positive encoding. The ambiguity in '*At last*' could be resolved by encoding GRADUATION:fulfilment more clearly as 'This process resulted in . . .'.

While it is assumed that the intended interpretation to this point is positive, the phase ends with an implied negative evaluation of this research in,

> '*compared with the work of West of Zimmerman, Roger, Bull and Smith did not relate interruptions with any social issue*'.

In order to accommodate this apparent shift in values the reader is required to insert a concessive conjunction to make sense of this shift. The inclusion of 'However', as in the rewording below, clarifies the shift in values for the reader. (See the discussion of concessives as an aspect of ENGAGEMENT in

Martin and Rose 2003.) 'However' functions to reinforce a positive inter-pretation of the preceding stance when followed by a negative evaluation, as in the reworded text below.

> Roger, Bull and Smith (1988) studied interruption in another angle. They formed the Interruption Coding System (ICS) for the classification of interruptions. . . . (detailed description of methodology) . . . At last there were 14 categories of interruptions in total. They were . . . (list of categories) . . . These classifications were based on the structure of turn-taking.
>
> However , compared with the work of West of Zimmerman, Roger, Bull and Smith did not relate interruptions with any social issue. (S2)

The changes reflected in the rewording below result in less ambiguity in evaluative meanings, in more clearly established prosodies of value, and in clearer relationships between one phase of text and the next.

> Roger, Bull and Smith (1988) **contributed** another angle to a study of interruption. They formed the Interruption Coding System (ICS) for the **detailed** classification of interruptions. . . . (detailed description of methodology) . . . This process resulted in a total of 14 categories of interruptions. They were . . . (list of categories) . . . These classifications were based on the structure of turn-taking.
>
> However , compared with the work of West of Zimmerman, Roger, Bull and Smith did not relate interruptions with any social issue. (S2)

9 Disjunctions in encoded values

A further issue that arises from an analysis of prosodies in the student texts is in the management of harmonies of attitudinal value. In Extract 15, different degrees of GRADUATION:enrichment are represented in '*to look into*' and '*be examined*', resulting in a discord in values across this phase.

> Extract 15
> In order to look into the relationship of the communication patterns of Chinese returnee children and their adaptation outcomes in Hong Kong, the following research questions will be examined. (S3)

Enrichment has to do with the infusing of a process with a circumstance of manner (Rothery and Stenglin 2000: 240). In the choices in Extract 15, different degrees of thoroughness or rigour are implied by the two pro-cesses. The rewording below realigns the values and restores an evaluative harmony.

> In order to examine the relationship of the communication patterns of Chinese returnee children and their adaptation outcomes in Hong Kong, the following research questions will be investigated

Discordant values are also evident in Extract 16.

Extract 16
Using the previous studies as foundations, this project is going to find out the relationship between power and interruption. This paper will also try to have a more thorough picture of the term 'power'. Since there is no unique definition of 'power' in the literatures, its meaning and some other related concepts in this research will be discussed first. (S2)

Here an enrichment of the research process, achieved through the intensified evaluative attribute '*more thorough*', is mitigated in the conation of the process, '*try to have*', suggesting a lack of fulfilment. The expression, '*to find out*' represents a neutral choice in that it says nothing about the manner of the process of research.

Discordant values are avoided in the following rewording by harmonizing the values evoked in '*explore*' and '*construct a more thorough picture*':

Using the previous studies as foundations, this project is going to explore the relationship between power and interruption. This paper will also construct a more thorough picture of the term 'power'. Since there is no unique definition of 'power' in the literatures, its meaning and some other related concepts in this research will be discussed first. (S2)

10 Confusion in phase boundaries

Extract 17 represents an introductory stage to a longer section of text in which other sources are discussed and evaluated.

Extract 17
Over the past decade [grad:scope + distance], written Cantonese has attracted the attention of linguists to study. Sociolinguists such as Bauer and Snow [grad:amount] have conducted a paper to discuss this question. Although both [grad:amount] of the papers are not mainly [grad:specificity] focus on advertisements, it gives a general [grad:specificity] picture of the growth [grad:amount] of written Cantonese in Hong Kong print media.

The text begins with a claim for the significance of the field.

Over the past decade, written Cantonese has attracted the attention of linguists to study. (S4)

This claim is weakly constructed through resources of GRADUATION. In the first instance the writer uses resources of scope and distance in the expression '*Over the past decade*' to encode extent of time and recent time, evoking positive APPRECIATION of the field of study on the grounds that it has had some lasting and recent interest to researchers. This is supported with quantification, although again weakly so, with the simple un-amplified plural form '*linguists*', representing a token of APPRECIATION:valuation. In summary, then, the field of research is weakly evaluated as having legitimacy through an unspecified measure of support over recent time. The confusion arises at the point of transition from the first to the second sentence. One interpretation is to take the first sentence only as realizing the functional stage of evaluating the field (written Cantonese) as a worthy research site. An alternative reading might see this stage extend to include the second sentence. Such an interpretation could flow from a reading of '*Sociolinguists, such as (. . .) and (. . .)*', as representing a further instance of GRADUATION:quantity, adding to the positive evaluation of the field as being supported. The potential confusion in where one stage of the texts ends and another begins results from a number of factors. First, the weak positive evaluation of the field of research in the opening sentence may encourage readers to look for reinforcement or enhancement of this stance in subsequent text. An anticipation of this kind would in fact be fulfilled in the opening words of the second sentence ('*Sociolinguists such as*'). The reading of this section of text is also made somewhat problematic by an apparent disjunction in the reference to '*linguists*' followed immediately by a reference to '*sociolinguists*'. With no explicit coding of the logic-semantic connection, the second sentence could be read as an elaboration of the opening sentence, that is, as an example of '*the attention of linguists*'. Alternatively, as is the interpretation made in this analysis, it could be read as a stage boundary, signalling the introduction to the evaluation of specific sources. The specific references to '*Bauer and Snow*' are subsequently evaluated, in terms of their relevance through GRADUATION:specificity (*not mainly, general*), which would support the latter interpretation. A writer's orthographic signals in the form of paragraph breaks, headings, etc. do not necessarily reflect the linguistic phasing or staging in texts (Martin and Rose 2003). However, in this case the section headings do align with an interpretation that the function of the opening paragraph is as an orientation to a longer section of text (macro-Theme in Martin 2003), as well as its function as an introduction to the subsequent phase. The reworded text below signals this more clearly.

> Over more than a decade, written Cantonese has attracted the attention of many linguists and sociolinguists. Bauer (1988) and Snow (1994) for example, have undertaken sociolinguistic studies, which although not specifically focused in the language in the context of advertisements, give a general picture of the growth of written Cantonese in the Hong Kong print media.

Ambiguities in interpretation are addressed by manipulating resources of GRADUATION, without relying on more explicit coding of ATTITUDE.

Note that in the rewording above, the publication dates for the two sources have been added. This not only eliminates the grammatical disjunction in the original between '*B . . . and S . . . have conducted a paper*' and '*both of the papers*', and conforms to the conventions of the academic discourse community, but also makes clearer the fact that two sources, not one, are being referred to. While a small change, it nonetheless contributes to enhancing the value through increased quantity.

It might be argued that Extract 17 could also be enhanced with a summative evaluation of the literature; for example, as inadequate in some respect. And as the body of this review is concerned with establishing a claim for the growth in written Cantonese, this might also be signalled in the opening stage. A further reworking of the text is included to illustrate these functions, relying predominantly on resources of GRADUATION to do so.

Over more than a decade [grad:scope], written Cantonese has attracted the attention of many linguists and sociolinguists [grad:amount]. While the literature offers considerable [grad:amount] evidence of growth [grad:amount] in the use of WC and suggests [grad:fulfilment] a range of [grad:amount] contributing factors, there is a need for further [grad:amount] quantitative studies that take into account more recent [grad:distance] developments.

Bauer (1988) and Snow (1994) [grad:amount] have undertaken sociolinguistic studies, which although not specifically [grad:specificity] focused in the language in the context of advertisements, give a general [grad:specificity] picture of the growth [grad:amount] of written Cantonese in the Hong Kong print media.

11 Conclusion

The evaluative functioning of academic writing is now well accepted and informs most EAP writing support programmes. It is reflected in our advice to students on how to structure their texts as generic stages or moves as they argue for their own research. It informs our teaching of the use of grammatical resources such as reporting verbs, concessive conjunctions, forms of citation, and even tense (e.g. Swales 1990; Hawes and Thomas 1997; Hyland 1999; Groom 2000; Swales and Feak 1994, 2000). What is lacking to date, though, are models and frameworks for guiding students in the integration of these resources and their management across stages or phases of discourse. In a sense what is missing is the middle ground, between genre and grammar. In the study reported here I have considered how one aspect of this middle ground is managed by a small number of published writers and novice undergraduate writers. The analyses elaborate some of the linguistic challenges facing novice academic writers. This study suggests that there is much more at issue than recognizing the intrinsic argument structure of the genre and the need to evaluate sources, or having access to a range of linguistic resource for doing so. A major challenge lies in recognizing and managing the effective deployment of resources in relation to fields of discourse. The study reported on here points for example to the different ways ATTITUDE is expressed in relation to aspects of the domain being researched as opposed to the evaluation of other research and sources. And, most importantly, consideration needs to be given to the co-articulation of resources in the dynamic construal of stance, in establishing and maintaining prosodies of attitudinal meaning, and managing harmonies of value.

Notes

1. Small caps are used to distinguish APPRAISAL systems as semantic systems.

References

Bizzell, P. (1992) *Academic Discourse and Critical Consciousness.* Pittsburgh: University of Pittsburgh Press.

Bloch, J. and Chi, L. (1995) 'A comparison of the use of citations in Chinese and English academic discourse', in D. Belcher and G. Braine (eds), *Academic Writing in a Second Language.* Norwood, NJ: Ablex, pp. 231–76.

Dudley-Evans, T. (1997) 'Genre models for the teaching of academic writing to second language speakers: advantages and disadvantages', in T. Miller (ed.), *Functional Approaches to Written Text: Classroom Applications.* Washington DC: United States Information Service, pp. 150–9.

Eggins, S. and Slade, D. (1997) *Analyzing Casual Conversation.* London: Continuum.

Francis, G. (1986) 'Anaphoric nouns'. Discourse analysis monograph. School of English Language and Literature, University of Birmingham.

Geisler, C. (1994) *Academic Literacy and the Nature of Expertise: Reading, Writing and Knowing in Academic Philosophy.* Mahwah, NJ: Lawrence Erlbaum Associates.

Groom, N. (2000) 'Attribution and averral revisited: three perspectives on manifest intertextuality in academic writing', in P. Thompson (ed.), *Patterns and Perspectives: Insights into EAP Writing Practice.* Reading: Centre for Applied Language Studies, University of Reading, pp. 14–25.

Halliday, M.A.K. (1985, 1994) *Introduction to Functional Grammar.* London: Edward Arnold.

Hart, C. (1998) *Doing a Literature Review.* London: Sage.

Hawes, T. and Thomas, S. (1997) 'Tense choices in citations', *Research in the Teaching of English,* 1(3), 393–414.

Hood, S. (2004) Appraising Research: Taking a Stance in Academic Writing. Unpublished PhD Thesis. University of Technology, Sydney.

Hunston, S. (1994) 'Evaluation and organisation in a sample of written academic discourse', in M. Coulthard (ed.), *Advances in Written Text Analysis.* London: Routledge, pp. 191–218.

Hunston, S. (1995) 'A corpus study of some English verbs of attribution', *Functions of Language,* 2(2), 133–58.

Hunston, S. (2000) 'Evaluation and the planes of discourse: status and value in persuasive texts', in S. Hunston and G. Thompson (eds), *Evaluation in Text: Authorial Stance and the Construction of Discourse.* Oxford: Oxford University Press, pp. 176–207.

Hyland, K. (1998) *Hedging in Scientific Research Articles.* Amsterdam: Benjamins.

Hyland, K. (1999) 'Academic attribution: citation and the construction of academic knowledge', *Applied Linguistics,* 20(3), 341–367.

Ivanič, R. (1998) *Writing and Identity: The Discoursal Construction of Identity in Academic Writing.* Amsterdam: Benjamins.

Johns, A.M. (1997) *Text, Role, and Context: Developing Academic Literacies.* Cambridge: Cambridge University Press.

Martin, J.R. (1992a) *English Text: System and Structure.* Amsterdam: Benjamins.

Martin, J.R. (1992b) 'Macro-proposals: meaning by degree', in W.C. Mann and S.A. Thompson (eds), *Discourse Description: Diverse Linguistic Analyses of a Fund-raising Text.* Amsterdam: John Benjamins, pp. 359–96.

Martin, J.R. (1997) 'Analysing genre: functional parameters', in F. Christie and J.R. Martin (eds), *Genre and Institutions: Social Processes in the Workplace and School*. London: Cassell, pp. 3–39.

Martin, J.R. (2000) 'Beyond exchange: appraisal systems in English', in S. Hunston and G. Thompson (eds), *Evaluation in Text: Authorial Stance and the Construction of Discourse*. Oxford: Oxford University Press, pp. 142–75.

Martin, J.R. (2003) 'Sense and sensibility: texturing evaluation', in J. Foley (ed.), *New Perspectives on Education and Discourse*. London: Continuum.

Martin, J.R. and Macken-Horarik, M. (eds) (2003) Special Edition of *Text*, 23(2).

Martin, J.R. and Rose, D. (2003) *Working with Discourse: Meaning Beyond the Clause*. London: Continuum.

Martin, J.R. and White, P.R.R. (in press) *The Language of Evaluation: The Appraisal Framework*. New York: Palgrave.

Nwogu, K.N. (1997) 'The medical research paper: structure and functions', *English for Specific Purposes*, 16(2), 119–38.

Paltridge, B. (1997) *Genre, Frames and Writing in Research Settings*. Amsterdam: Benjamins.

Rothery, J. and Stenglin, M. (2000) 'Interpreting literature: The role of Appraisal', in L. Unsworth (ed.), *Researching Language in Schools and Communities*. London: Cassell, pp. 222–44.

Samraj, B. (2002) 'Texts and contextual layers: Academic writing in content courses', in A. Johns (ed.), *Genre in the Classroom: Multiple Perspectives*. Mahwah, NJ: Lawrence Erlbaum Associates, pp. 163–76.

Swales, J. (1990) *Genre Analysis: English in Academic and Research Settings*. Cambridge: Cambridge University Press.

Swales, J.M. and Feak, C.B. (1994) *Academic Writing for Graduate Students*. Ann Arbor, MI: University of Michigan Press.

Swales, J.M. and Feak, C.B. (2000) *English in Today's Research World*. Ann Arbor, MI: University of Michigan Press.

Swales, J. and Lindemann, S. (2002) 'Teaching the literature review to international graduate students', in A. Johns (ed.), *Genre in the Classroom: Multiple Perspectives*. Mahwah, NJ: Lawrence Erlbaum Associates, pp. 105–19.

Taylor, G. and Chen, T.G. (1991) 'Linguistic, cultural, and subcultural issues in contrastive discourse analysis: Anglo-American and Chinese scientific texts', *Applied Linguistics*, 12, 319–36.

Thetala, P. (1997) 'Evaluated entities and parameters of value in academic research articles', *English for Specific Purposes*, 16(2), 101–18.

Thompson, G. and Ye, Y. (1991) 'Evaluation in the reporting verbs used in academic papers', *Applied Linguistics*, 12(4), 365–82.

Thompson, G. and Zhou, J. (2002) 'Evaluation and organization in text: The structuring role of evaluative disjuncts', in S. Hunston and G. Thompson (eds), *Evaluation in Text: Authorial Stance and the Construction of Discourse*. Oxford: Oxford University Press, pp. 121–41.

4 Scholar or consultant? Author-roles of student writers in German business writing[1]

Helmut Gruber

1 Introduction

Students' academic writing (as well as academic writing in general) is not a well researched area in German-speaking countries. Only a limited number of studies have investigated textual and stylistic properties of German academic texts (for a recent overview see Adamzik 2001; Gaberell 2001), some of them from a contrastive point of view (Clyne 1987; Fandrych and Graefen 2002), others from a 'critical perspective', which means that they aim to show how 'difficult' German academic prose is and why this is the case (Panther 1981; von Polenz 1981), others try to do the opposite (Ehlich 1983). However, while all of these studies used professional academic writing as their data, students' writing was not the analytic focus, although it is widely acknowledged now that writing may pose problems for students (Narr and Stary, 1999) and few German universities have established writing centres to support students with writing problems (see Kruse *et al.* 1999 for an overview).

In a recent study on students' writing, conducted at the Department of Linguistics at Vienna University in cooperation with the Vienna Business University (see details below), the analysis of the students' use of modal verbs and modal constructions revealed a number of differences from the use of modal constructions as currently described in the literature on German academic style. In particular, students seem to adopt two different roles in their texts: (1) the 'traditional role' of an academic writer and (2) the 'consultant role' of a management consultant. In their 'traditional role', writers use modals to mitigate claims or to formulate metacommunicative statements. In the 'consultant role', writers tell readers what they should do in certain situations in order to keep their business going. The nature and regularity of these patterns and supporting evidence from student interviews and questionnaires suggests that their use of modal construction is not defective in relation to 'standard' patterns, but rather is the effect of a basic tension between the demands of tertiary education at the university and the students' career wishes and job perspectives in the business world.

In this chapter, I will first present a short account of modality (sections 2 and 3), describe the project and data of the study in more detail (sections 4, 5 and 6), and then present the results of my investigation of epistemic and deontic modal constructions in students' writing (sections 7 and 8). In the last section of the chapter (section 9), I discuss the result with regard to the wider institutional context of the current situation of business universities in Austria.

2 The function of modality in language

I base my analysis on Halliday's model of systemic functional linguistics (SFL) (Halliday 1994) as the only alternative functional approach available ('functional pragmatics'; Brünner and Redder 1983; Ehlich and Rehbein 1972) does not give a comprehensive account of modality. SFL provides an integrative functional framework which explains why messages display certain features in regard to their content (ideational metafunction), the relation they establish between speaker and listener (interpersonal metafunction), and the way messages are organized (textual metafunction). As a socio-semiotic theory, SFL relates these three kinds of meaning to aspects of context (field, tenor, and mode; Halliday 1994; Martin 1992).

The system of modality, as part of the interpersonal function of language, offers language users the possibility to express various degrees of indeterminacy between the two poles of total positiveness and total negativeness of a statement (Halliday 1994). Modality is also involved in establishing a role relationship between speaker and listener.

Depending on whether a proposition (an utterance concerning 'information') or a proposal (an utterance concerning 'goods & services') is modalized, Halliday distinguishes between modalization and modulation.

By modalizing a proposition, speakers signal to their hearers how reliable the given information is; the speaker role they construe is that of a 'provider and evaluator of information'. The modulation of proposals establishes different degrees of obligation of the listener to do something or different degrees of inclination of the speaker to perform a certain action. Thus, in proposals, (normally) either the first person (offers) or the second person (commands, requests) occurs in the subject position; speaker roles are that of a 'commander' or 'somebody committed to do something'.

Halliday (1994) also mentions proposals in which speakers refer to obligations or inclinations of third persons (for instance 'the children should go to bed at 8 p.m.') and argues that utterances of this kind function as propositions which, however, do not lose their rhetorical force (that is, if the children are listening, they know when they have to go to bed). By uttering a proposition like 'the children should go to bed at 8 p.m.', a speaker may adopt the role of an 'adviser' or 'supervisor' of the hearer in a situation where the speaker is in a position to tell the hearer what he or she should get others to do.

As I will deal with this special kind of modalized proposals in this chapter, I will not use the SFL terminology which would subsume both modalization of propositions and modulated proposals with third person subjects under the heading of 'modalization', but rather use the terms 'epistemic' vs 'deontic' modality (Butler 1990; Brünner and Redder 1983; Coates 1983) to distinguish between the modalization of knowledge claims (epistemic modality) and modalization of proposals concerning third persons (deontic modality).

3 Research on modal constructions in academic texts

Although modal verbs are widely used in German academic prose, they have not yet received much interest in investigations of academic style. Panther (1981) and Clyne (1987) were the first to describe the modal verbs 'können', 'müssen', 'dürfen' (can, must, to be allowed to) in 'hedged performatives' (Fraser 1975) in German academic texts. Hedged performatives consist of a combination of a modal with a verbal process verb like 'sagen' (to say), 'feststellen' (to state), 'behaupten' (to claim) and include constructions like 'es kann festgestellt werden' (it may be stated), 'man kann behaupten' (one may claim). Panther concludes that hedged performatives in academic texts (together with impersonal construction) signal to the readers objectivity and legitimation of claims. That means that they are used to imply that statements, assertions, classifications, etc. are not expressions of writers' personal views or beliefs but rather 'dictated' by objective facts. Clyne argues that the use of hedged performatives is an immunization device which reduces the writers' risk of being contradicted by others. Of course, both interpretations are not incompatible: when Panther states that hedged performatives in academic texts are used to shift the responsibility for the correctness of a statement from the author to 'objective facts', he is implicitly describing 'an immunization strategy' of the author against critique.

Modality is also a widely used linguistic resource in English academic texts as: 'The modal verbs are among the most powerful devices available in English for the presentation of conclusions with a range of subtle gradations in strength and confidence' (Butler 1990: 138). In his study of modals in English academic texts, Butler (1990) found that epistemic modals were far more frequent than deontic modals and that most modals were found in the discussion section of academic papers or the explanation/discussion chapters of textbooks. According to Butler this is not surprising, because 'it is here (in the discussion sections) that the authors make claims about what is legitimate to conclude from the results, what may be the case, what phenomena are sometimes or generally observable and so on' (1990: 166).

However, in a series of publications, Hyland shows that metadiscursive devices (of which modal constructions are a part) are used differently in different disciplines (Hyland 1997, 1998b). Thus, the interpretation of certain patterns of use of modal constructions has to take into account disciplinary culture, for instance the 'professionally acceptable persona and a tenor consistent with the norms of a disciplinary community' (Hyland 1998b: 440). As Hyland (1998b) shows, 'hard' and 'soft' disciplines differ in their usage of metadiscourse.

4 Data and detailed research questions

The data of my study were collected in the summer semester of 1999 in a research project on students' academic writing skills, their demand for writing support and staffs' willingness and ability to support them.[2] We[3] followed one course for advanced students[4] at the Vienna Business University's Department of Personnel Management and obtained the following material:

- 13 students' papers (2 group papers and 11 single-authored papers).
- Semi-structured interviews with 20 students and several staff members on individual writing processes, students' and staff expectations towards students' writing and students' opinions of the course.
- A short questionnaire investigating students' academic aspirations, writing experience, and occupational wishes for the future.
- Participant observation of the seminar to triangulate the interview data.

This chapter will focus mainly on the students' texts. Only in the final interpretation of the results will I take into account results from the questionnaire and interview data.

Four research questions guided the analysis. In the following, they are grouped from a metafunctional perspective (this way of grouping shows how modal constructions, although they are part of the interpersonal function, 'cooperate' with elements of other metafunctions to create the author roles which writers establish in their texts):

Interpersonal metafunction: modality analysis
1 Which kind of modal constructions (epistemic vs deontic) occur in the data?

Ideational metafunction: transitivity analysis
2 With which kind of process types (verbal/mental vs relational vs material) are these modal constructions combined?
3 With which participant-realizations (theoretical/abstract concepts, 'classes of things and instances' vs concrete persons/enterprises in concrete situations) do modal constructions co-occur?

Textual metafunction: analysis of text structure
4 At which places in the textual macro-structure do modal constructions occur?

The first question is aimed at giving a general overview about the kinds of modality student writers use. The second question is intended to differentiate between modal constructions used in metacommunicative sequences (which are quite typical for German academic prose, see above) and modals which co-occur with other linguistic resources. The third question is especially relevant for investigating which roles writers adopt towards their readers in the papers. In answering this question, I study closely the subtle interplay of modalization, process types and degree of abstraction of participant realizations in the data. To approach the question of how 'abstract' a concept or participant is, I draw on van Leeuwen's work on the representation of social actors in discourse, especially on his categories of 'suppressed' and 'backgrounded' actors (van Leeuwen 1996: 39ff). Reconstructing 'hidden actors' helps us infer which role the writers adopt. The fourth question aims at showing correlations between generic stages of the texts and the occurrence of modality.

5 Results

The presentation of the results of my study is organized according to the four research questions above. I present an overview of the different kinds of modal constructions, their frequency and distributional patterns. After the discussion of the use of epistemic and deontic modal verbs in text commenting (metacommunicative) passages, I scrutinize how modal constructions were used in (non-)metacommunicative parts of the text.

Metacommunication is an important feature of academic writing as it helps readers to grasp the often rather complex structure of scholarly texts, and it has received broad attention in investigations of academic writing (Hyland 1998a; for a more recent overview see Fandrych and Graefen 2002). I differentiate between metacommunicative and (non-)metacommunicative uses of modal constructions here, as previous research has shown that German academic writers very often use modals in metacommunicative sequences (see section 3 above). If student writers thus use modals in metacommuncative sequences, this reflects that they are aware of one of the basic features of German scholarly prose.

6 Quantitative results

Table 4.1 offers an overview of the absolute and relative frequencies of deontic and epistemic modal constructions which occurred in the texts. Relative frequency counts are based on the number of clauses and clause complexes in the papers. Thus, the relative frequencies offer a rough impression of the numerical relationship between modal constructions and text-length.

Table 4.1 reveals two interesting details: first, it shows that the overall frequency of epistemic and deontic modals is rather low compared to the results Butler (1990) reported for English, and that deontic modals have a higher frequency than epistemic modal constructions. Only three papers (5, 11, 12) do not follow this general pattern.

The second interesting detail concerns the intertextual variation of frequencies. The use of epistemic modals varies between 0.9 per cent of modalized clauses and clause complexes (paper 8) and 11 per cent (paper 5). The same is true for the use of deontic modals which varies between 2 per cent

Table 4.1 Epistemic and deontic modality in the students' texts

Text no.	no. of clause complexes	no. of epistemic modals	rel. freq. of epistemic modals %	no. of deontic modals	rel. freq. of deontic modals %
1	333	24	7.2	25	7.5
2	847	45	5.3	121	14.3
3	1051	56	5.33	66	6.3
4	360	26	7.2	32	8.9
5	373	41	11	19	5.1
6	405	11	2.7	13	3.2
7	413	19	4.6	20	4.8
8	917	9	0.9	44	4.8
9	248	10	4.03	32	12.9
10	461	15	3.2	33	7.1
11	418	32	7.6	15	3.5
12	404	16	3.9	8	2
13	280	4	1.34	6	2.14
Total	6510	308	4.7	434	6.66

(paper 12) and 14.3 per cent (paper 2). Thus, the first, rough and descriptive analysis of the data shows a general tendency of most student writers to use more deontic than epistemic modality and large inter-individual differences in the use of modal constructions.

Apart from these general distributional features of modals, I was also interested in the textual distribution patterns of modal constructions (see research question four above). Therefore – in a second step of the quantitative analysis – I coded 'descriptive parts' and 'argumentative parts' of the texts. All stretches of texts which mainly described and defined concepts were coded as 'descriptive parts'. Those stretches of text where causes, consequences or preconditions of propositions were presented were coded as 'argumentative parts'.

Additionally, the structural labels the students themselves chose as headings for the sections of their papers were used to code 'introductions', 'problem definitions', and 'conclusions' of the texts. The code label 'case description' refers to a few stretches of text where students describe one or two 'real cases' which illustrate a general point in their papers. The codings for argumentative vs descriptive parts and the students' labels may overlap, as a problem definition may contain a description or an argumentation, etc. These two codings revealed the following 'prototypical structure' of the students' papers (optional elements in brackets):

introduction ^ problem definition ^ descriptive and argumentative discussion of several aspects of the problem(s) ^ (case description) ^ conclusion

Table 4.2 presents the overall frequencies of epistemic and deontic modals in the different macro-structural parts of the texts.

As can be seen, not all 13 papers correspond to the above mentioned text structure: one paper lacks an introduction, several papers have more than one 'problem definition' section and three papers present no conclusions. Table 4.2 also shows that, contrary to Butler's (1990) and Hyland's (1998a) findings for English academic texts, most of the modal constructions in the students' texts do not occur in the 'conclusion' sections but rather in argumentative and descriptive passages throughout the whole text.

Thus, the quantitative investigation revealed two interesting details about the students' use of modals: deontic modals are more frequent than epistemic modals, and modal constructions are used in all parts of the texts. However, one could tend to assume that in management studies – as an applied 'soft' discipline (Hyland 1998b) – deontic modals might be used differently from 'pure science' disciplines (Hyland 1998b). This might be the case because writers in applied disciplines may not only 'inform' their readership about their results, but they may also aim at advising them how to apply their results in practical contexts (see below). However, a qualitative analysis of a 'professional paper', which most of the students cited in their texts, shows that in this paper deontic modal constructions ('advice') also cluster at the end of the paper in the conclusion section (Gruber 2002). Thus, although 'advice giving' is a feature of applied science papers, such 'advice' has a fixed structural place, whereas in many students' papers, 'advice' is given throughout the text. Thus, the wide distribution of deontic modal constructions, as illustrated in Table 4.2, points to an interesting usage of modals in the students' texts.

7 Metacommunicative modal constructions – the 'typical' use of modals in German academic prose

In order to better understand the use of modals in the students' texts, it is important to first have some understanding of the 'traditional' use of modals in German academic prose, where epistemic (and deontic) modals are used

Table 4.2 Overall frequencies of epistemic and deontic modals in different parts of the texts

	Epistemic	Deontic
Introductions (12)	17	35
Problem definitions (16)	9	17
Argumentative parts (31)	121	222
Descriptive parts (37)	137	144
Case descriptions (3)	6	14
Conclusions (10)	22	21

in combination with verbs of saying or thinking. Typically, both types of modals co-occur with passive constructions and therefore in impersonal clauses.

On the textual level, epistemic modals serve as retrospective devices, which means that they occur in contexts where previous stretches of text (or primary and secondary sources) are summarized or commented on. But sometimes these constructions do not only refer back to the previous text but also contain a 'prospective' dimension as an announcement of the consequences of the previous stretch of text for the following text.

On the interpersonal level, epistemic modals in metacommunicative constructions are 'mitigating devices' which express a reluctance of the writer to 'impose' a certain discursive action (a summary, the introduction of a term) on the reader. Simultaneously, epistemic modals signal to the reader that alternative actions would have been possible at this stage of the text.

7.1 Epistemic modals in text commenting passages

I will now take examples of these general patterns from student texts, and examine the ways in which their texts reflect and adapt these standard patterns. Extract 1 presents an example of the use of an epistemic modal verb in a metacommunicative passage which serves to mitigate an evaluation of the author.

> Extract 1
> *Generell kann man sagen, daß hier grundlegende Punkte einer Implementation von personalwirtschaftlichen Maßnahmen durch Projekt eingehalten wurden und dies schlußendlich auch zum Erfolg führte.* (Text 3 (1747:1750))[5]
>
> Generally one may say that here basic issues of an implementation of personnel management measures by <a> project were kept and that this led eventually to success.[6]

In this example, the impersonal epistemic modal construction 'man kann sagen' ('one may say') refers back to a stretch of previous text (which is realized as a local adjunct ('hier', 'here') and introduces an evaluation of a previous descriptive passage. The clause complex consists of a modalized matrix clause and two projected clauses in which the evaluation is presented. The Actor(s) of the verbal process are weakly backgrounded by means of an impersonal construction ('man'). As this construction is very common in German academic texts I would like to call it a 'pseudo backgrounding' construction because it is clear for readers that 'man' refers to the author(s). The authorial stance (writer role) the writers adopt is that of a commentator/evaluator of previously given information.

Epistemic modal constructions are also used in metacommunicative passages which aim to help the reader in building up a mental, propositional structure of the text (Fandrych and Graefen 2002) as Extract 2 shows.

Extract 2

Entsprechend einer Expertenumfrage (vgl. Nippa, 1997, 37f) kann man Bremsen und Barrieren, welche einen reibungslosen organisatorischen Veränderungsprozeß stören, unter folgende Kategorien zusammenfassen: <. . .> (Text 10 (492:494))

According to an expert survey (cf. Nippa 1997, 37f) one may summarize hindrances and barriers which interfere with organizational change processes under the following categories: <. . .>

In Extract 2, the impersonal modal construction 'kann man zusammenfassen' ('one may summarize') occurs as part of an advance organizer which explicitly announces what follows ('the following categories'). As in the previous example, the author is 'pseudo backgrounded' by the use of impersonal 'man'. By the use of these constructions, authors offer their readers 'guidance' through the text, they 'manipulate the knowledge structure' of the readers (Fandrych and Graefen 2002). These constructions represent typical instances where students construe a writer role and help their readers to grasp structural or topical aspects of the text.

7.2 Deontic modals in text commenting passages

Deontic modals are used in advance organizers or when authors introduce new terminology. In advance organizers, the textual function of deontic modals is a 'prospective' one, where the future discursive actions of the authors are mentioned. In constructions which introduce terms, they refer backward and forward. The use of deontic modals in these contexts establishes a direct relation between authors and readers, where authors not only express their own intention to perform a certain discursive action in the (near) future but also invite the readers to do the same. This use of deontic modals in metacommunicative constructions are an indication for the 'process'-conception of academic texts which German scholars display according to Fandrych and Graefen (2002).

As the deontic and epistemic modals serve almost the same communicative functions in metacommunicative constructions, I do not present examples for this subtype in the following.

A special use of deontic modals in the students' texts concerns the mentioning of peripheral contents which could either be an indication for the 'digressive' German academic style (Clyne 1987) or a specific property of the genre 'seminar paper' (see below). In these modal constructions, concepts – which have some relation to the general topic of the paper – are mentioned, but not elaborated further.

Extract 3

In diesem Zusammenhang sind auch Cliquen und Koalitionen zu erwähnen. (Text 4 (96:97))

In this context, cliques and coalitions should also to be mentioned.

In Extract 3, the author mentions 'cliques and coalitions' without further elaborating on this topic. By the phrase 'in this context . . . should be mentioned', the writer signals to the reader that 'cliques and coalitions' may have some relevance in the actual context but does not specify which. The authorial stance the writer takes is again one of helping the reader to develop a propositional representation of the text (by recognizing that this proposition is of minor weight). As in the previous examples, passivization serves to suppress the Actor of the verbal process but this is easily retrievable for readers who are familiar with German academic text conventions. The use of the deontic modal implies that the writer is forced by an external force (the 'real world') to mention 'cliques and coalitions'.

Students' usage of these metacommunicative devices which mention but simultaneously exclude material from the text may be caused by the nature of a seminar paper in which writers want to show their instructor what they have read (and hence what they know), but what they think is of minor importance for their paper.

Examples 1–3 show that students adopt a rather traditional 'writer role' towards their readers by which they try to help readers to build up a propositional representation of, or to 'guide' them through, the structure of the text. The most frequent representational strategy for actors, namely 'backgrounding' and/ or 'suppression' of the writer, conforms to the norms of academic writing which demands an objective, distanced stance of the authors towards their texts (and their readers). This, however, is not the only role for modality in the student texts.

8 Modals in (non-)metacommunicative text passages

Using epistemic modality in (non-)metacommunicative text passages results in the construal of authorial roles which oscillate between authorial evaluations for readers and advice-giving. The use of deontic modality makes it much clearer that authors construe a consultant role for themselves.

8.1 Epistemic modality: weakening of claims and arguments

Epistemic modals in scholarly texts are 'mitigating devices' which indicate that a claim or an argument might not apply under all conditions or in all cases and thus they are also a rhetorical immunization strategy against criticism. On a more general level, epistemic modals may also show the authors' awareness of the course of academic inquiry in general, signalling the transitory character of knowledge production in academia which never comes to a definite end but rather proceeds from one step to the next. Thus, epistemic modals may express the awareness of writers that their texts are elements in a textual chain rather than its end points.

However, as Examples 4–7 will show, not all uses of epistemic modals mitigate statements. Depending on the level of abstractness of the partici-pants in the modalized clause, writers may construe their authorial role at different positions on the cline between 'author' and 'consultant'. By using epistemic modals in clauses with abstract concepts, writers adopt a rather 'traditional' role, signalling to the audience how confident they are towards their own statements and arguments.

Extract 4

Aber auch die Angst vor Machtverlust kann sinnstiftendes Moment für die Ausübung von Macht und Kontrolle, am Prozeß der Implementierung darstellen. (Text 1 (375:377))

But the fear of loss of power may also constitute a sense-making moment for the exertion of power and control in the process of implementation.

In Extract 4, two abstract concepts are being brought into a relationship by a modalized relational process. Both human participants of the relational process are 'abstracted' (van Leeuwen 1996: 59) by the use of grammatical metaphors (Halliday 1994) and only their characteristics are mentioned. Here the writer claims a relation between two impersonal (abstract and theoretical) entities but signals to the readers that this relationship may not apply in all instances. By assigning a certain probability to the proposition, the writer guides its integration into the readers' propositional representation of the text.

However, the abstractness of participants is not always as evident as in Example 4, as modals in (non-)metacommunicative text passages occur very often in impersonal constructions. In these constructions, it is not always clear whether the hidden actor is the author of the text (as it is the case with modals in metacommunicative passages). Thus, in these cases, it is crucial (but not always possible) to reconstruct from the context of an utterance who the hidden actor of an impersonal construction is in order to determine which role writers construe, as Extract 5 shows.

Extract 5

Die Kombination von Macht-, Fach- und Prozeßpromotoren kann beliebig gestaltet werden. Es hat sich aber gezeigt das die besten Ergebnisse durch ein Dreier-Gespann erzielt werden konnten (Text 3 (821:822))

The combination of power-, expert- and process-promoters may be structured arbitrarily. But it has turned out that the best results were obtained by a team of three.

By the use of a passive construction, the actor who may 'structure the combination of . . .' is hidden through suppression/backgrounding and from the context it does not become totally clear who he or she might be. What does this ambiguity mean for the writer role which is established through this utterance?

On the one hand, the writer's role may be construed in the same way as in the previous extracts and the writer may signal to the readers that his statement is only one possibility among others. This reading would be supported by the fact that the persons who are mentioned are the head of a nominal group with an abstract noun ('combination') as modifier and that they might be 'genericized' (van Leeuwen 1996: 47; which means that they are not referred to as concrete persons but as 'generic concepts'). On the other hand, if we try to reconstruct the social actor who is hidden in the passivized clause, it turns out that it must be either a member of a firm's management or a consultant. Thus, as the hidden actor is a concrete person, this passage may also be understood as advice the author gives to the reader. This second reading is supported by the context of the message (especially the second clause of the extract), as in the whole passage, the authors tell the readers what 'should be done' and what leads to the 'best results' in concrete situations. Thus, there is more support for the second reading, which suggests that the writers construe a 'consultant' role towards their readers, but the first reading cannot be totally rejected. This extract shows the multifunctionality of modality upon which writers may draw to change the relationship towards their readers in the course of a text.

In (the few) cases where epistemic modals co-occur with human participants, the writers' role towards their audience fluctuates even stronger between mitigating propositions and giving advice, although in the majority of modal constructions with human participants writers use deontic modality (see below). However, the number of epistemic modals in this context increases if we take into account all cases where a hidden actor is human and co-occurs with an epistemic modal.

Extract 6 shows how authors construe a rather traditional writer's role by using modal constructions in combination with genericized human participants, whereas Extract 7 presents an example where the authors construe a consultant role.

Extract 6

Wenn man diese Netze über mehrere Projekte hinweg aufbaut, kann ein Fachpromotor durchaus in die Rolle eines Prozeßpromotors oder sogar in die eines Machtpromotors schlüpfen. (Text 7 (467:469))

If one builds up these networks over several projects an expert promoter may slip into the role of a process promoter or even in the role of a power promoter.

In Extract 6, a higher level of abstraction is mainly realized through the use of the indefinite article for token and value which construes an abstract 'situational space' where the author locates the proposition semiotically. The human actors are genericized and taxonomized as a 'class' of participants rather than as individuals. In this example, the writer mitigates her argumentation by the use of the modal verb and thus adopts a 'writer' role rather than construing a 'consultant' role for herself.

Extract 7

Im Zuge der Implementierung von personalwirtschaftlichen Maßnahmen, könnte ein Mitarbeiter aus der Personalabteilung die Aufgabe des Fachpromotor übernehmen. (Text 3 (795:797))

In the course of an implementation of personnel management measures, an employee of the personnel department might assume the task of an expert promoter.

In Extract 7, the writer role tends more towards the 'consultant' model, as the situation which the clause describes is rather concrete. This concreteness is construed through the use of the singular for both token (an employee from the personnel department) and value (the task of the expert promoter) in the relational clause and by using the definite article for the value. Through these linguistic means, the writer construes a concrete, single situation in which he 'anchors' his statement. However, the genericized circumstantial adjunct at the beginning of the clause also allows a reading in which the writer hedges the proposition rather than offering advice.

In general, the investigation of the different types of modal epistemic constructions in (non-)metacommunicative contexts shows that the two author roles (author vs consultant) represent two poles of a cline on which the authors may locate themselves, rather than two distinct categories between which authors have to choose.

8.2 Deontic modals: 'giving advice'

As personnel management texts are part of an applied discipline where theoretical approaches from social psychology, sociology and other social science disciplines are combined to develop management strategies, the use of 'advice giving' sequences might be expected. However, as already mentioned above, in 'professional papers' of the discipline, deontic modal constructions tend to cluster in the 'discussion' section at the end of the paper.

Furthermore, on the Department of Personnel Management's web site, the students are given clear instructions that seminar papers have to be different from 'how to do' management guidebooks in regard to the 'stance' they take towards their topic. According to the web site, seminar papers present an 'academic argument' towards a topic whereas management guides tell readers how to deal with concrete situations.

Thus, the students' writing instructions as well as the distributional patterns of modals in professional papers would foster the expectation that (a) students do not use deontic modals very often and (b) that these modal constructions should cluster in certain parts of the texts. As the quantitative analysis has shown, neither of these expectations has been met and the students' use of deontic modals needs closer investigation.

Extracts 8–12 show different uses of deontic modals by the students. As with epistemic modals, the construction of an authorial role depends mainly on the abstractness of the participants in the clause. However, as Extracts 8–12 will show, by using deontic modals, the 'consultant' role becomes more prominent in the texts.

Extract 8
Politisches Handeln muß sich mit Erwartungsbrüchen, günstigen Momenten, Verzögerungen und Beschleunigungen, Zeitbindung auseinandersetzen. (Text 1 (303:305))

Political action has to look at ruptures in expectations, favourable moments, delays and accelerations, time commitment.

In Extract 8, the writer clearly adopts the role of a 'proposition evaluator' who formulates a general law-like relation between two abstract entities. Actors are abstracted by the use of grammatical metaphor (nominalizations which hide the participants of the mental process verb). Additionally, the entities are construed as general concepts by the lack of articles.

Extract 9
Gerade die Personalentwicklung soll auf die Linienmanager übergehen, da sie am besten die Entwicklungspotentiale ihrer Mitarbeiter einschätzen können. (Text 10 (466:468))

Especially personnel development shall pass to the line managers, because they are best able to estimate the developmental potentials of their employees.

In Extract 9, the author adopts an authorial stance which tends more towards the 'consultant' model. On the one hand, she uses the plural to refer to the human participants, thus construing a 'class of participants' rather than concrete persons. But, on the other hand, by referring to persons ('managers', 'employees') instead of abstract terms ('management', 'staff'), the level of abstraction is lower than in the previous extract and thus the writer's role tends more towards the 'consultant' pole of the cline.

As is the case with epistemic modals, deontic modals often occur in impersonal constructions where the hidden actor has to be reconstructed from the immediate context. In these cases, the 'consultant' role of the authors becomes more prominent than in the extracts with epistemic modals.

Extract 10
Besonders bei der Implementierung neuer Methoden oder Konzepte muß man mit Widerstand rechnen. (Text 7 (479:481))

Especially when implementing new methods or concepts one has to be prepared for resistance.

In Extract 10, it is paradoxically the use of the impersonal 'man' ('one') which makes it clear that a human agent (member of the management or consultant) is implied as the senser of a mental process (who can only be human). Also, the circumstantial adjunct[7] 'when implementing new methods or concepts' is a rather detailed description of the range in which resistance has to be anticipated. 'Resistance', additionally, is a grammatical metaphor for a process which needs a human actor (at least in this context). Thus, in this example, the writer construes herself as a consultant, as somebody who knows which course of action has to be anticipated.

Extract 11

In die Erarbeitung des Konzepts sind die Unternehmensleitung, Führungskräfte, Entscheidungsträger und Mitarbeiter des Unternehmens zu involvieren. (Text 2 (1351:1353))

In the process of working out the concept, the management, executives, decision-makers, and employees of an enterprise have to be involved.

Extract 11 shows the 'consultant' role the writers adopt even more strongly than the previous one. Although the actor is hidden through the use of a modal infinitive ('sind . . . zu involvieren'; 'have to be involved') the mentioning of the concrete and human goals ('management, executives, decision-makers and employees') of the relational process verb 'to involve' makes it clear that the hidden actor can only be a concrete human being (namely a consultant). This interpretation is also supported by the specific noun 'the concept' in the circumstantial adjunct. It refers back to the noun 'the payment-scheme' which is the topic of the whole section. Thus the low level of abstractness which renders the clause a description of a concrete situation together with the relational process show that the authors adopt a consultant stance in their text.

If a deontic modal co-occurs with a human participant, it is in most cases a genericized human participant in a concrete situation, as Extract 12 shows.

Extract 12

Der Mitarbeiter muß lernen und darf nie daran zweifeln, dass er die durch den Veränderungsprozeß bedingten, neuen Aufgaben, bzw. den neuen Kontext bewältigen kann. (Text 2 (1671:1672))

The employee has to learn and must never doubt, that he is able to manage the new context and new tasks respectively which are caused by the change process.

In Extract 12, the authors again construe a concrete situation by the use of the definite article for the complex nominal group which realizes the goal of the material process in the projected clause. The use of the definite article for the senser in the matrix clause, however, construes a 'generic, prototypical employee' rather than a concrete one. Through these linguistic devices the writers adopt again the role of consultants who tell their readers (members of the management) what to do 'with employees in general' in a concrete situation. Thus, in this example, by combining a genericized participant with a concrete goal, the authors 'locate' their message closer to the concrete end of the cline of abstractness/concreteness.

Examples 8–12 have shown that – as is the case with epistemic modals – the construal of an authorial role depends on the interplay between modals and the abstractness of participants in the clause. However, by using deontic modals, writers generally locate themselves closer to the 'consultant' pole.

9 Discussion of results

In discussing the results presented above, I first summarize the main findings and relate them to the two authorial roles (writer vs consultant) which were found in the students' texts. Second, I draw upon additional data (students and staff interviews, students' questionnaires) to offer an explanation for the results. In doing so, I differentiate between two layers of context which are relevant for interpreting the findings: the first layer concerns the occupational wishes of the students and the way these wishes may influence their use of epistemic and deontic modals. The second layer relates the results to a more general level of tension in the present organization of business studies in Austria and how these tensions may be reflected in the students' texts.

In general, the results show that the construal of a 'writer-role' depends not only on the use of certain modal constructions but also on their combination with other ideational linguistic choices in the clause. Of special importance is the level of abstractness of participants: the higher the level of abstractness, the more the writer role tends towards the 'conveyor and evaluator of propositions', whereas it tends towards the role of a 'consultant' if terms with a low level of abstraction co-occur with modal constructions. However, as the examples show, the two roles are not neatly separated but are rather the ends of a cline on which writers locate themselves.

Three different communicative purposes are associated with these roles:

1 By the use of modal constructions in metacommunicative sequences (especially through advance organizers, topical sentences, introduction of terms, etc.), the writer attempts to 'guide' the reader through the text. This feature may reflect a general rhetorical stance of German academic writers to present a text as an unfolding 'process' rather than as a finished 'product' (Fandrych and Graefen 2002).
2 Modals in specific metacommunicative sequences and epistemic and deontic modals in combination with abstract participants signal to readers the evaluation of propositions or arguments (in other words, the degree of confidence the reader should have in an utterance or the relative weight a proposition has in a certain context). Here again, writers adopt a text-oriented role, namely that of an 'evaluator of propositions'.

    Both kinds of use of modal constructions help the reader to build up a propositional representation of the text. The first usage is more concerned with helping readers to grasp textual structures (thus it is related to the textual metafunction), whereas the second usage is concerned with content matters (thus it is related to the ideational metafunction).
3 By using deontic modals (and to a lesser degree through epistemic modals) in combination with concrete participants, writers advise their readers what to do in specific situations. In these cases, writers construe a consultant or adviser role for themselves in their texts.

The first two uses are in line with the traditional role of an academic writer who is concerned with abstract theoretical matters and who wants to contribute to the theoretical development of a certain field, whereas the third shows a higher concern for practical matters. In principle, these findings should not come as a surprise, as personnel management is an applied discipline which aims, *inter alia*, at implementing theoretical constructs in concrete situations. Hyland (1998b) has shown that the use of interpersonal and textual metacommunicative devices is different in 'pure' and 'applied' disciplines. However, before accepting the unproblematic nature of these findings, two additional factors must be taken into account:

1 As was previously shown, modal constructions (epistemic as well as deontic) occurred throughout the texts and not only in the discussion sections. Thus, 'giving advice' to the readers was not a discursive action performed at the end of the texts based on theoretical considerations and arguments (or empirical findings) in the main body of the texts, but occurred almost everywhere.
2 The departments' writing instructions for seminar papers explicitly tell students not to write in the style of 'how to do' guides but in an 'academic style'.

These two additional factors would suggest that the students' use of deontic modality is not entirely to be anticipated in the context. What, then, might account for the patterns that have been found? To answer this question, I will refer to the students' questionnaires and interviews with students and staff.

In the questionnaire, the students were (among other things) asked about their occupational wishes. Table 4.3 gives an overview of the answers.

This result shows that the majority of the students want a managerial or a consultant position in the future. This is in line with the textual feature of deontic modality and the writer role of an adviser: these students may be anticipating in their texts the role they intend to play in their future job career. Further evidence for this interpretation comes from the interviews: most students complain about the 'theoretical character' of their training at the business university and demand a more 'practice-oriented' course of studies. None of them intends to make an academic career. On the contrary, they view their university instructors as 'failures' in their respective academic

Table 4.3 Occupational wishes of the seminar students (N=20)

Personnel manager:	8
Management consultant:	5
Marketing:	3
Other:	4
Total:	20

fields as they did not 'make it' into business and thus had to stay at university. This attitude offers an additional frame of interpretation for the use of non-abstract language in the texts. These students are not interested in abstract theorizing but want to deal with practical situations and to find solutions for practical problems (they are more interested in 'how to do' guidelines than in academic discussions). Thus, the occurrence of the 'consultant' role besides the 'traditional academic' role in the texts may reflect a tension in the students' attitudes towards their studies. Although they want to receive their degrees as soon as possible and thus have to conform to the rules of academia (and hence to the rules for writing academic texts), their texts also reflect the occupational role of their non-academic future.

Results of the staff interviews suggest a second, more general layer of interpretation. Most staff members address a basic dilemma of business universities in the current Austrian situation: for the last few years, not only do the business universities offer degrees in business administration but so do so-called 'business colleges'. The legal and administrative regulations for these colleges differ from those of universities. One of their major advantages (viewed from the colleges' perspective) is that they have different conditions for admission. Whereas public universities cannot restrict admission for their studies, colleges are allowed to do this. As a consequence, colleges offer much better training conditions for a limited number of students. Additionally, business colleges have the reputation of a strict 'practice orientation' and an avoidance of 'unnecessary' theoretical encumbrance. In this context, staff members at the university formulate the following problem: at present, business college graduates have a very good reputation in business circles (which are their prospective employers) and get very good jobs after graduation. As a result, many beginners try to get admission to these colleges. The universities are now in a dilemma. If they adapt to the college level and minimize the theoretical share of their courses in favour of 'practice orientation', they might attract more students. However, staff at the business university do have theoretical interests (contrary to the opinion of their students most of them are not failures but people who are interested in the theoretical problems of their fields) and view a university as a place where research and practice should meet (hence the writing instructions of the department: academic staff view seminars as theory-oriented; practical applications of theories are dealt with in other kinds of lectures). So far, this dilemma has not been resolved and the courses of study at the business university try to integrate these two, partly contradictory, endeavours.

The students' use of modal constructions and their oscillation between two different role models may thus reflect this basic tension of the whole university's course philosophy, which manoeuvres between a practice orientation, which would be appreciated by a majority of the students (and their future employers), and the interests of many staff members who want to further the theoretical development in their respective fields.

10 Summary

In an attempt to further describe the use of modals in a specific context of German academic writing by students at an Austrian business university, the findings have revealed that student writers use more deontic than epistemic modal constructions and that modals occur at all stages of the texts instead of clustering at certain stages. It has been shown that, to some extent, students use modals in a way which conforms to traditional norms of German academic writing. This was called the 'writer role' which students adopt towards their readers. However, in addition, by using (deontic) modal constructions in clauses with non-abstract participants, student writers also construe a second authorial role, called the 'consultant' role, by which students act 'as if' they were business consultants. Interestingly, the various authorial possibilities taken up by the student writers reflect a situational tension in the Austrian academic context between business universities and business colleges. Whereas business universities are research-oriented sites of tertiary education (and hence foster an 'academic' style for written texts), business colleges offer a practice-oriented education to (a limited number of) students. Interviews with students and staff revealed that students showed a strong inclination towards the practice-oriented model (hence their textual 'consultant role'). Staff members are aware of the tension between the two approaches but do not have a solution for the problem. While this paper does not propose any particular resolution of this tension, a more detailed and situationally specific account of the linguistic means by which these roles are constructed, and a greater understanding of the flexibility of these roles, may help both students and academics reflect more explicitly on the issues at stake.

Notes

1 Previous versions of this chapter were presented at the 27th ISFC conference in Melbourne, July 2000, and at the conference on Professional Discourse, Hong Kong, November 2000. I am grateful to Janet Jones for her comments on this previous version and also for her editorial comments on its text structure and English. The research which is reported here was funded by research grants of the Austrian Ministry of Science and the Austrian National Bank (project no. 7921) respectively.

2 At present, this study is continued in the context of a larger project in which textual features of students' papers from three academic programmes (personnel management, psychology of economy, and social history) are investigated and compared.

3 Research team: Patricia Herzberger, Karin Wetschanow; project co-ordinator: Helmut Gruber.

4 As the Austrian university system did not (and in most academic programmes still does not) offer a BA degree, these students cannot be referred to as 'graduate' students, therefore I use the term 'advanced students' as they are in their seventh or eighth semester of study. Most of them submitted their MA thesis shortly after the course.

5 The numbers in brackets refer to the line numbers in the original texts. Texts were coded using the Atlas.ti software package. All spelling errors remained unchanged and unmarked.
6 This (and the following) translation(s) of the German examples sticks very closely to the German original to preserve as much of the original linguistic 'flair' of the examples.
7 Which becomes a verbless clause in the English translation only.

References

Adamzik, Kirsten (2001) 'Grundfragen der kontrastiven Textologie', in Kirsten Adamzik (ed.), *Kontrastive Textologie. Untersuchungen zur deutschen und französischen Sprach- und Literaturwissenschaft.* Tübingen: Stauffenburg Verlag, pp. 13–49.

Brünner, Gisela and Redder, Angelika (1983) *Studien zur Verwendung der Modalverben.* Tübingen: Gunter Narr Verlag.

Butler, Christopher (1990) 'Qualifications in science: modal meanings in scientific texts', in Walter Nash (ed.), *The Writing Scholar. Studies in Academic Discourse.* London: Sage, pp. 137–71.

Clyne, Michael G. (1987) 'Cultural differences in the organization of academic texts. English and German', *Journal of Pragmatics*, 11, 211–47.

Coates, Jennifer (1983) *The Semantics of Modal Auxiliaries.* London: Croom Helm.

Ehlich, Konrad (1983) 'Denkweise und Schreibstil. Schwierigkeiten in Hegelschen Texten: Phorik', in Barbara Sandig (ed.), *Stilistik. Bd. 1: Probleme der Stilistik.* Hildesheim: Olms Verlag (= Germanistische Linguistik, 3–4/81), pp. 159–78.

Ehlich, Konrad and Rehbein, Jochen (1972) 'Einige Interrelationen von Modalverben', in Dieter Wunderlich (ed.), *Linguistische Pragmatik.* Frankfurt am Main: Athenäum, pp. 318–41.

Fandrych, Christian and Graefen, Gabriele (2002) 'Text commenting devices in German and English scientific articles', *Multilingua*, 21(1), 17–43.

Fraser, Bruce (1975) 'Hedged performatives', in Peter Cole and Jerry L. Morgan (eds), *Syntax and Semantics Vol. 3. Speech Acts.* New York: Academic Press, pp. 187–210.

Gaberell, Roger (2001) 'Das Problem der Linearität wissenschaftlicher Texte – Aspekte der Kohäsion und Kohärenz des Deutschen und Französischen', in Kirsten Adamzik (ed.), *Kontrastive Textologie: Untersuchungen zur deutschen und französischen Sprach- und Literaturwissenschaft.* Tübingen: Stauffenburg Verlag, pp. 287–329.

Gruber, Helmut (2002) 'Developing an own voice in academia'. Paper presented at the 2nd Knowledge and Discourse Conference, University of Hong Kong, 25–29 June, 2002.

Halliday, M.A.K. (1994) *An Introduction to Functional Grammar* 2nd edn. London: Edward Arnold.

Hyland, Ken (1997) 'Scientific claims and community values: articulating an academic culture', *Language and Communication*, 17(1), 19–31.

Hyland, Ken (1998a) *Hedging in Scientific Research Articles.* Amsterdam and Philadelphia: John Benjamins.

Hyland, Ken (1998b) 'Persuasion and context: The pragmatics of academic metadiscourse', *Journal of Pragmatics*, 30, 437–55.

Kruse, Otto, Jakobs, Eva-Maria and Ruhmann, Gabriela (eds) (1999) *Schlüsselkompetenz Schreiben – Konzepte, Methoden, Projekte für Schreibberatung und Schreibdidaktik an der Hochschule.* Neuwied, Kriftel: Luchterhand.

Leeuwen, Theo van (1996) 'The representation of social actors', in Carmen Rosa Caldas-Coulthard and Malcolm Coulthard (eds), *Texts and Practices.* London: Routledge, pp. 32–70.

Martin, James R. (1992) *English Text. System and Structure.* Amsterdam: John Benjamins.

Narr, Wolf-Dieter and Stary, Joachim (1999) *Lust und Last des wissenschaftlichen Schreibens.* Frankfurt am Main: Suhrkamp.

Panther, Klaus-Uwe (1981) 'Einige typische indirekte Handlungen im wissenschaftlichen Diskurs', in Theo Bungarten (ed.), *Wissenschaftssprache. Beiträge zur Methodologie, theoretischen Fundierung und Deskription.* Munich: Fink, pp. 231–60.

Polenz, Peter von (1981) 'Über die Jargonisierung von Wissenschaftssprache und wider die Deagentivierung', in Theo Bungarten (ed.), *Wissenschaftssprache. Beiträge zur Methodologie, theoretischen Fundierung und Deskription.* München: Fink, pp. 85–110.

5 Word power: negotiating success in a first-year sociology essay

Sue Starfield

1 Background

In 1993 and 1994, in response to repeated student demands, the Senate of a large, urban university in South Africa was debating whether the marking of essays and examinations should be anonymous. In a document supported by a number of student groupings calling for the introduction of anonymous marking, one of the black student organizations, the Azanian Students' Convention (AZASCO), referred to the 'anxiety and fear' (AZASCO 1993: 1) students had regarding assessment. 'Suspicions of bias along the line of race, sex, religion and person are common within the entire student community', stated the introduction to the motivation (ibid.: 1). The students argued that anonymous marking would 'go a long way towards our goals of total objectivity in evaluation' (ibid.: 1). One of the key points in their argument was that 'when the student advocates what the lecturer condemns, attitudes that are destructive to the learning process are bound to develop and might manifest themselves during the marking of scripts' (ibid.: 1). The document's contention was that the introduction of anonymous marking would result in an improvement in the performance of 'disadvantaged' students once the perceived sources of bias in assessment procedures were removed. 'Given that South African society abounds with prejudice on sex, race, religious and ideological grounds, there is suspicion that these prejudices might permeate the marking of essays and exams since [the] lecturers are also products of our society' an AZASCO representative told the *Wits Student* newspaper (1993: 2). These concerns led to the formation of a working group to investigate the possibilities of anonymous marking (Vice-Chancellor's Office 1994). By November 1994, it had been agreed that all examination scripts were to be identified solely on the basis of the student number. Student names were to be retained on essay submissions. It is worth noting that, after a meeting with the Registrar of the University early in 1994, it was reported that some members of the working group felt that anonymous marking would not solve the problem entirely, since markers would still 'readily be able to detect ESL speakers' (SRC 1994: 3).

From the early 1980s onwards, growing numbers of black students from segregated schools had been entering the formerly whites-only, urban universities. The socio-economic and educational effects of apartheid were such that many of the students from the schools of the Department of Education and Training (DET) were underprepared for academic study, leading to high attrition and failure rates, which perhaps prompted the student arguments outlined above.

The tenor of this discussion indicates the extent to which issues of identity are implicated in student success and failure and the extent to which the socio-historical context shapes the subject positions available to the participants in text production and interpretation. In my discussion of the Sociology One essay of Ben[1], a black student enrolled in a BA degree in1994, I argue that success in these unequal socio-political contexts is possible for black students but that it involves complex identity negotiations in the act of writing which, in Ben's case, are enabled by the discourses he brings with him from other spheres of his life.

2 Negotiating identity in academic writing

The view that academic writing is a 'social act' may have 'achieved a certain orthodoxy' (Candlin and Hyland 1999: 2), but the extent to which academic writing is a socio-political act negotiated in contexts of unequal power at both institutional and broader societal levels has been less well researched (see Clark and Ivanič 1997; Prior 1991, 1994, 1995). Within this perspective, individual writing is seen as shaped by complex interactions of social, institutional and historical forces (see Bakhtin 1981, 1986) which shape access to the privileged discourses of the academy.

In a discussion of student responses to English Language Testing Service (ELTS) writing test prompts, Hamp-Lyons refers to a test of writing as a 'discourse exchange, although a discontinuous one' (1991: 96). Unlike a face-to-face interaction in which the 'discourse exchange' is uninterrupted, in writing which is assessed, the feedback is not continuous. Essay topics can be seen as part of the Initiation–Response–Follow–Up sequence typical of pedagogic discourse (Hamp-Lyons 1991). The teacher/lecturer/marker initiates/sets the topic(s) – the written question or prompt – to which the student writer responds. This response, in the form of the academic essay or essay exam, is then marked either by the lecturer who set the question or by a marker (who may not necessarily be the lecturer). The essay can be seen as a dialogue between unequal participants. The lecturer, the institution and the discipline can be seen to map the parameters of both the topic and what might constitute an acceptable response and the lecturer/marker gives the feedback, at which point, in most instances, the sequence ends. What space is there in this tightly bounded sequence for students to challenge or respond by asserting their authority? Hamp-Lyons suggests that, as in oral discourse, it is possible to identify in written discourse interruptions which constitute a challenge to the 'making of meaning between writer and reader' (1991: 100). Hamp-Lyons identifies the possibility of marked and unmarked responses to essay topics. A challenge would be a marked response, as it would not conform to the expected discourse conventions, and the writer would be taking a risk. An unmarked response would be one that confirms the reader/marker's expectations.

Numerous studies of classroom interaction have pointed to the key role of the teacher in controlling 'what is and can be meant in the classroom' (Edwards and Furlong, cited by Brandt 1986: 101). Similarly, the writing task as assigned by the lecturer shapes what will be considered 'relevant, appropriate and correct' (ibid.: 101). As Ivanič and Simpson point out, the person who sets the assignment is 'usually the same as the reader of the assignment' and as such poses 'a challenge and a threat to the student – positioning him [sic] as a student writer and thereby exercising control over him [sic]' (1992: 146). There is, inevitably, an evaluative, face-threatening component to this sort of academic writing. The student, they argue, is not positioned as a 'writer with a responsibility to inform his [sic] reader, but as a student who has to perform a certain writing task in order to be assessed' (ibid.: 146). Power is exercised by the assignment setter through choice of 'form and content' (ibid.: 146). The feedback will definitely take the form of a mark or symbol appended to the essay on either the front or back page, and may or may not comprise written comments in the margins of the essay, in the body of the text, or at the end. The essay can therefore be seen as an extension into the written mode of the typical classroom routines identified in much of the literature (Sinclair and Coulthard 1975; Cazden 1988). In this type of writing, the roles of writers and readers are shaped by the constraints of the contexts: the mode of discourse is not only written to be read, it is written to be assessed.

If genres encode extant power relations (Kress 1985, 1993), students' academic essays may be considered as a 'discontinuous discourse exchange', produced and interpreted in contexts in which the exchange occurs between fundamentally unequal participants. The typical academic genres of essay, test and exams set up and reflect asymmetrical power relations in part through the so-called impersonal language forms (passive, avoidance of personal pronouns, nominalization, aspects of modality) and formal register (adoption of the standard or high variety; complex thematic structure; coded citation practices; conventions of formal written language; field-specific lexis, lexical density) and therefore set up unequal social and identity relations in discourse (Halliday 1994; Fairclough 1992). Kress identifies these features as central to what he calls broadly 'the genre of scientific writing with its insistence on suppressing any mention of the individual' (1993: 125), which he considers as part of the ideology of Western science. These generic constraints may, in fact, 'encourage the separation of students' private and public selves' (Chiseri-Strater 1991: 165).

While academic writing has traditionally been viewed as impersonal, recent research has argued for greater attention to be paid to the signifi-cance of identity in academic writing and on the ways in which writers, through the linguistic and discursive resources on which they choose to draw as they write, convey a representation of the self (Cherry 1988; Ivanič

1998; Ivanič and Camps 2001). The lexical, syntactic, semantic, visual and material resources writers employ construct 'writerly' identities, as do the various primary and secondary discourses which they bring to the academic writing process (Gee 1990; Ivanič 1998).

The 'writerly self' can be seen to be composed of several strands which shape the writer's representation of self (Ivanič 1998). The autobiographical self refers to the writer's life history and to the ways his or her beliefs, values and interests have been shaped by socio-economic and political factors and by the literacy practices with which he or she is familiar. Whether consciously or not, writers textually convey a sense of who they are, and the discursive practices they are able to draw on, as well as their understanding of who their potential reader is. This representation is their discoursal or textual self. The authorial self reflects the extent to which writers are able to project an identity for themselves as authoritative – as an authority who has 'something to say' (Clark and Ivanič 1997). First-year students, for example, may feel they cannot appear very authoritative in their essays, yet some students, through their personal histories, may be able to bring authority to their writing in ways in which other students cannot (Starfield 2002). A fourth, more abstract, aspect of writer identity concerns the 'socially available possibilities for self-hood' (Ivanič 1998: 28) that are available to writers within specific socio-cultural and institutional contexts. Some of these *subject positions* or identities – ways of thinking, feeling, believing, valuing, and acting – will have higher status than others (Gee 1990; Ivanič 1998). Writers may find themselves positioned by these possibilities, as were the black students whose views were reported on in the introduction to this chapter, or they may exercise agency and challenge these positionings as they write.

3 Methodology

The data referred to in this chapter are drawn from an ethnographic study, which I carried out in 1994, of the development of student academic writing in the Sociology One course of a large urban South African university. Ethnographic research provides a deeper understanding of the contexts of culture and the context of situation in which students negotiate the different texts and genres they are expected to produce as they develop as writers in a specific discipline (Halliday and Hasan 1989). I attended virtually every lecture, many tutorials and one of the weekly, adjunct, content-based, academic support tutorials aimed at students from disadvantaged educational backgrounds. Eleven students participated in the study, nine of whom were black South Africans who spoke English as a second language, while two were white, anglophone South Africans. I carried out in-depth interviews with these students and with all the teachers on the first-year course. I collected copies of all the students' assignments, observed two markers' meetings at which essay marking was discussed, and attended various other departmental meetings. I also analysed official university documents in order to provide a thick description (Geertz 1975) of the institutional contexts in which the students were studying. Ben's[1] essay, which is discussed in this chapter, was written for the first assignment of the year and was due in June 1994. It was marked by Lynne, a white, English-speaking woman who co-taught the first-year Social Theory course on Marx, Weber and Durkheim. Interview data from Ben and Lynne, in addition to observations from my fieldwork, are used to triangulate the textual analysis, providing a sense of the dynamic processes which shape text production and interpretation.

4 Negotiating an authoritative textual self

Ben's essay was successful – extremely successful – scoring 85 per cent[2] and a number of very positive comments. In this it posed a challenge to the expected (unmarked) performance of black students and I argue that it is by masking his identity and conforming to the traditional conventions of academic language in a subtle display of accommodation and challenge that Ben subverts the expected positioning of black students in the university. Ben succeeded in creating a powerful textual self as author and constructing a reader/marker who affords him recognition and respect as a writer and grants him full rights of entry into the new discourse community. His authority is displayed in a variety of subtle ways.

Ben chose Topic Two: *Why is the concept of exploitation fundamental to Marx's desired endpoint of socialism?* The marker's memorandum for this topic was a list of the following points:

1 Explain the concept of exploitation through an examination of class formation in society – will particularly focus on capitalism.
2 Need to be able to show where exploitation comes from – expropriation; lack of ownership; not the same as profit.
3 Show how Marx links this up to key problems in modern society – can also speak of alienation here.
4 Root cause – private property and the division of labour.
5 Need to show how logical end point is socialism – linked to key social problem and its root. Need for elimination of private property.
6 Would need some examination of what socialism is according to Marx.

Ben's essay was the only typed one in my batch of first essays. It was beautifully laid out with a cover sheet containing his personal details and the essay topic is centred inside a neat, black-bordered box[3] (see Appendix 1, page 82). Clear bold headings designate the essay's four sections:

Introduction
The concept of exploitation
The implications of exploitation; Socialism: Marx's desired end point
Conclusion.

These headings in themselves constitute an embryonic answer to the question. They match several of the points made in the memorandum, which was unseen by the students, and echo the topic, underlining the extent to which Ben shares a context with his assessor and structures his essay as a response. As Prosser and Webb have argued, 'successful essays reveal their organisational structure explicitly' (1994: 131). The headings in Ben's essay function as a 'predictive scaffold' (ibid.), signposting for the reader what the essay's structure is to be.

The typed essay both reveals and conceals. It reveals a student who can type, can use a computer, and has access to a computer – none of which could be presupposed in as far as black students in 1994 were concerned – and it also suggests a student who realizes the value of handing in a typed essay. What is largely concealed is Ben's 'blackness' (although his surname would have indicated this), his history as a trade unionist, his educational origins and his second language status. The writing of former DET students often literally bore the traces of their educational backgrounds as many lecturers claimed they could identify a 'DET handwriting' – signifying a difficult to read script, frequently correlating with poor presentation and poor use of English. They also claimed that they could 'detect ESL students', through the 'typical' language errors they made, confirming the students' perceptions outlined in the introduction to this chapter. Typescript and an impeccable layout were therefore already a challenge to received ideas about what African students' texts might look like and a bid to construct an identity as a successful student which involved the construction of a reader who would respond positively to the presentation of the essay. For, as Fairclough (1989) has argued, texts contain 'built in', 'ideal' subject positions for readers who will infer certain preferred readings of the text.

It is ironic that, given African students' desire for anonymity, signs of educational background could be read in ways other than purely from the student's name, especially in the case of essays. The choice to type his essay is perhaps one of the first of many of the choices Ben makes as he constructs his authorial persona as he writes his first essay for Sociology One. Ben actively chooses amongst the possibilities of self-hood available to him, drawing on discursive resources he brings with him to the new community of which he is attempting to become a member.

In his essay, Ben establishes his textual authority from the outset. His introduction (see Appendix 2, see page 83) invokes the comment 'Good Introduction' from the marker, immediately below the end of this first section. Instead of beginning with the typical 'in this essay', he inverts the standard generic format and begins with a brief overview of Marx's understanding of exploitation and of the link between the eradication of exploitation and the inauguration of socialism in Marx's theory. Two large ticks (✓) are further indications of his marker's satisfaction with his opening sentences. In these introductory sentences, Ben clearly links the two key semantic fields of exploitation and socialism, signalling the relationship between them. This use of the ideational metafunction was also found by

Prosser and Webb (1994) to be characteristic of successful essays. Ben also signals to his reader that he is operating at a high level of abstraction – dealing with the *concepts* (my emphasis) of exploitation and socialism. The introductory sentences contain definitions of exploitation ('it refers to a situation') and socialism ('where the ownership of private property') which Ben seems to feel are 'quite broad' and lead him to perform a fairly sophisti-cated move which involves a challenge to what he has just argued: 'The explanation of the concepts of exploitation and socialism given above is quite broad and it offers little understanding.' That the marker was quite happy with his definitions is indicated by her positive verbal and non-verbal feedback and Ben's self-criticism or perhaps a criticism of a view expounded in the Department was not commented on but served to increase the sense of authority conveyed in the paragraph as a whole.

All verbs in the three opening sentences are categorical, which also helps to create an impression of an authoritative writer. When I asked Lynne, his marker, whether Ben did in fact develop the critique which the sentence quoted above seemed to suggest, she replied that he did not in fact do this but, nevertheless, gave a most comprehensive and competent account of the issues. Ben ends his introduction with what for many students is the habitual point of departure but for him it functions more as a summing up of the complex understandings he has put forward: 'Therefore, this essay will attempt to discuss firstly, the concept of exploitation in more detail. Secondly, the implications of exploitation and finally the concept of socialism.' His verbless sentence is not corrected or commented on by Lynne. He has, however, made use of the logical connectors often recommended to students which signal the development of an argument (firstly, secondly, finally) in conjunction with a conclusive 'therefore' in theme position which all seem to carry more weight with his reader than does the grammatical error.

Ben takes charge of his text through adopting a clearly recognizable 'academic' voice and using many of the linguistic features typically associated with academic writing (see above). His tenor is at the formal end of the continuum and interpellates a reader who is almost an equal in 'expertise'. The traces of his own intervention in the process of text production are found in complex nominalizations, the use of the passive and impersonal constructions. All traces of first or second person personal pronouns have been removed from the text and only the third person singular pronoun remains and it refers solely to Marx himself and his theory. Ben uses the introductory impersonal trope 'this essay will attempt to discuss' instead of a more personal form, with an academic task word 'discuss', although he hedges this with 'attempt to' which is partly a politeness form and partly a sign of junior status. However, as his marker realized, he is not a typical first-year student.

Ben uses a dense, conceptual, highly nominalized language in which the participants are mainly abstract concepts like: 'capitalism'; 'concept of exploitation'; 'the conditions of the capitalist mode of production' or 'Marx' and 'the worker'. Ben typically uses clauses like 'This statement definitely require [*sic*] more investigation' – using the indirect, impersonal language of written argument rather than saying 'I will investigate this further'. He makes little use of evaluative strategies – 'verbal items which interpret the ideational content for the reader and express a value judgement' (Peters 1986: 175) and there is little evidence, other than the collocation of three abstract nouns to evoke the condition of the working class faced with mechanization: 'poverty, agony and misery', to suggest that Ben has first-hand knowledge of the situation of the working class. This suppression of the personal is a powerful strategy for Ben as a student writer.

Ben's citation practices are interesting in that he only cites one authority: he references Giddens[4] three times and these are his only citations. Unlike many of the other students, he never refers to the *Course Reader*[5] and has only one quote in quotation marks (from Giddens). It is interesting to compare Giddens' words with Ben's:

> The conditions of modern manufacturing and industrial production allow the worker to produce considerably more, in an average working day, than is necessary to cover the cost of his subsistence. Only a proportion of the working day, that is, needs to be expended to produce the equivalent of the worker's own value. Whatever the worker produces over and above this is surplus value. If, say, the length of the working day is ten hours, and if the worker produces the equivalent of his own value in half that time, then the remaining five hours' work is surplus production, which may be appropriated by the capitalist. Marx calls the ratio between necessary and surplus labour the 'rate of surplus value' or the 'rate of exploitation'. (Giddens 1971: 49)

Here are Ben's words:

> Marx also contended that the conditions of the capitalist mode of production allow the worker to produce more, in an average working day, than is necessary to cover the cost of the worker's subsistence and that quantity which the worker produces above his cost of subsistence, according to Marx is surplus value (Giddens 1992). Marx calls the ratio between necessary and surplus labour the 'rate of surplus value' or the 'rate of exploitation' (Giddens 1992: 49). This concept can be illustrated by the following example: Assuming that a worker is expected to work nine hours per day and he manages to expend only five hours to cover his cost of subsistence. The four hours' output that he produces is the surplus value and it is appropriated by the capitalist.

Although Ben's text stays close to Giddens' original text, Ben is not perceived by his marker as having plagiarized. Perhaps this is due to Ben's taut paraphrase of Giddens. His use of 'contended' – a verbal process verb specific to the lexicon of academic or legal argument – and of the passive transformation of yet another 'academic discourse' verb in 'this concept can be illustrated,' in conjunction with appropriate citation and referencing, are all traces of Ben's intervention in his essay which help make it 'his own'. The large black tick at the end of the 'concept of exploitation' section of his

essay, and the absence of any negative comments, suggest that the marker
had no quarrel with Ben's use of words and his conceptual understandings.
Lynne (the marker) in fact praised Ben's use of Giddens to me, explaining
that Giddens' text was very difficult and should probably not be prescribed to
first-year students. Ben had 'amazingly, tackled and understood Giddens'
and was, in her view, 'more like a second or third-year student'.

Similarly in the 'implications of exploitation' section several paragraphs
receive ticks. The final two sections, each consisting of one paragraph, also
receive an approbationary tick each. When I asked Lynne for her reasons for
awarding such a high mark to Ben, her response was interesting. She felt that
his essay demonstrated a high conceptual ability at a first-year level and felt
that what she had rewarded was 'the fact that he's done reading . . . extra
reading from the reading package [in addition to] . . . and is able to develop
quite a clear argument in terms of what he's trying to say.' As she re-read the
essay, however, she commented, 'he hasn't really developed the concept per
se of exploitation which I think should have been looked at more by me.
Probably . . . at a comparative level, he got that mark because it's clearly
much better than other first-year students'. As we talked, it became clearer to
me that Ben's success could be understood as an accumulation of all those
'signs' which pointed to his 'academic persona' or to academic 'distinction'
which distinguished him from the mass of students and which he had conveyed via his construction of his discoursal and authorial selves. He had
created what Bourdieu (1977) calls an 'authority effect', which distinguishes
legitimate speakers from 'impostors'. Lynne elaborated on this:

> and a clear introduction, which most students don't do. Which means that he has a
> sense of where he's going to which is really important . . . also what seems import-
> ant is that there's an understanding of the broader paradigm in which he's writing.
> You know the kind of theoretical framework of that particular theorist which
> I think is really important. Instead of looking at concepts in isolation . . . I think
> that what he shows is a real engagement with the theorist which is really nice.
> He's clearly interested in the theorist as well which obviously affects the way that he
> writes and thinks.

5 Negotiating between autobiography and anonymity

In fact, it is Ben's autobiographical self which has played a large role in the
constitution of these other 'writerly' selves and the choices he is able to make
regarding the possibilities of self-hood rather than accepting conventional
positionings of black, ESL students. So much of who Ben is has been conveyed in a text which, superficially, would appear not to say much about
its writer. Ben was an older student who had worked in a factory in the
Eastern Transvaal (a region about four hours north-east of Johannesburg)
for ten years – first in the processing plant and, subsequently, in the administration department. A staunch trade unionist and Marxist, he was thoroughly
familiar with the works of Marx and other socialist writers through years of
union education. In fact, I suspect he was better read, on certain topics, than

some of his teachers and he certainly did not always share their interpretations. Retrenchment at the factory had led him to consider university
study on a full-time basis as he had already completed five courses through a
distance-learning university for which his current institution had only been
prepared to give him one credit. The union had helped him obtain a bursary
for his studies and he had a strong sense of commitment to the union and his
home locality. He had left his family behind to come to Johannesburg to
pursue his academic career but was already working part time for an NGO,
doing policy work in his area of interest, and he intended to work full time
for them on completion of his degree, which was to be in economics,
mathematics and sociology. I witnessed him engage in a complex political
debate on an important topic with the head of department and saw evidence
of his strong convictions and ability to argue verbally.

Ben believed that success lay, at least in part, in meeting a set of departmental and institutional expectations and that these would vary in relation to
the lecturers' own ideological standpoints, thus reducing the likelihood of
objectivity. He gave as examples of this a lecturer who did not believe in
capitalism who might find it difficult to 'objectively' assess a pro-capitalism
essay or the subjectivity which might arise if a gay person were to mark
a psychology essay on lesbians and gays: 'So if really I believe, if really I
don't believe in capitalism, really to see things very objectively sometimes
is difficult, although you can claim that, "no", I'll try to be as objective as
possible.'

When we talked about his experience as a first-year student he seemed to
be consciously operating from two different subject positions which were not
easily reconcilable. The one position was articulated in these words:

> what I've also learned or discovered, is that if you're a first-year student, you are
> always viewed that you are not really academically equipped to deal with criticism
> effectively. You are still learning. You are quite new in the field. So we don't expect
> much from you.

The use of 'we' is exclusive of Ben and seems to refer to a generalized
university authority figure to which Ben gives a voice. He does use the first
person pronoun but it is to give 'voice' to the words of an imaginary
academic who has 'written a book or something' and 'think[s] that every-
body has to think the way I think'. When describing how this makes him feel
about possibly putting forward his own point of view – 'arguing otherwise' –
Ben puts these words into the mouth of a 'second person' (not himself). Ben,
the new student, has considered challenge but has come to the realization
that

> once they've decided on certain things it's very difficult to actually influence them
> to change certain things ... If, for instance, I've written a book or something
> [laughs] in a way I believe and I think that everybody has to think the way I think.
> You can't come and argue otherwise, as long as we are within my territory, this how
> we have to do things.[6]

The older, mature-age students in the study, who had experienced adult life after school, before university, had a strong sense of having to surrender or disguise something of themselves in order to succeed. Ben gave a resigned laugh when he explained to me how difficult he believed it was for lecturers to accept explanations that differed from the beliefs which they held. To be a successful student, one would have to accept being on the lecturer's turf and recognize an essentially unequal power relation. A lecturer might be a published authority in the field in which they were teaching the first-year course and might hold views quite dissimilar to those dear to the student. Yet Ben is not only a first-year student, he is also a trade unionist, and the characters who populate the texts (see Ivanič and Simpson 1992) prescribed for the first essay are familiar to him:

> I mean especially when it come to Marx' theory and other things, this field, those discussions and everything. I mean, trade unions really elaborate on those and discuss them a lot, and we have got different perspectives, different interpretations. So on certain things we don't agree really with what they're saying especially from an empirical evidence [*sic*].

When he talks about the unions, the reference for the 'we' has shifted to include Ben himself: 'on certain things, really, we don't agree with what is said'. This is the source of the textual power Ben brings to his essay on Marx and which his marker recognized. While she responded to his passion and the breadth of his reading, she did not, however, recognize his 'unionist' self as it was carefully disguised by his 'academic self'. Not knowing who his marker would be, he needed some camouflage but did not want to/was not able to appear as a total novice. His essay successfully juggled a complex range of subject positions shaped by his understanding that 'in an academic world, of course, things are approached differently'.

As I had frequently heard lecturers say in the lectures that students could put forward their own opinions, provided that they substantiated their arguments with evidence, I asked Ben whether he thought there were circumstances in which he could put forward views that differed from those held by the lecturer. He responded, 'the problem is that [laughs], is the lecturer agreeing with what you say, although you back it up. I think it's how he's going to respond to give your marks'. The issue of students wanting some sort of institutional recognition of their personal experience, of their unique identity was raised slightly differently by Ben as he considered whether he might be able to challenge the accepted rules of evidence. Ben wondered if he could draw on his experiences of working in a chrome factory when writing about the social theories of Karl Marx and Max Weber. He seemed to abandon this idea and told me, 'For them, empirical evidence must always be documented. I do understand that in an academic world things are approached differently.' He felt that saying 'this is what I have experienced in the last ten years' as evidence in support of an argument would not be recognized by the academic world as it would be undocumented and reduce rather than increase his power.

Ben is conscious of operating in a very specific context, bounded by conventions which he should not transgress if he wishes to succeed. His success so early in his academic career is, in part, I suspect, a function of this awareness. Despite little or no referencing, he is not found guilty of plagiarism, his arguments are not judged as too sophisticated for a first-year student. On the contrary, he 'passes' for a third-year student. He has textually created sufficient authority to ensure that much of what he says is accepted as common ground and does not require referencing.

Less important than the pellucid exposition of the topic is a constellation of other criteria, one of which is his 'engagement with the theorist' – a criterion I never heard or saw enunciated to students at any stage during 1994. Despite this, Ben succeeds in conveying his 'engaged identity' to his reader, evoking a very positive response. In a similar vein, she acknowledged that he was being 'rewarded for reading outside of the course material', which she felt had lead to his developing a greater understanding of the issues. It should, however, be recalled that his wide reading has taken place within his trade union context and not strictly within his 'first-year student' context.

6 'You can't come to argue otherwise'

A successful writer can flout the strictures which the less successful may need to adhere to, but success can come in a variety of forms and, most significantly, success is accomplished in a complex interaction between reader, writer, the discursive worlds which they inhabit and always something more than this – the acts of identity and investment (Norton 2000) accomplished in attempting to make and share meaning. When writing, a student makes the sorts of choices and takes the sorts of bets which Ben is able to consciously articulate. When a student comes from a community and an educational world very dissimilar to that which has shaped the potential markers and readers, these choices are all the more complex and the risks of failure are greater. And while authority is in part discursively constructed, its origins are social and political: they lie in the capital – economic, symbolic and discursive (Starfield 2002) – which students as social agents bring to the university and these cannot be divested from power structures and struggles in the wider society.

Paradoxically, Ben's flouting is to comply. Through his appropriation of the forms of academic discourse, and because his sophisticated understandings of Marx, garnered in the non-academic world of the trade union movement, enable him to speak as an equal, he receives the following end comments:

85%
An excellent essay showing:

1) Understanding
2) Ability to develop an argument
3) Coherence
4) Reading

Ben's 'ownership' of the words of others has conferred authority on him.

Ben was one of the few students who used 'we' instead of 'I'. His trade union background and the reading he had done appeared to give him the power to resist the sense of having to surrender one's own views and identity in order to succeed. In his successful essay, he masked his trade union identity and was able to adopt a new academic one. Nevertheless, he explained to me that at the university, 'within this short space of time', he had learned that 'once they've decided certain things it's very difficult to actually influence and to change certain things'. Ben can be viewed as having adopted an identity of accommodation but one which, in his case, is very successful, at least when writing essays. He ultimately submits his authority to that of the lecturers and markers but is left with a sense of having compromised a part of himself in this act of choosing to invest in an 'academic' identity.

Ben did seem able to negotiate, to an extent, the demands of the course. He scored very highly in his essays but was, however, very disappointed by his low exam marks and was unable to explain why he did so poorly, other than to suggest it might be because he did not work well under pressure.[7] Reading both Ben's essay and his marker's comments, it was obvious that Ben could write academically and sociologically. Was it merely the stress of having to perform under exam conditions which gave rise to such differing identities? Was Ben highly successful or rather mediocre? If Kress' (1993) understanding of genre is correct – that it is primarily about social relations – and essays, tests, and exams are all different pedagogic genres that embody different types of social relationships and identities, then Ben's highly successful essay identity can be seen to be related to his ability to satisfy the generic demands. The degree of power and authority enacted in the essay exam genre is much greater than in the essay, the social relations much more distant and the task demands less easy to satisfy. When Ben wrote an essay he was able to redraft it a number of times, to invest more of himself, to work on how he would use language to present his arguments, unlike under the pressure of an exam or test. The possibilities of negotiating a successful identity within the 45 minutes per question in the exam room were greatly reduced.

Ben never mentioned race as an issue to me but he did emphasize how he felt he could not express his lived experience of his union views on Marx. It must be borne in mind that I, the interviewer, was white as were all of the lecturers on the first-year course,[8] which may have made certain things 'unsayable' too.

Textually there are different paths to success and success is a complex outcome in which students' social identities and the social relations they develop in and outside of the text as they negotiate meaning help constitute successful texts. Moreover, students' prior life histories, the socially structured opportunities and the more or less privileged discourses they have had access to, affect how they engage in the essay-writing sequence. Success is also accomplished through the relationship between writer and reader that the text constructs. Authoritative writers seem able to construct positions for their readers in ways which the readers accept. Markers (who are always readers) may bring different criteria to bear in the moment of interpretation (as Lynne did with Ben, when she responded to her positioning by Ben as the reader of what could pass for a third-year essay but written by a first-year).

Ben was highly successful in his first essay as he brought authority to his essay through his prior trade union engagement with the works of Marx. He was able to engage with the themes of the topic at a highly sophisticated level, using complex, traditional academic discourse. He negotiated his authority textually and created a powerful writer identity that earned success by drawing on resources from his symbolic capital and from discourses which he brought with him into Sociology One. He also drew simultaneously on extra-discursive authority from the social contexts which had shaped his identities prior to coming to university. He successfully appropriated the conventions of academic discourse to the extent that his essay writing was like that of a second or third-year student. Ben chose a path to success which was partly determined by his previous experiences both of writing and of living in specific social contexts, but he also exercised choices in and around his writing which shaped it. His identity as a successful student was constituted in the act of writing as he erased the textual traces which might identify him as an 'ESL speaker'.

Successful students seem to be those who can negotiate the complex intertextuality of academic texts and the pedagogic demands this makes on students. Those whose home and school-based discourses (including the discourses of non-formal schooling like Ben's trade union education discourse) are 'better prepared' (as opposed to 'underprepared') to enter the new community. If we believe in the power of human subjects to exercise agency and that the relationship between social structures and practices is dialectical, then, as I have tried to argue in this chapter, students can, as Ben does, respond to opportunities and obstacles in 'conventional or creative ways' (see Giddens 1984, cited in Heller and Martin-Jones 1996: 8).

Notes

1 All names of participants are pseudonyms and informed consent was obtained from all participants. English first names were selected if the participant identified as having an English first name and African first names chosen if the participant used an African first name.

2 In terms of the university's grading conventions, 50 per cent was a pass; 50–59 percent a third-class pass; 60–69 per cent a second-class pass; 70–74 per cent an upper-second-class pass and 75 per cent and above a first-class pass. In the South

African university system, upper-second-class passes are rare and first-class passes are exceptional.

3 His name and student number have been deleted.

4 Anthony Giddens is a very highly regarded social theorist whose book was recommended to the class. I have used the 1971 version of his book, while Ben refers to a later version.

5 The *Course Reader* was a compilation of photocopied texts from the works of Marx, Weber and Durkheim put together for the students. Most students used it as their primary source.

6 Hewlett's interviews with black students at the same institution revealed student anger at the perceived negation of their 'political' identities by marker feedback which questioned the relevance of students' political comments to the given essay topic. This appeared to be a particularly sensitive issue when the marker was 'white and unfamiliar to the student' (1996: 94).

7 The discrepancies between Ben's essay marks and those for his tests and exams were striking. His essay marks were extremely high: 85 per cent for each of the two essays assigned for the course. However, on the three class tests written during the year he scored 53 per cent, 72 per cent and 44 per cent, while in the mid-year exam he got 50 per cent, improving to 65 per cent in the final in November. His final mark at the end of the year, 61 per cent, was a weighted combination of these marks, as the exam counted 70 per cent towards the final mark.

8 It is noteworthy that 71 per cent of the Sociology One students in 1994 were black.

References

AZASCO. (1993) 'Anonymous marking: A brief outline'. Document presented to the Senate of the University of the Witwatersrand, 29 November 1993 by Branch Executive Committee, AZASCO-Wits.

Bakhtin, M. (1981) *The Dialogic Imagination.* Austin: University of Texas Press.

Bakhtin, M. (1986) *Speech Genres and Other Late Essays.* Austin: University of Texas Press.

Bourdieu P. (1977) 'The economics of linguistic exchanges', *Social Sciences Information*, 16(6), 645–68.

Brandt, D. (1986) 'Text and context: How writers come to mean', in B. Couture (ed.), *Functional Approaches to Writing: Research Perspectives.* London: Frances Pinter, pp. 93–119.

Candlin, C. and Hyland, K. (1999) 'Introduction: Integrating approaches to the study of writing', in C. Candlin and K. Hyland (eds), *Writing: Texts, Processes and Practices.* London: Longman, pp. 1–17.

Cazden, C.B. (1988) *Classroom Discourse.* Portsmouth, NH: Heineman.

Cherry, R. (1988) 'Ethos versus persona: Self-representation in written discourse', *Written Communication*, 5(3), 251–76.

Chiseri-Strater, E. (1991) *Academic Literacies: The Public and Private Discourse of University Students.* Portsmouth, NH: Boynton-Cook.

Clark, R. and Ivanič, R. (1997) *The Politics of Writing.* London: Routledge.

Fairclough, N. (1989) *Language and Power.* London: Longman.

Fairclough, N. (1992) *Discourse and Social Change.* Cambridge: Polity Press.

Gee, J.P. (1990) *Social Linguistics and Literacies: Ideology in Discourses.* London: The Falmer Press.

Geertz, C. (1975) *The Interpretation of Cultures.* London: Hutchinson.

Giddens, A. (1971) *Capitalism and Modern Social Theory*. Cambridge: Cambridge University Press.

Halliday, M.A.K. (1994) *Introduction to Functional Grammar* 2nd edn. London: Arnold.

Halliday, M.A.K. and Hasan, R. (1989) *Language, Context, and Text: Aspects of Language in a Social-Semiotic Perspective*. Victoria: Deakin University Press.

Hamp-Lyons, L. (1991) 'Pre-text related influences on the writer', in L. Hamp-Lyons (ed.), *Assessing Second Language Writing in Academic Contexts*. Norwood NJ: Ablex, pp. 87–107.

Heller, M. and Martin-Jones, M. (1996) 'Introduction to the special issues on education in multilingual settings: Discourse, identities, and power', *Linguistics and Education*, 8(1), 3–16.

Hewlett, L. (1996) 'How can you discuss alone?: Academic literacy in a South African context', in D. Baker, J. Clay and C. Fox (eds), *Challenging Ways of Knowing: In English, Mathematics and Science*. London: Falmer Press, pp. 89–100.

Ivanič, R. (1998) *Writing and Identity: The Discoursal Construction of Identity in Academic Writing*. Amsterdam: John Benjamins.

Ivanič, R. and Camps, D. (2001) 'I am how I sound: Voice as self-representation in L2 writing', *Journal of Second Language Writing*, 10(3), 3–33.

Ivanič, R. and Simpson, J. (1992) 'Who's who in academic writing?', in N. Fairclough (ed.), *Critical Language Awareness*. London: Longman, pp. 141–73.

Kress, G. (1985) *Linguistic Processes in Sociocultural Practice*. Victoria: Deakin University Press.

Kress, G. (1993) *Learning to Write*. London: Routledge.

Norton, B. (2000) *Identity and Language Learning*. Essex: Pearson Education.

Peters, P. (1986) 'Getting the theme across: A study of dominant function in the academic writing of university students', in B. Couture (ed.), *Functional Approaches to Writing: Research Perspectives*. London: Frances Pinter, pp. 169–85.

Prior, P. (1991) 'Contextualising writing and response in a graduate seminar', *Written Communication*, 8(3), 267–310.

Prior, P. (1994) 'Response, revision, disciplinarity: A microhistory of a dissertation prospectus in Sociology', *Written Communication*, 11(4), 483–533.

Prior, P. (1995) 'Redefining the task: An ethnographic examination of writing and response in graduate seminars', in D. Belcher and G. Braine (eds), *Academic Writing in a Second Language: Essays on Research and Pedagogy*. Norwood, NJ: Ablex, pp. 47–81.

Prosser, M. and Webb, C. (1994) 'Relating the process of undergraduate essay writing to the finished product', *Studies in Higher Education*, 19(2), 125–38.

Sinclair, J.McH. and Coulthard, R.M. (1975) *Towards an Analysis of Discourse*. Oxford: Oxford University Press.

SRC. (1994) Minutes of meeting. University of the Witwatersrand. 15 February.

Starfield, S. (2002) ' "I'm a second-language English speaker": Negotiating writer identity and authority in Sociology One', *Journal of Language, Identity, and Education*, 1(2), 121–40.

Vice-Chancellor's Office. (1994) Minutes of meeting, Vice-Chancellor's Office. University of the Witwatersrand, 28 March.

Wits Student. (1993) 'Azasco for no names', *Wits Student*, 45(3), 2. Johannesburg: University of the Witwatersrand.

Appendix 1: Cover sheet of Ben's essay

NAME   :   *Ben*.

STUD. No.   :

TUTOR   :

TUT. TIME   :   14h00 at CB41

STREAM   :   D

ESSAY TOPIC   :   Why is the concept of exploitation
                            fundamental to Marx's desired endpoint of
                            socialism ?

85½.

Appendix 2: Introduction to Ben's essay

Introduction

According to Marx, exploitation is one of the predominant features in the capitalist mode of production and it refers to a situation where the capitalists are maximizing profits at the expense of the labour power of the proletariat. Marx also argues that the perpetuation of capitalism is actually intensifying exploitation, consequently exacerbating pauperisation in the working class. Marx, in his theory, pointed out that the only way to eradicate exploitation and other related problems experienced under capitalism, is to usher in socialism where the ownership of private property and class antagonism will be non-existent. The explanation of the concepts of exploitation and socialism given above is quite broad and it offers little understanding. Therefore, this essay will attempt to discuss firstly, the concept of exploitation in more detail. Secondly, the implications of exploitation and finally the concept of socialism.

Good   Introduction

6 The exegesis as a genre: an ethnographic examination

Brian Paltridge

1 Introduction

This paper examines the exegesis in art and design Masters degrees. The exegesis is a written text which accompanies a visual project submitted as the research component of the Masters degree. These texts are similar in some ways to what is called the thesis[1] genre, but, in many ways, are also quite different. The exegesis expands on the methodology, parameters, and context of the visual project, rather being a stand-alone piece of work in its own right. The study reported on in this chapter is a 'textography' (Swales 1998) of the particular genre; that is, an examination which looks at the texts themselves, as well as the context of production and interpretation of the texts. The study draws on the notion of the ethnography of writing (Grabe and Kaplan 1996) where key participants in the production and evaluation of the genre are asked about its role, purpose, and discourse community expectations. The study examines the interaction between texts, roles, and contexts (Johns 1997) as a way of understanding the characteristics of the particular genre and the role it plays in its particular academic setting. As Fairclough (1989) and Lea (1994) have argued, any examination of texts needs to take into consideration the relationships between texts, the processes of their production and interpretation, and the social and cultural context of their production and interpretation. This study aims to do this. Data includes student, supervisor, programme leader, and examiner interviews. The course prospectus, guides to students and examiners, examiners' reports, and the annual programme report are also examined. A range of exegeses is also described.

2 Thesis writing

Apart from a few exceptions, most of the literature on thesis writing includes very little analysis of actual texts. There are a number of reasons why this might be the case. One of these is that theses are often difficult to get hold of in university libraries, and even more difficult to get hold of from outside a university. Often a researcher has to know what thesis they want in order to get it, and when they do, they cannot take it away with them to read and refer to for their analysis. Some universities will send a copy of a thesis to another university on an inter-loan agreement and some will not. And sometimes a university will send a copy of the thesis on microfiche which requires particular equipment (and a particular location) to read it. In some countries, copies of theses can be obtained electronically, but again the researcher needs to know exactly which thesis they want in order to obtain it.

Another difficulty is the size of theses as texts for analysis. This often places limits on what a researcher is able to look at as well as the number of texts they are able to analyse. There is often also considerable variation in expectations across disciplines, fields of study, and supervisors, in terms of what a thesis should look like, what it should contain, and what it should do.

Theses in some areas of study, furthermore, are changing. A thesis written in some academic disciplines is now very different from one that might have been written ten or more years ago, particularly with the influence of post-modernism and other views of knowledge, and what is now considered to be valid 'research' (Best and Kellner 1997). A further problem is that although theses are similar in some ways to other pieces of research writing, they are also in many ways quite different. Apart from the size of the texts and the scale of the projects they report on, they also vary in terms of their purpose, readership, and the kind of skills and knowledge they are required to display (Atkinson 1997).

There are also often very particular requirements that theses are expected to meet. For example, an examiner may be asked to consider the extent to which the text they are assessing provides evidence that the writer has carried out 'a sustained piece of work demonstrating that a research apprenticeship is complete' and that the student 'should be admitted to the community of scholars in the discipline' (University of Melbourne 2001: 1) (or not).

Swales (1996) describes yet another issue in his discussion of the 'occluded' nature of genres in the academy. By this he means many important high-stakes genres, such as examiners' reports, which are 'out of sight' and not accessible to public view. It is often difficult, without this kind of information, to know what is a highly regarded example of a thesis and what amount of revision was required by the examiners before the final copy of the thesis was accepted by the university. As a result, it is often difficult for researchers (and students) to know what is a 'best example' of a thesis and why. This is certainly also the case with the art and design exegesis.

3 Audience and academic writing

An important aspect of the context of reception and interpretation of a student's text is the audience of the text, the student's perception and understanding of that audience, and what this means for his or her text. Johns (1990) describes the expert, all-powerful reader of students' texts who can either accept or reject their writing as coherent and consistent with the conventions of a field of study, or not. In her view, knowledge of this audience's attitudes, beliefs, and expectations is not only possible, but essential, for students to succeed in academic settings. As Canagarajah (2002) has argued, the notion of audience influences all aspects of the writing process. Writers need to 'take into account the fact that matters such as knowledge, conventions, genre, and register are defined and used differently by each community or audience' (ibid.: 161).

Brookes and Grundy (1990) discuss the notion of 'primary' and 'secondary' readerships, which is especially important for students writing theses and exegeses. The student's text typically has a primary readership of one or more examiners, but also has a secondary readership of the student's supervisor and anyone else the student decides to show their work to for comment and feedback. The student may also have in mind a broader academic audience, such as readers of academic journals, participants at academic conferences, and other students in their area of study. It is the primary reader, however, that makes the final judgement as to the quality of the student's work, rather than any of their secondary readers. As Kamler and Threadgold point out:

> Thinking about who the examiners are, will/must shape the thesis and a variety of questions related to its production, including what are the interdisciplines it will cross and what tendacious issues it might address and how. (1997: 47)

As Kamler and Threadgold (1997: 53) argue, a dominant, or 'primary' reader, within the academy, 'quite simply counts more than other readers'.

4 Genre and academic writing

In recent years considerable attention has been given to the notion of genre in discussions of academic writing. Berkenkotter and Huckin (1995) provide an important contribution to this discussion. Their interest, in particular, is in the ways in which language users draw on genre knowledge in order to communicate in academic and professional communities. Their perspective on genre is based on five key principles.

The first principle of Berkenkotter and Huckin is that genres are dynamic rhetorical forms which have developed as responses to recurring communicative situations. Genres, in their view, both 'stabilize experience and give it coherence and meaning' (ibid.: 4). Genres change over time, however, in response to users' needs and changes in the situations in which they occur. Genres can, and should, be modified according to particular communicative circumstances and the particular setting of the text. Students need to be aware, then, that what they are writing is not *the* thesis (or exegesis) but an instance of a genre that is strongly influenced by a number of important factors. It is easy for a student to think that what applies in one seemingly similar situation may also apply in another. Students need to consider the ways things are done in the situation in which they are writing, and orient their text to account for these expectations.

Berkenkotter and Huckin's second principle is that genre knowledge is acquired through participation in the communicative activities of daily and professional life. Genre knowledge, further 'continues to develop as we participate in the activities of our culture' (ibid.: 7). As Prior (1998) has argued 'knowledge construction and communication are achieved by engagement, participation, and performance, not by detached learning of abstract rules' (Canagarajah 2002: 166). This tells us that, rather than simply comparing surface level features of a text with a prototypical example of the genre, we should also examine the processes through which writers and speakers acquire genre knowledge and what it is that people learn in this process that is needed for the successful performance of the genre.

Their third principle is that genre knowledge includes both form *and* content. This includes a sense of appropriate content for a particular purpose, in a particular setting, at a particular point in time. Students need to understand how what they are writing fits in with current discussions and assumptions in the setting in which they are communicating. A genre used without this sort of knowledge may fail to achieve its goal, or be rejected because it simply does not 'understand' the key issues of the discussion.

The fourth of Berkenkotter and Huckin's principles is that as people use genres and engage in communicative activities, they both constitute and reproduce particular social structures and social relations. As Threadgold has argued, genre is not an ideology-free, objective process, which can be 'separated from the social realities and processes which it contributes to maintaining' (1989: 103). For Threadgold, genres are not just linguistic categories but 'among the very processes by which . . . ideologies are reproduced, transmitted and potentially changed' (ibid.: 107).

Berkenkotter and Huckin's fifth principle is that a genre's conventions reveal much about the norms and ideologies of a discourse community. Performing a genre is never just the reformulation of a linguistic model, but always the performance of a politically and historically significant process. The analysis of genres should, as much as possible, aim to 'make visible' the social construction and transmission of ideologies, relationships, and identities (Threadgold 1989).

Students, then, need to consider general discourse community expectations and conventions for their text, as well as the particular expectations, conventions and requirements of the particular communicative setting (Dudley-Evans 1993, 1995). They need to consider the intended audience for their text, how their audience will react to what they read, and the criteria they will use for evaluating and responding to what they have written. Students need to consider the background knowledge, values, and understandings it is assumed they will share with their audience, including what is important to their audience and what is not (Johns 1997).

This 'situated' view of genre is clearly highly relevant for discussions of academic writing in that it takes us beyond the language and form of the text to a consideration of the ways in which a genre is embedded in the communicative activities of the members of a particular discourse community. It also gives us insights into the ways a person both acquires and uses genre knowledge as they participate in the knowledge-producing activities of their field or profession.

As Bazerman reminds us, genre 'is not simply a linguistic category defined by a structural arrangement of textual features' (1988: 319). There is a need to go 'beyond the text' (Freedman 1999) into the social and cultural context which surrounds the genre, in order to fully understand its purpose and use. Students need to be aware of this as much as they need to have command of the language needed to use to perform particular genres.

It is clear, then, that not all culturally relevant information can be derived from the text itself. There is, as Tickoo (1994) has argued, also the need to go beyond the text into ethnographic examinations of the social and cultural context in which the genre occurs as well as to explore 'insiders' views' on the genre in order to make genre-based descriptions pedagogically most useful.

5 An ethnography of writing

Grabe and Kaplan's (1996) notion of an ethnography of writing provides a useful framework for carrying out a context analysis which examines some of these issues. In the case of academic writing, an analysis of the social and cultural context in which the writing occurs considers the various components of the communicative situation and how these might impact upon what a student writes. It considers who writes what to whom, for what purpose, why, when, where, and how.

The analysis focuses on important contextual aspects of the genre and situation in which it occurs, each of which is strongly interconnected, and interacts with each other. The first of these is the actual setting of the text. For example, is the text written in a first or final year of a university course? Is the course undergraduate or postgraduate? What area of study is the text being written in? The analysis also considers the purpose of the text. For example, is the purpose of the text to display knowledge and understanding in a particular area, to demonstrate particular skills, to convince a reader, to argue a case, to critique, to break new ground – or all of these? The analysis also considers the content of the text, asking questions such as what is appropriate content for the text? What points of view and claims are acceptable in the particular area of study, and what points of view and claims are not – and why? Another issue is the intended audience for the text. For example, what is the intended audience for the text, their role and purpose in reading the text (Johns 1997)? How will the reader/s react to the text? What criteria will they use for assessing the text? What is important to their audience and what is not? A further issue is the relationship between the writer and reader/s of the text and how will this impact on what the student says. For example, are the students novices writing for experts? Or are they 'apprentices' writing for admission to an area of study? Or are they 'novices' writing for experts – or both? And to what extent do students have to tell their audience what they already know?

Other issues include discourse community expectations for the text, shared understandings between writers and reader/s of the text, and the background knowledge assumed by the text. For example, what *are* the general discourse community expectations and conventions for the text? What particular expectations, conventions, and requirements apply in the particular area of study? What genre is required by the assessment task? How is the text typically organized? What style of language should be used? How should students use source texts and how should they refer to other texts in their area of study? How should students quote and paraphrase other texts? How long should the piece of writing be? How is the piece of work weighted in terms of academic grades? What level of critical analysis is required (or not) of students at their particular level of study? What level of originality is expected of students? What background knowledge, values, and understandings is it assumed that students will share with their readers? And what amount of negotiation is possible in terms of all of this?

The analysis also considers the relationship the text has with other academic texts and other genres. Where is the text located within the systems of genres (Bazerman 1994) and genre networks (Swales and Feak 2001) that surround the text? And how is the student's text related to previous texts, such as other academic work and research in the area of study, and anticipated texts, such as examiners' reports, journal articles, and conference presentations?

5.1 Data collection and analysis

In order to carry out a context analysis of the art and design exegeses, the MA prospectus, MA publicity material, postgraduate student handbook, guide to examiners, examiners' reports, and annual report on the MA programme were examined. Student, supervisor, programme leader, and examiner interviews were also conducted. Six students, three supervisors, three examiners, and the programme leader were interviewed for the study. Eleven exegeses were examined (see Table 6.1).

Each of the interviews followed the same basic format (see Appendix) although space was allowed for interviewees to provide extra information and to elaborate on particular points that had not been covered in the initial set of questions. Interviewees were given an information sheet that explained the project to them and a consent form to sign indicating their agreement to take part in the study. Anonymity of project participants was guaranteed.

The framework for analysis of the data drew on Grabe and Kaplan's (1996) notion of the ethnography of writing presented above. The results of the analysis that follow are presented as a set of aspects of the context of production and interpretation of the texts. Each of these aspects are strongly related to, and impact on, each other and there are significant associations between. It should not be read, then, that they are as separate and discrete as their presentation here might suggest.

5.2 The setting of the texts

The texts that were examined were written for a Master of Arts degree in art and design at a university of technology in New Zealand. Until very recently, the university had been an institute of technology and had only one year previously acquired university status. The Masters degree in art and design had, however, been on offer for four years and had recently been externally moderated by a visiting professor from a British university. The School of Art and Design in which the Masters degree is taught is very highly regarded in the field and its staff have strong reputations as art and design theorists and practitioners. Some of these Members of staff had taught on similar programmes in other New Zealand and Australian universities so had a strong understanding of art and design as a field of study in academic settings other than their own.

The MA in art and design is a two-year full-time degree. The first year of the degree is made up of core courses which focus on contextual, technological, methodological, and interdisciplinary issues, and art and design practice. The second year of the degree is devoted to the development of an independent visual project and the accompanying exegesis. The programme of study moves from directed study, theory, and practice, through to self-directed research, development, and production of the visual project and exegesis.

Art and design could be described as a 'divergent' area of study in that research perspectives are often drawn from other areas of study and there is a broad view of what is considered 'research' (Becher and Trowler 2001). The MA is interdisciplinary in nature with students being encouraged to explore a range of processes, technologies, and cultural perspectives in the development of their work. Two or more supervisors work with each student in order to support the interdisciplinary potential of the student's project as well as to provide specific specialist support.

The MA prospectus points out how in the traditional practice of art and design education, means of visual expression such as painting, sculpture, typography and printmaking have, in the main, been separate disciplines. Today, they argue, the demarcations of those specializations are being challenged and broadened by technological innovations and cultural and theoretical developments that are rapidly reordering traditional paradigms of art and design practice. Art and design, thus, is no longer organized around exclusive definitions of particular mediums, or on the basis of particular practices, but through a view of connective practices which encourage students to pursue new horizons in the face of constant, and at times rapid, change.

5.3 The content of the texts

The collection of exegeses examined covered a range of different topics and kinds of visual project. These are summarized in Table 6.1.

Table 6.1 Titles of the exegeses and their visual projects

Title of the exegesis	The visual project
Being Chinese	An installation of artwork pieces (paintings, Chinese papercuts and cabinet boxes)
Seeing beyond sight: The poetics of line	A compilation of line drawings presented in a loose-leaf atlas, a public exhibition of line drawings, and an extended piece of poetry in spoken and written form.
Public outdoor furniture design: Capturing the ethos of the city	A series of benches and tables designed for an outdoor public space
Myth of the cave: Art (?) and the dissection of meaning	A set of paintings presented as a CD-ROM
Dressing the tarot	A set of costumes presented as a portfolio of photographic images, an installation, and a choreographed performance
The new pencil: Towards developing a challenging curriculum in computer imaging for art and design undergraduate education	A poster session of computer generated images
Natural dying: An evocative expression	An exhibition of hand dyed and knitted wearable art
Deconstructing the inscrutable: Wabi Sabi, a Japanese evaluation of beauty and design	A CD-ROM and installation using ceramics and mixed media
Still life re-framed	An installation of paintings, fruit and vegetables, and mixed media
Secret site: A investigative narrative of the notion of artistic identity	An exhibition of photographs
Fade away and radiate	A set of public installations, incorporating video and work placed on a web site

The perspectives taken in these exegeses could be described as neither quantitative nor qualitative in the traditional sense of research but rather descriptive, evaluative, and reflective. One student described his methodology as 'personal, intuitive, and reflective', a view that was reflected in many of the interviewees' comments on their research.

Many of the exegeses, in part, documented the creation of the student's visual project. Some had a section on the methodology employed for the development of the project (rather than the exegesis). Some drew on theories which had been presented to students in a course on cultural investigations they had taken in their first year of study. This course covered a range of intellectual positions rather than a single overarching theory. As a result, the exegeses were based on a range of different theoretical points of view which came from a number of different sources. One example of this is the student who wrote the exegesis titled 'Fade away and radiate' which covered the areas of architecture, sculpture, and filmmaking. The student said in her interview that she found the theoretical drive for her work changed while she was working on the exegesis from phenomenology to a range of theories which came from the areas of architecture and film. In her exegesis she 'played off' the tension between these disciplines to produce a commentary on both the disciplines and her visual project.

5.4 The purpose of the texts

The postgraduate handbook says the purpose of the exegesis is to elucidate the relationship between the personal concept of the candidate and the perceptual context of the body of work presented for examination. The course material adds to this by saying the purpose of the exegesis is to develop, critically analyse, process, and evaluate a body of work which may be social, cultural, technical, or aesthetic, in focus. The aim of the exegesis, it says, is to set the creative work in its relevant theoretical, historical, critical, and design context. The exegesis also seeks to explain and defend both the applied research methodology and theoretical base of the visual project.

The exegesis may also develop a topic in some depth which is closely related contextually or methodologically to the overall visual project. Where the development of this topic becomes a more independent and in-depth investigation, the issue arises, one of the supervisors suggested, of whether the exegesis might then be better described as a thesis or dissertation. This raises questions, he said, of definition and demarcation, and expectations including the size of the written text in proportion to the practical visual component.

The exegesis also plays a role in legitimizing a mode of writing institutionally and the place of creative areas of study in universities. As one of the supervisors said, the students are in a curious position in that they do not need the Masters degree in order to become a successful artist. There is, however, something different that happens, he said, because a student is in an institutional setting. Part of this difference is that there is a certain kind of requirement, in the institution, to formalize in some way the questioning of and reflecting on the student's own practice. The exegesis, he said, serves the role of demonstrating that reflexive moment. The exegesis also assists the students in sorting out the agenda for their oral examination.

One of the students said in her interview that the exegesis, for her, worked both as a support document and as a philosophical articulation of the practical component of her work. It was also a documentation of her visual project. In many cases, she said, it is the only documentation that remains after the visual project has been dismantled. She saw the exegesis as analogous to subtitles in a film in that they are not a complete translation of the dialogue of a film but rather a sketch of what is taking place. To make sense of a film, a viewer has to search constantly between the subtitles and the action of the film, remembering that subtitles are not a transcription but a rough approximation. The reader of an exegesis also needs to do this. For her, the exegesis provided an umbrella for theorizing and contextualizing what was driving the practical component of her project, bringing together a strong correlation between practice and theory. Another student said in her interview that there was a reciprocal exchange between the practical work and her visual project. The exegesis produced a dialogue between these two components as well as a pause from the process of creating art works. She described her exegesis as being both reflexive and constitutive of the practical work.

5.5 The intended audience for the texts

An important issue is who the students are writing their exegesis for. Some students may think they are writing for their supervisors, for the friends or colleagues that might read the drafts of their text, or for other students and academics working in the field of art and design. A further issue is who counts the most in judging whether the exegesis meets its particular requirements, or not.

The intended audience for the exegesis, the supervisors said, is two people: the two examiners. One supervisor said:

> The exegesis is a curious document in that it's only read by two people. I say you're writing for the examiners because the student has to be able to pitch his or her text to a certain level of refinement. I believe, however, I'm at odds with a certain kind of prescription about the exegesis. I've been told by a couple of students who've said 'we've been told you write for the most general audience, for somebody who doesn't know much about the field'. I say, well, that's ridiculous. You're a higher degree student who should be writing for an informed audience and an examiner who we have selected because they have expertise in the field, and you're pitching your work at the level of that expertise.

If students want a different audience for their writing, the supervisor added, they then need to revise their text in some way. In order to be published, for example, the exegesis needs to be reworked for its different audience and its different purpose.

One student, however, said she was writing the exegesis 'for herself'. She had no sense, she said, that she was writing her text for her examiners, nor for the institution. Her exegesis and visual project, notwithstanding, received the highest possible grade from her examiners. They said her exegesis was an exceptional submission, that it excelled in its understanding of contemporary theory, and that the project was remarkably persuasive at the level of both craft and critique.

5.6 The relationship between the writer and readers of the texts

There is an important difference between the writers and readers of texts such as research articles and writers and readers of theses and dissertations, which is not immediately obvious to many student writers. This relationship changes, further, for other academic genres, such as conference presentations. Writers of research articles are generally 'experts writing for experts' whereas writers of theses and dissertations are often 'novices writing for experts' and writing 'for admission to the academy'. Conference presentations, for graduate students, are often written as a mixture of the two.

One of the supervisors said he felt this issue goes right back to the question of what art and design is doing in universities. The exegesis, in part, he felt validates creative works as research and the exegesis is caught up in all of this. At other universities where he had worked he was not allowed to use the word 'research' for his students' work. Rather, he had to talk about 'research training', even at the doctoral level. It was not until students got on to a postdoctoral fellowship that they were viewed as actually being engaged in 'research'. Visual arts students, however, he felt, fell into the anomalous situation that when they leave the university, they are no longer required to do the writing that they do there, which is quite different from the sort of research where people continue to do print-based work. What is more, art and design students do not need the Masters degree to validate their position in the field in the same way that Masters students in other areas of study might. Exegesis writers, then, are not always writing 'for admission to the academy' in the sense that thesis and dissertation writers in other areas of study often are. The students, one of the supervisors said, see the exegesis as a test of their capacity to make sense of the work to somebody who they would recognize as being a significant player in the field.

5.7 Discourse community expectations for the texts

The degree regulations for an exegesis at the university state that there is a minimum written requirement of 3,000 words. There is a variation to this regulation published by the School of Art and Design which suggests a minimum of 6,000 words for the exegesis. This variation is, to some extent, due to the fact that for a student to develop a topic in the depth appropriate to Masters level study, extra word length is generally required. It is also based on exegesis requirements in equivalent programmes at other universities in New Zealand and Australia. In reality, however, most exegeses are between 10,000 and 12,000 words.

There are currently no guidelines, for either students or examiners, which discuss the relative weighting of the exegesis and the visual project. This is, in part, because the weighting is not the same for every student. The student handbook states that an appropriate exegesis length should be negotiated with the supervisor. Students can establish a balance between the exegesis and the visual project anywhere along a continuum from 10 per cent to 100 per cent. While this provides great flexibility, it also raises questions about the differential nature and requirements of the written component and at what point the exegesis becomes a dissertation or a thesis. It also raises questions about appropriate examiners for assessing the two components of the project. This is generally addressed by appointing examiners whose collective expertise gives the required balance. During assessment, however, the visual project and the exegesis are treated as one unit, and the grade recommended by each of the examiners is given equal weighting by the postgraduate board of studies when the overall grade and level of honours are considered.

Notwithstanding differences in length and weighting, some conventions still hold for written exegeses. For example, an exegesis has to have a coherent structure to it. One student had wanted to do a piece of creative writing as his exegesis and his supervisor had insisted that the student still have a 'front ending' that linked that piece to the visual project and that provided a guide for the reader as to what this piece of writing was doing and why it was there. The student was also told he needed to provide a framework so the piece of creative writing would be seen as appropriate to the situation. In this sense, the supervisor said, the exegesis and the thesis have some sort of commonality in that students have to make the structure and framework of what they are doing clear, even though an exegesis in an art and design school has much more latitude for the modes of writing that students may end up engaging in.

One of the supervisors said students were expected to provide a short methodological statement that says what the broad area of enquiry is that they are working in. For example, is it an empirical piece of work or are they working within a certain way of thinking – and why are they doing this? He also added:

> I'm a bit old fashioned as far as syntax goes. I think attention to syntactic structure is still important. I think bibliographic referencing is still quite important. You also have the same kinds of micro-structural moves as in a thesis. For example, you're introducing arguments, making a point, giving the outcomes of arguments, and building on that. That's still there.

One student said she did not want to interrupt the reading of her text by using footnotes so she added them into the text in a lighter font. She also used a less conventional way of placing references in her text that she took from writing in the area of architecture. Instead of showing the author and date in brackets within her text, she placed the full reference in a lighter font above the place in the text where she had drawn on the author's work. This unusual way of writing and citing other work was not commented on by the examiners. They said in their reports, however, that her writing had involved a number of 'risk taking operations' but that the outcome of the piece of work was among the best they had ever seen.

This same student had obtained agreement from the department to hand in her exegesis after her oral examination so that she could include visual documentation of her project in the final text. Her examiners were given a four-page extract from her exegesis prior to the oral examination and read the completed exegesis only after they had met with the student and viewed the visual work. The student said she was well aware that she was going against general conventions and expectations for submitting an exegesis by doing this, but that it was crucial to her work to do it this way. She had done this, she said, by 'side stepping' the people in her department that she thought would have been more conventional in their view of what she wanted to do.

5.8 Shared values and understandings between writers and readers of the text

Becher and Trowler (2001) describe each academic discipline as an academic tribe that has its own academic culture, its own sets of norms and values, its own bodies of knowledge, its own modes of inquiry, in short, its own academic territory. Sometimes students can 'border cross' (Giroux 1992) between these territories, and sometimes they cannot (Swales 2000). Academic tribes and territories are not, however, monolithic and unitary (Hyland 2000). As Hyland (ibid.: 9) points out, academic disciplines 'are made up of individuals with diverse experiences, expertise, commitments and influence'. There may be considerable variation in which members of these disciplines identify and agree with the goals, methods, conventions, histories, and values of their academic community, even though they may disagree with each other in agreed ways. This is as true of art and design as an area of study as it is of other academic areas.

One of the supervisors said a good exegesis should contain critical reflection, not only on the work, but also on the frameworks whereby the work is possible; that is, 'the horizons that have led to what comes into view as the project for the work'. This kind of exegesis was clearly much more highly valued by examiners than a solely descriptive piece of work. While this demonstration of critical awareness is often put forward as a requirement for a post-graduate qualification, such a requirement, one of the supervisors said, often conflicts with aspects of the methodologies employed by many artists and designers. The supervisor also said it can be argued that the notion of critical awareness is of little consequence in the consumption and legitimation of a work of art. In his view, students attempting to outline and justify the methodology they have employed are likely to get only so far through analytical or deconstructive approaches. Furthermore, this critical reflection may contribute little of value to the body of knowledge, have little predictive value for the artist, and even induce a self-consciousness that is counterproductive to the students' methodology. He felt that this problem could often be circumvented by discussing the implications and limitations of the intuitive method as a whole, rather than attempting to define the stages of the research and defend the internal logic of the process. Examiners, however, he said, need to be sensitive to this and not penalize students for not describing their research methodology in more traditional terms.

5.9 The relationship the text has with other texts

An important development in genre theory is the notion of 'systems of genres' (Bazerman 1994); that is, the way the use of one genre may assume or depend on the use of a number of other interrelated genres. An example of this is the academic essay, which may draw from, and cite, a number of other genres such as lectures, specialist academic texts, and journal articles. Academic essays also interrelate closely with assignment guidelines, statements of assessment criteria, tutorial discussions, and teacher–student consultations. Each of these genres, thus, interacts with each other within their own particular system of genres. It is also often the case that only certain genres may appropriately follow other genres. Also, one genre is often dependent on the outcome of another genre. The sequence of genres may be highly constrained in some circumstances and less so in others. Nonetheless, our students need to be able to perform each of the genres well when the appropriate occasion arises (Bazerman 1994). Swales and Feak (2001) use the term 'genre networks' to capture this interrelationship of genres.

The notions of genre systems and genre networks are an important aspect of genre knowledge 'outside the text' that can be usefully explored in a context analysis. One of the students interviewed for the study discussed the genre networks she moved through in the production of her exegesis. Some of these were, perhaps, predictable while some of them were much less so. The most obvious genres in her network were the exegesis proposal which she presented for admission to the degree, the development of the proposal which she wrote for her research methods course, the student/supervisor consultations she engaged in as part of the development of the visual project and exegesis, the oral examination she took part in at the time of the public presentation of her work, and the exegesis itself. Other genres were the presentation of the visual project, conversations she had with other students, artists, and friends she knew outside of the institution, and discussions she had with academic staff who were no longer working at the university. She also attended a writing class for postgraduate students at another university to help her write her exegesis. Other genres that were part of her genre network were the course description she read at the beginning of the degree and the research material she read for writing the exegesis. She did not know there was a handbook for postgraduate students so did not refer to that document for the writing of her exegesis. Hidden, or 'occluded', genres she did not have access to were the guidelines that were given to her examiners, the examiners' reports, conversations between the examiners, and the postgraduate board of studies meeting where her final grade was discussed and decided on by a group of people she largely did not know.

5.10 The structure of the texts

Previous research into the typical structure of theses suggests that there are a number of main ways in which these texts are typically organized. A study carried out at the University of Melbourne which looked at masters and PhD theses found four main kinds of thesis being written at that institution (Paltridge 2002). These were 'traditional: simple', 'traditional: complex', 'compilations of research articles' and 'topic-based' types of theses. The first three of these thesis types are all variations on the type of thesis which has 'introduction', 'review of the literature', 'materials and methods', 'results', 'discussion', and 'conclusion' type sections. The 'topic-based' thesis typically commences with an introductory chapter which is then followed by a series of chapters which have titles based on sub-topics of the topic under investigation. The thesis then ends with a 'conclusions' chapter.

The exegeses that were examined in this study did not fall into 'traditional' groupings of organizational structures. They were all largely 'topic-based', although some of them commenced with a section that outlined the methodology that was followed in the development of the visual project and had a number of chapters that also drew from the more traditional type of thesis. For example, the thesis that was titled 'Dressing the tarot' was made up of an 'introduction', a 'methodology' section, a 'commentary' section, and a 'conclusions' section. This was followed by endnotes, a 'survey of relevant literature' (an alternative title for the bibliography) and reproductions of a set of images. The 'commentary' section included a section titled 'Investigation of resources' where the student outlined where she had drawn the resources from for her project, and included a budget which outlined what the visual project had cost. This section, she noted, had been added at the request of her examiners.

Some of the exegeses, however, took quite different approaches to laying out the text. The exegesis that crossed the areas of architecture, film, and sculpture, for example, was laid out in three simultaneous strands of text appearing in continuous blocks of text across the page. Instead of reading the text from the top to the bottom of each page, the reader had to read each strand of the text from page to page, then return to the next, then the next. The student said she did this to spatially lay out the tension between the three distinct bodies of theory she had been working with. She said she thought that as this was a visual arts degree she should be consistent in her writing with the practices she was employing elsewhere in her visual arts practice. This non-linear format was highly praised by the examiners, even though they acknowledged that she had taken a substantial risk in using it.

5.11 *The language of the texts*

An examination of the language of the texts is a necessary complement to ethnographic studies. Such an examination is, however, beyond the scope of the present chapter. The requirements of the texts described by the supervisors, written guidelines presented to the students, and the views and practices of the examiners all have important implications for the use of language. Together, they present an extremely complex picture with a number of important tensions in terms of what actually happens in the texts, what is successful, what is accepted, and what is not. How all of this is done, in language, can only be seen by looking at the texts themselves. For example, what linguistic resources do the students use to negotiate their position in the text? How do they negotiate their relationship with the audience of their text? What amount of linguistic variation is allowed in the texts? And how are the students' arguments presented and supported in the texts?

There may be considerable variation in how students, supervisors, and examiners identify and agree with the goals and values of their area of study and the ways in which these are expressed in language. The question for students writing art and design exegeses is, what *are* these ways? And what amount of variation and negotiation is possible among these ways? There is very often a 'hidden curriculum' (Christie 1989) in the use of language that is followed in the awarding of academic grades. What then, in the area of art and design, is this 'hidden curriculum'? It is interesting to note that the student who consistently flouted the conventions for exegesis writing was, at the same time, highly rewarded. The interview with the student showed that she was well aware of the 'rules of game' for this kind of writing, even though she chose not to follow them. Being aware and in control of the conventions of her area of study, she then negotiated a strategy for resisting them.

One of the supervisors, who also played the role of an examiner on occasions, said he advised his students to take a largely conventional approach to writing their exegesis. He said clarity of expression in the exegesis is important as it takes on the role of indicating how generic assessment criteria might be appropriately applied to the student's text. Other approaches, however, which are consistent with the methodology of the practical work and which reinforce a particular methodological approach might, he said, on occasion be appropriate. For example, an exegesis might incorporate a number of narratives, or other kinds of written expression, such as poetry, or be developed through a number of competing narratives that reflect certain poststructural approaches.

Another supervisor said that the exegesis generally falls short in its ability to represent experiential aspects of making and 'reading' practical work. In his view, unusual and sophisticated writing skills are needed to transcend the limitations of written language in order to articulate matters that are key to the success and quality of the practical work, which is often subtle, complex, and contingent. Such skills, he felt, go beyond the requirements of normal academic writing suitable for a written thesis.

Some of the students actually talked about language in their texts. The writer of the exegesis titled 'Myth of the cave: Art (?) and the dissection of meaning', for example, had a section titled 'Why I write the way I do'. She said it is important for writers to write in a style they are comfortable with so as to make 'the mind as comfortable as possible for the challenging task of thinking'. She wrote that the question of style plagued her writing and that it seemed impossible to maintain a similar style of writing throughout the exegesis.

6 Conclusions

This chapter has considered the exegesis as an instance of the thesis genre. Often writers use the term 'thesis' to refer to an exegesis even though, in many ways, they are referring to quite a different kind of text and quite a different site of production and reception from that of the more traditional 'thesis' (or dissertation). For example, the academic setting of an exegesis is different from that of many other academic areas of study in that it is based on a less traditional view of what 'research' is, and how it is conceptualized. The weighting of the exegesis also varies from piece to piece of writing making it hard, in some ways, to compare one outcome with another.

The boundaries between art and design as an area of study and other academic disciplines are also much less clear than more 'convergent' (Becher and Trowler 2001) areas of study which may have clearer sets of norms, bodies of knowledge, and modes of inquiry. The purpose of exegeses is also somewhat different from that of a more traditional thesis in that there may be less display of knowledge in the students' texts, even though students are still writing to convince their reader of what they know and the depth to which they know it. The place of the exegesis in the students' future lives is also very different from that of many thesis writers.

While some academic conventions still hold for exegesis writers, such as the need to acknowledge sources and to list references, there is much more latitude in exegeses in how this can be done. Students are still expected to present a coherent argument and to convince their readers, but the ways in which they can do this vary much more than in traditional theses, or dissertations. There were several cases of students submitting their exegesis after their oral examination, a situation that would never occur within the context of a more traditional approach to thesis examination. Students in art and design, then, are more able to 'resist' some of the academic conventions for thesis writing and examination that might hold in more traditional areas of study which have a more established place in the academy.

As Zamel and Spack have argued, 'it is no longer possible to assume that there is one type of literacy in the academy' (1998: ix) and that there is one 'culture' in the university whose norms and practices simply have to be learnt in order for our students to have access to our institutions. Writing in the academy requires a repertoire of linguistic practices that are based on complex sets of discourses, identities and values (Lea and Street 1998). This has enormous implications for students writing in new and emergent academic areas (Baynham 2000), such as art and design, where they may write texts which cross a number of disciplinary boundaries and where conventions and expectations of how they present their text might be more fluid and open than in other areas of study. We, as researchers, need to work to make these complexities as visible as possible to our students as well as help our students understand how they can negotiate academic conventions and academic boundaries in ways which help them achieve their goals, yet maintain their academic voices and identities.

Note

1 The terms 'thesis' and 'dissertation' are used in different ways in different parts of the world. In the US, honours and masters students write 'theses' whereas in Britain, they write 'dissertations'. At the PhD level, a US student writes a 'dissertation' and a student at a British university writes a 'thesis'. In Australia and New Zealand, the term 'thesis' is used for both the Masters and doctoral degrees. The term 'thesis' is used throughout this chapter as the focus here is on the exegesis and as instance of the (Masters) thesis genre.

References

Atkinson, D. (1997) 'Teaching and researching the thesis/dissertation in ESP'. Colloquium introduction, TESOL '97, Orlando, Florida.

Baynham, M. (2000) 'Academic writing in new and emergent discipline areas', in M. Lea and B. Stierer (eds), *Student Writing in Higher Education: New Contexts*. Buckingham: Open University Press, pp. 17–31.

Bazerman, C. (1994) 'Systems of genres and the enactment of social intentions', in A. Freedman and P. Medway (eds), *Genre and the New Rhetoric*. London: Taylor and Francis, pp. 79–101.

Bazerman, C. (1988) *Shaping Written Knowledge*. Madison, WI: University of Wisconsin Press.

Becher, T. and Trowler, P.R. (2001) *Academic Tribes and Territories: Intellectual Enquiry and the Cultures of Disciplines* 2nd edn. Buckingham: Open University Press.

Berkenkotter, C. and Huckin, T.N. (1995) *Genre Knowledge in Disciplinary Communication: Cognition/Culture/Power*. Hillsdale, NJ: Lawrence Erlbaum.

Best, S. and Kellner, D. (1997) *The Postmodern Turn*. New York: Guilford Press.

Brookes, A. and Grundy, P. (1990) *Writing for Study Purposes*. Cambridge: Cambridge University Press.

Canagarajah, S. (2002) *Critical Academic Writing and Multilingual Students*. Ann Arbor, MI: University of Michigan Press.

Christie, F. (1989) *Language Education*. Oxford: Oxford University Press.

Dudley-Evans, T. (1993) 'Variation in communication patterns between discourse communities: The case of highway engineering and plant biology', in G. Blue (ed.), *Language, Learning and Success: Studying through English*. London: Modern English Publications in association with The British Council, Macmillan, pp. 141–7.

Dudley-Evans, T. (1995) 'Common core and specific approaches to the teaching of academic writing', in D. Belcher and G. Braine (eds), *Academic Writing in a Second Language: Essays on Research and Pedagogy*. Norwood, NJ: Ablex, pp. 293–312.

Fairclough, N. (1989) *Language and Power*. London: Longman.

Freedman, A. (1999) 'Beyond the text: towards understanding the teaching and learning of genres', *TESOL Quarterly*, 33, 4, 764–8.

Giroux, H. (1992) *Border Crossings: Cultural Workers and the Politics of Education*. New York: Routledge.

Grabe, W. and Kaplan, R. (1996) *Theory and Practice of Writing: An Applied Linguistic Perspective*. London: Longman.

Hyland, K. (2000) *Disciplinary Discourses: Social Interactions in Academic Writing*. Harlow: Longman.

Johns, A.M. (1990) 'Coherence as a cultural phenomenon: employing ethnographic principles in the academic milieu', in U. Connor and A.M. Johns (eds), *Coherence in Writing*. Alexandria, VA: Teachers of English to Speakers of Other Languages, pp. 211–26.

Johns, A.M. (1997) *Text, Role and Context: Developing Academic Literacies*. Cambridge: Cambridge University Press.

Kamler, B. and Threadgold, T. (1997) 'Which thesis did you read?', in Z. Golebiowski (ed.), *Policy and Practice of Tertiary Literacy*. Proceedings of the First National Conference on Tertiary Literacy: Research and Practice. Volume 1. Melbourne: Victoria University of Technology, pp. 42–58.

Lea, M. (1994) ' "I thought I could write till I came here": student writing in higher education', in G. Gibbs (ed.), *Improving Student Learning: Theory and Practice*. Oxford: Oxford Centre for Staff Development, pp. 216–26.

Lea, M.R. and Street, B. (1998) 'Student writing in higher education: an academic literacies approach', *Studies in Higher Education*, 23, 157–72.

Paltridge, B. (2002) 'Thesis and dissertation writing: an examination of published advice and actual practice', *English for Specific Purposes*, 21(2), 125–43.

Prior, P. (1998) *Writing/Disciplinarity: A Sociohistoric Account of Literate Activity in the Academy*. Mahwah, NJ: Erlbaum.

Swales, J.M. (1996) 'Occluded genres in the academy: The case of the submission letter', in E. Ventola and A. Mauranen (eds), *Academic Writing: Intercultural and Textual Issues*. Amsterdam and Philadelphia: John Benjamins, pp. 45–58.

Swales, J.M. (1998) *Other Floors. Other Voices: A Textography of a Small University Building*. Mahwah, NJ: Erlbaum.

Swales, J.M. (2000) 'Further reflections on genre and ESL academic writing'. Abstract, Keynote presentation, Symposium on Second Language Writing, Purdue University, USA.

Swales, J. and Feak, C. (2001) *English in Today's Research World: A Writing Guide*. Ann Arbor, MI: University of Michigan Press.

Threadgold, T. (1989) 'Talking about genre: Ideologies and incompatible discourses', *Cultural Studies*, 3, 101–27.

Tickoo, M.L. (1994) 'Approaches to ESP: Arguing a paradigm shift', in R. Khoo (ed.), *LSP – Problems and Prospects*. Anthology Series 13. Singapore: SEAMEO Regional Language Centre, pp. 30–48.

University of Melbourne (2001) 'Information for PhD thesis examiners'. School of Graduate Studies, The University of Melbourne.

Zamel, V. and Spack, R. (eds), (1998) *Negotiating Academic Literacies*. Mahwah, NJ: Lawrence Erlbaum Publishers, pp. ix–xviii.

Appendix

Interview questions

What do you think is the purpose of an exegesis?

What you would describe as appropriate content for an exegesis?

Who would you say is the intended audience for an exegesis?

What do you think is the audience's role and purpose in reading an exegesis?

How would you describe the relationship between the reader/s and writer of an exegesis?

How would you describe the particular expectations and conventions of an exegesis?

What background knowledge, values, and understandings do you think it is assumed the writer of an exegesis will share with their reader?

How would you describe the relationship between the exegesis and the visual project?

Do you have other comments about the role and nature of an exegesis?

7 Signalling the organization of written texts: hyper-Themes in management and history essays

Louise J. Ravelli

1 Introduction

Among the many demands made of emergent academic writers, the resources to 'technicalize' and 'rationalize' are paramount. That is, writers must be able to give names to things, and to connect these names to each other, in order to theorize about the world around them. Many resources interweave to enable these fundamental processes, but they depend initially on the two key motifs of a stratified linguistic system: the potential to refer, and the potential to expand. In a discussion of scientific discourses, Halliday (1998: 195) argues:

> In these [scientific] discourses, the semiotic power of *referring* is being further exploited so as to create *technical taxonomies*: constructs of virtual objects that represent the distillation of experience (typically experience that has itself been enriched by design, in the form of experiment). The semiotic power of *expanding* – relating one process to another by a logical-semantic relation such as time – is being further exploited so as to create *chains of reasoning*: drawing conclusions from observation (often observation of experimental data) and construing a line of argument leading on from one step to the next.

Through the reconstrual possibilities afforded by stratification and its inherent metaphoric power, processes and qualities can be named, and connected to each other. Thus, a picture of the world can be technicalized, and reasoned about. This becomes a critical component of success in academic writing, enabling writers to shift *up* in levels of abstraction. Importantly, however, it is not enough to simply provide a list of 'names'; abstraction and theorization need to be explicitly signalled, and connected in some overt framework. The student who can successfully predict where they are going, flag where they are, and reiterate where they have been, is more likely to be able to convince through their writing than the student who cannot. In this chapter, I will examine how the fundamental processes of technicalizing and rationalizing are inflected in the higher-level structuring of written texts via *hyper-Themes*. Through an examination of first year university essays in management and history, the role of hyper-Themes in the development of basic argumentative frameworks will be identified. It will be seen that hyper-Themes have a dual function, establishing retrospective and pro-spective connections to the argumentative framework, and that they have distinctive lexicogrammatical and colligational patterns, according to the discipline.

2 Data: First-year management and history essays

Two sets of 20 essays were collected[1] from first-year subjects in management and history. For management, each essay answered the question: 'Explain how country differences make international management a different proposition from management in a purely domestic context.' The essay was the final assignment for their subject. Each essay was already graded and commented upon by their subject lecturer, and grades ranged from 80 per cent down to a fail, with writing quality deteriorating rapidly in association with the grade. Essays were ranked in descending order of merit from 'M1' to 'M20'. Many of the writers are not native English speakers, and there are a number of infelicities in expression which indicate this, although 'surface' errors, such as the incorrect form of a verb, are not relevant to the current discussion.

For history, essays were also already graded by the subject lecturer, and ranked in descending order of merit, from 'H1' to 'H20'. The history essays answered several different questions: H1, H2 and H3 answered the question 'How did Dutch colonialism foster the development of Indonesia's present ruling class?'; H7 answered the question 'How did Javanese society change as a result of Dutch influence?' and so on. Extracts from both sets of essays are included in the appendix and are referred to in the chapter. The essays are used illustratively as evidence of trends in each set.

It is apparent that the history students are generally more sophisticated in their grasp of the written mode than their management counterparts. More relevant for this chapter, however, is a basic contrast in approach between the two disciplines in terms of structuring the fundamental argument. While to a certain extent they each rely on similar resources to achieve successful structures, there also seem to be distinct disciplinary differences. As many scholars have observed, the disciplines have their own distinctive characteristics, their own ways of semiotically reconstruing, reasoning about, and participating in the world,[2] yet they do so with the 'same' resources. This would suggest that, if we are to maximize our potential for assisting students in their moves towards demanding forms of literacy, then we need to continue to explore these differences, both analytically and pedagogically.

3 Basic argumentative frameworks of the management and history essays

To begin to understand how the essays are organized, it is useful to examine the relations between paragraphs. Given that a paragraph tends to be organized around one key idea, that is, it 'has a relatively strong sense of internal coherence' (Greenbaum and Quirk 1990: 464), it is in the relationship of paragraphs to each other that we can begin to see the essay's organization of ideas, or the conceptual framework around which it is based. Of course, as is well known, the paragraph is itself just an orthographic unit, and can be a very problematic category to work with (particularly when examining the work of apprentice writers), nevertheless, we will use it as our basic unit of structure here, at least to begin with (but see Le 1999 for further discussion). In addition, we will focus on paragraph beginnings only; while the beginning of the paragraph is not *necessarily* where links have to be foregrounded, it usually is, so this will be our point of departure.

The fundamental argumentative structures of each set of essays can be viewed either synoptically or dynamically. A synoptic view of the conceptual organization of ideas for M1 is presented in Figure 7.1 (relevant extracts of M1, awarded 80 per cent, are presented in the appendix).

The introductory paragraph establishes the main area of concern, variation in management style, and outlines the paper. The following paragraph spends some time defining 'management' and its components, then the remainder of the essay is organized around three factors explaining variation in management styles, arising from cultural differences, social behaviour and values, and the external environment. Each of these points is then developed in further detail.

This synoptic overview represents a kind of 'cleaning up' of the essay's organization; a willing and cooperative reading of the text. If we follow the text dynamically, paragraph by paragraph, this conceptual map does not necessarily coincide with the linear development of the text. For example, the major point about 'cultural differences' introduced in P3, is not further developed until much later in the essay, in P7; clearly pointing to a weakness in the student's organization of the essay.

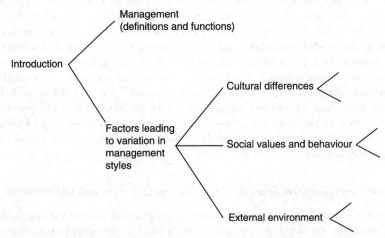

Figure 7.1 Synoptic view of the first management essay (M1)

In addition to highlighting possible strengths or weaknesses in the underlying structure, a more dynamic view of the paragraph relations reveals how one step in the argument leads on from another. In order to examine the relation of ideas to each other, at the level of the paragraph, we will use Halliday's description of logico-semantic relations as a basis (cf. Halliday 1994; Matthiessen 1995). While Halliday explores these primarily to account for relations between clauses, he also notes (1998: 202) that the logico-semantic relations 'are not limited to the clause complex, but represent basic semantic motifs that run throughout the language as a whole'.[3]

Briefly, then, the logico-semantic relations fall into the two key types of expansion and projection. Most relevant to this study are the categories of expansion, given the particular role that they have in creating chains of reasoning, that is:

Elaboration: 'i.e.', symbolized by '='
one clause expands another by elaborating on it (or some portion of it): restating in other words, specifying in greater detail, commenting or exemplifying.
Extension: 'and', symbolized by '+'
one clause expands another by extending beyond it: adding some new element, giving an exception to it, or offering an alternative.
Enhancement: 'so, yet, then', symbolized by 'x'
one clause expands another by embellishing around it: qualifying it with some circumstantial feature of time, place, cause or condition. (Halliday 1994: 220)

4 Preferred frameworks in the management essays

Figure 7.2 presents a dynamic view of organizational relations in M1. In this Figure, elaborating relations are presented with an arrow to the right; extending relations with a downward arrow, and enhancing relations with a downward curved arrow.

Elaborating relations can be seen between P1 and P2. The first paragraph, P1, begins with a thesis statement that international and domestic management will differ as a result of cultural differences, social behaviour and values, and the external environment. The second paragraph, P2, provides a definition of management, so it *elaborates* the first, as it specifies in further detail something which has already been introduced.

Enhancing relations can be seen between P2 and P3. Paragraph 3 argues that variation in management styles arises from cultural differences between countries. This paragraph thus also elaborates something introduced in paragraph 1; at the same time it is in an enhancing relation to P2, because it explains one of the causes of variation in management styles, as introduced at the end of P2.

Extending relations can be seen between P3 and P4. In P4, factors other than cultural differences are introduced (social structure, religion, values and history). This paragraph thus also elaborates the introduction; and, in

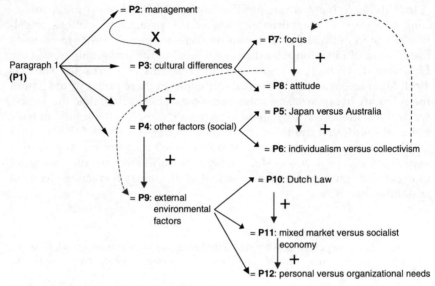

Figure 7.2 Dynamic view of the first management essay (M1): logico-semantic relations

this case, it is in a clear extension relation to the immediately preceding paragraph, as it adds something new to the conceptual framework.

Thus, in this essay, the preferred expansion relations are in terms of elaboration and extension, that is, they mostly elaborate on given concepts, and extend points in a list. (Enhancement is certainly present but is generally not used as a core structural element). This pattern also emerges as the core of M2 (awarded 75 per cent), where P5–8 lists those factors which differ between countries, following an introduction which defines management and the problems faced by multinational corporations (P1–4). These relations are illustrated in Figure 7.3.

M3 (awarded 70 per cent) uses a similar structure; at the end of its introductory section, P4, it uses a macro-Theme to predict the core argument: 'There are four important differences relevant to international management. These include culture, communication, motivation and leadership.' The paper is then structured into four sections, clearly signalled by headings, again with each major section simultaneously elaborating and extending the basic structure.

These descriptions, while not definitive, begin to reveal the argumentative framework that the students build in the texts. There are clear groupings of content, arising because the students can develop superordinate categories like 'cultural differences', and 'external environmental factors'; this is evidence of their ability to technicalize. At the same time, there are clear relationships and connections between these groupings; the named elements are linked together, to rationalize.

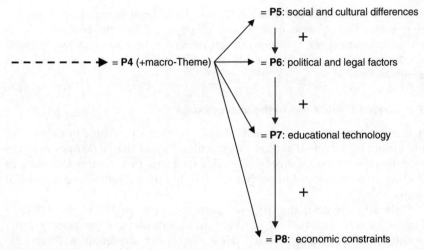

Figure 7.3 Dynamic view of the second management essay (M2 partial)

Thus, each essay builds up an argument about the differences between international and domestic management; they construct their own picture, in this case a taxonomy, of key ideas in the essay and the relations between them. Taxonomies 'classify and name (things) . . . within a larger system, according to their similarities and differences' (Sinclair 1987). The two main types of taxonomic relations are superordination, 'based on sub-classification' and composition, 'based on the relation of parts to wholes' (Martin 1992: 295).

Most familiar from their use in scientific classification systems, taxonomies are also 'a feature of everyday language' (Halliday 1998: 197), as well as being found in many domains of academic writing, where control or under-standing of content can be at least partly manifested by the development of field-related and instantial taxonomies (ibid.: 221). That which is repre-sented in this, and the other, management essays is not necessarily the same as a scientific taxonomy, but it is analogous to it, and so I will refer to it as a *conceptual* taxonomy.

As illustrated, the taxonomies in the management essays are primarily structured around classification: types of factors (which vary across countries/ cultures). It seems that they are answering the question: 'What are the factors which vary between international and domestic management?' Yet the actual essay question was: 'Explain how country differences make inter-national management a different proposition from management in a purely domestic context' – which would seem to suggest the explanation genre as the preferred answer. While still successful, the students' essays are not, in fact, structured to answer the question which was asked. Note that the causal explanation *is* (sometimes) present in their essays, and is found as post-modification, 'a further cultural difference *that affects management practices amongst different countries*'; 'political and legal factors *that are likely to exert heavy direct influence on multinational organizations*', etc. However, this is secondary to the core argument structure, where the post-modifiers indicate a simple listing about 'factors which vary': 'many other factors *which vary across countries*'.

5 Preferred frameworks in the history essays

A taxonomy is not the only way of representing the world, however, and the history essays reveal a different structure. Rather than a taxonomic structure, the history essays show a cascading-type structure, with one argument leading on to the next. Enhancing relations are the preferred organizational device.

A dynamic view of the argumentative relations in H1 is presented in Figure 7.4. H1, awarded 90 per cent, in fact challenges the basic presupposition behind the question, 'How did Dutch colonialism foster the development of Indonesia's present ruling class?'. H1 argues that the New Order rose to power independently of the Old, and so cannot be said to have been fostered by it, even though they are similar across a number of dimensions. Thus in terms of Coffin's (1997) description of history genres, it is a clear example of a *Challenge*.

The first half of H1, paragraphs 2–4 (just over half the essay) explains how the army in Indonesia has come to be the ruling class, in terms of economic activity (P2), the political and economic circumstances of 1942–65 (P3), and the history of the military (P4). The second part describes the similarities between the New and Old Orders, in terms of similarities in administration (P5), economic and technical advancement combined with political repression (P6), and reliance on force (P7). However, the conclusion (P8) under-

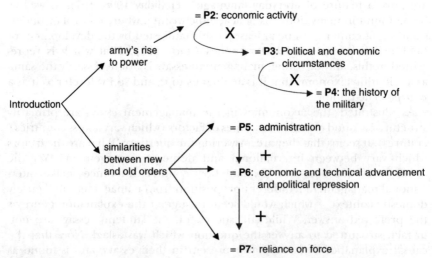

Figure 7.4 Dynamic view of the first history essay (H1)

scores that these similarities 'are not evidence that Dutch colonialism fostered the development of the ruling elite'.

The two 'halves' of the essay, P2–4, and P5–8, are quite different in their structure. Only in the second half of the essay do taxonomic-like structures appear. The first half of the essay is structured around enhancement, not elaboration or extension. One paragraph is used to qualify another.

For example, P2 introduces the economic policies of the military since 1965; an aspect of this is initially elaborated in P3 (ownership being foreign/ Chinese), but then this elaboration is used as Agent (anaphoric 'This') to explain the consequence of the ownership of capital on the indigenous bourgeoisie (Agentive 'this' in: 'This in turn has served to inhibit the development of an indigenous bourgeoisie'). Thus a sequence of events (the economy of that time) is 'picked up' and related causally to another.

It is notable that among the history essays, only the second half of H1 includes any kind of 'branching' structure similar to the patterns found in management. H2 and H3, awarded 85 and 80 per cent respectively, do not challenge the basic thesis underlying the question, but give an explanation which answers the question directly. So, they are significantly different in genre,[4] and as with the first half of H1, they each build up a description of an event and connect it causally to another, to create an explanation sequence. As Coffin notes (1997: 218), 'causality becomes a staging and ordering device'. For example, from H2 (awarded 85 per cent) in Figure 7.5, we see connections such as the following: P9 introduces the 1830s, and Dutch administration via the cultivation system; these are linked to changes in the ruling class in P10, linked to regent corruption and exploitation in P11.

And in H3 (awarded 80 per cent) in Figure 7.6, P2 introduces the Forced Cultivation System and double bureaucracy; linked to the native nobility as official governing body in P3, which also introduces the dismantling of the cultivation system, this being linked to the expanding economy in P4.

P9: (the 1830s; *Dutch administration* via the cultivation system)

 X

P10: The effect which this period of Indonesian history had on fostering a political structure which still retains much of what was initiated by the cultivation scheme, was most significant in the *changes it brought about to the functioning of the ruling class.*

 X

P11: The concept of supervision under the cultivation system became an increasingly profitable avenue for *regent corruption and exploitation.* ...

Figure 7.5 Extracts from H2

P2: (Forced Cultivation System; *double bureaucracy*)

P3: This notion of indirect rule via the Inlandsch Besturr, was contained in a Regulation of 1854, stating that "Insofar as circumstances permit, the native population is to be left under the supervision of its own, government-appointed or recognized chiefs." This therefore allowed the *native nobility* to become an official governing body, a colonial 'policy of enoblement' ... (and further details of cultivation system, inc' being *dismantled* in 1860s)

P4: The dismantling of the Forced Cultivation System saw the beginning of an era of an *expanding economy* as private capitalism replaced the government monopoly ...

Figure 7.6 Extracts from H3

Thus, the preferred structuring relation in history is that of enhancement; elaboration and extension are also used, but only in H1 are they used to frame (part of) the core argument. So, instead of a basic branching structure, a cascade-like structure, supporting the genre of explanation and challenge, is preferred. While this description is only a simple indicator of underlying structures, it suggests that these two disciplines, at least at this level, have distinct preferences for basic organizational relations.

6 Signalling the organization through hyper-Themes

If, then, these are some of the basic frameworks and preferred logico-semantic relations in the management and history essays, how is it that these relations are signalled? Of course, as with connections between clauses, certain relations will hold with or without an explicit marker of that connection (such as a conjunction), but generally they are explicitly signalled, and one of the main resources for signalling and foregrounding the conceptual framework of the essay is the hyper-Theme.

Hyper-Themes are an extension of the general principle of thematic organization in text, where theme is used to signal a point of departure (cf. Halliday 1994).[5] The term was introduced by Daneš (1974) to account for one particular pattern of Theme-Rheme progression, namely that whereby 'successive Themes can be related to a single preceding Theme' (Martin 1992: 437). This principle is extended by Martin to account for 'the Theme of a paragraph', defining a hyper-Theme as 'an introductory sentence or group of sentences which is established to predict a particular pattern of interaction among [lexical] strings, [reference] chains and Theme selection in following sentences' (ibid.) That is, the hyper-Theme functions predictively.

This is, of course, closely aligned to the school-rhetoric notion of the *topic sentence*. When discussed in academic writing textbooks, the topic sentence is usually described as something relevant to the paragraph, which encapsulates 'general' and 'specific' levels of detail in the paragraph. It is described by Oshima and Hogue, for instance, as 'stating the topic and the controlling idea of the paragraph (1991: 19) (Similar definitions can be found in many other academic writing textbooks, for example Rooks 1988; Arnaudet and Barrett 1990). In formal terms, the definitions given of topic sentences tend not to be very specific in elucidating exactly what it is, lexically or grammatically, which constitutes the 'general' idea/topic and 'limiting' or 'specific' idea/topic.

Martin, however, does describe the hyper-Theme in further lexico-grammatical detail. The range of devices he discusses include the following:

(i)   grammatical metaphor (nominalisations), especially Vocabulary 3 items (Winter 1977) and Anaphoric Nouns (Francis 1985). Examples include 'difference' and 'similarity'

(ii) conjunctive relations, realized explicitly (*'Furthermore'*) or incongruently ('A *further* similarity')

(iii) relational processes, used to classify and describe, as well as to construe logical connections ('A further similarity *is*') (Martin 1992: 440ff, 1993)

All these features are typically characteristic of hyper-Themes, although none are obligatory. Also, while 'Theme' in SFL is associated with point of departure, equating with first position in English, the 'topic sentence' of traditional rhetoric is often described as being able to occur in the middle, or even at the end, of a paragraph, so its realization seems hard to pin down. Thus there is scope to expand on the description of hyper-Themes in terms of their function and realization.

7 Hyper-Themes in management 1

A key distinguishing feature of the hyper-Theme in management and history essays is that, in addition to predicting the development of the paragraph, they also connect 'back' to the unfolding conceptual framework of the essay. Not every paragraph will realize this function, of course, only those paragraphs which have a core role to play in outlining the framework of the essay. But this does accord with Martin's suggestion (1992: 447) that the hyper-Theme is a metaphorical marked Theme for the text. Just as a marked Theme in a clause tends to signal a shift in the method of development of a text, so too the hyper-Theme, at least in its dual role, signals a shift in the conceptual development of the text as a whole. The point of departure is not, then, an orthographic place, that is, the beginning of the paragraph, but a structural place, namely a step in the argument.

So, for example, in M1 we see a number of examples which clearly fulfil this dual role.

M1:P2:S10   Leadership and motivation styles will be different across countries . . .
M1:P3:S1:   *Variations in management styles between international and domestic organisations* will primarily arise from *the cultural differences present in various countries.*

Towards the end of P2, the writer says that 'Leadership and motivation styles will be different across countries . . .' and this is encapsulated and picked up as given information in the opening sentence of P3, 'Variations in management styles between international and domestic organisations (will primarily arise from the cultural differences present in various countries)', using lexical and grammatical metaphor to enable the shift ('down in rank, and sideways in class and function'; Halliday 1998) from 'will be different' to 'variation'. This opening nominal group points retrospectively to something already established, presenting it as given, and creates an instantial node in the unfolding taxonomy. The remainder of this sentence relates this variation causally ('will primarily arise from') to the presence of cultural differences in various countries ('the cultural differences present in various countries'). 'Cultural differences' is New information (other than having been presented in the introduction) and has not yet been lexicalized, so it functions to predict forward for this paragraph.

The opening sentence of P3, then, simultaneously creates a new node for the conceptual taxonomy, connects retrospectively to a preceding node, and predicts forward to the development of the remainder of the paragraph. It thus acts as a nexus point for the organizational relations of the essay, distilling these prospective and retrospective functions, enabling connections to be made to an unfolding conceptual taxonomy.

M1:P4:   *Along with cultural differences,* there are also *many other factors that differ across countries.*

The opening of P4, 'Along with cultural differences, there are also many other factors that differ across countries', clearly marks that this paragraph is moving on to a different point. The conjunctive phrase 'along with' marks extension in terms of an addition, an addition to the lexically repeated preceding node of 'cultural differences'. Thus, this sentence locates itself very explicitly in relation to the unfolding taxonomy. It thus extends the immediately preceding node, but *in relation to* that which is established in the introduction, in P1, so it is also an elaboration of P1. At the same time, it suggests that there are factors other than cultural differences which vary across countries ('there are also many other factors that differ across countries'). So this sentence predicts forward, as well as connecting backward.

In history, there are connections which also fulfil this dual function, of facing forward and back.

H2:P10:   The effect which this period of Indonesian history had on fostering a
           political structure which still retains much of what was initiated by the
           cultivation scheme, was most significant in the changes it brought about
           to the functioning of the ruling class.

(*points back* to P9, which discusses Dutch influence in the 1830s; and *points forward*
by enhancing in terms of explaining the changes it brought)

H3:P4:   The dismantling of the Forced Cultivation System saw the beginning of
           an era of an expanding economy as private capitalism replaced
           government monopoly.

(*points back* to P3, which discusses the demise of the Forced Cultivation System, and
points forward by enhancing in terms of explaining the consequences of this
demise.)

While these sentences from history are dual facing, they tend not to point
(back) to an over-arching framework, as is the case for the management
examples. The connections in history are more local, moving from one part
of an unfolding explanation to another. As already noted, this effect arises
because of the preference for enhancing relations in these history essays,
producing a cascade structure instead of a taxonomic one. The connections
between 'points' (such as they are) in a cascade are very local – one level
flows on to another; in a taxonomy, nodes are explicitly connected 'up'
to higher levels of abstraction/generality and 'down' to lower levels of
specificity, so location of any one node reveals (at least part of) the larger
picture.

But in both cases, the successful hyper-Themes face both directions. This
expanded notion of the function of hyper-Themes enables us to begin to
differentiate these connections from those which face in one direction
only.

Thus in M1:P6: 'Many countries tend to encourage individualism' –
'countries' of course repeats an existing lexical chain, and 'individualism'
could be connected hyponymically to 'ideology' (as introduced in P5) so
it is not unconnected to the remainder of the essay, but unlike some of the
other sentences, there are no explicit markers of the taxonomic connections.
As it is, the cooperative reader can work out the relevance of this paragraph
to the essay as a whole, but that relevance is not made explicit for the reader.
Similarly, there are a number of other examples from management which
seem to point forward, but which fail to connect to any overarching
framework.

M1:P11:   Australia is a mixed market economy.
M2:P11:   Japanese companies have taken such a commanding lead in doing
           business that other countries have a slim chance of catching up.
M3:P22:   Motivations vary across countries.

Also in history, there are examples which certainly connect with preceding
parts of the text, usually through lexical repetition, but which do not seem
to bring that connection 'forward' into an explanatory (i.e. enhancing)

framework. There are relationships here, but, again, the nature of that relationship (i.e. enhancing, causal, etc.) is not made explicit. For example:

H1:P2:   The current Indonesian ruling group could be better described as a military caste than a class.

H2:P3:   Political power in pre-colonial Indonesian society, featured at its apex the divine power of a king.

H3:P5:   Education was slow in coming to the native population despite the fact that the 1854 constitution stressed Dutch responsibility for it.

Thus in both history and management, these might still count as topic sentences in terms of traditional descriptions, as they are 'general' ideas which the remainder of the paragraph can make more explicit. They can also be said to fulfil the predictive function of the hyper-Theme. However, in terms of the retrospective function of the hyper-Theme, they are ineffective.

This dual-function of the hyper-Theme enables us to distinguish different kinds of paragraph beginnings. When both functions are fully and success-fully realized, a clear and unambiguous hyper-Theme results; however, when only one function is realized, identification of the hyper-Theme becomes less certain, though there is still what might be called a 'topic sentence'.

At the same time, this dual-function of the hyper-Theme also enables us to separate the hyper-Theme from orthographic position (i.e. first sentence in the paragraph). Based on this functional understanding, there can be sentences functioning as hyper-Theme which are *not* in first position.

It is important to note, however, that *signals* of structure are not in them-selves enough to actually achieve a successful structure. Even the clearest of hyper-Themes does not necessarily fulfil its promises. Consider the following:

M1:P3:   Variations in management styles between international and domestic organisations, will primarily arise from the cultural differences present in various countries. Culture will affect an individual's social behaviour and their way of communicating with others. The culture in a particular country is an important contributor to an individual's personality. It determines such factors as a person's independence, aggression, competition and coordination.

M1:P4:   Along with cultural differences, there are also many other factors that differ across countries.

M1:P7:   A cultural difference is also shown . . .

M1:P8:   A further cultural difference . . .

M1:P3 promises to explain 'cultural differences', but it goes on to simply give further definitions of 'culture', ('Culture will affect . . .; The culture in a particular country is . . . ; It . . . ') and examples of cultural differences are not actually presented until P7 and P8. So, the opening of P3 looks quite effective as a link, and enables us to see how it functions to scaffold a framework for this essay, but it is in fact a false lead. Similar problems can be found in the management essays, and as the essays become less successful overall, these problems become endemic, indicating that basic control of conceptual structure, as well as its signalling, is one of the key areas for literacy development.

8 Structure and colligational patterns in the Hyper-Themes

When the hyper-Themes are used effectively, they add an enormous amount to the organizational framework of the essays. What then are the lexico-grammatical resources which enable the hyper-Themes to fulfil this dual-function of retrospective and prospective connections? In the first instance, there is the familiar resource of grammatical metaphor, used to name, and so encapsulate, a figure or a sequence (Halliday and Matthiessen 1999: 236). In M1:P3, for example, 'variations' refers back to the preceding clause 'will be different'. This is – as we know – one of the most important ways of beginning to technicalize: to provide names to processes and sequences, and then to use those names as a further point of departure.

At the same time as using grammatical metaphor in this way, other closely related devices are also deployed, including generic nouns, and semiotic abstractions (Martin 1992; Halliday and Matthiessen 1999); these are not quite metaphor 'proper' (cf. discussions in Derewianka 1995), but, developmentally, can be seen as steps on a continuum, moving from the concrete towards a general notion of 'abstraction'. See Figure 7.7.

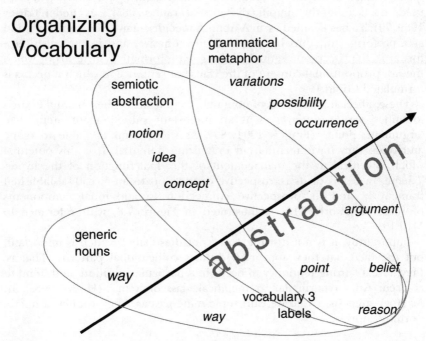

Figure 7.7 Organizing Vocabulary

The organizing role of these items has been well documented by Winter, with his description of Vocabulary 3 items (Winter 1977), Hoey, with lexical signals (Hoey, *passim*) and Francis, with metalinguistic labels (Francis 1994). The various descriptions of these categories overlap, both with each other and with grammatical metaphor 'proper'. They share the features of being metadiscursive, able to refer to text, and of facilitating semantic connections between sections of text, either prospectively or retrospectively.

Winter's original suggestion of Vocabulary 3 was proposed to account for one group of 'organizing' Vocabulary items (as opposed to Vocabulary 1, which includes subordinators, like 'by, after, unless, although', and as opposed to Vocabulary 2, which includes 'sentence connectors like "thus"' (Carter 1989: 75) which 'fulfil an anticipatory function. They project the reader forward by creating expectations of what is to ensue in the next part of the discourse' (ibid.: 75). Vocabulary 3 includes items such as 'cause; ontrast; fact; point; reason; way'.

Later scholars argue that these relations can also be established instantially in text, and that the organizational link can be backward as well as forward (cf. Hoey 1998a, Francis 1994).

Francis, for example, proposes the category of *advance* and *retrospective* labels (Francis 1994; building on her work on anaphoric nouns, Francis 1985) extending Halliday and Hasan's (1976) category of general nouns, to include those nouns which are, in the first instance, *metadiscursive*, that is, used 'to talk about the ongoing discourse' (Francis 1985: 3, as cited in Carter 1989: 79). To be classified as an A-noun, a metadiscursive item must function as a proform, and thus be anaphorically cohesive, and it must also 'face forward', that is, 'be presented as the *given* information in terms of which the *new* propositional content of the clause or sentence in which it occurs is formulated.' (ibid.).

These labels are an aspect of nominal group lexical cohesion, and Francis identifies *metalinguistic labels* as an important subset; again, items like 'argument, point' (Francis 1994: 83). As these items are able to name and refer, they have an inherent organizing potential. It is this potential which is critical to the management of the dual function of the hyper-Theme, in terms of its retrospective connection to an already established framework, and its prospective connection to additional components of that framework. This is illustrated in Figure 7.8, with reference to M1:P10.

Importantly, it is not just the *presence* of these labels which is important, but the fact that they appear in distinct colligational patterns. That is, they have a 'strong tendency to occur in a particular position' and 'tend to co-occur with a particular grammatical class of items' (Hoey 1998a: 3). As Hoey suggests, (what we call) topic sentences are the product of micro-wording choices:

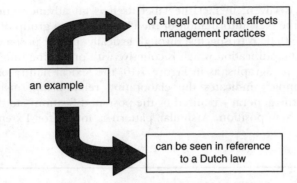

Figure 7.8 Retrospective and prospective connections

M1:P7:S1	
A cultural **difference**	is also shown in the **way** countries tend to be focussed ...
retrospective label (to paragraph 3)	*advance label (to current paragraph)*
Head Noun	*Head Noun*
Theme/Given	*Rheme/New*

Figure 7.9 Colligational patterns

the topic sentence is dead. It is not the case that the decision to make a topic sentence affects the wording of the beginning of that sentence. What appears to be the case is that the wording at the beginning of the sentence dictates whether we perceive it to be a topic sentence. In other words, topic sentences are the product of micro-wording choices, they do not dictate such choices.

For example, as Francis observes (1994), the retrospective labels are typically associated with Given (information), in Theme position. The advance labels tend to be associated with new information, in Rheme position. The labels are typically the Head noun (see Figure 7.9).

However, this does not always have to be the case (for instance, advance labels can occur in Theme position) and it seems that it may be possible to describe more delicate colligational patterns associated with the use of these labels.

8.1 Post-modification

In most cases, and especially in Elaborating paragraphs, while the label in Theme position is presented as 'Given' information, it is not the label *as such* which is Given; in fact the label itself is an advance one, pointing forward to the New information of the clause, but the group of which it is part is made to be retrospective through lexically specific post-modification. It is the post-modification which is cohesive with preceding information. In Elaborating paragraphs, as in Figure 7.10, the lexical nature of the Head noun, 'example', indicates the elaborating relationship, mediating the move from the general – realized by the post-modification – to the specific, realized in New position. A similar pattern is found for Extending paragraphs.

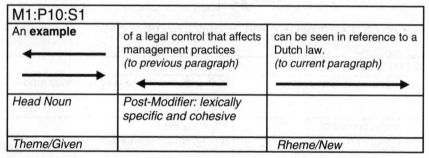

M1:P10:S1		
An **example**	of a legal control that affects management practices *(to previous paragraph)*	can be seen in reference to a Dutch law. *(to current paragraph)*
Head Noun	*Post-Modifier: lexically specific and cohesive*	
Theme/Given		*Rheme/New*

Figure 7.10 Colligational patterns: lexically specific post-modification (Elaborating)

8.2 *Textual markers and pre-modification*

In the hyper-Theme of extending paragraphs, the Theme typically includes a textual marker, realized congruently as a conjunction (such as 'Furthermore') or metaphorically as a pre-Modifier in the nominal group ('A further difference ...'). Also, the label may be pre-modified by a Classifier which is retrospective, that is, lexically cohesive with a pre-ceding node (as well as the post-modification already seen above). Again, this pattern is to be anticipated; as the function of extension is to add, it seems logical to find explicit markers of that which is being added. The label itself is 'made' to be retrospective by virtue of the pre-classification; at the same time, the textual marker 'makes' it prospective; we anticipate lexicalization of this item in the near context. In the Extending paragraph, we also find a label in Rheme position. Again these occur as a Head noun, and may be relexicalized by its own Qualifier, but there is a sense in which these labels also 'point forward' to the remainder of the paragraph (i.e. they will be relexicalized there) (see Figures 7.11 and 7.12).

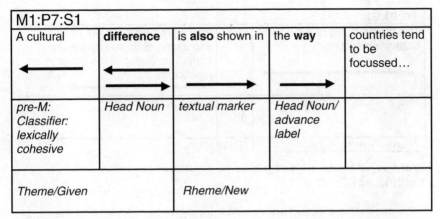

Figure 7.11 Colligational patterns: textual markers (Extending)

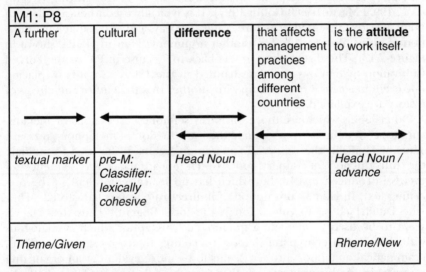

Figure 7.12 Colligational patterns: pre-modification and textual markers (Extending)

8.3 Grammatical metaphor

In the hyper-Themes of Enhancing paragraphs, we see similar colligational trends as observed elsewhere; labels as Head noun in Theme/Given and Rheme/New positions, and specific lexicalization in pre- and post-modifying position. But what tends to characterize these hyper-Themes is a clearer preference for grammatical metaphor (as opposed to something more identifiable as, say, a semiotic abstraction), as well as a relational process which itself encodes an enhancing connection between the two Participants in the clause.

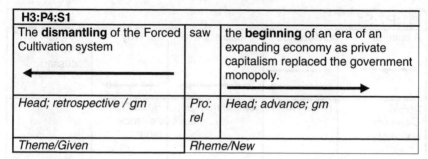

H3:P4:S1		
The **dismantling** of the Forced Cultivation system	saw	the **beginning** of an era of an expanding economy as private capitalism replaced the government monopoly.
Head; retrospective / gm	Pro: rel	Head; advance; gm
Theme/Given		Rheme/New

Figure 7.13 Colligational patterns: grammatical metaphor (Enhancing)

The hyper-Themes in history make more frequent use of (clear) grammatical metaphors than is the case for management. The use of grammatical metaphor is already well established as a feature of history writing (Eggins *et al.*, 1993; Martin 1993; Coffin 1997). It is typically used to encapsulate an event already presented in a more congruent way, and to use that encapsulation as point of departure for another argument. Thus in H3:P4, shown in Figure 7.13, 'The dismantling' refers back to a clause in P3 'As the Forced Cultivation System was slowly dismantled in the 1860s'. So, it is by placing one event in a causal relationship with another that the nature and effects of history are explained.

Other labels which are more obviously semiotic abstractions or metadiscursive seem to be used to mediate the introduction of metaphors 'proper'. Thus in H2:P11: 'the *concept* of supervision' seems to be used to mediate the introduction of 'supervision', which encapsulates the sequence of events introduced in P10, but which has no lexical equivalent in the preceding text. In H2:P3: 'this notion of indirect rule' refers back to P2, 'They [the Dutch] chose to rule through the local Regent.' Thus these labels seem to be used to mediate a grammatical metaphor which is analogous with, but not directly parallel to, a preceding figure or sequence. Thus, grammatical metaphor 'proper' seems to be more evident as an organizing resource in the history texts, which prefer the enhancing relation between paragraphs.

9 Difference: referring to and expanding on a different basis

The management and history essays have different preferred logico-semantic connections between paragraphs, resulting in different underlying frameworks for their essays. The foregrounding of semiotic abstractions and metadiscursive labels in management means that that which is referred to, or named, is an aspect of the text itself. In history, the foregrounding of metaphorical processes means that a figure or sequence is repackaged to become an intrinsic component of the text; a covert move which effectively absorbs its own processes of textual manipulation.

While generic nouns, semiotic abstractions and metaphor all contribute towards increasing abstraction in text, with the first two, the move is, so to speak, still 'visible'; with the latter, it is no longer transparent. This supports Coffin's description of the 'gatekeeping' function of history, with the covert manipulation of text providing a more powerful (because more valued) resource for argumentation.

However, it is not just the organizing vocabulary which is important; control of the supporting colligational patterns is also crucial. Even in the more successful essays, from both disciplines, there are many points where the students would be able to improve their writing by accessing the resources of analysis and abstraction, both the appropriate organizing vocabulary and the colligational structures which support them. The student who can only write 'the first factor, the second factor, the final factor', without explaining what the factors are, is not in fact creating a strong structural framework.

If we return to M1:P4, 'Along with cultural differences, there are also many other factors that differ across countries', we can see here that, while this seems to function quite explicitly and successfully as a link in the essay's unfolding structure, it is in fact rather vague. 'Cultural differences' is not Qualified, and 'many other factors' is Qualified by the slightly vague 'that differ across countries'. In other words, the explicit lexical marking of the exact taxonomic link, 'variation in management styles' has been lost (and note that it is at this point in this essay that the student slides from the enhancing framework established in P3, to the elaborating/extending framework of this and subsequent paragraphs).

This is just one example, among dozens and dozens in these essays, where the overall framework could be improved with attention to the organizing vocabulary and supporting colligational structures. Among the weaker essays, these problems become endemic, to the point that there is no evident argumentative framework at all. While there is not space in this chapter to demonstrate these weaknesses, the absence of a clear argumentative framework is evident in the failure to use effective metadiscursive labels and appropriate supporting colligational structures. Students are confined to a descriptive listing of 'factors', which are linked by lexical cohesion to the general topic, but which are not linked to any more abstract framework, that is, a position on the topic.

10 Conclusions: similarities and differences in the signalling of structure between management and history

Most teachers of academic writing would be very familiar with these kinds of weaknesses, where there is a need to move students away from description, and 'up' to analysis and abstraction. This is a general requirement of academic writing and, of course, goes far beyond the demands of hyper-Themes, but it *is* particularly important to foreground analysis and description in the hyper-Themes, in order to provide the initial scaffolding for the argument.

The stronger essays in both management and history are able to use lexicogrammatical resources to develop analysis and abstraction. They are able to refer to and name key points in their texts, whether via metaphor, a semiotic abstraction, or a metadiscursive label, and so to move from a congruent representation of content to a metaphorical encapsulation of significant steps in an argument. In conjunction with the associated colligational patterns, these devices (the metaphors, the labels) are fore-grounded in the hyper-Themes, providing a metaframework for the essay, and functioning as a nexus, pointing forward and back, enabling a writer to connect the points they have named. The successful student is thus able to use these resources to shift between levels of abstraction; the weaker writers are unable to do this.

In examining these resources in further detail, I have claimed that hyper-Themes have a dual, not a singular function, that they may be used to create and support different kinds of frameworks, according to the main logico-semantic patterns they realize, and that there are distinctive lexico-grammatical resources which characterize the hyper-Themes. With this enhanced understanding of hyper-Themes, we can begin to explain different degrees of success (or otherwise) in the hyper-Themes of particular texts, and begin to differentiate them from the traditional notion of topic sentences.

In some ways, the hyper-Themes and associated resources are used to similar effect in management and history. That is, their core function is to shift the ground: to move from the familiar to more abstract and analytical levels of discussion. With their dual face, pointing back and forward to the overarching framework, they foreground the processes of technicalizing and rationalizing, that is, naming a particular view of the world, and weaving that into a larger picture. Many resources are harnessed to this effect, but it begins with the ability to name, or refer, through grammatical metaphor, semiotic abstractions, and metadiscursive labels, and is dependent on the ability to expand, or rationalize, about these things in relation to each other. The colligational patterns supporting these structures are critical to their success.

But despite these inherent similarities, it is also the case that management and history prefer different patterns, confirming the now well-established notion that the disciplines are, indeed, of different 'tribes and territories'. The essays examined here show clear preferences for fundamentally differ-ent argumentative structures: taxonomic classification versus cascading argument, each of which is supported by its own particular patterns of hyper-Theme. The variations here point to the need for much more vigorous exploration of disciplinary differences, and the need to incorporate such findings into pedagogical materials and practices.[6] As long as universities and other institutions continue to struggle with the literacy demands of a broad demographic in the student population, these needs remain paramount.

Notes

1 From the University of Wollongong, Australia.
2 See, for example, Christie and Martin (1997) for discussion of a number of different educational and bureaucratic discourses; Bhatia (1999) on the specificities of 'genre knowledge' required in different contexts; Bazerman (1998), Becher (1989), and Hyland (2000) on the 'tribes and territories' of academia.
3 There are certainly other frameworks which can provide complementary pictures of the relations we are trying to capture here, including Martin's description of conjunctive relations (1992); Rhetorical Structure Theory, as developed by Mann *et al.* (1992), and exemplified in relation to academic language by Stuart-Smith (1998) and Benwell (1999); or Winter and Hoey's descriptions of lexical signals (Winter *passim*; Hoey, *passim*).
4 See papers in Christie and Martin 1997, which observe the topographical relations between genres across a number of different disciplines.
5 See also Halliday 1994; Fries 1981, 1995; and Martin 1992 for detailed theoretical background, and Martin 1999 for an effective and accessible explanation.
6 See Thurston and Candlin 1997 for an interesting beginning here, and Jones 2000, for extensive materials on taxonomies.

References

Arnaudet, M.L. and Barrett, M.E. (1990) *Paragraph Development: A Guide for Students of English* 2nd edn. Englewood Cliffs, NJ: Prentice Hall.

Bazerman, Charles (1998) 'Emerging perspectives on the many dimensions of scientific discourse', in J.R. Martin and Robert Veel (eds), *Reading Science: Critical and Functional Perspectives on Discourses of Science*. London: Routledge, pp. 15–30.

Becher, Tony (1989) *Academic Tribes and Territories: Intellectual Enquiry and the Cultures of Disciplines*. Buckingham: Open University Press.

Benwell, Bethan (1999) 'The organisation of knowledge in British tutorial discourse: Issues, pedagogic discourse strategies and disciplinary identity', *Pragmatics*, 9(4), 535–66.

Bhatia, V.J. (1999) 'Disciplinary variation in business English', in Martin Hewings and Catherine Nickerson (eds), *Business English: Research Into Practice*. London: Longman, pp. 129–43.

Carter, R. (1989) *Vocabulary: Applied Linguistic Perspectives*. Routledge: London.

Christie, Frances and Martin, J.R. (eds) (1997) *Genre and Institutions: Social Processes in the Workplace and School*. London: Cassell.

Coffin, Caroline (1997) 'Constructing and giving value to the past: an investigation into secondary school history', in Frances Christie and J.R. Martin (eds), *Genre and Institutions: Social Processes in the Workplace and School*. London: Cassell, pp. 196–230.

Daneš, F. (1974) 'Functional sentence perspective and the organisation of the text', in F. Danes (ed.), *Papers on Functional Sentence Perspective*. The Hague: Mouton, pp. 108–28.

Derewianka, Beverly (1995) 'Language development in the transition from childhood to adolescence: The role of grammatical metaphor'. Unpublished doctoral thesis, Macquarie University, Australia.

Eggins, S., Wignell, P. and Martin, J.R. (1993) 'The discourse of history', in M. Ghadessy (ed.), *Register Analysis: Theory and Practice*. London: Pinter, pp. 75–109.

Francis, G. (1985) *Anaphoric Nouns.* Discourse Analysis Monographs no. 11. Birmingham: English Language Research Unit, University of Birmingham.

Francis, Gill (1994) 'Labelling discourse: an aspect of nominal-group lexical cohesion', in M. Coulthard (ed.), *Advances in Written Text Analysis.* Routledge: London, pp. 83–101.

Fries, Peter H. (1981) 'On the status of Theme: arguments from discourse', *Forum Linguisticum,* 6(1), 1–38.

Fries, Peter H. (1995) 'Themes, methods of development, and texts', in Peter H. Fries and Ruqaiya Hasan (eds), *On Subject and Theme: A Discourse Functional Perspective.* Amsterdam: Benjamins, pp. 317–60.

Greenbaum, S. and Quirk, R. (1990) *A Student's Grammar of the English Language.* Harlow: Longman.

Halliday, M.A.K. (1994) *Introduction to Functional Grammar* 2nd edn. London: Edward Arnold.

Halliday, M.A.K. (1998) 'Things and relations: regrammaticising experience as technical knowledge', in J.R. Martin and Robert Veel (eds), *Reading Science: Critical and Functional Perspectives on Discourses of Science.* London: Routledge, pp. 185–235.

Halliday, M.A.K. and Hasan, R. (1976) *Cohesion in English.* London: Longman.

Halliday, M.A.K. and Matthiessen, C.M.I.M. (1999), *Construing Experience through Meaning: A Language-based Approach to Cognition.* London: Cassell.

Hoey, Michael (1979) *Signalling in Discourse.* Discourse Analysis Monograph no. 6. Birmingham: English Languge Research, University of Birmingham.

Hoey, Michael (1983) *On the Surface of Discourse.* London: Allen & Unwin.

Hoey, Michael (1997) 'The interaction of textual and lexical factors in the identification of paragraph boundaries', in M. Reinhardt and W. Thiele (eds), *Grammar and Text in Synchrony and Diachrony: In Honour of Gottfried Graustein.* Vervuert: Iberoamericana, pp. 141–67.

Hoey, Michael (1998a) 'Some text properties of certain nouns'. Forthcoming in *Proceedings of the Colloquium on Discourse Anaphora and Reference Resolution.* Lancaster.

Hoey, Michael (1998b) 'The hidden lexical clues of textual organisation: a preliminary investigation into an unusual text from a corpus perspective'. Forthcoming in *Proceedings of the 3rd International Conference on Teaching and Learning Corpora.* Oxford: Keble College.

Hyland, K. (2000) *Disciplinary Discourses: Social Interactions in Academic Writing.* Harlow: Longman.

Jones, Janet (2000) 'Applying SFL to teaching tertiary literacy'. Paper presented to the 27th ISFC, Melbourne, Australia.

Le, Elisabeth (1999) 'The use of paragraphs in French and English academic writing: towards a grammar of paragraphs', *Text,* 19(3), 307–43.

Mann, W.C., Matthiessen, C.M.I.M. and Thompson, S.A. (1992) 'Rhetorical structure theory and text analysis', in W.C. Mann and S.A. Thompson (eds), *Discourse Description: Diverse Linguistic Analyses of a Fund-Raising Text.* Amsterdam: Benjamins, pp. 39–78.

Martin, J.R. (1992) *English Text: System and Structure.* Benjamins: Amsterdam.

Martin, J.R. (1993) 'Life as a noun: arresting the universe in science and humanities', in M.A.K. Halliday and J.R. Martin (eds), *Writing Science: Literacy and Discursive Powers.* London: The Falmer Press, pp. 221–67.

Martin, J.R. (1999) 'Close reading: functional linguistics as a tool for critical discourse analysis', in Len Unsworth (ed.), *Researching Language in Schools and Communities: Functional Linguistic Perspectives.* London: Cassell, pp. 275–303.

Matthiessen, C. (1995) *Lexicogrammatical Cartography: English Systems*. Tokyo: International Language Science Publishers.

Oshima, A. and Hogue, A. (1991) *Writing Academic English: A Writing and Sentence Structure Handbook* 2nd edn. USA: Addison-Wesley.

Rooks, G. (1988) *Paragraph Power: Communicating Ideas through Paragraphs*. Englewood Cliffs, NJ: Prentice Hall.

Sinclair, J. (ed.) (1987) *Collins Cobuild English Language Dictionary*. London: Collins.

Stuart-Smith, Virginia (1998) 'Constructing an argument in psychology: RST and the analysis of student writing', in C. Candlin and G. Plum (eds), *Researching Academic Literacies*. Sydney: Macquarie University/NCELTR, pp. 31–146.

Thurston, Jennifer and Candlin, Christopher C. (1997) *Exploring Academic English: A Workbook for Student Essay Writing*. Sydney: Macquarie University/NCELTR.

Winter, Eugene (1977) 'A clause relational approach to English texts: a study of some predictive lexical items in written discourse', *Instructional Science*, 6(1), 1–92.

Winter, Eugene (1982) *Towards a Contextual Grammar of English: The Clause and its Place in the Definition of Sentence*. London: Allen & Unwin.

Winter, Eugene (1992) 'The notion of unspecific *vs* specific as one way of analysing the information of a fund-raising letter', in W.C. Mann and S.A. Thomson (eds), *Discourse Descriptions: Diverse Analyses of a Fund-raising Text*. Amsterdam: Benjamins, pp. 131–70.

Appendix 1

Management: 'Explain how country differences make international management a different proposition from management in a purely domestic context.'

M1 (80%): Extracts

P1 Within any organization, people and their attitudes will vary widely. International management will often be completely different to management in a purely domestic context. This arises primarily as a result of the cultural differences present amongst countries. Along with these differences, comes varying social behaviour and values, which management must take into consideration when adopting a leadership style. In particular, management practices in Japan often reflect a different attitude to employees, than is seen in our own domestic environment. The external environment in different countries will also contribute to variations in management styles. As a result, management functions will vary accordingly.

P2:S1 Management is the process of coordinating the activities of individuals and groups in order to attain some objective.

P3:S1 Variations in management styles between international and domestic organizations, will primarily arise from the cultural differences present in various countries.

P4:S1 Along with cultural differences, there are also many other factors that differ across countries.

P5:S1 A particular example between a managers perception of employees in an international organization compared to that in the domestic context, is demonstrated by comparing the ideology of Japanese and American management.

P6:S1 Many countries tend to encourage individualism.

P7:S1 A cultural difference is also shown in the way countries tend to be focused.

P8:S1 A further cultural difference, that affects management practices amongst different countries, is the attitude to work itself.

P9:S1 The impact of external environmental factors in different countries, will also reflect in management styles.

P10:S1 An example of a legal control that affects management practices can be seen in reference to a Dutch law.

P11:S1 Australia is a mixed market economy, with little government interference.

P12:S1 Within the external environment, a dilemma also exists between an individual's need for satisfying personal goals and an organizations need for efficiency.

P13 (Conclusion) Country differences, particularly in cultural beliefs, makes international management quite different to management in our domestic context.

Appendix 2

M2 (75%): Extracts

P4:S8 The following paragraphs includes many of the significant differences between cultures that affect the practice of multinational, and for which managers are often unprepared.

P5:S1 Firstly, there is social and cultural differences, which can and does affect the operations of multinational organizations.

P6:S1 Secondly, there is political and legal factors that are likely to exert heavy direct influence on multinational organizations, since there are different political and legal policies in the 170 or so countries in the world.

P7:S1 Thirdly, there is education and technology.

P8:S1 Finally, there are economic constraints.

Appendix 3

M3 (70%): Extracts

P4 There are four important differences relevant to international management. These include culture, communication, motivation and leadership.

P5:S1–2 Culture can be thought of as a set of values and morals that are generally accepted and followed by most members of a society. One factor that makes international management a problem for organizations is adjusting to foreign cultures.

Appendix 4

History: 'How did Dutch colonialism foster the development of Indonesia's present ruling class?'

H1: (90%): Extracts

P1 The contention that Dutch colonialism 'fostered the development' of the present Indonesian ruling class' is dubious. This paper will argue that the present ruler of Indonesia, the Indonesian army, has emerged not as the product of Dutch colonialism, but from the circumstances of the collapse of the Dutch empire in Indonesia and the economic and political difficulties encountered by the Indonesian republic in the 1950s and 60s. These circumstances, and the army's response to them, created the opportunity for a military takeover in 1965. While it is true that there are strong elements of similarity and continuity between the New Order regime and the Dutch colonial administration, these occur in the nature of the state apparatus and the policies it pursues, and not in the group that is in control of it. The present directors of that state, and not its functionaries, constitute the Indonesian 'ruling class'.

P2:S1 The current Indonesian ruling group could be better described as a military caste than a class.

P3:S1–2 In this type of economic activity, ownership (but not control) of capital rests with foreign or Chinese firms. This in turn has served to inhibit the development of an indigenous bourgeoisie.

P4:S1 The Republican army was originally the creation of the Japanese during their occupation of Indonesia from 1942 to 1945, and they not only armed and trained an Indonesian-officered military force, but also imbued it with an Indonesian nationalist ideology.

P5:S1 The similarities and elements of continuity between the New Order government and Dutch rule can be found in the manner in which both have administered the country, but not in the social group or class which rules it.

P6:S1 Both colonial and New Order regimes have pursued a policy of economic and technical advancement, with a corresponding repression of political activity, which serves to facilitate the economic exploitation of the country for the benefit of the ruling caste.

P7:S1 A further similarity is that both systems have relied ultimately on force.

P8 (Conclusion) All these elements of Dutch colonial rule appropriated by the New Order government serve to facilitate its complete political and economic exploitation of the country.

Appendix 5

H2 (85%): Extracts

P9 (. . . the 1830s; Dutch administration via the cultivation system . . .)

P10:S1 The effect which this period of Indonesian history had on fostering a political structure which still retains much of what was initiated by the cultivation scheme, was most significant in the changes it brought about to the functioning of the ruling class.

P11:S1 The concept of supervision under the cultivation system became an increasingly profitable avenue for regent corruption and exploitation . . .

Appendix 6

H3 (80%): Extracts

P2 (. . . Forced Cultivation System; double bureaucracy . . .)

P3:S1–2 This notion of indirect rule via the Inlandsch Bestuur, known in indigenous terms as the Pangreh Praja, was contained in a Regulation of 1854 stating that '. . . insofar as circumstances permit, the native population is to be left under the supervision of its own, government-appointed or-recognized chiefs'. This therefore allowed the native nobility to become an official governing body, a colonial 'policy of ennoblement'. (+ further details of cultivation system, inc. being dismantled in 1860s)

P4:S1 The dismantling of the Forced Cultivation System saw the beginning of an era of an expanding economy as private capitalism replaced the government monopoly . . .

8 Developing discipline-specific writing: an analysis of undergraduate geography essays

Ann Hewings

1 Introduction

Research and pedagogy on the subject of writing for academic purposes has focused for some time on the significance of discourse communities (Bizzell 1992; Swales 1990). More recently the discussion has moved, via investigation of the features of science discourse (Bazerman 1988; Halliday and Martin 1993; Martin and Veel 1998), to the role of disciplines in creating and governing communities. In particular, the effect of disciplinary norms, expectations and methods of knowledge creation have come under scrutiny (Becher 1994; Hyland 2000; Myers 1990). This narrowing of focus has been partly in response to interest in what constitutes knowledge in different academic fields and partly to concerns about how to help those trying to learn the practices of their chosen discipline. This has resulted in work on the disciplinary writing produced by school students, undergraduates, post-graduates and professional academics in diverse academic fields such as history, biology, psychology and business studies. For example, history texts have been studied in secondary schools (Coffin 2000; Veel and Coffin 1996), at undergraduate level (McCabe 1999) and in academic articles (MacDonald 1994). Generally, however, undergraduate writing has received less attention from applied linguists than, for example, research articles, and writing in the discipline of geography has focused mainly on secondary school writing and textbooks (Kay 2001; van Leeuwen and Humphrey 1996; Wignell *et al.* 1989/1993). The research reported here, therefore, focuses on undergraduate writing in geography and seeks to contribute both to our understanding of the discipline and to ways in which students can be assisted in their writing at tertiary level.

2 Disciplinary communities

Work on writing at university level has taken place across and within different disciplinary areas and for different purposes. It was led, at least in part, by academics working with international students who were writing in English. A branch of applied linguistics known as English for Academic Purposes (EAP) was concerned to tease out the features of academic writing which could be passed on to students, mostly postgraduates. Early EAP work on genres by among others Swales (1981), Dudley-Evans (1987) and Bhatia (1993) looked at generalizable features of texts, that is, how they were structured as particular text-types or genres, and the language that accomplished this. It was not enough for students to know about and have ideas on a subject. They needed to be able to convey the knowledge and ideas *in writing* using formats which would accord with the expectations of their readers. This approach, then, recognized the significance of the expectations of the academic community on writing. The construct of the academic discourse community represented the generalized scholarly audience for whom certain standards and norms might be assumed to be universal.

The concept of the discourse community was further refined as practical experience in classrooms and lecture theatres served to highlight that there was significant variation within the norms of academia. Certain generic features might occur in similar texts written for say biology and psychology, but areas where they differed were often as, if not more, important. There has, therefore, been a noticeable shift in recent years towards looking at writing within the context of its disciplinary community (Hyland 2000; MacDonald 1994).

As well as the pedagogic push to understand more about academic writing in the discourse and disciplinary communities, there has also been work within the field of the sociology of knowledge. Here interest has been focused particularly on scientific knowledge (Bazerman 1988; Latour and Woolgar 1986; Myers 1985). How the scientific research paper has evolved into its present form, how scientific knowledge claims are negotiated and the hidden persuasion at the heart of much writing have all been described and discussed. This detailed research into scientific articles together with pedagogic need has helped to highlight not only the norms of science writing but also the significance of the socio-cultural setting.

Earlier, I mentioned the scholarly audience for academic writing, but in many ways this can been seen as a shorthand reference to the wider array of social and cultural factors which affect writing. Work outside linguistics in ethnography and anthropology has been influential in extending our view of writing and literacy more generally. Malinowski's work (1994) at the beginning of the twentieth century with the Trobriand Islanders highlighted the importance of the 'context of situation' to language, a notion that was subsequently incorporated into Halliday's systemic functional grammar (1994). More recently, the work of anthropologists such as Brian Street has widened again the view of factors which affect what Street calls 'literacy practices':

> I prefer to work from what I term an 'ideological' model of literacy, that recognises a multiplicity of literacies; that the meaning and uses of literacy practices are related to specific cultural contexts; and that these practices are always associated with relations of power and ideology. (1994: 139)

This view of literacy practices has influenced work on what, in the United

Kingdom, is becoming known as 'Academic Literacy', that is, research and pedagogy associated with writing at tertiary level, particularly as it relates to making clear to all students the writing practices used in higher education (Coffin *et al.* 2003; Lea and Street 1999; Lillis 2001). This view is, as Street makes clear, ideological in nature and in that respect has much in common with the work in schools undertaken by applied linguists working within the systemic functional linguistics (SFL) tradition. (For a discussion of the ideological foundations of SFL work see Cope and Kalantzis 1993.)

The literacy practices that students bring with them when they enter higher education are as varied as their backgrounds. However, once within the institution they are expected to produce writings which conform to disciplinary and institutional expectations as assessed by the academic staff reading and judging their work. These academic staff will in turn be influenced by their own interpretations of these norms and which particular aspects they think are essential and which of lesser importance. It is not the intention in this research to look at the effect of individual marker expectations on students' writing (see, for example, Prior 1995, 1998). Rather, it is to look at writing produced within a single department which, while it may carry departmental characteristics, is taken to represent writing at this level in the discipline as a whole. I shall discuss the characteristics of the discipline of geography first, and then look at a corpus of essay writing by first and third year geography students concentrating on how they manage the textual development of their essays, or in SFL terms, their use of the resource of Theme.

2.1 The disciplinary background

Historically, geography as a discipline was concerned with describing and accounting for natural and man-made landscapes and this led to the development of two sub-disciplines – physical and human geography. As the discipline evolved, different methodologies became associated with physical and human geography. Physical geography adopted the methods used in the sciences where it has much in common particularly with geology and biology. Scientific methods are used to research phenomena and processes such as volcanoes and soil erosion where quantifiable results are obtainable and hypotheses can be generated and tested. Human geography remained for some time highly descriptive and decried the quantitative methods of the physical geographers. They saw such methods as highlighting generalizations at, what they considered to be, the expense of detailed descriptions of the unique. There are indeed some geographers today who are still working along lines which resist the dominance of the scientific methods paradigm, but for the most part this paradigm is now the main influence in both the physical and the human wings.[1] Human geographers are as likely to be looking for patterns in demographic data or statistics on disease and housing location as physical geographers are to be measuring rates of river flow and making computer forecasts of bank erosion.

The dominance of the scientific method throughout geography and particularly on research has not led to a reintegration of the discipline. The phenomena studied dominates, and there are still prestigious journals which ally themselves with one wing or another. For students entering the discipline, the polarization of the two wings is often institutionally signalled through the presence of professors of human geography and professors of physical geography. Courses may well be divided into similar categories and students will have opinions on the interest and difficulties of the sub-disciplines which initially will be based on their experiences prior to entering university. Academics too, may consider that the two wings are very different and may have different expectations of writing depending upon whether they are physical or human geographers.

The research reported here concentrates on a single aspect of undergraduate geography writing in order to further our knowledge of the discipline and to examine the contrasts between truly novice undergraduate students and those who have undergone the full undergraduate degree programme and are close to graduating. Although only reporting one linguistic feature studied, the wider research (Hewings 1999) examined aspects of the disciplinary context through interviews, questionnaires and document analysis as well as further linguistic analysis. This wider study helps to inform the analysis and discussion of results reported here. The study as a whole looks for contrasts in the essays produced by first- and final-year geography students. The essay was chosen as the most widely produced written genre and the one which students had to produce both at the beginning and at the end of their studies. Other genres, such as the research report or dissertation were not repeated during the period of undergraduate studies and therefore could not be used to examine changes which might be happening in response to disciplinary, or wider academic, pressures or expectations.

3 Methodology

3.1 The data

Essays were collected from students who were studying geography as their main subject in the School of Geography at the University of Birmingham, UK. All the students were native speakers of English and had studied geography to advanced level at school and received good final grades. A corpus of 56 scripts was selected to represent writing by first- and third-year students and to cover both human and physical geography. From this a further selection was made of 16 essays, eight each from the first and third years. These were equally balanced between human and physical geography and represented the top and bottom of the range of marks awarded, though all were at a level to secure a pass grade.

3.2 *Method of analysis: the significance of Theme*

The essays were analysed on the basis of their thematic structure, where Theme choice is seen as indicative of wider rhetorical patterning. Themes are the initial elements of clauses or clause complexes and together with the Rheme (the rest of the clause) they make up the entire clause or clause complex. The description of Theme used was based on Halliday (1994) and Fries (1981/83) and takes its theoretical rationale from systemic functional grammar (SFG). The choice of Theme was based on the usefulness of the beginning of the clause as an indicator of the types of meanings being foregrounded in a text. The choices made at the beginning of a clause are significant in two ways. First, they create the framework for the interpretation of the rest of the clause. In the example below, from the beginning of a children's book, *Bye Bye Baby*, the Theme elements of the main clauses (in italics) serve to highlight the central character *This baby*, *He* and in the final Theme to alert the reader to changes that are about to happen. By placing baby in the Themes, the writers are constantly contrasting the information which follows with the unusual situation of a lone child. Matthiessen (1995: 27) refers to this aspect of Theme as creating 'the angle on the message'.

> *There* was once a baby who had no mummy. *This baby* lived in a little house all by himself. *He* fed himself and bathed himself. *He* even changed his own nappy. *It* was very sad. *Then, one night* . . . (Ahlberg and Ahlberg 1991)

The second area of significance has been referred to as 'method of development' (Fries 1981/83) or 'thematic progression' (Danes 1974). Themes are central to the creation of coherence within a text, often containing reference items both to earlier parts of the text and forward referencing to what is to come. They, therefore, tie in a clause to the surrounding text. This is clearly visible in the example of the baby, where *This baby* refers back to the information introduced in the previous sentence and *He* picks up on this in the next two clauses. *It* encapsulates all the earlier information and *Then, one night* moves the story on. Similar patterning can be seen in the example from a geography essay below. The first two Themes are the same, with *it* being a pronominal reference back to *The essay*. The third Theme, and particularly *these trends*, picks up on the final element of the Rheme in the previous sentence.

> *The essay* will begin with a brief assessment of the advantages and disadvantages of communal housing, in order to contextualise subsequent sections of the essay. *It* will then consider temporal patterns of supply and demand for residential care homes, and will offer an analysis of recent trends. *The spatial implications of these trends* will be discussed.

In this chapter, I shall not deal with thematic progression (see Hewings 1999 for a discussion of thematic progression), but instead concentrate on the importance of Theme in creating an angle on the message. By looking at the different functional messages that Theme can convey and then comparing the findings for first- and third-year geography essays, I will exemplify some of the changes that can be identified between the two groups of essays.

The Theme of a clause can contain up to three functional elements, one or all of which can influence the angle on the message. Following Halliday (1994), the multifunctional potential that exists within Themes is divided into:

- our experience of the world (the ideational function)
- our relationships and viewpoints (the interpersonal function)
- how a particular clause fits in with others to make a coherent whole (the textual function).

The Theme thus has the potential to influence the reader's interpretation of the rest of the clause and ultimately of the text and can take on a significant role in the domains of evaluation and persuasion. It is this evaluative or persuasive role which will be investigated in detail. It is not that such a role is only contained within the Theme element, but rather that an investigation of Theme helps to indicate whether such roles are being used in the student essays. Using this indicator, it is possible to identify differences between the rhetorical functions in the first- and third-year essays examined.

Signals of persuasion or evaluative purpose can occur anywhere in a text as the various contributors to Hunston and Thompson's (2000) collection of papers on evaluation demonstrate. Similarly, Hyland's (1998) extensive study of hedging in scientific research articles makes no distinctions based on position in the clause. However, a focus on the beginning of the clause is supported by, for example, Conrad and Biber (2000). In their corpus study of stance adverbials, they note that in prose, including academic writing, stance adverbials tend to come early in the clause either as the initial element or before the verb. Their explanation given for this focuses on both the clause and the discourse roles played:

> From a processing perspective, these positions [at the beginning of the clause] are 'user-friendly' in that they provide the author's framing for a proposition before actually presenting the proposition. In addition, stance adverbials in initial position often serve a secondary function as linking adverbials. (Conrad and Biber 2000: 71)

This parallels the dual functions of the Theme as the starting point of the message and as the place where the whole clause is tied into its context; that is, within which elements from the preceding discourse are reiterated, reintroduced or reinterpreted.

Support for the significance of initial position is also given by Thompson and Zhou (2000) in their discussion of disjuncts. They note that while the role of conjuncts (*thus, therefore*, etc.) has been recognized as fulfilling a textual function, disjuncts such as *unfortunately* and *obviously* are discussed mainly as sources of evaluation. However, as their examples demonstrate, they frequently occur in sentence initial position establishing what they call 'evaluative coherence'; that is, they both convey evaluation and serve to link parts of the text together as in the next example:

> And who in the world could possibly make a mistake about a thing like that? *Admittedly* it was painted white, but that made not the slightest difference. (Thompson and Zhou 2000: 125)

For this study, Themes were analysed only in independent clauses in the clause complex (with the exception of fronted dependent clauses which were classed as marked clausal Theme). The emphasis on independent clauses accords with Halliday's (1994: 61) observation that the main contribution to the method of development of text comes from the 'thematic structure of independent clauses'. Specifying the extent of thematic elements has presented problems to theorists, but the approach adopted widely has been to classify everything as thematic up to and including the first part of the clause that has an ideational function. In SFG these are clause participants (e.g. the subject), circumstances (e.g. adjuncts specifying place, time, etc.) or processes (verbs). While the Theme must contain an ideational element, it can also include preceding optional textual and interpersonal elements. Where there are such optional elements, the Theme is classified as 'multiple'. Themes are said to be 'unmarked' if in declarative clauses the ideational element is the grammatical subject. If a different ideational element is chosen to appear before the subject then the Theme is said to be 'marked'. Marked Themes can also be preceded by textual and interpersonal Themes and so be considered in the multiple Theme category.

The classification system used is summarized in Table 8.1 and largely follows Halliday (1994) with the exception of an extension of the coding for interpersonal Theme elements.

The realization of interpersonal Theme is extended to include grammatical metaphors encoded as *it*-clauses with extraposed subjects, which clearly project an angle on the proposition to follow. This follows Martin's analysis of

> It would be irresponsible to ignore Australia's pleas to reform antiquated gun law policies! (1995: 244)

into interpersonal Theme (It would be irresponsible) and an ellipted topical Theme, 'Mr Greiner', the person to whom the exhortation is addressed. Similarly, Cloran considers 'It's lucky' in

> It's lucky that we left early (1995: 378)

to be interpersonal Theme, giving an evaluative point of departure and Whittaker classifies all the following as interpersonal Theme on similar grounds:

It has been suggested that . . .
Of course, it may be counter-argued that . . .
It is often argued that . . . (1995: 111)

Davies (1997) discusses these structures in terms of the presentation of 'viewpoint' from an invisible subject. Thus, in the example on page 139, taken from the data examined here *and* is textual Theme, *it has been suggested that* is interpersonal and *Such long-term cycles* is topical Theme.

Table 8.1 Summary of Theme choices analysed and coding system used

Theme type	Description and example	Abbreviation
Topical	Theme is congruent with the grammatical subject, e.g. *The soft rock* is eroded relatively rapidly. Thematic equatives (pseudo-clefts) are also included in this group, e.g. *What is indisputable,* is that women . . . Clauses beginning with existential *there* are classed as topical Theme, e.g. *There* is great prestige associated with being innovative.	i
Marked	A circumstantial adjunct occurring before the grammatical subject is the first ideational element and therefore thematic, e.g. *From here,* water would follow the stream. Fronted dependent clauses are analysed as marked clausal Themes, e.g. *If water becomes sufficiently concentrated* it might begin to cut a channel. Similarly, predicated Themes (clefts) are classified as marked, e.g. *It is perhaps the shorter lifespan of mobile homes* that prevents . . .	m
Textual	These are structural elements such as conjunctions and relatives which occur at the beginning of the clause, e.g. . . . *but* it is still a significant amount.	t
Interpersonal	These are any combination of vocatives, modals and mood-markings, e.g. *Indeed*, Hartmann argues that the basis of male power . . . Clauses such as those with anticipatory *it* followed by an extraposed subject are treated as interpersonal grammatical metaphors, e.g. *It is obvious from the descriptions of the various processes that* soil creep is a very slow form of movement.	int
Unclassified	Clauses are marked as unclassified when punctuation and grammatical errors make it impossible to infer a 'correct' version.	U

and it has been suggested that 'Such long-term cycles characterize most glacier dammed lakes'.

Such interpersonal Themes frequently have embedded within them textual Themes such as 'therefore' in the next example:

It is therefore important that models of hillslope runoff explicitly distinguish rill flow from inter-rill flow.

An alternative to classifying these elements as interpersonal Theme is given by Thompson (1996) who groups fronted *it*-clauses as 'Thematized comment', presumably fulfilling an ideational function and therefore requiring no further elements to be included in the Theme. By thus classifying them as topical Theme the affective function of such elements may be lost and therefore in this analysis they are assigned an interpersonal thematic label.

3.3 Analysis and findings

A total of 1,272 clause complexes were analysed and in Table 8.2 the percentage of clause complexes that consisted of ideational elements only (unmarked topical Themes and marked Themes) together with the number of Themes which comprised multiple elements is shown. This was broken down into sub-groups corresponding to year groups and whether the essays were on physical or human geography topics.

Table 8.3 shows the percentages of textual and interpersonal thematic elements within the multiple theme category.

The most obvious areas of contrast are in the uses of unmarked topical, multiple and textual Themes. First-year students make use of 12 per cent more unmarked topical Themes than do third-year students. Third-year students, in contrast, use over 11 per cent more multiple Themes, with the

Table 8.2 Theme choice analysis I

| Sub-group | Single element Themes | | | | No. of clause complexes |
	Unmarked topical Themes	Marked Themes	Multiple Themes	Unclassified clauses	
1st year physical	66.88%	15.63%	17.50%	0.30%	320
1st year human	63.04%	16.73%	19.07%	1.20%	257
1st year sub-total	65.16%	16.12%	18.20%	0.69%	577
3rd year physical	51.03%	16.52%	32.45%	0.00%	339
3rd year human	54.34%	16.90%	27.53%	1.23%	356
3rd year sub-total	53.24%	16.26%	29.93%	0.57%	695

Table 8.3 Theme choice analysis II: textual and interpersonal thematic elements within the multiple Theme category

Sub-group	Interpersonal Themes	Textual Themes
1st year physical	2.19%	15.94%
1st year human	7.00%	15.56%
1st year sub-total	4.33%	15.77%
3rd year physical	6.49%	28.32%
3rd year human	5.90%	23.60%
3rd year sub-total	6.19%	25.90%

majority of those being textual Themes. There is little overall variation between physical geography and human geography. However, first-year physical geography essays are generally the least similar to either third-year physical geography essays or third year essays as a whole. They have the highest percentage of unmarked topical Themes and the lowest percentage of marked, multiple and interpersonal Themes.

In discussing the results, I shall examine what an analysis of Theme can tell us about writing in geography at two points in an undergraduate career and particularly what the increased use of multiple Themes in more experienced students' essays indicates about disciplinary writing in geography.

4 The role of unmarked topical Themes

Students entering the School of Geography were given information about what was expected and would be rewarded in their essays. In outlining the top three grades the word *argument* and its synonyms was prominent together with *criticism, insight* and *imaginative discussion/analysis* (School of Geography 1996). It is clear from reading the essays that some students, mostly those in their first year, did not understand what *argument, criticism* and so on entailed within an academic essay (see also, Coffin *et al.* 2003). There was extensive use of unmarked topical Themes where subject and Theme are conflated; that is, Themes identify people, places, things or abstract qualities and these are often the same as a previous Theme or pick up on a previous rheme. This can contribute to texts sounding descriptive or expository. The example below is a paragraph from a first-year physical geography essay written in response to the title 'River channel types'. (Themes are in italics.)

There are three different forms of delta.   i

The Nile is an arcuate delta which has a rounded convex outer margin.   i

Where the material brought down by a river is spread out evenly on either side of   m
    the channel, like the Tiber, it is called Cuspate.

The final type of delta is a birds foot.   i

This is where a river has many distributaries bounded by sediment and   i
   which extend out to sea like the claws of a bird.

The Mississippi delta is the best example of this.   i

The student has interpreted the task as one of describing and categorizing
river channel types. The lack of any words in the assignment title such as
discuss, compare or *account for* indicating ways in which such a title could be
focused has perhaps understandably led the student to reproduce the type
of writing with which they are familiar. At the beginning of the first year,
students are likely to have read mostly textbooks. These tend to present
a synthesized and unproblematic account of a discipline and therefore
may not be the best writing model to follow (Hewings 1990; Myers 1992).
As Hyland (1999) points out, they are not representative of academic discourse in general and may not be capable of conveying both scholarship
and discipline-specific rhetorical and linguistic practices.

In the next example taken from a third-year physical geography essay
entitled 'Advances in hillslope erosion modelling', the student is discussing
a model known as the Universal Soil Loss Equation (USLE). (Different types
of Theme are divided by /.)

The USLE also contains theoretical problems.   i

Firstly, / *many of the factors* are interdependent.   t/i

and / *as a result* / *the importance of some of the factors* will clearly be   t/t/i
   overstated in relation to others.

The USLE also made two simple and seemingly reasonable   i
   assumptions that have since been proved to be incorrect.

Firstly / *the model* works on the basis that increases in vegetation   t/i
   cover lead to reduced erosion.

In actual fact / *changes in microtopography associated with vegetation*   int/i
   cover appear to encourage rilling, until the vegetation cover
   exceeds approximately 15%,

soil erosion as a result of this rilling is believed to be higher than   i
   losses from bare soil.

The USLE also works on the assumption that erosion increases with   i
   length of slope.

However, / *the important factor* is the capacity of the flow to transport   t/i
   sediment,

and / *over longer slopes* the chances of the capacity being reached are   t/m
   greater

and / when the capacity is reached the erosion downslope will not   t/m
increase but remain the same.

The USLE also ignores the fact that some deposition of sediment   i
may occur on the hillslopes.

Here we see exploitation of Theme position to signal organization *Firstly* and angle on the message *In actual fact.* If the first clause complex is seen as thematic for the paragraph (see Martin 1992 for a discussion of Theme above the level of the clause), then we have a whole section of text set up as an evaluation of a particular model. Some of that evaluation is signalled by Themes such as *However, the important factor* but much is also carried in the Rhemes. Both Themes and Rhemes use more abstract and technical lexis than the first-year example above with greater use of grammatical metaphor (e.g. *soil erosion, deposition of sediment*) and complex nominal groups (e.g. *microtopography associated with vegetation cover, the capacity of the flow to transport sediment*). Importantly, this paragraph demonstrates not only the student's familiarity with certain discipline specific material, but also shows that they are able to evaluate its significance or usefulness rather than just describe its characteristics. This student has moved beyond description and categorization and has interpreted the requirements of the discipline in terms of content knowledge *and* critical stance. A further distinguishing element in the Themes of final-year as opposed to first-year students is frequent references to the literature of the discipline. These occur as both unmarked topical and marked Themes as in the next example from a paragraph in a third-year human geography essay.

As Ermisch (1991) comments, this has significant . . .   m

Laing and Buisson (1993) predict that if the proportion . . .   i

In addition, / as Sinclair (1988) observes, '[further] pressures on   t/m
residential accommodation . . .

Use of attributed opinion and evidence is much more common within Theme position in third-year essays and demonstrates not only an ability to integrate the ideas of others but perhaps also an understanding of the significance of the accumulation of research into a topic. The importance of cumulative knowledge building has been identified as typical of the scientific method (Becher 1994) and attribution itself is typical of tertiary level academic writing.

Finally, in this discussion of the contrasts in the use of unmarked topical Theme between first- and third-year writers, the types of meanings made are also noticeably different. In a study of school-based geography, Wignell *et al.* observed that the:

discipline of geography is concerned with making order and meaning of the experiential world, through observing, classifying, and explaining phenomena . . .

> [G]eography observes the world by setting up a technical lexis; . . . [and] it orders the world by arranging these terms into taxonomies. (1989/1993: 165)

This description was found to be particularly apt for the physical geography essays analysed and particularly those written by first-year students. Within first-year essays, writers defined, categorized and classified the natural world as exemplified in the following Themes:

> *The third type of flood that can occur* is . . .
>
> . . . *these six categories* can be classed as . . .
>
> *The term afforestation* refers to . . .

Attribution, exploration of different theories and evaluation are all features which were more typical of those essays in the third-year group which were awarded high marks. More third-year students' simple Themes were oriented towards theories, hypotheses and evaluation. Such Themes often fore-grounded synthesis and evaluation, as in the following examples.

> *The reason for this* is . . .
>
> *A second interpretation* was . . .
>
> *This argument* can be extended to . . .
>
> *Academic thought* has seen a confrontation of . . .
>
> *The theoretical assumption underlying these reforms* is that . . .

The observation that first-year students use more unmarked topical Themes and ways in which such usage contrasts with that of third-year students gives an insight into how successful students learn to fulfil the expectations of their discipline at tertiary level. The importance of not just knowledge display but also synthesis and evaluation highlighted in third-year essays can also be traced in the use of multiple Themes.

5 The significance of multiple Theme

As third-year writers use 12 per cent fewer unmarked topical Themes than first years, this allows a greater variety of starting points. Third-year students show a greater willingness to exploit thematic potential for ends other than, or in addition to, what might be described as topic maintenance. This change is not brought about by a significant increase in marked Theme choices. Rather, it is the result of an increase in multiple Themes; that is, textual and/or interpersonal Themes preceding a marked or unmarked topical Theme. Thus 'what the message is concerned with' (Halliday 1985: 36) is not just the ideational content (topical Themes) but text building (textual Themes) and the conveying of social relationships (interpersonal themes). This exploitation of the different functions within Theme position is further extended by the use of more than one textual Theme at a time;

typically this is *and* or *but* followed by logical connectors such as *as a result* and *thus* as in the next examples. (In these examples, the whole Theme is italicized and unmarked topical Themes are underlined. The '/' is used to separate different types of Theme element and multiple uses of the same type of Theme.)

> *and/ as a result/ the importance of some of the factors* will be clearly overstated in relation to the others
>
> *and/ thus/ his analysis* was fundamentally flawed

These types of Theme are less common in first-year essays. There are fewer multiple textual Themes of the *and* type followed by logical connectors. The decrease in *and* and *but* appears to illustrate a favouring of shorter sentences or more subordinated rather than co-ordinated clauses – hypotaxis rather than parataxis (Halliday 1994: 218ff). (Findings on the length of the grammatical subject (Hewings 2002) also indicate that first-year students use shorter subjects than do third-year students.) The lower number of logical connectors also means that more often the reader is left to try and intuit connections and relationships.

Textual Themes serve the purpose of most clearly indicating the 'linking function' (Martin *et al.* 1997: 25) of the textual metafunction. This linking function, particularly when not just realized by *and* or *but*, also serves to highlight the unfolding or logical structure of the essays. This is particularly important in the light of the significance given to argument, insight, criticism, discussion and analysis in the guidance supplied to the students. Logical connectors allow writers to make connections and pursue a line of argument. In addition, interpersonal Themes are strongly associated with presenting an angle on the matter of the clause and, as a result, their rhetorical role is more visible. The analysis of multiple Themes, therefore, points to one way of indicating the relative presence or absence of an unfolding, possibly argument-based, structure within essays. The use of conjunctive adjuncts in Theme position indicates a text which has been formulated to show how the different elements connect through the resources of the textual metafunction, what Halliday refers to as 'creating relevance to context' (1994, p. 36). Investigating the types and configurations of Themes is one way of investigating how a writer creates such relevance. Multiple Themes allow the writer to exploit the textual metafunction to a greater degree, allowing relevance to context to be grounded through textual conjunctive Themes as well as through the ideational content of topical Themes. In addition, the writer's viewpoint can be overtly signalled using interpersonal Themes.

Rhetorical motivation and interpersonal Theme

I have argued above that multiple Themes allow the encoding of a greater number of meanings in the opening of the clause and that these are indicative of some of the differences between first- and third-year geography essays.

In particular, by the third year, students are learning to write a more sophisticated form of argument essay that includes logical exposition and evaluation as well as categorization and synthesis. Evaluative or persuasive intent can be traced through the greater use of interpersonal Themes in third-year essays.

The next two examples are typical of the types of interpersonal Themes found in the data. (The whole multiple Theme is in italics and the final ideational element, the topical Theme, is underlined.)

> *and/ in general/* the nations being affected would classify as peripheral or semi-peripheral countries
>
> *However,/ it is often felt that/* Dual Labour Market Theory lacks precision as an explanation of gender segregation. *Indeed/* it fails to explain women's inferior labour market position beyond their being female

In the first, the interpersonal Theme element *in general* conveys the writer's notion of usuality for the rest of the clause. Through its use, the writer is able to mediate the amount of commitment they show to the statement. Similarly, in the second example, *it is often felt* makes the opinion sound more objective without attributing it to the author or anyone else. The author, however, goes on to show agreement with the statement through the use of *indeed* in the Theme of the following sentence.

The extensive example below is the final paragraph from the third-year physical geography essay which received the highest mark in the whole corpus. The evaluative and persuasive nature of this paragraph permeates more than just the Themes, but is particularly indicated through the use of interpersonal Theme elements: *unequivocally, it is fair to say, perhaps.* It is the presence of these interpersonal elements which can help distinguish writers who are creating essays which do more than recount facts. The writer is prepared to intrude more openly into the text, albeit often in a disguised, objectivized way. That this engagement by the essay writer with the subject is valued can be gauged from its greater frequency of occurrence in third-year essays and especially in those receiving higher marks. It also accords with the 'Guidelines' produced by the School of Geography mentioned earlier.

Unequivocally / hillslope erosion models have advanced since the first one in 1940,	int/i
but/ these models are still not perfect.	t/i
Currently/ it is fair to say that / results from the models although representative of soil loss in an area are far from accurate.	t/int/i
Perhaps/ the most promising advances in modelling are not the predictions made, but the theoretical advances in the model base.	int/i
Significant advances in the understanding of hillslope erosion processes have been made recently,	i

and / the latest model (De Roo, 1996) attempts to incorporate these   t/i
processes.

Currently/ the model is not perfect   t/i

but / it shows almost a breakthrough in erosion modelling   t/i
because of the inclusion of some of the most up to date
advances in the understanding of hillslope erosion processes.

This engagement with the subject matter and the disciplinary dialogue is highlighted by an analysis of the interpersonal metafunction and is picked up here in the interpersonal element of Theme. However, interpersonal Theme elements do not constitute a large proportion of the Themes analysed and in two first-year essays were entirely absent. To understand the significance of interpersonal Theme elements it is, therefore, necessary to examine their distribution in some individual essays and to consider the essays in relation to the marks they received.

Analysis of third-year essays shows interpersonal Theme elements occurring more frequently than in first-year essays. This is particularly so in the case of those essays which were most highly rated. To illustrate the contrast, I shall examine their use in physical geography essays written by first- and third-year writers. The top two physical geography essays written by third-year students contained interpersonal Theme elements in 10 per cent and 9.09 per cent respectively of their Themes. This is the highest proportion in any of the essays and in greatest contrast to the scarcity of interpersonal Themes in first-year physical geography essays, two of which had no interpersonal Theme elements. One of these first-year essays was given a high mark. It contained a wealth of technical detail, clearly demonstrating a depth of knowledge on the subject. The essay, entitled 'The weathering of building stone in urban areas', discussed the processes of weathering, particularly the chemical basis, and the effects on different stone types. The final section summarizes a report and concludes from it:

> *The report* clearly illustrated that future stone weathering is inevitable with so many contributing aspects.

The information in the report is not questioned and no other evidence is considered. The writer while finding a source of evidence has not moved to the point of critically evaluating that source or contrasting it with other research.

The top third-year physical geography essay, by contrast, is a model of focused comparison. In this essay interpersonal Theme elements commonly occur when evaluations are taking place:

During the year a farmer may traverse up to 80% of a field,   m

and / the wheelings which are used even more regularly will become   t/i
extremely compacted,

Clearly/ the properties of the soil change as a result of this   int/i
  compaction,

but / so far none of the models discussed include this as a factor.   t/m

Clearly signals the writer's evaluation of the significance of the evidence just presented and a marked Theme *so far* highlights the inadequacies of the 'models discussed'. The writer's purpose in this essay contrasts with that of the first-year writer discussed above. Displaying a wide knowledge of geomorphological processes is not sufficient; evaluation is also required.

These examples from physical geography may be taken as suggestive of a change in the rhetorical function of essay writing between first and third years. The predominance of unmarked topical Themes in first-year essays is indicative of their more descriptive and non-evaluative style. Third-year essays, and particularly those which received high marks, showed a more complex rhetorical structure signalled in Theme position by complex unmarked topical Themes, textual Theme elements highlighting a logical argument structure and interpersonal Theme elements providing an evaluative or persuasive angle.

6 Conclusion

I started this chapter by reviewing the recent history that has led to the interest in disciplinary writing. The realization of the complexity of factors influencing writers has resulted in different groups of researchers focusing on different aspects of academic writing. Within the sphere of disciplinary studies, the emphasis in the past has been on the two poles of schools-based and published academic writing. Here, I have argued for attention at the level of the undergraduate student new to tertiary-level disciplinary study. Through analysis of a small corpus of undergraduate writing we can begin to describe more precisely the product which students are expected to produce. We can also start to make explicit the types of knowledge valued by particular disciplines at this level.

One of the main expectations of academic essays is that they will contain synthesis, evaluation or critique and that these will be bound within a rhetorical framework, most typically of argument. The students reported on here were given information that these qualities were required by their department. Analysis of their writing has looked at contrasts between first- and final-year students in the search for ways to map linguistically how these expectations were realized in one disciplinary community. The research has pedagogic implications as well as contributing to the description of the discipline of geography at undergraduate level. In addition, it indicates a possible research tool for looking at the gradual development of students' writing in other disciplines. Using similar techniques we can examine aspects of the academic conventions and disciplinary epistemic norms of a variety of disciplines and students' increasing ability to adopt and adapt them as they proceed through their studies.

The analysis presented suggests that Theme is a useful lexicogrammatical indicator of how students rhetorically frame their essays. The predominance of unmarked topical Themes in first-year essays, often combined with simple thematic progression patterns, resulted in some texts which resembled narratives or textbook descriptions. This mirrors the types of texts that most students have been exposed to at the point of entry into undergraduate study. It may be as a result of this type of reading that students are perhaps not aware at the beginning of their university careers of the conflicting theories *within* their chosen discipline. Their concern up to this point has been with learning more and more disciplinary content. If this content is seen as 'received wisdom', it may then be difficult for students to understand what is to be synthesized and argued over. There may also be problems of voice, in that students may not feel comfortable evaluating published works other than in glowing terms, or be familiar with the language in which to accomplish such critical evaluation.

In contrast to the writing produced by students beginning their under-graduate degrees in geography, most essays written by third-year students are impressionistically qualitatively different and this is shown quantitatively in the types of Themes chosen. Theme, as a resource for encoding 'angle on the message' is exploited to a greater degree particularly by those who are most successful. The increased use of multiple Themes means that third-year students can exploit Theme position to signal such things as the logical basis of their assertions, or their particular stance on the ideational material being presented, as well as topic continuity. Use of structures such as *It may be argued that* or *It is obvious that*, which here are treated as interpersonal Theme choices, enable students to encode evaluations and comparisons without the necessity of owning them outright by using *I*. Use of such structures may be attributed to an understandable wish to avoid direct critique by students, or as an indication that they are assimilating a pseudo-objective scientific norm in their writing.

It should be noted, of course, that Theme is only one mechanism through which students can present evaluation, argument or angle. Other mechanisms include metadiscourse, lexis, grammatical structures, appraisal and discourse patterns. (For overviews see Hunston and Thompson 2000; Hyland 2000). However, looking at this first constituent of the clause does appear to give an insight into how students are appropriating disciplinary discourse practices. The differences between first- and final-year students' writing can be traced through the patterns of Themes employed. These students have been given little in the way of writing instruction after their first semester, so we can only speculate as to how this development has come about. The common thread for all the students will have been exposure to writing in the discipline – textbooks, collections of articles and journal literature. Their bibliographies show that textbooks become less influential by the third year, so they are likely to be absorbing aspects of disciplinary writing while reading journals and books written primarily for professionals in the discipline. This is not necessarily the most efficient or effective way of encouraging students to write in the ways deemed most appropriate. Indeed for some students relying on 'demystifying' the acceptable practices of academic writing largely through exposure to professional genres, those written by people already approved by the academic community, may result in frustration and failure.

This brings me finally to possible teaching implications of the findings reported here. Explicit teaching about Theme has been used in the past to help students with coherence in essays (Webb 1991), but the insights from this study show how Theme can also highlight the rhetorical or evaluative expectations of the genre within the discipline. A focus on the beginning of the clause in both essays and published texts can be used as an initial consciousness-raising exercise. Questions about why a writer has chosen as point of departure one Theme rather than another can lead into discussion of rhetorical purpose. The ways in which writers encode evaluation and how visible they make themselves in the text may be traced through the use or non-use of personal pronouns or phrases such as *in my opinion . . .* or *it has been found that . . .* in Theme position. Similarly, the functions of multiple and marked Theme in maintaining not only topic coherence but also indicating evaluative or interpersonal standpoints and logical frameworks (*As a result of . . .; So, although . . .; Indeed, Drury's explanation . . .*) can indicate how disciplinary writing is structured and what types of argument and evidence are valued. Discussion of why other researchers and their work often occur in Theme position can bring to light the importance of building arguments around the work of others. Such discussion and explanation can help avoid the often-seen marginal remarks from those marking scripts 'Who says?' and 'Where is your evidence?', which might otherwise be an unhelpful form of feedback.

The research reported here focused on a small corpus and is therefore subject to the problems of small sample size. Nevertheless, it indicates one aspect of texts that can be isolated for comparative purposes in order to indicate patterns of organization that may be valued in academic writing in the disciplines. As a research tool, it allows us to better understand the epistemology of a discipline and as a teaching resource it helps focus on the particular wordings used by student writers and to begin to evaluate their appropriacy. As Theme in English is recognized by position at the beginning of the clause or clause complex, it may also prove of use to subject-specialist lecturers who are non-linguists as a recognizable component for them to discuss with student writers.

Notes

1 For a detailed historical account of the evolution of geography as a discipline see Bird 1989.

References

Ahlberg, J. and Ahlberg, A. (1991) *Bye Bye Baby*. London: Little Mammoth.

Bazerman, C. (1988) *Shaping Written Knowledge: The Genre and Activity of the Experimental Article in Science*. Madison, WI: University of Wisconsin Press.

Becher, T. (1994) 'The significance of disciplinary differences', *Studies in Higher Education*, 19, 151–61.

Bhatia, V.K. (1993) *Analysing Genre: Language Use in Professional Settings*. London: Longman.

Bird, J. (1989) *The Changing Worlds of Geography: A Critical Guide to Concepts and Methods*. Oxford: Clarendon Press.

Bizzell, P. (1992) *Academic Discourse and Critical Consciousness*. Pittsburg, PA: University of Pittsburg Press.

Cloran, C. (1995) 'Defining and relating text segments: subject and theme in discourse', in R. Hasan and P.H. Fries (eds), *On Subject and Theme*. Amsterdam: John Benjamins, pp. 361–403.

Coffin, C. (2000) 'History as discourse: construals of time, cause and appraisal'. Unpublished PhD thesis, University of New South Wales, Sydney, Australia.

Coffin, C., Curry, M.J., Goodman, S., Hewings, A., Lillis, T. and Swann, J. (2003) *Teaching Academic Writing: A Toolkit for Higher Education*. London: Routledge.

Conrad, S. and Biber, D. (2000) 'Adverbial marking of stance in speech and writing', in S. Hunston and G. Thompson (eds), *Evaluation in Text: Authorial Stance and the Construction of Discourse*. Oxford: Oxford University Press, pp. 56–73.

Cope, B. and Kalantzis, M. (eds) (1993) *The Power of Literacy*. London: Falmer Press.

Danes, F. (1974) 'Functional sentence perspective and the organization of the text', in F. Danes (ed.), *Papers on Functional Sentence Perspective*. Prague: Academia, pp. 106–28.

Davies, F. (1997) 'Marked theme as a heuristic for analysing text-type, text and genre', in J. Piqué and D.J. Viera (eds), *Applied Languages: Theory and Practice in ESP*. Valencia: Universitat de Valencia, pp. 45–79.

Dudley-Evans, T. (ed.) (1987) 'Genre Analysis and E.S.P.' *ELR Journal 1*. Birmingham: English Language Research, University of Birmingham.

Fries, P.H. (1981) 'On the status of theme in English: arguments from discourse', *Forum Linguisticum* 6(1), 1–38. Reprinted in J.S. Petöfi and E. Sözer (eds) (1983), *Micro and Macro Connexity of Texts*. Hamburg: Helmut Buske Verlag, pp. 116–52.

Halliday, M.A.K. (1985) *Spoken and Written Language*. Victoria: Deakin University.

Halliday, M.A.K. (1994) *An Introduction to Functional Grammar* 2nd edn. London: Edward Arnold.

Halliday, M.A.K. and Martin, J.R. (1993) *Writing Science: Literary and Discursive Power*. London: Falmer Press.

Hewings, A. (1990) 'Aspects of the language of economics textbooks', in A. Dudley-Evans and W. Henderson (eds), *The Language of Economics: The Analysis of Economics Discourse. ELT Documents: 134*. London: Modern English Publications in association with The British Council, pp. 29–42.

Hewings, A. (1999) 'Disciplinary engagement in undergraduate geography writing: an investigation of clause-initial elements in geography essays'. Unpublished PhD thesis, University of Birmingham, Birmingham.

Hewings, A. (2002) 'Shifting rhetorical focus in student and professional geography writing', in C.N. Candlin (ed.), *Research and Practice in Professional Discourse*. Hong Kong: City University of Hong Kong Press, pp. 441–62.

Hunston, S. and Thompson, G. (eds) (2000) *Evaluation in Text: Authorial Stance and the Construction of Discourse.* Oxford: Oxford University Press.

Hyland, K. (1998) *Hedging in Scientific Research Articles.* Amsterdam: John Benjamins.

Hyland, K. (1999) 'Talking to students: metadiscourse in introductory textbooks', *Journal of English for Specific Purposes,* 18(1), 3–26.

Hyland, K. (2000) *Disciplinary Discourses: Social Interactions in Academic Writing.* Harlow: Longman.

Kay, H.L. (2001) 'A site for soaring eyes: a sociocognitive study of secondary school geography texts'. Unpublished PhD thesis, University of Birmingham, Birmingham.

Latour, B. and Woolgar, S. (1986) *Laboratory Life: The Social Construction of Scientific Facts.* Princeton, NJ: Princeton University Press.

Lea, M. and Street, B. (1999) 'Writing as academic literacies: understandng textual practices in higher education', in C.N. Candlin and K. Hyland (eds), *Writing: Texts, Processes and Practices.* London and New York: Longman, pp. 62–81.

Lillis, T.M. (2001) *Student Writing: Access, Regulation, Desire.* London: Routledge.

MacDonald, S.P. (1994) *Professional Academic Writing in the Humanities and Social Sciences.* Carbondale and Edwardsville, IL: Southern Illinois University Press.

Malinowski, B. (1994) 'The problem of meaning in primitive languages', in J. Maybin (ed.), *Language and Literacy in Social Practice.* Clevedon Multilingual Matters in association with The Open University, pp. 1–10.

Martin, J.R. (1992) *English Text.* Philadelphia and Amsterdam: John Benjamins.

Martin, J.R. (1995) 'English Theme', in M. Ghadessy (ed.), *Thematic Development in English Texts.* London: Pinter, pp. 223–58.

Martin, J.R. and Veel, R. (1998) *Reading Science: Critical and Functional Perspectives on Discourses of Science.* London: Routledge.

Martin, J.R., Matthiessen, C.M.I.M. and Painter, C. (1997) *Working with Functional Grammar.* London: Edward Arnold.

Matthiessen, C.M.I.M. (1995) 'Theme as an enabling resource in ideational "knowledge" construction', in M. Ghadessy (ed.), *Thematic Development in English Texts.* London: Pinter, pp. 20–54.

McCabe, A. (1999) 'Theme and thematic patterns in Spanish and English History texts'. Unpublished PhD thesis, Aston University, Birmingham.

Myers, G. (1985) 'The social construction of two biologists' proposals', *Written Communication,* 2, 219–45.

Myers, G. (1990) *Writing Biology: Texts in the Social Construction of Scientific Knowledge.* Madison, WI: The University of Wisconsin Press.

Myers, G. (1992) 'Textbooks and the sociology of scientific knowledge', *English for Specific Purposes,* 11, 3–17.

Prior, P. (1995) 'Redefining the task: an ethnographic examination of writing and response in graduate seminars', in D. Belcher and G. Braine (eds), *Academic Writing in a Second Language: Essays on Research and Pedagogy.* Norwood, NJ: Ablex, pp. 47–82.

Prior, P. (1998) *Writing/Disciplinarity: A Sociohistoric Account of Literate Activity in the Academy.* London: Lawrence Erlbaum.

School of Geography (1996) *Year One Handbook.* Birmingham: The School of Geography, University of Birmingham.

Street, B.V. (1994) 'Cross-cultural perspectives on literacy', in J. Maybin (ed.), *Language and Literacy in Social Practice.* Clevedon: Multilingual Matters in association with The Open University.

Swales, J. (1981) *Aspects of Article Introductions*. Birmingham: The University of Aston, Language Studies Unit.

Swales, J.M. (1990) *Genre Analysis: English in Academic and Research Settings*. Cambridge: Cambridge University Press.

Thompson, G. (1996) *Introducing Functional Grammar*. London: Edward Arnold.

Thompson, G. and Zhou, Jianglin (2000) 'Evaluation and organization in text: the structuring role of evaluative disjuncts', in S. Hunston and G. Thompson (eds), *Evaluation in Text: Authorial Stance and the Construction of Discourse*. Oxford: Oxford University Press, pp. 121–41.

Van Leeuwen, T. and Humphrey, S. (1996) 'On learning to look through geographer's eyes', in R. Hasan and G. Williams (eds), *Literacy in Society*. London and New York: Longman, pp. 29–49.

Veel, R. and Coffin, C. (1996) 'Learning to think like a historian: the language of secondary school history', in R. Hasan and G. Williams (eds), *Literacy in Society*. London and New York: Longman, pp. 191–231.

Webb, C. (1991) *Writing Practice for University Students: Writing an Essay in the Humanities and Social Sciences*. Sydney: Learning Assistance Centre, University of Sydney.

Whittaker, R. (1995) 'Theme, processes and the realization of meanings in academic articles', in M. Ghadessy (ed.), *Thematic Development in English Texts*. London: Pinter, pp. 105–28.

Wignell, P., Martin, J.R. and Eggins, S. (1989) 'The discourse of Geography: ordering and explaining the experiential world', *Linguistics and Education*, 1, 359–91. Reprinted in M.A.K. Halliday and J.R. Martin (1993), *Writing Science: Literary and Discursive Power*. London: Falmer Press, pp. 136–65.

9 IELTS as preparation for tertiary writing: distinctive interpersonal and textual strategies

Caroline Coffin and Ann Hewings

1 Introduction

Across English-speaking countries such as the USA, Australia and the UK, it is now common for universities to request proof of a particular level of English language ability from non-native speakers of English wishing to enrol in undergraduate and postgraduate courses. Levels of English language competence can be measured in many ways. A test specifically designed to measure language competence relevant to academic study is the object of a research study reported on in this chapter. Referred to as the International English Language Testing System (IELTS), it is a test that measures candidates' listening, reading and writing abilities. In the following, our focus is on the IELTS component labelled 'academic writing', which measures candidates' competence in writing a short argumentative essay. Specifically we aim to examine the kinds of written texts that such a component solicits and to describe aspects of argumentative styles adopted by the candidates as revealed in our corpus. In particular, we consider argumentative strategies associated with high-scoring texts and present insights into the ways in which factors such as test design and candidates' understanding of academic genres may influence the structure and style of the arguments produced.

Our theoretical framework for exploring such areas is that of systemic functional linguistics (SFL), which allows us to take account of variation in linguistic style by reference to the social and cultural context in which linguistic interactions take place. In the study reported on here, we draw on the SFL notion of Theme (concerning the way in which meaning is structured and foregrounded) and APPRAISAL[1] (concerning the way phenomena are evaluated and judged). These areas of meaning, both of which are further elaborated below, serve to illuminate aspects of argumentation that were seen to be of particular interest.

Within the functional tradition linguistic studies of university-level non-native speaker academic writing under test conditions have, to date, been relatively small in number, in that research has tended to concentrate on published academic discourse, particularly research articles and textbooks and, to a lesser extent, on student writing (Ghadessy 1998; Hewings 2002; Hyland 1999a, 2000; McCabe 1999; Myers 1990; Swales 1990; Whittaker

1995). The relative paucity of recent research focusing on student writing of the type produced by IELTS candidates (see, however, Hamp-Lyons 1991) meant that we were reliant on other less appropriate descriptions of academic writing in formulating our expectations. Influenced by the findings of available research we initially expected that successful argumentative essays in our student corpus would reflect elements of the relatively objective orientation to a topic typical of much academic discourse, with the writer favouring an impersonal and analytical style. We were surprised, therefore, when a preliminary reading of the texts gave the impression that the writer's voice and subjective opinions, rather than being in the background, were, in fact, made rhetorically prominent. As a consequence, our focus shifted to an exploration of the lexico-grammatical resources that were being used to construct this much more personal and involved stance. Our findings (both quantitative and qualitative) are reported below. First, however, we provide further details on the IELTS test.

1.1 The IELTS test

The section of the IELTS test of interest in this chapter requires candidates to write a short argumentative essay by responding to a controversial issue (for example, 'expenditure on space research'). Candidates have 40 minutes under test conditions in which to produce their response with no access to sources or references to serve as evidence for their argument. The standard format and wording for this task is shown in the example below:

> Present a written argument or case to an educated reader with no specialist knowledge of the following topic.

> Controversial proposition
> It is now 30 years since man landed on the moon. Since then more and more money has been spent on space research and exploration. Some people think that this is not a good use of our resources and that any hope of establishing human colonies in space is unrealistic.

> To what extent do you agree or disagree with this opinion?
> You should write at least 250 words.
> You should use your own ideas, knowledge and experience and support your arguments with examples and relevant evidence.

In order to complete the task, candidates typically draw on either a discussion or exposition genre.[2] Although not the focus of this chapter, the stages of discussion or exposition genres prove relevant when considering the types of persuasive strategy deployed by candidates. Illustrated below, therefore, is a sample essay written by a candidate from China, analysed to show the typical stages (labelled in bold) comprising an exposition genre. It was written in response to the task prompt given above:

Thesis
This year marks the 30th anniversary of man landing the moon. In these 30 years, we see more and more money and resources has been spent on space research and exploration for investigating the possibility of establishing human colonies in space for the future.

However, some people think that further funding the research is a waste of resources. This article aims at clarifying some of the views and tries to establish and reiterate the importance of further research on outer space.

Argument 1
First of all, we talk about resources. Resources is said to be misused if the balance of 'supply and demand' is not reached. Most of the researches, if not all, are being carried out by developed countries which they hold a great bundle of reserves, should it be money, gold or natural resources. Up till now, there is no one report or any evidence to suggest that there are people starved because of the ongoing research. Yet the research has not produced any known environment pollutants that would adversely affect human existence. Those countries only use their 'excess' resources for the research, nevertheless, we must not forget the researches may lead to new job opportunities or new resources found in outer space or even lead up to human beings being able to emigrate to the outer space in case the Earth is not suitable for human living resulting from increasing environmental pollution problems because of industrialization and modernization. We could say the researches some form of investment, yet we don't know whether we will gain or lose. But we cannot say we are wasting the resources since we are not spending at the expense of others, let alone sacrifice.

Argument 2
Secondly, I would like to throw some light on idea that establishing human colonies in space is unrealistic. Up to this present moment, no one can tell the research result. It is not substantial to abandon the programmes now. People have always said 'What can be imagined can be achieved'. Imagine for how many times of failure Addison experienced before he invented light bulbs. I think we should allow time for the research since outer space is a new subject and the research has only been going on for 30 years.

Position/Recommendation
We must not forget if it comes to the time when the food is not edible or the water is not drinkable on Earth than we do research, the comment will be very simple. It is really too late. I very much hope that this article help clarify some of the sceptical views on outer space research and funding.

As shown by the preceding analysis of the main argumentative stages, the writer of the sample essay is able to shape and structure their 'case'. There are, of course, some IELTS candidates who fail to produce a clearly organized text and it is important to remember that candidates may be complete novices at tertiary level writing, or, if they have completed a degree in their own country, novices at academic writing in English. In the corpus of texts that form the data for this study, however, most reflect a basic argumentative structure.

2 The study

2.1 The data

The corpus of texts comprised 56 essays ranging in length from approximately 230 to 280 words. These were selected from a far larger corpus which formed the basis of a research study examining a broader range of issues concerning the writing of students preparing to enter English medium higher education (Mayor *et al.* forthcoming). The corpus was balanced along three dimensions as follows:

- linguistic/cultural background of candidates defined by their first language (in this case either Chinese or Greek)
- High/low scores obtained for the test (high scores are defined as 7 to 8 on a 9-point scale and low scores as 5. In terms of marks needed to enter English medium higher education 7 or 8 is considered more than adequate, while 5 is unacceptable in many institutions)
- the test version – either Test A or Test B (all quoted essays in this chapter are drawn from Test A, the prompt for which is included in Section 1.1 above).

Each of the texts in the corpus was analysed using the tools of Theme and APPRAISAL. First, we consider the significance of Theme choice as a descriptive tool for capturing and quantifying the way in which particular patterns of meaning are foregrounded in specific types of language use. Then we move to a relatively recent innovation in SFL theorizing – the APPRAISAL system – and consider its value as an analytical tool when combined with Theme analysis in particular. We draw attention to possible modifications in the way in which Theme is identified and classified which would enable analysts to better explain the choices being made in the texts examined.

Below we set out our initial methodology for analysing Theme, and our findings with regard to different combinations of Theme choices made. Subsequently, (Section 2.3) we outline the way in which aspects of the APPRAISAL system used within Theme position were identified.

2.2 Theme – analysis and findings

At its simplest, Theme in English can be thought of as that element in a clause or larger unit of text which comes first. Theme and Rheme (the rest of the clause after the Theme) is a major component of the textual metafunction, that is, in the organization of a text as a message. As Thompson puts it:

> When we look at language from the point of view of the textual metafunction, we are trying to see how speakers construct their messages in a way which makes them fit smoothly into the unfolding language event . . . As well as interacting with their

listeners and saying something to them about the world, speakers constantly signal to them how the present part of their message fits in with other parts. (1996: 116)

Theme is used to signal what a message is about and the writer's angle on that message, and to signpost the development of the text. A similar position is taken by Conrad and Biber (2000: 71), who through analysis of large text corpora note that 'an author's framing for a proposition before actually presenting the proposition' frequently occurs in initial or pre-verbal position, that is, it is often thematic. Studies of metadiscourse, that is, interpretative and evaluative content matter, also often concentrate on first position (Crismore *et al.* 1993; Hewings and Hewings 2002; Hyland 1999b; Vande Kopple 1985). More abstractly, Theme has been described by Halliday (1994: 52) as a 'movement from the beginning of the clause', a description which highlights what elsewhere has been referred to as the wave-like structure of English (Martin 1992). The fluidity or dynamic quality of these descriptions is significant and will be returned to below. However, to allow identification of thematic elements we need to have a workable definition of what constitutes Theme and how to sub-divide its functional constituents. For analytical purposes, the Theme of a clause is said to extend up to and include the first ideational element, that is 'the first constituent that is either Participant, Circumstance, or Process' (Halliday 1994: 52). The remainder of the clause is referred to as the Rheme. It is this description that our initial thematic analysis is based on.

Theme was analysed at the level of independently conjoined clause complexes following categories based on Halliday (1994) and Fries (1981/83). In declarative clauses, Theme most often coincides with the grammatical subject and is referred to as topical Theme. However, additional elements, such as conjunctions and modal adjuncts, can also occur before the grammatical subject and these are thematic too. Because they play a role in the textual or interpersonal function of a clause they are classified as textual Themes and interpersonal Themes. We were particularly interested in isolating different functional roles within the Theme element, and especially in seeing whether the interpersonal stance which we had noted on reading the scripts was observable in the use of interpersonal Theme. While topical Theme, possibly preceded by textual or interpersonal Themes, is seen as the most common choice, other starting points are also possible, but less likely. These are known as marked Theme. The categorization used can be summarized as:

- **Topical Theme** – the grammatical subject (in declarative clauses), e.g. *Man* landed on the moon 30 years ago.
- **Interpersonal Theme** – any combination of vocatives, modals and mood-markings, e.g. *Maybe* we would live still in the caves.
- **Textual Theme** – structural elements such as conjunctions and relatives occurring at the beginning of the clause, e.g. . . . . *but* it is still a significant amount.

- **Marked Theme** – two main types: (a) circumstantial adjuncts occurring before the grammatical subject, e.g. *In the 1970s* the first man landed on moon; (b) fronted dependent clauses, e.g. *If we first take a glance in the disadvantages of space research and exploration* we will mention the enormous amounts that are spent every year for these 'trips'.
- **Multiple Theme** – where the topical Theme is preceded by either or both an interpersonal or textual Theme (the preceding interpersonal or textual Theme is separated from the topical Theme by '/'). They can be either marked, e.g. *However,/ from my point of view,* this is a result from the great development of the society; or unmarked, e.g. ... *and,/ people* need to adapt to the environment to catch up with the changing world.

It should be noted that within the corpus as a whole a number of fragments were unclassifiable; for example, in cases where it was not possible to identify a finite verb and therefore to delimit the clause complex.

Across the corpus of 56 essays, 1036 independent clauses were identified and analysed. Table 9.1 shows the number and percentage of different Theme types.

Table 9.1 Theme patterning in student test essays

	Topical	Textual	Interpersonal	Marked	Multiple marked and unmarked
No. of clauses	466	338	44	195	375
% of total clauses	44.98	32.63	4.25	18.82	36.20

On the evidence of this study, international students writing for the IELTS examination were adept at using complex Themes as shown by the relative frequency of multiple Themes. The use of multiple Theme allows writers to encode coherence markers such as *thus* and *therefore,* and to signal interpersonal concerns such as attitude (e.g. *Surprisingly* ...), and modality (e.g. *Probably* ...). The IELTS candidates also made use of marked Themes which are traditionally associated with the marking of coherence and emphasis (Eggins 1994: 298). This is demonstrated in the example below – the opening of the text quoted fully at the beginning of this chapter. (The letters A and B indicate the paragraphs and the numbers refer to the clause complexes.) The Theme in A1 is simple topical. In A2 the marked Theme picks up on '30' from the previous Rheme. B1 exemplifies multiple Theme with the textual Theme (*However*) preceding the topical Theme.

A1 *This year* marks the 30th anniversary of man landing the moon.

A2 *In these 30 years*, we see more and more money and resources has been spent on space research and exploration for investigating the possibility of establishing human colonies in space for the future.

B1   *However, / some people* think that further funding the research is a waste of resources.

The finding that was least expected was the relative infrequency of inter-personal Theme. Our expectation had been that the personalized nature of the arguments that we had noted on reading the essays would be reflected in the use of interpersonal Themes. However, where the interpersonal stance was signalled by pronouns such as *I* or *we* in Theme position they were categorized as topical not interpersonal Themes. This would help to account for the relatively low figure of 4.25 per cent of all Themes with an inter-personal element. Such low figures are not uncommon however. Ghadessy (1998) in a corpus described as 'academic prose' only found 5.3 per cent of Themes were interpersonal and Hewings (Chapter 8, this volume) had a similar finding of 5.4 per cent in her corpus of undergraduate geography essays.[3]

So, a traditional Theme analysis had shown that IELTS candidates were often competent users of relatively sophisticated thematic choices, but it had failed to isolate the personalized arguments that we had noted on reading the essays. To recap, on first reading the essays we had been surprised at the amount of use made of phrases such as *in my view . . ., I personally believe . . .*, etc. signalling strong interpersonal involvement and had expected this to be apparent in thematization, particularly interpersonal Theme. This con-trasted with our original expectation based on the research literature that a linguistic analysis of successful essays (i.e. ones that scored more highly) would show a favouring of lexical and grammatical patternings construing the writer as an objective and neutral arbiter of knowledge. In order to try to capture the personalized nature of the arguments we embarked on a second, additional stage of analysis (focusing on the semantic properties of Theme). This revealed, in contrast to our expectations but in accordance with our observations, that in many of the high-scoring essays the subjective nature of the argument was made explicit in Theme position.

2.3 Semantically oriented Theme analysis – the role of APPRAISAL

In our second phase of analysis we decided to incorporate the semantic categories of the APPRAISAL system into our Theme analysis. This was in order to capture the way in which evaluations of phenomena are made salient in the student texts, an area of research which has recently received con-siderable attention (see, for example, Fuller 1998; Hunston and Thompson 2000; Hyland 1999a, 1999b; Rothery and Stenglin 1999; White 1998).

APPRAISAL (Martin 1997, 2000; White 1998), as outlined in Figure 9.1 below, refers to the set of interpersonal systems which give language users choice in terms of how they grade and give value to social experience. Thus, within the system of ATTITUDE, the three sub-systems of AFFECT, JUDGEMENT and APPRECIATION comprise a set of language resources for appraising experience in terms of:

- the emotional effect of an event (AFFECT)
- the moral nature of human behaviour (JUDGEMENT)
- the social significance of processes and products within a particular culture, social grouping or institution (APPRECIATION).

The two other systems included within the framework of APPRAISAL are GRADUATION and ENGAGEMENT. GRADUATION is a system for grading evaluations – 'turning the volume up or down', while ENGAGEMENT is a set of resources for negotiating the play of voices and perspectives around an issue; for example, the use of modality in allowing other possible viewpoints and the use of projection to source alternative positions:

> *Perhaps*, there *may* be something out there that constituted the cause of existence of human species. (modality)
>
> *They say that* any hope of human colonies established in space is something absurd. (projection)

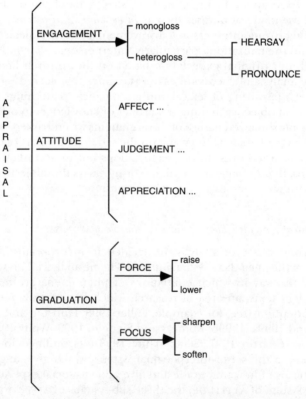

Figure 9.1 An outline of APPRAISAL resources in English (after Martin 1997)

Two key resources within the system of ENGAGEMENT, referred to as HEARSAY and PRONOUNCE, were found to be of particular importance to the study. HEARSAY refers to a set of resources for reporting on utterances where the speaker/writer is not specified. For example:

People have always said 'What can be imagined can be achieved'.

PRONOUNCE, on the other hand, refers to the interpolation of a speaker/ writer into the text. The form of interpolation may be explicit whereby a writer is clearly the source of a particular perspective. For example:

In my opinion more and more money should be spent on space research

or it may be less direct and expressed through an intensifying comment adjunct. For example:

Really, more and more money should be spent on space research

Equally it may be expressed through stress on the auxiliary. For example:

They *did* spend more money on space research

or through structures such as:

It's a fact that they spent more money on space research.

Regardless of form of expression, the rhetorical effect of such a stance is to increase the interpersonal cost of any doubting or rejection (by the listener/ speaker) of the writer/speaker's views.

In this chapter, rather than considering each category of APPRAISAL as manifested in the sample texts (see Coffin and Mayor 2000, for a broader discussion), we focus on PRONOUNCE and HEARSAY and discuss their role in developing an argument, namely the way in which they bring into play a range of voices and perspectives around an issue. In particular we are interested in the way in which thematizing these resources develops a contextual 'frame' for, or 'angle' on, the proposition that follows. For example:

Some hold that this way abuses our resources. (HEARSAY)

In my view space research and exploration should be encouraged. (PRONOUNCE)

Inclusion of such resources within an interpersonal Theme analysis, while departing from traditional approaches to Theme (e.g. Halliday 1994), is not without precedent. We noted earlier the description of Theme as a movement and the metaphor of a wave, but that for ease of analysis the transition from Theme to Rheme was generally coded as occurring after the first ideational element in the clause. Not all analysts have followed this route. Work by, among others, Berry (1989, 1995), Davies (1988, 1997), Mauranen

(1993), and Ravelli (1995) has argued for an extension of the Theme element to include everything up to, but not including, the main verb. Of particular relevance to this study is the extension of components of interpersonal Theme. Hewings (Chapter 8, this volume) and Whittaker (1995) argue for the inclusion of certain anticipatory *it*-clauses as fulfilling an interpersonal role and not exhausting the thematic potential. Martin (1995) reminds us that as a functional category Theme cannot be defined and warns against a tight mapping of Theme onto grammatical elements such as circumstantial adjuncts or grammatical subjects.

With these more semantically based views of thematic analysis in mind, we set about using the APPRAISAL system to help us identify interpersonal Theme. To provide an extended interpersonal perspective on Thematic patterning, a number of analytical decisions were taken. The first was to treat a unit of PRONOUNCE or HEARSAY (where it appeared in initial position) as the interpersonal element of the Theme whereby any subsequent ideational element was analysed as topical Theme. Thus *in my view* in the following clause was analysed as interpersonal Theme, followed by *space research and exploration* as the topical Theme:

In my opinion, / *space research and exploration* should be encouraged.

In cases of the interpersonal element serving to project (e.g. *I personally believe* . . .), the projecting clause was treated as behaving in a similar way to marked hypotactic clauses whereby one clause in a clause-complex may serve to thematize the other. Hence in the following examples, rather than treat instances of PRONOUNCE such as *I believe* as a form of grammatical metaphor realizing a unit of modality within the clause (see Halliday 1994: 58), we decided to treat the projecting clause as a thematizing clause, creating an interpersonal lens through which the projected clause is interpreted (cf. Whittaker 1995):

I personally believe that money should be spent on space research and exploration, provided that each state has taken care of certain more important priorities.

This has implications for standard SFL Theme analysis, as traditionally *I personally believe* would be classified as marked Theme. Thus, a recategorization using the resources of APPRAISAL might lead to a decrease in the number of instances of marked Theme and an increase in interpersonal Theme.

2.4 *The* APPRAISAL *analysis findings – bringing into play alternative perspectives*

Drawing on a wider interpretation of interpersonal Theme, in which the APPRAISAL categories of PRONOUNCE and HEARSAY were included, analysis revealed some interesting patterns. For example, it emerged that many candidates chose to foreground their own voice by deploying between one to five instances of PRONOUNCE in Theme position. With regard to HEARSAY, findings were less consistent, that is, only approximately half of the total texts placed HEARSAY in Theme position.

With regard to PRONOUNCE, the most significant finding was the frequent use of the writer's subjective view as the contextual 'frame' for the arguments and evidence put forward to prove the overall thesis of the essay. In Text 1, reproduced below, for example, the writer increasingly interpolates and foregrounds his own personal position regarding the issue under discussion, particularly as he moves towards the final Recommendation stage.

Given that the sample essay (Text 1) scored highly, we can assume that such a rhetorical strategy is not contrary to the expectations of the marker. One reason for its success may be the authority the writer assumes through the location of his personal views in Theme position. In other words, by making his angle on the issue the starting point, the writer is positioning himself as an expert.

In addition, if we extend the notion of Theme to refer to a paragraph Theme, traditionally referred to as the *topic sentence* in a pedagogic context, we can see how the writer further increases the strength of their position. That is, in paragraph 4 of Text 1, the topic sentence or opening generalization (in Martin's (1992: 437–9) terms the hyper-Theme) in which the writer is directly inscribed (*I would like to throw some light on . . .*), invests the writer with a degree of authority regarding the subsequent set of propositions. Moreover, this position of authority is reinforced through the thematization of PRONOUNCE in the final clause of the paragraph (*I think we . . .*). According to Martin (1992: 453–6) the final clause in a paragraph (the hyper-New) often serves to pull together and summarize information built up in the rest of the paragraph and, therefore, as in the case of hyper-Theme, can be seen as textually prominent.

Similarly, the writer of Text 1 exploits the meaning potential of the final sentence of the final paragraph in the text to thematize and make prominent their own personal stance (*I very much hope . . .*) in the process of summarizing the overall message of the text (in Martin's terms, the macro-New), i.e. the clarification of sceptical views towards space research.

Text 1 – Extract
(*italics* = Theme (including simple, multiple and marked Theme)

<u>double underlining</u> = Theme + PRONOUNCE

<u>dotted underlining</u> = Theme + HEARSAY)

Bold font indicates where PRONOUNCE is placed in hyper or macro-Theme or hyper or macro-New.

Paragraph 4 (Argument)
  Secondly, **I would like to throw some light** on idea that establishing human colonies in space is unrealistic. *Up to this present moment*, no one can tell the research result.

It is not substantial to abandon the programmes now. People have always said '*What* can be imagined can be achieved'. *Imagine* for how many times of failure Addison experienced before he invented light bulbs. I think we should allow time for the research since outer space is a new subject *and the research* has only been going on for 30 years.

Paragraph 5 (Recommendation)

We must not forget if it comes to the time when the food is not edible or the water is not drinkable on Earth than we do research, the comment will be very simple.

It is really too late. **I very much hope** that this article help clarify some of the sceptical views on outer space research and funding.

The pattern of Theme and PRONOUNCE illustrated in Text 1 above is not unique to the sample essay. Other high-scoring texts in our corpus employ similar patterns of ENGAGEMENT, with authorial viewpoints being frequently made salient through their strategic location in the overall structure of the argument, that is, in hyper and macro-Theme and hyper and macro-New. Such a texturing of authorial stance serves to inject a strong subjective orientation – both prospectively and retrospectively – to the unfolding arguments and evidence. The following extracts from high-scoring essays provide further illustration:

Text 2 – sample extract
Thesis

. . .

In my view, *space research and exploration* should be encouraged.

(PRONOUNCE in Theme and hyper-New position)

Argument 1

. . .

From this point of view, *space research and exploration* is a very important channel.

(PRONOUNCE in Theme and hyper-New position)

Recommendation/Thesis

. . .

In my view, *establishing human colonies in space* is a very challenging idea, *it* is very possible to be realized, *and this* will solve the problem that the earth will not undertake the heavy burden of population-exploding.

(PRONOUNCE in Theme and macro-New position)

Text 3 – sample extract
Thesis

. . .

I personally believe that money should be spend on space research and exploration, provided that each state has taken care of certain more important priorities.

(PRONOUNCE in Theme and macro-Theme position)

Argument 1

I believe that if a country has assured the better living conditions for its citizens, then, money on space research and exploration should be spent . . .

(PRONOUNCE in Theme and hyper-Theme position)

Argument 2

Furthermore, **I believe** that there is another important reason in favor of the establishment of human colonies in space, which is totally realistic . . .

(PRONOUNCE in Theme and hyper-Theme position)

Argument 3

Apart from this option, **I strongly believe** that it is our natural charisma to have the willingness to learn new things . . .

(PRONOUNCE in hyper-Theme position)

Recommendation

In concluding **my agreement with this opinion I would like to add the fact** that money should be spend on space since it constitutes an important aspect of human life and of our world specifically.

(PRONOUNCE in Theme and macro-New position)

In terms of the HEARSAY findings, patterns of use are more varied than in the case of PRONOUNCE. For example, whereas of the total number of instances of PRONOUNCE in the high-scoring texts, 93 per cent appear in Theme position, only 84 per cent of the total instances of HEARSAY do. And, in approximately 50 per cent of texts, HEARSAY is not drawn on at all (neither in Theme position nor elsewhere in the clause). However, it is clearly an important resource in the interpersonal repertoires of many student writers, and in the case of the Chinese cohort, could possibly be a criterion in distinguishing high- and low-scoring essays (i.e. more high-scoring Chinese writers use more instances of HEARSAY than low-scoring Chinese writers).

The importance of the resource can primarily be attributed to its role in bringing into the argument perspectives, opinions and evidence that belong to society at large rather than exclusively to the individual writer. Thus, whereas we have seen PRONOUNCE resources draw attention to the subjectivity of the writer, we can see how HEARSAY deflects attention away from individual opinion and emphasizes broader community views. Such views may or may not confirm the individual opinion of the test candidate. Of importance here is that by actively engaging with social diversity, the writer avoids construing an audience as sharing the same, single worldview. This is a common and effective argument strategy.

Typically, HEARSAY functions to either contrast the opinions of others with those of the writer or to corroborate and reinforce authorial stance. The following extracts illustrate both patterns:

(*italics* = Theme

<u>dotted underlining</u> = Theme + HEARSAY)

However, <u>some people think</u> that further funding the research is a waste of resources. *This article* aims at clarifying some of the views and tries to establish and reiterate the importance of further research on outer space.

(HEARSAY functioning to contrast with authorial stance)

Secondly, I would like to throw some light on idea that establishing human colonies in space is unrealistic. *Up to this present moment,* no one can tell the research result. *It* is not substantial to abandon the programmes now.

<u>People have always said</u> '*What* can be imagined can be achieved'.

(HEARSAY functioning to corroborate authorial stance)

Generalizing beyond the individual opinion of the essay writer and actively promoting (or at least acknowledging) diversity is effective not only in terms of accumulating additional authority for the writer's views but also in terms of opening them up to alternative positions and contestation. By introducing negotiability into propositions and by not assuming solidarity between writer and reader, the effectiveness and persuasiveness of an argument text is increased. In the sample text (Text 1), it appears to play a particularly important role in counter-balancing the overt subjective stance which, as we have seen from sample extracts in the corpus studied here, is frequently made thematically prominent. Indeed APPRAISAL analysis shows that high-scoring text writers use a range of resources in order to avoid appearing categorical or biased in their line of argumentation. HEARSAY is one such resource, commonly deployed in the test essays to foreground the heteroglossic nature of the issue under discussion.

Use of HEARSAY is seen to be a highly effective strategy in these test essays, but its role in other academic writing texts is still largely unknown. Although comparisons with tertiary level undergraduate and postgraduate writing are not yet available, data does exist for argumentative writing in upper secondary school in the subject of history (Coffin 2000). In this study, Coffin found that the average use of HEARSAY was low (i.e. 1 instance per 500 words either in Theme or non-Theme position). More commonly, voices additional to those of the writer were integrated into a text through direct quotations or through a paraphrase of the original wording of a source (referred to as EXTRAGLOSS in the APPRAISAL system). Clearly, in an argument text written under test conditions, in a field that many students may only have common-sense experience of, referencing specific sources is not possible. In many ways, therefore, HEARSAY can be seen as a less sophisticated, but, nevertheless, necessary device for bringing in perspectives located beyond those of the writer.

3 Theme, rhetorical thrust and the student essay corpus

Theme analysis, particularly when APPRAISAL resources are taken into account, provides some interesting insights into the rhetorical strategies deployed by non-native speaker writers in order to fulfil the requirements of a test assessing academic writing competence. Significantly, whilst some of these strategies resemble those used in tertiary-level academic writing, there are several surprising disjunctures.

First, the attention drawn to the subjectivity of the argument put forward, namely through the use of thematized PRONOUNCE resources, is at odds with the view of academic argument as a dispassionate and objective process. Although the interpolation of the writer into a text may arise in the context of professionally or vocationally oriented disciplines (such as business studies, education, social work, etc.) and in professional academic writing (namely the research report and article), it is frequently discouraged in undergraduate writing (Smyth 1994: 3). While it has been argued in this paper that, within the constraints of a test situation, PRONOUNCE can be effectively used to construe writers as authoritative in relation to the views put forward, it is also the case that the wrong balance of the resource can over-inflate the authority of the writer's voice to the point where pomposity rather than a sense of expertise and knowledge is communicated. This is particularly the case in texts where a general paucity of persuasive evidence highlights the writer's lack of expertise in the field, thus making the use of PRONOUNCE seem inappropriate.

While the use of PRONOUNCE may be justified in the test essays examined here, the findings also point to a propensity for overstatement by international students writing in English. In an analysis of writing by postgraduate students of business administration, Hewings and Hewings (2002) note their tendency to make more emphatic statements *It must be emphasized . . .*, *It is a fact that . . .*, *It is pointless . . .* and to use hedges *It is likely that . . .* to a more limited degree than published academic writers in the same field. An excess of authorial intrusion on the part of novice academic writers, particularly where persuasive supporting evidence is absent, may weaken rather than strengthen the overall argument. Overuse of PRONOUNCE may also draw attention to the writer rather than allowing the argumentative process itself to be foregrounded (e.g. *the main reason . . .*, *another factor . . .*), the latter generally being a more favoured orientation in novice academic argumentation (Martin 1993).

It is, of course, difficult to establish the extent to which interpolating oneself into an academic essay is culturally conditioned. Some research, for example, indicates that non-Anglo-based academic culture does not follow the English tendency to downplay the role of writer in interpreting and presenting knowledge. A question to be asked, therefore, is whether students are following familiar tacit cultural processes and assumptions when they foreground their own position (Atkinson and Ramuna than 2000) and whether they would position themselves differently if teachers made explicit the typical patterns of interpersonal meaning in English medium academic writing.

A second key difference between the academic writing style adopted by test candidates and that generally favoured within Western-based tertiary education is the former's use of HEARSAY. That is, as mentioned earlier, academic argumentation, even at secondary level, encourages the integration of expert voices through direct quotations or paraphrases of the original wording of a source. HEARSAY functions rather differently in that although it may serve to introduce alternative and contrary views, these views derive authority less from expertise and more from the weight of collective views expressed by certain (anonymous) sectors of society. Nevertheless, HEARSAY can, to some extent, be viewed as a nascent form of conventional academic referencing providing helpful practice for students to widen their range of views and perspectives in relation to the issue under discussion. In particular, it is interesting to observe that, just as in academic referencing where the writer often incorporates their views towards the referenced source (e.g. *Jones claims* as opposed to the more neutral *Jones says*), HEARSAY is deployed in similar ways, as the following extracts exemplify:

> *Everyone claims* there is not enough money to fund the research program.
>
> Now *some people think* that this is not a good use of our resources.

Even so, the use of such a rhetorical strategy, where the source of a view is not specified, would be relatively unconvincing in the target academic register.

Equally interesting is the possibility that it is a feature of non-native speaker 'interlanguage' to be direct rather than tentative in putting forward claims and in rejecting and confirming other scholars' opinions. For example, a study of Bulgarians writing academic articles in English (Vassileva 2001) suggests that these writers are more likely to show high degrees of commitment to their argument (including the use of 'boosters' whereby the writer states unequivocally that they are convinced of what they are saying) than when writing in their native language. As a consequence, 'the generally higher degree of commitment ... may ... make the texts sound inappropriately assertive and imposing' (Vassileva 2001: 87). One possible explanation for this phenomenon is the writers' limited repertoire of interpersonal resources.

An alternative explanation for the use of PRONOUNCE and HEARSAY, features not commonly found in academic writing, could be that those teaching towards and marking the IELTS tests do not expect candidates to make use of all the specific conventions of the academic essay genres. There is no reason, for example, why those working in English language teaching outside tertiary education institutions should have extensive knowledge of the genre characteristics of tertiary writing. As a consequence, teachers are likely to prepare students to write arguments using the limited resources available. This could result in unsupported assertions and strongly affirmed opinions (as seen in the examples of HEARSAY and PRONOUNCE) which serve to fulfil the argumentative function specified in the test prompt.

Finally, although HEARSAY is clearly a means of introducing a diversity of views into the text, a strategic 'norm' in academic argumentation, it is a relatively unsophisticated technique. Obviously one explanation for its use is related to the situational context of producing an essay in a field that is not the candidate's area of expertise. Thus the student writer has to rely more on opinion than evidence and on common consensus rather than expert sources. It may also be seen as an interim stage in learning the generic requirements of academic writing. In a study of native-English speaking undergraduate writers, it was found that at the beginning of their degree programme students were likely to make generalized unreferenced assertions (e.g. *It is believed that . . .*). By their final year, however, they approached the more valued attribution style of professional academic writers (Hewings 1999). The IELTS candidates may be in the same position as first-year undergraduate students: they do not yet know enough about the conventions of tertiary level academic argument to perceive any problems with arguing using the resources of HEARSAY and PRONOUNCE.

Traditionally, academic argument and persuasion has been seen as taking place within a rhetorical framework which highlights objective detachment and minimizes authorial intrusion. The apparent objectivity is achieved through careful lexical, grammatical and discoursal choices. The essays written by candidates for the IELTS examinations show argumentative and persuasive strategies which appear very different from this norm. Through an examination of the use of Theme resources and particularly the mapping of elements of the APPRAISAL system on to interpersonal Theme, we have begun a description of the ways in which the candidates' strategies vary. On the basis of the sample essays, students appear to be practising, and perhaps developing, a very different interpersonal positioning. This is, nevertheless, institutionally valued as candidates using this variety of written genre are being rewarded with high marks. There are good pragmatic reasons why this should be the case. IELTS requires the candidates to present a written argument in a test paper entitled 'Academic Writing'. Candidates are not given any material on which to base their case and they are therefore forced into using other resources. This results in a distinctive argumentative style which cannot be closely modelled on professional academic genres. Its mastery, however, may be a good indicator that a student will be able to cope with the language demands of studying in English.

Notes

1 Small caps are used to distinguish APPRAISAL systems as semantic systems.
2 Whereas in an exposition genre, a writer puts forward a single argument or interpretation, in a discussion genre, a writer considers alternative interpretations prior to reaching a position.
3 It should be noted that Hewings categorizes clauses with anticipatory *it* and extraposed grammatical subjects (e.g. *It is obvious from the descriptions of various procedures that soil creep is a very slow form of movement*) as multiple Theme, with the *it*-clause constituting an interpersonal element.

References

Atkinson, D. and Ramanathan, V. (2000) 'On Peter Elbow's response to "Individualism, Academic Writing and ESL Writer" ', *Journal of Second Language Writing*, 9, 71–6.

Berry, M. (1989) 'Thematic options and success in writing', in C.S. Butler, R.A. Cardwell and J. Channell (eds), *Language and Literature – Theory and Practice: A tribute to Walter Grauberg*. Nottingham: Nottingham Linguistic Circular Special Issue in association with University of Nottingham Monographs in the Humanities.

Berry, M. (1995) 'Thematic options and success in writing', in M. Ghadessy (ed.), *Thematic Development in English Texts*. London: Pinter, pp. 55–84.

Coffin, C. (2000) 'History as discourse: construals of time, cause and appraisal'. Unpublished PhD thesis, University of New South Wales, Sydney, Australia.

Coffin, C. and Mayor, B. (2000) 'Perspectives on the collective and the individual voice in academic writing'. Paper presented at the Education and Research in Learning and Instruction Writing Conference 2000, Verona, Italy.

Conrad, S. and Biber, D. (2000) 'Adverbial marking of stance in speech and writing', in S. Hunston and G. Thompson (eds), *Evaluation in Text: Authorial Stance and the Construction of Discourse*. Oxford: Oxford University Press.

Crismore, A., Markkanen, R. and Steffensen, M.S. (1993) 'Metadiscourse in persuasive writing: a study of texts written by American and Finnish university students', *Written Communication*, 10, 39–71.

Davies, F. (1988) 'Reading between the lines: thematic choice as a device for presenting writer viewpoint in academic discourse', *The ESPecialist*, 9, 173–200.

Davies, F. (1997) 'Marked Theme as a heuristic for analysing text-type, text and genre', in J. Piqué and D.J. Viera (eds), *Applied Languages: Theory and Practice in ESP*. Valencia: Universitat de Valencia.

Eggins, S. (1994) *An Introduction to Systemic Functional Linguistics*. London: Pinter.

Fries, P.H. (1981) 'On the status of theme in English: arguments from discourse', *Forum Linguisticum*, 6(1), 1–38. Reprinted in J.S. Petöfi and E. Sözer (eds) (1983) *Micro and Macro Connexity of Texts*. Hamburg: Helmut Buske Verlag.

Fuller, G. (1998) 'Cultivating science: negotiating discourse in the popular texts of Stephen Jay Gould', in J.R. Martin and R. Veel (eds), *Reading Science: Critical and Functional Perspectives on Discourse of Science*. London: Routledge, pp. 81–98.

Ghadessy, M. (1998) 'Textual features and contextual factors for register identification', in M. Ghadessy (ed.), *Text and Context in Functional Linguistics*. Amsterdam: John Benjamins, pp. 125–39.

Halliday, M.A.K. (1994) *An Introduction to Functional Grammar* 2nd edn. London: Edward Arnold.

Hamp-Lyons, L. (ed.) (1991) *Assessing Second Language Writing in Academic Contexts*. Norwood, NJ: Ablex.

Hewings, A. (1999) 'Disciplinary engagement in undergraduate writing: an investigation of clause-initial elements in geography essays'. Unpublished PhD thesis, The University of Birmingham, Birmingham.

Hewings, A. (2002) 'Shifting rhetorical focus in student and professional geography writing', in C.N. Candlin (ed.), *Research and Practice in Professional Discourse*. Hong Kong: City University of Hong Kong Press, pp. 441–62.

Hewings, M. and Hewings, A. (2002) ' "It is interesting to note that . . .": a comparative study of anticipatory "it" in student and published writing', *Journal of English for Specific Purposes*, 21, 367–83.

Hunston, S. and Thompson, G. (eds) (2000) *Evaluation in Text.* Oxford: Oxford University Press.

Hyland, K (1999a) 'Disciplinary discourses: writer stance in research articles', in C. N. Candlin and K. Hyland (eds), *Writing: Texts, Processes and Practices.* London and New York: Longman, pp. 99–121.

Hyland. K. (1999b) 'Talking to students: metadiscourse in introductory coursebooks', *English for Specific Purposes,* 18, 3–26.

Hyland, K. (2000) *Disciplinary Discourses: Social Interactions in Academic Writing.* Harlow: Longman.

Martin, J.R. (1992) *English Text.* Philadelphia and Amsterdam: John Benjamins.

Martin, J.R. (1993) 'Technology, bureaucracy and schooling: discursive resources and control', *Cultural Dynamics,* 6(1), 84–130.

Martin, J.R. (1995) 'More than what the message is about: English Theme', in M. Ghadessy (ed.), *Thematic Development in English Texts.* London: Pinter, pp. 223–58.

Martin, J.R. (1997) 'Analysing genre: functional parameters', in F. Christie and J.R. Martin (eds), *Genres and Institutions: Social Processes in the Workplace and School.* London: Pinter, pp. 3–39.

Martin, J.R. (2000) 'Beyond Exchange: APPRAISAL Systems in English', in S. Hunston and G. Thompson (eds), *Evaluation in Text.* Oxford: Oxford University Press, pp. 142–75.

Mauranen, A. (1993) *Cultural Differences in Academic Rhetoric: A Textlinguistic Study.* Frankfurt/Main: Peter Lang.

Mayor, B., Hewings, A., North, S. and Swann, J. (forthcoming) 'A linguistic analysis of Chinese and Greek scripts for IELTS academic writing task 2', *Studies in Language Testing.* Cambridge: UCLES/Cambridge University Press.

McCabe, A. (1999) 'Theme and thematic patterns in Spanish and English history texts'. Unpublished PhD thesis, Aston University, Birmingham.

Myers, G. (1990) *Writing Biology: Texts in the Social Construction of Scientific Knowledge.* Madison WI: University of Wisconsin Press.

Ravelli, L.J. (1995) 'A dynamic perspective: implications for metafunctional interaction and an understanding of Theme', in R. Hasan and P.H. Fries (eds), *On Subject and Theme.* Amsterdam and Philadelphia: John Benjamins, pp. 187–234.

Rothery, J. and Stenglin, M. (1999) 'Interpreting literature: the role of APPRAISAL', in L. Unsworth (ed.), *Researching Language in Schools: Functional Linguistic Perspectives.* London: Cassell, pp. 222–44.

Smyth, T.R. (1994) *Writing in Psychology: A Student Guide.* Brisbane: John Wiley and Sons.

Swales, J. (1990) *Genre Analysis in Academic and Research Settings.* Cambridge: Cambridge University Press.

Thompson, G. (1996) *Introducing Functional Grammar.* London: Arnold.

Vande Kopple, W.J. (1985) 'Some exploratory discourse on metadiscourse', *College Composition and Communication,* 36, 82–93.

Vassileva, I. (2001) 'Commitment and detachment in English and Bulgarian academic writing', *English for Specific Purposes,* 20(1), 83–102.

White, P. (1998) 'Telling media tales: the news story as rhetoric'. Unpublished PhD thesis, Department of Linguistics, University of Sydney, Australia.

Whittaker, R. (1995) 'Theme, processes and the realization of meanings in academic articles', in M. Ghadessy (ed.), *Thematic Development in English Texts.* London: Pinter, pp. 105–28.

10 Technical writing in a second language: the role of grammatical metaphor

Mary J. Schleppegrell

1 Second language writers in university courses

In US contexts, and especially in California, we are seeing a new kind of second language student in tertiary education in recent years. This student is not the international student from an English as a Foreign Language (EFL) learning context where English was developed after or in conjunction with mother-tongue literacy skills, and where a focus on language and grammar was a typical aspect of how English was learned. Instead, the new second language student is an immigrant who came to the USA as a child or adolescent. These students have often not had the opportunity to develop first language literacy and have developed spoken English proficiency in contexts where most interlocutors are other speakers of English as a Second Language (ESL) or speakers of non-standard varieties of English. In addition, they have often attended secondary schools where little attention was paid to language structure or to raising awareness about language in functional ways.

These students have not been able to base their development of ESL on a firm foundation of knowledge about 'schooled' ways of using language in their mother tongues, nor have they had opportunities to focus on different ways that lexical and grammatical options are typically taken up in different kinds of writing tasks, and so they have not developed the ability to draw on academic registers effectively in their writing. Their immersion in English-speaking contexts has not provided opportunities for them to develop awareness of how English is structured for technical and academic purposes. Although their performance in secondary school and on standardized exams qualified them for the university, they still lack experience with and knowledge about the ways of using language that are highly valued in the kinds of texts that are typical of the learning tasks in their disciplines.

These students make second language errors related to word choice, morphology and syntax, but correcting their grammatical errors is not enough to make their writing effective for the discourse contexts in which they write. Even with all their errors corrected, their writing still often construes more informal contexts that fail to make the meanings they intend. If instruction for these students is to be effective in helping them write in the ways their disciplines and instructors expect, we need to understand the more complex patterns of language that they are expected to draw on and help them see how particular grammatical choices can contribute to the construction of texts that will be highly valued. A focus on patterns of meaning-making across a text is not typical of current ESL writing instruction in the USA, which tends to focus more on rhetorical strategies. Teachers find it difficult to teach grammar in ways that are functional for the writing students need to do (Brinton and Holten 2001; Frodesen and Holten 2003).

Current controversies in L2 writing instruction focus teachers on the consequences of providing or not providing feedback to students on errors (Ferris 1999; Truscott 1996), or on how to value and respect the ways of knowing and learning that students bring to writing classrooms (see, for example, the papers in Zamel and Spack 1998). While these are important concerns for ESL students in certain contexts, they are not the most pressing issues in the context of the science and technical subjects that enroll the majority of students at my university. More than a third of these students come from homes where a language other than English is spoken, and about 10 per cent of the first-year students are second language learners of English whose placement exams indicate a need for further development of academic English registers. In this context, then, it is not surprising that some second language writers, even as third- and fourth-year university students, still have difficulty with the technical and scientific writing required in their fields of study. Although these students may have lived in the USA for several years and speak English fluently, many of them have not developed the register features of scientific and technical English that they need in the new disciplinary contexts of tertiary education. For these upper-level university students, writing in mainstream courses in science and technical fields, the surface errors that do not impede understanding are of less concern than the control of language needed for broader text structuring and presentation of an authoritative stance. The disciplines they have chosen to study require them to write in genres which have particular features that they need to control.

2 Writing technical registers

This chapter focuses on student writing in chemical engineering laboratory courses where students write reports on experiments. It looks at instructors' expectations of the students and analyses what students need to be able to do to meet those expectations. For these students, just fixing grammatical errors is not enough; they need to develop a wider range of choices for structuring their writing and incorporating their evaluative stance towards what they write. These science and engineering students are aware of the genre expectations of the lab report and want to be able to write effectively in their courses, but need help realizing the relevant register options. This chapter demonstrates how we can use systemic functional linguistics (SFL) to analyse student writing and make explicit the choices that are functional for achieving the purposes of the genres students need to write.

Constructing particular instances of a genre calls for the coherent presentation of meanings at the clause level. This means that writing any genre necessarily requires attention to the lexical and grammatical elements that realize the registers of academic disciplines. The register features required for academic assignments differ in significant ways from the registers of ordinary spoken interaction, making it necessary for even those students whose English is already well developed for everyday tasks to expand their linguistic repertoires and learn to be more precise in their linguistic formulations to meet the demands of academic tasks (Schleppegrell 2001). While all students face this challenge, non-native speakers are at a particular disadvantage, because they may have both limited resources in English and less experience with the genres and registers expected in the assignments they are given. This means that their attempts to tackle new genres with new register expectations not only result in texts with second language errors in morphology and syntax, but also may miss the mark in terms of register choices.

This chapter focuses in particular on register elements related to the use of what systemic functional linguists call *grammatical metaphor*. Halliday (1994) proposes the term grammatical metaphor to refer to making the same 'meaning' with different 'wording', where two layers of meaning result from grammatical choices. Grammatical metaphor is a resource for construing meanings in ways that depart from the grammar through which 'ordinary life' is typically construed; for example, by realizing as a nominal element something that is congruently a process. Halliday (1993: 111) calls grammatical metaphor 'the key for entering into . . . knowledge that is discipline-based and technical'. Through grammatical metaphor, a text can be developed in ways that highlight technicality, that enable reasoning within rather than between clauses, that allow for clear structuring of a text, and that present the writer's point of view as something objective, not subjective (Martin 1992; Halliday 1998). This chapter demonstrates how grammatical metaphor in each of these four manifestations (its contributions to technicality, reasoning within the clause, text structuring, and the construal of authoritativeness) is crucial to writing in ways that are highly valued in scientific and technical contexts. It shows that second language writers of English may lack the resources for drawing on the options for meaning-making that grammatical metaphor enables.

The SFL analysis presented here also points to ways that the teaching of grammar topics can be enhanced by an understanding of how the grammar is functional in the broader discourse context. The focus on word- and sentence-level infelicities that is typical of ESL instruction, when grammar is taught at all (Celce-Murcia 2002), typically does not engage students in the broader discourse structuring and semantic issues that are crucially at stake in the construction of disciplinary texts. Students need to go beyond word- and clause-level instruction to focus on text development and the effective construal of interpersonal meaning in order to draw on the register options that realize the disciplinary context in ways that are valued. Going beyond a focus on clause-level errors, an SFL approach to analysis of student writing provides a broader view of the challenges students face and a framework for addressing their writing development needs. Rather than dealing with grammar as a set of rules to apply, SFL lets us look at the *choices* students make in their writing. In seeing grammar as a set of choices, we can work with students to help them develop and use new options.

3 Grammatical metaphor in laboratory reports

This chapter analyses reports written in an upper level (third or fourth year) chemical engineering university course. These reports were written following an experiment in which students determined the diffusion coefficients for three solvents. Assignment guidelines inform students that 'the purpose of the written report is to provide a summary of techniques used in the experiment and to present and evaluate the results and compare them with results of established theories and/or literature values' (course syllabus). Table 10.1 lists the seven major divisions that the course syllabus specifies for each

Table 10.1 Expectations for the laboratory report

Section	Purpose
Abstract	To summarize the information in the report in half a page or less
Introduction	To explain the background and importance of the work, the goals of the work, why it was done, and how it relates to published work
Theory	To state the basis needed to interpret the data obtained in the experiment.
Experimental Methods	To provide sufficient information to allow another worker to reproduce the experiments.
Results	To provide a summary of results in reduced form (not raw data) in tables and graphs and a comparison of them with appropriate theoretical values and/or literature results.
Discussion	To evaluate the results, including an assessment of reliability and precision (error analysis), and a statement of what the results mean.
Conclusions	This short section is entirely a *repetition* of the most important points in the results and discussion sections.

Source: course syllabus

laboratory report: Abstract, Introduction, Theory, Experimental Method, Results, Discussion, and Conclusions. With these guidelines students are supplied with information on what is expected in each section; for example, in the introduction, to 'explain the background and importance of the work, the goals of the work, why it was done, and how it is related to published work' (course syllabus).

As Table 10.1 indicates, the stages and purposes of each stage in the lab report genre are made clear to students, but no guidance is given regarding the linguistic features that would construe the various meanings anticipated by the generic demands. At this upper level of university work, the proficient writer is able to draw on a set of linguistic options that enables the presentation of meanings in ways that realize academic, rather than everyday, registers. On the other hand, less proficient writers, including many second language writers, experience difficulty with this. Even with guidelines about the general structure and purpose of the genre, they do not have the repertoire of linguistic choices available to them to construe their meanings in the more academic ways that are expected. Often, they have not had opportunities to focus on the alternative linguistic realizations of the multiple complex meanings that need to be made in writing a text of this type.

This chapter first looks at what instructors for this course expect in terms of register, and then analyses the linguistic choices that a proficient student writer and three less proficient second language writers make in writing these lab reports. The 'proficient writer' is a student whose work was judged by the course instructors to be exemplary of the kind of writing that is valued in the field. The 'second language writers' wrote reports that their instructors found difficult to read and respond to because of many errors and infelicities typical of second language learners of English. In this case, the 'proficient writer' is a native speaker of English.

'Native speaker' is not a clearly definable category, especially in this context where many students are bilingual to varying extents and have had different experiences and opportunities to develop proficiency in academic registers. Contrasting the ways that the second language writers and the proficient native speaker make different grammatical choices, and identifying the implications of those choices for the kinds of texts they create, requires simplifying the notions of 'native speaker' and 'second language writer'; clearly much more complex categories than are presented here. The point of comparing these examples is to highlight areas that teachers can focus on in the instruction of language learners. Analysis of these texts indicates that second language learners of English may not have available to them the range of meaning-making resources that good native speaker writers in their peer groups draw on. The resources of grammatical metaphor enable the proficient writer to achieve the technicality, reasoning within the clause, text-structuring, and authoritativeness that the instructors value, while the second language writers' choices limit their meaning-making potential.

3.1 Technicality and reasoning within the clause

Two aspects of students' writing that are often commented on by instructors are their 'wordiness' and 'informal style'. Following are some typical comments, written by an instructor on students' draft lab reports:

- At the beginning of a section: 'State concisely how you did it in a sentence or two and then expand it.'
- 'This is a nice draft abstract. Try to reduce its size a bit.'
- 'You have the right idea for starting this, but think again about the wording.'
- 'Think of a better phrase or word. This is much closer to what you would say rather than what you would write.'

These comments indicate that the instructor is focused on conciseness and register, asking the students to make their points in a few words and to adopt a way of writing that is appropriate for the task and discipline. The instructor does not use grammatical terminology in these comments, but responding appropriately to the comments means making the grammatical choices that enable conciseness and clear expression of technical content. Making these choices requires that the students draw on a grammar that 'is much closer to what you would write rather than what you would say', to paraphrase the instructor. A primary resource for construing meanings with 'written' grammar is grammatical metaphor. Proficient writers use grammatical metaphor in their chemical engineering lab reports to adopt the technicality, structure, and interpersonal stance that are expected in this genre and discipline. Second language writers of English, on the other hand, have difficulty managing the texturing that grammatical metaphor enables.

Consider the instructor's admonition to the students to be 'more concise', or 'reduce its size'. One of the grammatical resources for doing this is *technicality*. Example 1 compares sentences written by the proficient writer and a second language writer (D_{AB} = diffusion coefficient):

Example 1
Proficient writer:

D_{AB} has a *temperature dependence*.

Second language writer:

Diffusion coefficient among other things *depend largely on temperature*.

The proficient writer uses a technical term, *temperature dependence*, a grammatical metaphor that presents the temperature dependence as an attribute of the diffusion coefficient. The second language writer 'says the same thing' in a more congruent way, with *depend* as the verb. This student's statement is not wrong, but it is not 'concise' and may not be valued by the instructor in the same way.

'Sounding written' is also enabled through the resource grammatical metaphor presents for reasoning within rather than between clauses, also more highly valued in science registers. For example:

Example 2

Proficient writer:

The three temperatures of acetone that were investigated produced calculated D_{AB} values which increased *with increasing temperature.*

Second language writer:

The diffusivity is higher *when the temperature is raise.*

Example 2 shows how the proficient writer uses a clause structure where two complex nominal groups (*The three temperatures of acetone [that were investigated]; calculated D_{AB} values [which increased with increasing temperature]*) are linked with a verb, here a relational process, *produced.* Both nominal groups are expanded with embedded clauses (marked with brackets). The point that the second language writer makes, that diffusivity is higher at higher temperatures, is made by the proficient writer in the embedded clause by saying the D_{AB} *values (the diffusivity) increased with increasing temperature.* Grammatical metaphor enables the proficient writer to present the causal explanation of temperature's effect in the prepositional phrase *with increasing temperature.* Rather than drawing on the grammar of time sequence as the second language writer does, using *when* to link the clauses about the effect of temperature, the proficient writer realizes the relationship of cause as a circumstance; presenting a conjunctive relationship through a prepositional phrase which itself is embedded in a relative clause within a nominal construction. The proficient writer is able to manipulate the resources of the grammar in sophisticated ways that enable her to pack a lot of information into each clause. The second language writer, on the other hand, uses a more congruent way of making the causal links, drawing on an oral style of explanation that is causally explicit but perhaps less highly valued than the nominalized grammatically metaphorical style (Martin 1989). (See Mohan 1997; Mohan and Huxur 2001; Mohan and Van Naerssen 1997 for studies that explore these kinds of differences in the construal of causality.)

3.2 Structuring a text

Examples 1 and 2 show how grammatical metaphor helps structure a clause in ways that allow more information to be incorporated and greater conciseness to be achieved. Grammatical metaphor is also a resource for structuring a text beyond the clause, as the shifts in grammatical realization that it allows (e.g., from verb to noun, as in Example 1, or from conjunction to preposition as in Example 2) enable manipulation of thematic elements in the clause in ways that allow for more options in the structuring of the information in a text (Halliday 1998; Ravelli 1988). Grammatical metaphor also operates at a broader level within the text through the resources of *textual metaphor*, lexical items that organize text (e.g., terms like *reason, example, point*) (Martin 1992: 416; Ravelli, this volume). Drawing on these resources for text structuring is difficult for second language writers.

This difficulty emerges most prominently in the Discussion section of these lab reports. The Discussion section, which follows the Results section, is where the writer needs to evaluate the outcome of the experiments. From a linguistic perspective, this is the most challenging part of the lab report. In the Theory and Results sections, students can use mathematical formulas or tables and charts to make their points and present their data, but in the Discussion section, they have to use language to interpret their results and locate them in relation to the theoretical assumptions that they made in conducting the experiment. This calls for a nuanced use of language to present a clear interpretation of results; a challenging linguistic task that may be impossible to do well without control of the range of grammatical resources that enable such presentation.

The challenges of this task can be seen in comparison of paragraphs from Discussion sections written by the proficient writer (Example 3) and a second language writer (Example 4). The proficient writer found that her results met the expectations of the theoretical constructs that guided her experiment. The second language writer, on the other hand, found that her results corresponded to what the theoretical constructs she used would have predicted for some of the compounds, but not the others. So the task that each of these writers confronted in writing the Discussion section was different. What is being compared here is not the experiential meanings that are construed, but the ways the students draw on resources for textual meaning to structure their paragraphs. Grammatical choices enable the proficient writer to structure her text so that the point of her discussion is clear, while the second language writer's choices limit the effectiveness of her discussion.

Example 3 is the beginning of the proficient writer's Discussion section:

Example 3
Proficient writer:

The results demonstrate the trends predicted by theory. D_{AB} has a temperature dependence. The three temperatures of acetone that were investigated produced calculated D_{AB} values which increased with increasing temperature. A large molecular weight is expected to retard the compound's rate of diffusion. N-Hexane was the heaviest compound investigated and it produced the smallest calculated D_{AB} value, as was expected. Values calculated for D_{AB} of acetone at 40, and 45°C as well as the value of D_{AB} calculated for ethanol at 40° were within 10% of the literature and theoretical values. Acetone and N-Hexane at 35°C produced data leading to calculated D_{AB} values within an order of magnitude of the diffusion coefficient values expected.

This paragraph begins with a topic sentence (**bold**), what Martin (1996) calls a hyper-Theme; providing a clear point of departure for the paragraph as a whole. The writer uses the nominal groups *results* and *trends,* textual metaphors that highlight the goal of this paragraph, the linking of results with theory. By using these terms the writer is able in one clause to refer to the two previous sections of the report and at the same time to highlight the way she will organize her paragraph. Her next sentence picks up on the 'new' element in the previous clause (the trends *predicted by theory*) by stating the theoretical prediction, the assumption of temperature dependence. She then gives her results for acetone as evidence for this, followed by another theoretical statement about the role of molecular weight. Specific results supporting the molecular weight theory are presented next, followed by further evidence that her results agreed with the theoretical predictions. This writer is able to move skilfully between the general and the specific to illustrate the congruence of her findings with the theoretical values that had been predicted. She exploits Theme/Rheme structure by drawing on passive voice and nominalization, resulting in a well-structured paragraph. The writer uses textual metaphors, drawing on the 'organizing vocabulary' that includes nominalization through grammatical metaphor, generic nouns, semiotic abstractions, and metalinguistic labels that are key resources for this kind of advanced literacy (Ravelli, this volume).

With this clear structure, the instructor responding to this report is able to focus in his comments on the content of what the student says (for example, he takes issue with the student's point about the values being 'within an order of magnitude' of the expected values). In contrast, the instructors reading the second language writers' reports are often distracted by the linguistic infelicities that characterize them. This leaves the second language writers disadvantaged in the feedback they receive. Example 4 comes from the Discussion section of a second language writer:

Example 4
Second language writer:

Analysis of the data in this experiment illustrated that the experimental diffusion coefficients of Methanol and n-Hexane agreed with the Chapman Enskog diffusion coefficient with the different of 5% and 4% for the 30°C experiment, of 6% and 1% for the 37°C experiment respectively. These experimental diffusion coefficients satisfy the property of diffusion coefficients of species increasing as the temperature increasing. The results of the two experiments for the two compounds agreed with Chapman-Enskog values, but these results did not agreed with Yaws' correlation values, with the percent difference of 39% and 31% at 30°C and 101300 Pa, and 31% and 29% at 37°C and 101300 Pa respectively (Table 4). **So different methods gave different diffusion coefficients**. The diffusion coefficient of Acetone as function of temperature was shown on the Figure 4 in the pervious section. The experimental diffusion coefficients of Methanol and n-Hexane in 45°C experiment and Acetone's coefficients in 30°C, 37°C, and 45°C experiments had very large percent different with theoretical values with the average percent difference were above 30%. In general, the difference between the experimental and the theoretical values were within and without the error bound limit.

The second language writer has a great deal of difficulty with this part of the lab report, and the instructor's comments show that the lack of clarity in the organization and presentation of the discussion makes it difficult for him to understand the writer's point. The student does not begin with a hyper-Theme or topic sentence, and provides no textual metaphors to scaffold her text. Instead, she begins with a statement of her specific results as evidence that these data agreed with one of the theoretical values she had used. In a sense she is doing the same thing as the proficient writer, who also began by saying that her results agreed with theory. However, this point is not made in general terms, and, in addition, the writer's main point, revealed later in the paragraph, is that only *some* of her results were in line with the theoretical predictions. She does not draw on grammatical resources at the beginning of her paragraph that help the reader understand that this is the contrast she will draw. It is not until the third sentence that she introduces this contrast in a clause introduced with *but*, followed by her real topic sentence (in bold), the generalization that helps the reader understand the point of the paragraph: that different methods gave different results.

Keep in mind that the reader here is looking for reasoning about the results. Just giving the results is not enough; this student needs to generalize as the proficient writer does. This paragraph has little generalizing of results and does not draw on resources for moving between the general and the specific. For example, comparing the first sentences of these two paragraphs, we see that *analysis of the data in this experiment* in Example 4 is the 'same' as *the results* in Example 3. But rather than refer generally to *the trends predicted by theory*, as the proficient writer does, the second language writer gives specific results. Even her topic sentence construes a lesser level of generality, as she refers to the *diffusion coefficients*, rather than to her *results*, which would generalize beyond the diffusion coefficients. In addition, the overall structure of the paragraph does not help the reader understand the point she is making.

This paragraph does show some academic register features, including use of the kind of experiential and logical grammatical metaphor illustrated in Examples 1 and 2 in this chapter. For example, the writer does adopt the kind of causal reasoning that the proficient writer used in Example 2, as illustrated in Example 5:

Example 5
Second language writer:

These experimental diffusion coefficients satisfy the property of diffusion coefficients of species increasing as the temperature increasing.

This writer still needs to correct some surface forms (e.g., *as the temperature increases*), but she is using grammatical metaphor to construe the causal relationship here; different from the second language writer whose construal of cause in Example 2 draws on clause structures that are more congruent, realizing cause as temporality.

But this second language writer does not use text-structuring resources that enable a clear presentation of her discussion. At the end of the paragraph, the student again shows the limitations of her control of the grammatical resources she needs. She ends with *In general, the differences were within and without the error bound limit.* A proficient writer might have said that *in summary,* some of her results were within the range expected and some were not; this is clear from how she proceeds in the next two paragraphs of her discussion, where she first presents the results that agreed with the theoretical predictions and then those that disagreed. The statement as written makes no sense, however, and the instructor's reaction is that the differences cannot be both within and without the error bound limit. While the instructor reacts to this as a lapse in logic, there are clearly grammatical issues at stake here. Not only is *in general* the wrong choice of conjunctive adjunct, the use of *within* and *without* is non-idiomatic. Constructions using *with* and *within* are common in this lab report genre, having specific technical meanings that this register construes. Example 2 shows how constructions using *with* can construe grammatically metaphorical realizations of cause. Constructions using *within* are also functional for discussing the congruence of particular results with the theoretical values predicted by the research literature. But second language writers do not automatically know how to use this resource. Example 6 compares how the expression *be within* is used in Examples 3 and 4:

Example 6
Proficient writer:

Values calculated for D_{AB} of acetone at 40, and 45°C as well as the value of D_{AB} calculated for ethanol at 40° *were within 10% of the literature and theoretical values.*

Second language writer:

The experimental diffusion coefficients of Methanol and n-Hexane in 45°C experiment and Acetone's coefficients in 30°C, 37°C, and 45°C experiments *had very large percent different with theoretical values with the average percent difference were above 30%.*

The proficient writer uses the relational process *be within* to present the values she obtained and compare them with the theoretical predictions. Not having the construction *be within* in her grammatical repertoire, the second language writer struggles to make the meaning she intends and ends up with the circumlocution *had very large percent different with theoretical values with the average percent difference were above 30%.* The student does not have a problem with technical terms more generally; she uses expressions like *experimental diffusion coefficients* and *theoretical values,* but the 'grammatical' technical and academic terms like *in general/in summary* and *be within* are challenging features of this register that this second language writer does not yet control. Manipulation of grammatical resources to construe these technical meanings requires control of a range of options and an understanding of the different kinds of meaning that these resources can construe.

3.3 Intersubjective meaning

We have seen that grammatical metaphor is a resource for construing technicality, reasoning, and text structuring in ways that are functional in this genre. Grammatical metaphor is also a resource for construing intersubjective meaning in ways that appear objective. Intersubjective meanings in academic discourse, like ideational and textual meanings, are inevitably construed in every clause, and failing to construe these meanings in ways that are valued and expected can have negative consequences for the student writer. The kinds of intersubjective meanings that are presented in these lab reports, as in other kinds of academic writing, include how explicit the writer wants to be about where her assessments are coming from, how subjective or objective she wants them to appear, how definite they are, and so on (Martin 1995). Halliday (1994) uses the notion of *interpersonal grammatical metaphor* to compare four ways that intersubjective meaning can be realized as speakers/ writers construe modal responsibility in more or less congruent ways. He categorizes these as *explicit* or *implicit* and *objective* or *subjective*. Examples of each of these types are presented in Example 7:

Example 7

- Explicit subjective: I believe that these results are in error.
- Explicit objective: It is obvious that these results are in error.
- Implicit subjective: These results must be in error.
- Implicit objective: Clearly these results are in error.

From Halliday's perspective, it is the explicit presentations of modal responsibility that are grammatically metaphorical, as they are realized in clauses projected by or embedded in other clauses. With explicit subjective modality, grammatical metaphor presents the evaluation as a projection of what the writer believes. With explicit objective modality, interpersonal grammatical metaphor is used to construe the evaluation as fact, rather than opinion. Implicit presentations are congruent; the presentation of evaluation is not construed as a projected belief or as an embedded 'fact'. Instead, the evaluation is presented in the modal verb (*must be*) or in the modal adjunct (*clearly*).

What is interesting about interpersonal grammatical metaphor is that, in contrast to the experiential, logical, and textual grammatical metaphors discussed above, interpersonal grammatical metaphor does not always construe the more highly valued ways of making meaning in academic registers. The explicit subjective metaphor, *I believe that these results are in error,* may in fact construe tentativeness rather than authoritativeness. It is the objective options that are more highly valued. With subjective presentation, metaphorical or not, it is clear who is making the evaluative comment – the writer. With objective presentation, the responsibility for the evaluative comment is not individuated. Second language writers tend to overuse the subjective options, either through the explicitly subjective forms with *I* or through the overuse of modal verbs (Hyland and Milton 1997; Schleppegrell 2002).

The proficient writer, in the report analysed here, has greater control of resources for construing evaluative meanings in ways that are objective, as we see in Example 8:

Example 8
Proficient writer:

Explicit objective:

- Given the error bounds on the calculations, it is not possible to draw any firm conclusions about this from the data.
- Having said this, however, it is difficult to draw any firm conclusions from the results about the dependability of the Stefan diffusion tube method for measuring diffusivities.

Implicit objective:

- A large molecular size is expected to retard the compound's rate of diffusion.
- A great degree of uncertainty is attached to these results.

This writer realizes the modal responsibility for her statements as something objective rather than using a subjective modality such as *this may be* or *I did not expect* or *it might be wrong*. The explicitly objective realizations involve theme predication (*it is not possible; it is difficult*), a structure which construes probability, usuality, and inclination as ideational facts for which she is not the apparent source. Even in the implicit evaluation, the student does not individuate herself as an authority as she presents objective expectations and suggests a degree of uncertainty.

This writer often realizes implicit objective modality in the use of *perhaps*, which she draws on to suggest optional interpretations related to the discussion of possible error in the experiment, as shown in Example 9:

Example 9
Proficient writer:

- Perhaps a variation in experimental design and not a large degree of variability in the length measurements is to blame.
- As the confidence intervals consider a 'worse case' scenario, and the values calculated are not far from those predicted by theory, perhaps it would be safe to assume the error bounds are larger than they need to be.
- Perhaps a variation in flow rate over the tubes contributed to the variation in results seen between the tubes.

This implicit objective presentation is a useful device that construes modal responsibility as something outside the author and enables the presentation of options to which the author does not have to be completely committed.

The second language writers' reports, on the other hand, use almost no instances of explicitly objective realizations of modal responsibility. Instead, they draw heavily on implicit subjective modality, highlighted in Example 10, a paragraph from the discussion section of a second language writer:

Example 10
Second language writer:

There were a lot of assumptions associated with this experiment which *could* cause some discrepancy in the final results. It was assumed that the temperature at the interface was the temperature of the liquid and this *may* not be the case. This assumption *could* have some effect on the final result because as stated earlier, the diffusion coefficient is a function of the temperature. It was also assumed that air is an ideal gas and single species, and that *may* be not case because air is mixture of different species. This also *may* affect the final results.

Contrast this explanation with the way the proficient writer uses *perhaps* in Example 9. While the proficient writer uses the implicit objective presentation, the second language writer relies on the implicit subjective use of modals (*could, may*) to construe the alternative possibilities operating in the experiment which might have affected her particular results; a less authoritative presentation than the proficient writer achieves with grammatical choices that realize a more objective stance. In addition, the writer juxtaposes the construal of *certainty* with the construal of *low* probability in this paragraph. She uses *it was assumed* to introduce the assumptions that are at stake, explicitly objective and construing high probability, but then uses *could* and *may*, construing low probability, to challenge that certainty. This gives these conclusions a great deal of tentativeness. The juxtaposition of the certainty of *it was assumed* and the tentativeness of *may* and *could* contributes to the lack of authoritativeness in this text.

Although the proficient writer also occasionally uses implicit subjective modality, she uses it to construe high obligation, demonstrating her awareness of what is needed for appropriate control of the experimental context. Examples are provided in Example 11:

Example 11
Proficient writer:

- The accumulation term can be neglected if one assumes a quasi-steady state condition.
- For an accurate determination of D_{AB}, efforts to minimize these effects must be made.
- Conclusions about the relationship of vapor pressure and polarity of compounds with the accuracy of the Stefan method can not be drawn from the data.

Hunston (1993) has shown how evaluation pervades published scientific articles, where there is no sharp distinction between fact and evaluation. This means that the student must present information and arguments in terms that fit with the value system of the discourse communities they are being socialized into through their writing. Getting control over the grammar that enables such evaluation is difficult. The second language writers are either too definite where some tentativeness would be called for, or, on the contrary, they are tentative where they should be definite. The proficient writers have greater resources available for construing interpersonal meaning, including objective modality.

4 Discussion and conclusions

Martin (1992: 491) has suggested that, through grammatical metaphor, method of development (identification), point (conjunction), cohesive harmony (ideation), and modal responsibility (negotiation) are texturing resources for discourse semantics. These examples have shown the different ways that students handle the technicality, reasoning, text structuring, and authoritativeness that grammatical metaphor enables in these lab reports. These various roles for grammatical metaphor are laid out in Table 10.2. As Table 10.2 shows, grammatical metaphor is a valuable resource for construing experiential, logical, textual, and interpersonal meanings in ways that are valued in this technical and scientific discourse.

Knowing how to make the choices that involve grammatically metaphorical presentations is a key aspect of realizing academic registers that construe disciplinary meanings effectively. Second language writers often fail to draw on the relevant resources and so produce texts which are less highly valued by their instructors. The analysis of these lexicogrammatical options points to topics that instructors who work with students like these could fruitfully focus on at the level of the text and broader discourse structuring.

For example, the technicality afforded by grammatical metaphor is already part of what a typical ESL programme would address, by helping students learn technical terms or practising transcategorization of lexis; for example, changing verbal to nominal forms of lexemes. But what a functional approach to text suggests is that just doing such exercises will not give language learners control of the way technical terms can be used in the textual structuring required in technical subjects. They also need to consider how the technical terms can participate in clause structures that compact information and move effectively from what is known to what is new in their texts.

Table 10.2 Roles of grammatical metaphor

Type of metaphor	What it enables	Example
Experiential	Technicality	*temperature dependence*
Logical	Reasoning	values which increased *with increasing temperature*
Textual	Text structuring	The *results* demonstrate the *trends . . .*
Interpersonal	Authoritativeness	*it is difficult* to draw any firm conclusions

The grammar that is functional for the kind of reasoning enabled through grammatical metaphor is also addressed in many ESL courses, as students learn different kinds of subordinate clause structures and a range of academic verbs. But again, a narrow focus on clause types and lexis is not enough to help learners see how such structures and terms can be employed to construe more 'written', academic modes of meaning-making. Exercises that help learners analyse how texts are constructed with the kind of clause structures we have seen in the proficient writer's report in this chapter can raise students' awareness of how the logical relationships they currently construe in congruent ways, using the grammar of temporality, for example, can be construed through clause structures and verb choices that address the issues of conciseness and 'writtenness' that instructors value.

Students also need help with overall structuring of their writing and with moving from the general to the specific, and back again to the general. Textual metaphors that help organize text and point to overall structure can be taught in textual contexts where students can see their value in the kinds of meanings and text structuring they enable. Challenging features of science registers – such as 'ordinary' terms like *be within* that have more specifically 'technical' meanings, and the appropriate use of discourse-structuring terms such as *in general* also need to be explicitly addressed and practised in authentic contexts.

Finally, beyond textual structuring, students also need to adopt an inter-personal stance that enables the authoritative presentation of meanings which is highly valued in academic discourse. This is a very difficult area for ESL writers, as they find the modal systems in English challenging even in their more congruent realizations. Adopting objective or metaphorical construals of these meanings is a greater challenge. Teachers are rarely prepared to explicate the range of meanings that are available through different expressions of modality. There is also a major cultural aspect to the use of interpersonal resources that still needs much study. SFL approaches that focus on the expression of judgements and attitudes rather than on the meanings of particular modal verbs (e.g., Lock 1996; Hood, this volume) demonstrate how the functional meanings can be construed in various ways related to the demands of the particular context. Having opportunities to focus on the options available in the grammar for realizing the same function in different registers is crucial for enabling language learners to embed their evaluative stance and signal membership in the larger academic discourse community in the objective ways that are more highly valued.

ESL writing instructors may avoid grammar teaching because they are not acquainted with grammatical frameworks that would enable them to address grammar in ways that are functional for the kind of writing students are expected to do in disciplinary contexts. SFL offers a functional linguistic framework within which ESL writing instruction can focus on the grammatical and lexical issues related to the kind of reasoning and text structuring under discussion here. There is a growing body of research on ESL pedagogy from an SFL perspective (e.g., Christie 1999; Drury and Webb 1991; Er 1993; Hasan and Perrett 1994; Jones *et al.* 1989; Martin 1996; Mauranen 1996; Melrose 1991; Perrett 2000; Schleppegrell and Colombi 1997), with some work focused on technical writing in tertiary contexts (e.g., Drury 1991; Schleppegrell 2002). More research from an SFL perspective can contribute to the participation in technical contexts of students from backgrounds that have not provided them with ways of developing such language skills.

References

Brinton, D.M. and Holten, C.A. (2001) 'Does the emperor have no clothes? A re-examination of grammar in content-based instruction', in J. Flowerdew and M. Peacock (eds), *Research Perspectives on English for Academic Purposes.* Cambridge: Cambridge University Press, pp. 239–51.

Celce-Murcia, M. (2002) 'On the use of selected grammatical features in academic writing', in M.J. Schleppegrell and M.C. Colombi (eds), *Developing Advanced Literacy in First and Second Languages: Meaning with Power.* Mahwah, NJ: Lawrence Erlbaum, pp. 143–58.

Christie, F. (1999) 'Genre theory and ESL teaching: a systemic functional perspective', *TESOL Quarterly,* 33(4), 759–63.

Drury, H. (1991) 'The use of systemic linguistics to describe student summaries at university level', in E. Ventola (ed.), *Functional and Systemic Linguistics.* Berlin: Mouton de Gruyter, pp. 431–56.

Drury, H. and Webb, C. (1991) 'Teaching academic writing at the tertiary level', *Prospect,* 7(1), 7–27.

Er, E. (1993) 'Text analysis and diagnostic assessment', *Prospect,* 8(3), 63–77.

Ferris, D. (1999) 'The case for grammar correction in L2 writing classes: a response to Truscott', *Journal of Second Language Writing,* 8, 1–11.

Frodesen, J. and Holten, C. (2003) 'Grammar and the ESL writing class', in B. Kroll (ed.), *Exploring the Dynamics of Second Language Writing.* Cambridge: Cambridge University Press, pp. 141–61.

Halliday, M.A.K. (1993) 'Towards a language-based theory of learning', *Linguistics and Education,* 5(2), 93–116.

Halliday, M.A.K. (1994) *An Introduction to Functional Grammar* 2nd edn. London: Edward Arnold.

Halliday, M.A.K. (1998) 'Things and relations: regrammaticising experience as technical knowledge', in J.R. Martin and R. Veel (eds), *Reading Science: Critical and Functional Perspectives on Discourses of Science.* London: Routledge, pp. 185–235.

Hasan, R. and Perrett, G. (1994) 'Learning to function with the other tongue: a systemic functional perspective on second language teaching', in T. Odlin (ed.), *Perspectives on Pedagogical Grammar.* Cambridge: Cambridge University Press, pp. 179–226.

Hunston, S. (1993) 'Evaluation and ideology in scientific writing', in M. Ghadessy (ed.), *Register Analysis: Theory and Practice.* London: Pinter, pp. 57–73.

Hyland, K. and Milton, J. (1997) 'Qualification and certainty in L1 and L2 students' writing', *Journal of Second Language Writing,* 6(2), 183–205.

Jones, J., Gollin, S., Drury, H. and Economou, D. (1989) 'Systemic-functional linguistics and its application to the TESOL curriculum', in R. Hasan and J.R. Martin (eds), *Language Development: Learning Language, Learning Culture.* Norwood, NJ: Ablex, pp. 257–328.

Lock, G. (1996) *Functional English Grammar: An Introduction for Second Language Teachers.* Cambridge: Cambridge University Press.

Martin, J.R. (1989) *Factual Writing.* Oxford: Oxford University Press.

Martin, J.R. (1992) *English Text: System and Structure.* Philadelphia: John Benjamins.

Martin, J.R. (1995) 'Interpersonal meaning, persuasion and public discourse: packing semiotic punch', *Australian Journal of Linguistics,* 15(1), 33–67.

Martin, J.R. (1996) 'Waves of abstraction: Organizing exposition', *The Journal of TESOL France,* 3(1), 87–104.

Mauranen, A. (1996) 'Discourse competence – evidence from thematic development in native and non-native texts', in E. Ventola and A. Mauranen (eds), *Academic Writing: Intercultural and Textual Issues.* Amsterdam: John Benjamins, pp. 195–230.

Melrose, R. (1991) *The Communicative Syllabus: A Systemic-functional Approach to Language Teaching.* London: Pinter.

Mohan, B. (1997) 'Language as a medium of learning: academic reading and cause', *Ritsumeikan Educational Studies,* 10, 208–17.

Mohan, B. and Huxur, G. (2001) 'A functional approach to research on content-based language learning', *Canadian Modern Language Review,* 58(1), 133–55.

Mohan, B. and Van Naerssen, M. (1997) 'Understanding cause-effect', *English Teaching Forum,* 35(4), 22–9.

Perrett, G. (2000) 'Researching second and foreign language development', in L. Unsworth (ed.), *Researching Language in Schools and Communities: Functional Linguistic Perspectives.* London: Cassell, pp. 87–110.

Ravelli, L. (1988) 'Grammatical metaphor: an initial analysis', in E.H. Steiner and R. Veltman (eds), *Pragmatics, Discourse and Text: Some Systemically-inspired Approaches.* London: Pinter, pp. 133–47.

Schleppegrell, M.J. (2001) 'Linguistic features of the language of schooling', *Linguistics and Education,* 12(4), 431–59.

Schleppegrell, M.J. (2002) 'Challenges of the science register for ESL students: errors and meaning making', in M.J. Schleppegrell and M.C. Colombi (eds), *Developing Advanced Literacy in First and Second Languages: Meaning with Power.* Mahwah, NJ: Lawrence Erlbaum, pp. 119–42.

Schleppegrell, M.J. and Colombi, M.C. (1997) 'Text organization by bilingual writers: clause structure as a reflection of discourse structure', *Written Communication,* 14(4), 481–503.

Truscott, J. (1996) 'The case against grammar correction in L2 writing classes', *Language Learning,* 46, 327–69.

Zamel, V. and Spack, R. (eds) (1998) *Negotiating Academic Literacies: Teaching and Learning Across Languages and Cultures.* Mahwah, NJ: Lawrence Erlbaum Associates.

11 Problems with the metaphorical reconstrual of meaning in Chinese EFL learners' expositions

Youping Chen and Joseph A. Foley

1 Introduction

Exposition texts are the linguistic manifestations of the genres valued in English-speaking cultures for challenging or defending the existing order of social reality (Martin 1985). One of the features that contributes to the effectiveness of expository writing is buried reasoning[1] (ibid.), which can be achieved mainly through the deployment of the linguistic resource of grammatical metaphor. In a non-English-speaking culture where English is taught as a Foreign Language (EFL) or perhaps in a culture where English is taught as a Second Language (ESL), the effective teaching of exposition writing should involve turning learners' attention to the lexicogrammatical realization patterns that may realize the features of such writing.

Previous research on the use of grammatical metaphors by Chinese EFL students in their construction of expository texts (Chen 2001) suggests that one of the most problematic aspects of their expository writing is an inappropriate deployment of lexicogrammatical resources. The present chapter will focus on the exploration of this aspect of language use in EFL students' exposition writing and adopt a systemic functional approach to investigate how meaning is realized in the lexicogrammar, so as to provide an additional perspective on first language interference in EFL students' factual writing (Ellis 1994).

2 Theoretical rationale

The theoretical rationale for this study is derived from systemic functional linguistics in that it views grammar as a theory of human experience (Halliday 1994, 1995, 1998; Halliday and Matthiessen 1999: Ravelli 1988). According to this view, grammar plays an essential role in construing human experience into meaning, and its categories (clause complex, clause, and group) stand in a natural relationship with those of meaning (sequence, figure, and element) that are construed through grammar. For example, 'sequence' would involve the processes of expansion and projection in clause complexing; 'figure' is the semantic representation of a 'process' such as *doing, sensing, saying* and *being,* while 'elements' would be the process (verb group), participant (nominal group), circumstance (adverbial group) and relator (conjunction). The significance of the existence of grammar as a purely abstract coding system of the human language, according to Halliday (1998), is the potential for remapping between grammatical and semantic categories. The contexts for the remapping can be characterized as the result of language change that happens across the three time-frames of phylogenesis (language evolution through human history), ontogenesis (language development in individuals), and logogenesis (unfolding of meaning in text) in the semohistory of language (Halliday and Martin 1993; Martin 1997; Halliday and Matthiessen 1999). The result of the three kinds of language change is the creation of two kinds of realization relationship between lexicogrammar and semantics, known as congruent and metaphorical, which are represented as in Figure 11.1 (where solid lines represent congruent realization and broken lines stand for metaphorical realization).

Congruent realization is a kind of realizational relationship between lexicogrammar and semantics. This kind of relationship, or mode of meaning, represents a natural realization relation in that it occurs earlier in the evolution of language, it is learnt by children at an early age and it occurs at the beginning stage of an unfolding text (see Halliday and Mathiessen, 1999). In 'congruent mode of meaning', any phenomenon, or event that happens around us or inside us, once perceived, can be construed through language into a semantic category called figure and this semantic category is realized in lexicogrammar in the form of a clause. Halliday's (1998) example of 'the rapid downhill driving of the bus caused the brake failure' can serve as an illustration. When we see a bus running, we may say 'a bus is running very fast down the hill' or 'the driver is driving the bus very fast down the hill'. Each of the statements represents a semantic configuration of figure with elements of participants (bus, driver), processes (run, drive) and circumstances (fast, down the hill) realized by lexicogrammar as a ranking clause. Sometimes, another event may occur simultaneously and has been observed. If the relationship between the occurrence of two events is perceived as a causal one, then, we can say 'The driver was driving the bus very fast down the hill, so the brake failed.' On this occasion, a sequence of events is construed through language as a sequence at semantic level which is realized in lexicogrammar as a clause complex.

Contrary to the congruent mode of meaning which is typical of the

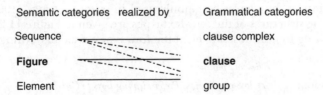

Semantic categories	realized by	Grammatical categories
Sequence		clause complex
Figure		**clause**
Element		group

Figure 11.1 Congruent and metaphorical realization of meaning in lexicogrammar

language in children and the language of the spoken mode is the meta-phorical mode of meaning, involving a remapping between semantics and lexicogrammar (as shown in Figure 11.1 by broken lines). For the same phenomenon of experience or the same sequence of events that can be construed congruently by grammar as clause (e.g., 'the driver was driving the bus very fast down the hill') or a clause complex (e.g. 'the driver was driving the bus very fast down the hill, so the brake failed'), it is possible to reword them or to reconstrue them metaphorically through the grammar into a nominal group (e.g., 'the driver's fast downhill driving of the bus') or a ranking clause (e.g., 'the driver's fast downhill driving of the bus caused a brake failure'). To reconstrue a semantic category of sequence in the form of a clause in the lexicogrammar is an important linguistic resource by which buried reasoning in expository texts is achieved.

3 Hypothesis

The study reported here hypothesizes that some of the major grammatical problems associated with the use of written language by Chinese EFL students in their expository texts can be attributed to the interfering effect of the mother tongue in the way meaning is construed in the grammatical system of English (Ellis 1986). The effect of interference is perceptible in the context where EFL students attempt to use a metaphorical mode of meaning which involves the semantic shift from Quality and Process to Thing, and the rank shift from clause to group. Such interference may result in the inappropriate choice of a grammatical unit for realizing the participant roles in the structural configuration of figures of being. This thereby inhibits the EFL students from successfully burying reasoning in their writing.

4 Research methodology and data

A total of two hundred texts were sampled for the study. Since the study also involves exploring the effect of the context of culture (i.e., types of genre) on the use of grammatical metaphor, four different topics were chosen. Each topic was addressed by 50 Chinese EFL tertiary-level students, majoring in science and engineering. The topics were designed to elicit four types of factual writing – Report, Explanation, Exposition and Discussion.[2] The last three text types can be characterized as expository writing. The characteriza-tion of the generic structures of these four text types is based on Foley's classification of the genres commonly used in school settings (1994: 268). The generic structures of the four text types are given in Figure 11.2.

The writing topics chosen to elicit the four types of factual writing were:

Report: *Decline of Smallpox*

Explanation: *Why do Some Couples Prefer Having Boys to Girls?*

Exposition: *Is 'One Couple One Child' Policy Necessary in China?*

Discussion: *Do 'Lucky Numbers' Really Bring Good Luck?*

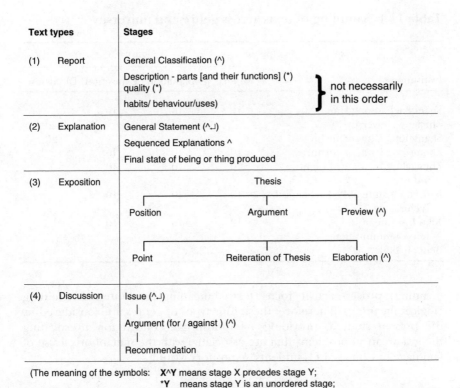

(The meaning of the symbols: **X^Y** means stage X precedes stage Y;
                              ***Y**   means stage Y is an unordered stage;
                              ⌐X stage X is a recursive stage)

Figure 11.2 Generic structures

The sample texts included in the Appendix are representative of the texts produced by the students in this study.

The first three topics were designed by the researcher and written by the students in their English class. The last topic was taken from the Writing Section of National College English Test (band 4), which was administered in June 1998. Regardless of the different situations of the text production, the time allocated and the length of the composition were similar. The students involved were required to write a 120-word composition with three distinct paragraphs in 30 minutes based on an outline or topical sentences provided in the writing instructions. The number of the texts sampled across genres and universities is summarized in Table 11.1.

The study found that the dominant lexicogrammatical resources used in the four types of genres are those of relational processes and the realization of logical meaning within clauses. The deployment of these two resources, both of which depend on grammatical metaphors for relating grammar to its context, are essential to expository texts that foreground what Martin (1997) identifies as the contextual features of thesis appraisal (interpersonal

Table 11.1 Sampling of texts across genre and university

Institutions	Genre			
	Report	Explanation	Exposition	Discussion
Shanghai Jiaotong Univ	10	10	10	
Zhejiang University				20
Shangdong Univ. of Techn				20
Zhengzhou Univ. of Techn	10	10	10	
Zhengzhou Institute of Light Industry	10	10	10	
Jiangsu Institute of Petrochemical Technology	10	10	10	
Xian Institute of Telecommunications	10	10	10	
Bengbu Tank				10

meaning), process/activity focus (textual meaning), and internal unfolding (logical meaning). Therefore, these four types of genres are considered by the present study as providing an appropriate context for investigating the grammatical problems that are associated with the metaphorical use of language in Chinese EFL students' expository writing.

5 Method of analysis

In proposing a method of analysis, it seems that in the most general terms, there are two types of grammatical problems with the use of metaphorical language in Chinese EFL students' expository texts. The first type is purely grammatical in nature, because it occurs only at the grammatical stratum of content plane. The occurrence of the problem of this kind is simply the result of mistaking one grammatical class for another, usually adjectives for nouns or verbs for nouns as in the following:

Example
Nominalized Quality and Process that should have been realized in the lexico-grammar through both prefixation and suffixation: *No equal between men and women make some couples prefer having boys to having girls* (no equal: inequality).

However, the grammatical problem that will be the focus of this study involves a situation that cannot be accounted for simply in grammatical terms. It has to be approached by adopting the 'from above'[3] perspective of considering how meaning is construed by grammar (for detailed discussion, see Halliday 1994: 342). More specifically, consideration is given to how a semantic category of figure is reconstrued metaphorically by the grammatical category of nominal group as an element of Thing that may fill the participant roles of Token, Value, or Carrier and Attribute in relational processes. We will only focus on those instances which the EFL students have realized as simple things when they should have been construed as macro-things or nominalizations of Quality and Process. These instances can be classified into the following three groups with reference to Halliday and Matthiessen's (1999: 67) taxonomy of things, as shown in Figure 11.3.

1 Conscious things for macro-things.
2 Figures for macro-things.
3 Qualities for things.

Among these three categories, the most salient problem is the failure in the reconstrual of figures as macro-phenomena. Macro-phenomena refer to 'figures downranked to function as ordinary elements' (Halliday and Matthiessen 1999: 102), and they can be realized either in the form of a pronoun for anaphoric reference or in the form of an extended nominal group through the nominalization of processes or qualities. The two realization patterns can be illustrated by Halliday and Matthiessen's example (1999: 102).

They broke a Chinese vase.
(i) **That** was careless. (pronoun for anaphoric reference)
(ii) **The breaking of a Chinese vase** was careless. (extended nominal group)

The actual method of analysis we use in this study is based on the taxonomy of types of elemental metaphor proposed by Halliday (1998), developed and elaborated by Halliday and Matthiessen (1999), and the model of general semantic shift of elemental metaphor towards Thing (see Halliday 1998: 211; Halliday and Matthiessen 1999). Halliday (1998) categorized grammatical metaphors into a taxonomy of 13 types which can be characterized according

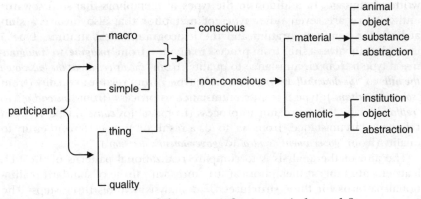

Figure 11.3 Taxonomy of the types of THINGS (adapted from Halliday and Matthiessen 1999)

to the type of semantic shift involved in the metaphorical realization of a meaning. The occurrence of any instance of grammatical metaphor follows a general principle of 'shift to entity' at the semantic stratum where semantic categories of relator, circumstance, process and quality can be metaphorically realized as 'thing'. Whenever there is a semantic shift, there would be a shift in grammatical categories as a result of the realization in lexicogrammar. Of the 13 types of metaphors, 11 types have been focused on for the present research, as exemplified in the following.

Type 1 metaphor: Semantic shift: from quality to entity
                    Grammatical shift: from adjective to noun
                    *The society is **stable**.*   *The **stability** of society*

Type 2 metaphor: Semantic shift: from process to entity
                    Grammatical shift: from verb to noun
                    *The driver **drove** the*   *The **driving** of the bus*
                    bus.

Type 3 metaphor: Semantic shift: from circumstance to entity
                    Grammatical shift: from adverb/prepositional
                                                 phrase to noun
                    The driver drove the   *The **speed** at which the driver drove*
                    *bus **very fast***   *the bus*

Type 4 metaphor: Semantic shift: from relator to entity
                    Grammatical shift: from conjunction to noun
                    The driver drove the bus   *The **result** of fast driving is that the*
                    *very fast, and **so** the*   *brake failed.*
                    brake failed.

These four types of metaphors are generally referred to as nominalizations or nominalizing metaphors, the presence of which is a typical feature of written language. In addition to the types of metaphors that shift towards entity, there are seven other types of metaphor that also involve a shift at both the semantic stratum and the lexicogrammatical stratum. Type 5 metaphor involves a shift from process to quality (from '*imagine*' to '*imaginative*'); type 6 from circumstance to quality (from '*the driver drove the bus **down the hill**' to '*the **downhill** driving of the bus*'); type 7 from relator to quality (from '*so*' to '*resultant*'); type 8 from circumstance to process (from '*instead of*' to '*replace*'); type 9 from relator to process (from '*so*' to '*cause*'); type 10 from relator to circumstance (from '*so*' to '*as a result of*'); type 13 from entity to quality (from '*government decided*' to '*government's decision*').

The aim of the analysis is to compare realizational patterns of the EFL learners' attempts at metaphorical structures with those of standard realizational patterns for these structures. The analysis involves three steps. The first step of the analysis involves classifying all the instances of elemental metaphors found in the data in terms of Halliday's taxonomy, as described above. The second step is concerned with identifying the instances of nominalizing metaphor that occur in two kinds of syntagmatic relations labelled by Halliday (1998) as 'lower rank syndromes' and 'higher rank syndromes'.[4] The structural configuration of lower rank syndromes can be expressed as $1/2 + [6]/[13]$. This can be interpreted as the configuration of type 1 metaphor (from Quality to Thing), and type 2 metaphor (from process to thing) as controlling metaphors, with type 6 metaphor (from Circumstance to quality) and type 13 metaphor (from thing to quality) as secondary metaphors (see Halliday 1998). The structural configuration of higher rank syndromes can be expressed as $1^{st} \{1/2 + [6]/[13]\} + 9 + 2^{nd} \{1/2 + [6]/[13]\}$ which can be interpreted as two lower rank syndromes joined by type 9 metaphor (from relator to process, e.g. 'so ... caused'). The final step involves sorting out the instances of 'nominalizing metaphor' that were intended by EFL students to be the metaphorical realization in lower rank syndromes and higher rank syndromes. Through these three steps of analysis, an attempt was made to explore whether the actual realization patterns employed in EFL learners' expository texts deviate from the typical realization patterns of $1/2 + [6]/[13]$ for lower rank syndromes and $1^{st} \{1/2 + [6]/[13]\} + 9 + 2^{nd} \{1/2 + [6]/[13]\}$ for higher rank syndromes. The instances with the deviating realization patterns are then analysed in functional terms with reference to the EFL learners' mother tongue, the Chinese language.

The following analysis will demonstrate how EFL students tend to construe as simple things what should be construed as macro-things.

6 Analysis

6.1 The choice of conscious Things for macro-Things

The problem in this category involves the construal of meaning as conscious Things instead of the reconstrual of meaning as macro-Things. The clauses in the following example are typical of this problem.

Example
First, with the development of society, people have been aware that boys and girls are same important. Second, for the reason of economy, to the family that isn't rich enough, girls means to save much money in the future.

Obviously, the figure construed by the underlined clause is intended to be a figure of being, where one participant functions as Token and the other as Value which elaborates the Token. To understand what the writer intended to say and what should be the appropriate realization of that meaning, it is necessary to understand the relevant cultural background behind this meaning. In China, there is a long-established tradition that the parents of a girl who is to marry should receive a dowry from the family of their would-be son-in-law. Thus, the parents who have a daughter do not have to worry about

Girls	*means*	*to save much money in the future*	Original
Token		Value	wording
Conscious thing		Figure (realized as non-finite)	

↓

Macro-thing	*means*	Macro-thing		Suggested
Token		Thing	Qualifier	wording
(Having girls	means	the **saving**	of a lot of money in the future.)	

Figure 11.4 Identifying relational process (elaboration)

the considerable expenses needed for their daughter's future marriage. In this sense, bringing up a daughter is more economical for parents. Under this circumstance, we can infer that what the writer actually wanted to say might be something like 'as far as parents are concerned, if their baby is a daughter, it would mean that they would be saved (relieved) from the burden of paying a lot of money for their daughter's marriage'. Or it can be reworded metaphorically as 'as far as parents are concerned, having daughters means the saving of a lot of money in the future'. We can compare a suggested metaphorical wording (in parentheses) with the original one in terms of types of things that have been construed and grammatical functions in the structural configuration of transitivity (see Figure 11.4).

This is demonstrative of what Halliday (1998) calls 'higher rank syndrome' structure in which two participants that function as Token and Value[5] are each supposed to be a nominalized process or quality joined by a verbalized process. The typical structural configuration of this kind, which can be expressed in terms of the types of metaphor that co-occur simultaneously in the form of $\{1/2 + [6]/[13]\} + 9 + \{1/2 + [6]/[13]\}$, can be unpacked into a clause complex of hypotactic relation of cause. Theoretically speaking, any metaphorical wording with the higher rank syndrome structure is subject to further unpacking into a less metaphorical wording of a clause complex. This is because the two participants involved in the higher rank syndrome structure already include the semantic features of either process or quality that can be realized nominally. However, the way the above example (i.e. *Girls means to save much money in the future*) is worded suggests that any further unpacking into a clause complex seems impossible because none of the two participants involves the nominalization of the semantic features of process or quality.

Here are more examples found in the data in which participants are realized as human conscious beings instead of macro-Things.

Examples
Too much people lead to the lack of food, water and source (resource).

(**Overpopulation** leads to the lack of food, water and resources.)

More than people will hold back our development.

(**Overpopulation** will hold back our development.)

6.2 The choice of figures for macro-Things

The problem in this category is similar to that in the previous category, except that what has been realized as participant is the grammatical unit of clause with its semantic status as figures. The two examples in Figure 11.5 illustrate the problem.

6.3 The choice of qualities for Things

The students' problem in this category differs from those in the previous two categories in that no downrank movement (i.e. from clause to group) is involved between what has been construed and what should have been construed. The problem occurs within the nominal group and lies in the confusion of whether an element in the group should be construed as Thing or as the quality of a Thing. The examples in Figure 11.6 illustrate the problem.

6.4 Impact of the mother-tongue interference

From the above analysis, we can see that Chinese EFL students' writing seems to be characterized by the congruent (clausal) mode of meaning rather than the metaphorical (nominal) mode of meaning. The occurrence of grammatical problems of this kind may result from the interfering effect

A girl must be married and became other family's member,

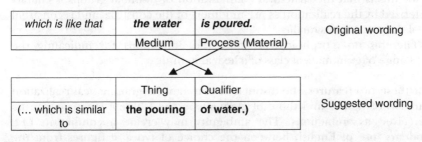

which is like that	the water	is poured.	
	Medium	Process (Material)	Original wording

	Thing	Qualifier	
(... which is similar to	the pouring	of water.)	Suggested wording

Identifying relational process (enhancement)

People	is	more	will bring us many social problems	Original
Carrier	Process	Attribute		wording

Epithet	Thing	Qualifier		
(The rapid	increase	of population)	will bring us many social problems	Suggested wording

Figure 11.5 Attributive relational process

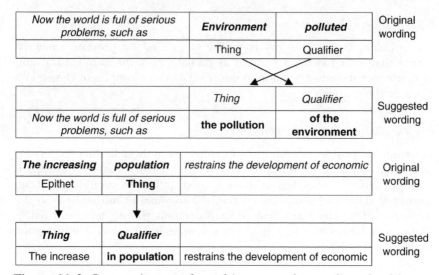

Figure 11.6 Construing words as thing or as the quality of a thing

of the Chinese language, which has, significantly for this study, the two following grammatical features:

- The congruent grammatical realization of a figure in the form of clause and its metaphorical realization in the form of nominal group may have the identical ordering of elements in grammatical structure. The reason for this is that the structural configuration of nominal groups is characterized by the realization as pre-modifiers of the construal and reconstrual of the meaning as quality.
- There is no morphological signal (i.e. inflection) for indicating the change of grammatical class of a lexical item.

For these two features, the distinction between the grammatical realization patterns of figures and those of elements in the Chinese language can be perceived as ambiguous. The ambiguity may create a conflict in EFL students' use of English between the choice of types of figures from the ideational potential of semantic system (i.e. a figure of being) and choice of grammatical units for realizing the participant roles of the figure of being that has been selected. Semantically, the types of genres concerned impose certain semantic constraints for realizing figures as if elements of a figure, and for realizing logical relations as if processes. But the grammatical realization of these semantic constraints seems to have been affected by interference from the grammatical system of Chinese language (Ellis 1986, 1994).

　　The impact of the mother-tongue interference can be explored through the comparison of the possible versions of the word-for-word translation in Chinese as follows.

Too	*many*		*people*	will	cause	*our*	*living*	*environment*
Guo duo		**de renkou**		jiang	daozhi	**wo men**	**sheng cun**	**huan jing**
过	多	的 人口		将	导致	我们(的)	生存	环境

bad.
e hua
恶化。

So	*some*	*couples*	*prefer*	*having*	*boys*	*to girls*	have	two	factors.
Suo yi	**you xie**	**fu qi**	**pian ai**		**nan hai**		you	liang ge	yuan yin
所以	有些	夫妻	偏爱		男孩		有	两个	原因。
所以	有些	夫妻	对偏爱		男孩		有	两个	原因。

People	*is*		*more*	*will*	*bring*	*us*	*many*	*social*	*problems*.
Renkou		**guo duo**		jiang	dai gei	wo men	xu duo	she hui	wen ti
人口		过 多		将	带给	我们	许多	社会	问题。

All	*of*	*that*	*(reason)*	*cause*	*the couples*	*prefer*	*having*	*boys*	*to having girls*.
Suoyou		zhexie	**(yuan yin)**	dao zhi	**fu qi**	**pian ai**		**nan hai**	
所有		这些	（原因）	导致	夫妻	偏爱		男孩	
所有		这些	（原因）	导致	夫妻	对偏爱		男 孩	

Now	*the world*	*is*	*full of*		*serious*	*problems,*	*such as*	*environment*
Muqian	shi jie		chong man	le	yan zhong	wen ti.	Li ru	**huan jing**
目前	世界	充	满 了	严 重		问题，	比如	环 境

polluted.
wu ran
污 染。

Although the English versions are seriously impaired, their Chinese equivalents can be judged as being free from any serious grammatical problems and can be accepted as correct Chinese. The reason for this is that, in Chinese, the congruent grammatical realization of a figure in the form of a clause and its metaphorical realization in the form of a nominal group may have an identical ordering of elements in the grammatical structure. To distinguish whether the wording is the construal of a figure or the reconstrual of a figure as an element, one has to resort to the linguistic context for interpretation because there is no morphological change of words in the Chinese language (i.e. inflection) for signalling the function of the grammatical units. The ambiguity of grammatical functions of the elements in Chinese can be exemplified as shown in Figure 11.7.

Although it seems that the Chinese translation of 'couples prefer having boy' only allows for its interpretation as the construal of a figure of sensing, an alternative wording in Chinese 夫妻对男孩偏爱 (literally means 'couples to boys prefer'), which is an equally popular way of expressing the same

	我们 (的) wo men (de)	生存 sheng cun	环境 huan jing	恶化 e hua
Figure	**Our** Deictic	**living** Classifier Carrier	**environment** Thing	**deteriorated.** Event Attribute
Element	**our**	**living** Qualifier	**environment**	**deterioration** Thing

	人口 **ren kou**	过 多 **guo duo**
Figure	**Population** Carrier	**is too large** Attribute
Element		**overpopulation** Qualifier Thing

	环 境 **huan jing**	污 染 **wu ran**
Figure	**The environment** Medium	**was polluted** Process (Material)
Element	**the environmental** Qualifier	**pollution** Thing

Figure 11.7 The ambiguity of the grammatical functions of some elements in Chinese

meaning, is subject to the construal as a figure and reconstrual as an element, as shown in Figure 11.8.

The types of grammatical problems we have explored above tend to occur in relation to figures of being, particularly the identifying type, in which one participant enhances another along the circumstantial dimension of causal relation. Since the typical lexicogrammatical realization pattern of this domain of the ideational potential is 'favourite clause type' construction in the form of higher rank syndrome pattern (Halliday 1998), it is useful to explore the distribution of this lexicogrammatical resource across the four types of genre under study, as well as the extent to which the deployment of this resource is negatively affected by the mother tongue. The study found that EFL students tend to have more grammatical problems with the 'favourite clause type' construction in writing exposition texts. The number of problematic instances that occur across the four genres can be summarized as shown in Table 11.2.

7 Discussion and pedagogical implications

The comparative analysis with the Chinese language has shown that Chinese EFL students' problem with construing participant roles arises from the interfering effect of the grammatical system of their mother tongue on the way meaning is construed in the grammatical system of English. At the same time, the study also shows that grammatical metaphor, which is the outcome of the interplay between semantics and lexicogrammar in

	夫妻 fu qi	偏爱 pian ai	男孩 nan hai
	Couples	**prefer**	**sons.**
Figure	Senser	Process: Affection	Phenomenon

	夫妻 fu qi	对 男孩 dui nan hai	偏爱 pian ai
	Couples	**(for sons)**	**have preference.**
Figure	Senser	Phenomenon	Process: Affection
	the couples'	**(for sons)**	**preference**
Element	Qualifier	Qualifier	Thing

Figure 11.8 Different ways of construing meaning in Chinese

Table 11.2 Grammatical problems with 'favourite clause type' construction across genre

	Explanation	Exposition	Discussion	Report
No. of type 9 metaphor	8	47	19	17
No. of problematic instances	2	17	5	1
Percentage of problematic instances	25%	36%	26%	6%

the content plane, can be exploited by Chinese EFL learners as an important resource in constructing expository texts. The semantic evidence for this claim is the general tendency of the metaphorical move from the logical towards the experiential through which the domain of sequences is reconstrued as the domain of figures of being and having. By adopting the 'from above' perspective of considering how meaning is construed by grammar, we can see that in EFL students' use of language in expository texts, there exists a conflict between the choice of figures of being as the metaphorical reconstrual of sequences from the ideational potential of the semantic system and the choice of the grammatical units for realizing participant roles. The outcome of the conflict is manifested in the inappropriate construal of the participants either as figure or as things other than macro-things, with the realization pattern in lexicogrammar deviating from the typical pattern of higher rank syndrome structure.

If the claim that one of the problems with the Chinese EFL students' expository writing lies in the metaphorical use of language can be accepted, it follows that in China's EFL context, more attention should be given to the teaching of grammar in expository writing. However, the teaching of grammar should be undertaken from a perspective which is able to relate the semantics to the lexicogrammar, as in systemic functional linguistics. If we adopt the systemic functional perspective, we may find that more work can be done in the teaching of vocabulary and the teaching of grammar through translation.

Practice in the transcategorization of one grammatical class to another should not be aimed simply at increasing students' vocabulary. Rather, students' attention should be directed to their grammatical functions in the context of a lower rank syndrome and higher rank syndrome structures. For example, some modifications can be made in the existing word formation exercises that can be found in almost all the English textbooks to incorporate the rewording practice that involves the rankshift from clause to group and from clause complex to clause. Practice can be designed in a way that may provide a step-by-step understanding of the change of grammatical functions when a downrank movement occurs. The step-by-step practice may take the form of a pyramid such as the following (the illustration is taken from Halliday's 'driver' example, 1998).

Clausal mode	Nominal mode
The driver was driving.	the driver's driving
The driver was driving the bus.	the driver's driving of the bus
The driver was driving the bus fast	the driver's fast driving of the bus
The driver was driving the bus fast down the hill.	the driver's fast downhill driving of the bus

This type of exercise can be more meaningful than the exercise that only requires students to provide the noun form of the verb 'drive'. By doing this kind of practice, students are more likely to notice the impact of changing from a verb form to a noun form on the change of the grammatical functions of the other elements of the clause. Once students become familiar with the structure of extended nominal groups, the practice can proceed to the construction of 'favorite clause type' structure which involves, in addition to realizing figure as element, the realization of relator as process in the form of a verb (as in 'so' → 'caused').

The traditional translation approach to the teaching of English should not be employed simply for understanding and learning the vocabulary and grammar of the target language. It should be adopted in a way that may sensitize students to the different linguistic features of the clausal and nominal modes of meaning in Chinese and English. This can be achieved through comparing the syntactic features of clauses as the lexicogrammatical realization of figures with those of nominal groups as the metaphorical realization of figures as if they were elements.

8 Conclusion

Mother-tongue interference is inevitable in the learning of a foreign language. It is true that the problem of mother-tongue interference may vary with the kind of foreign language that is being learned and the mother tongue of the language learner. However, the basic and underlying cause that leads to the occurrence of the problem may be similar because the ways the semantic stratum and the lexicogrammatical stratum interact in different languages are different.

It is therefore important that such studies be conducted on 'whole texts' so that the findings reflect the process of language in use. It may also be argued that what has been found in this study may only be applicable in the educational context of China where English is very much an EFL. Obviously, further research will be needed to establish any general principles underlying the present study, that is, the possibility of the way meaning is construed in the mother tongue impacting on the way the meaning is construed in the foreign language(s) the learners are learning.

Notes

1 Buried reasoning is a mode of realization whereby the logico-semantic meaning of cause and effect is realized in lexicogrammar inside one clause rather than across clauses. In spoken language, causal relations, for example, are typically realized by conjunctions or prepositions as in the following:

> *Because modern science has developed very fast, the disease of smallpox becomes curable.* (Hypotactic relation with the conjunction '*because*' linking two clauses.)

> *Thanks to the development of modern science, the disease, which ever was impossible to cure, had become curable.* (The causal relation is realized as prepositional phrase '*because of*' within one clause.)

> In written language, especially in exposition texts, causal relations are often realized as verbs or nouns. The effect is that reasoning is realized within one clause. For example:

> *The decline of smallpox can be attributed to the development of modern science.* (The causal relation between two events '*the decline of*' and '*the development of*' is realized as verb '*attributed to*')

> *There are some reasons for the decline of smallpox.* (The causal relation is realized as noun '*reasons*'.)

> The reason for the deployment of this resource in exposition texts, according to Martin (1985), is that by using buried reasoning, 'an argument is presented not as supposition but as an unassailable fact. In our culture burying the reasoning in this way has the effect of strengthening one's case' (ibid.: 26).

2 As shown in Table 11.2, the number of problematic instances with the higher rank syndrome structure varies with the types of genre under study. As only one problematic instance is found in the Report genre, this genre is not discussed in this chapter.

3 The 'from above' perspective is an approach adopted by systemic functional model of language in dealing with the relationship between meaning and form. This approach is concerned with how a given meaning selected from the semantic system of language gets realized in lexicogrammar. This approach forms a contrast to the 'from below' perspective on language which is concerned with what a given expression means (Halliday 1994: 342).

4 Instances of grammatical metaphor seldom occur as an isolated phenomenon. Rather, they often occur in syndromes. Syntagmatically, grammatical metaphors often find themselves in either lower rank syndrome structures or higher rank syndrome structures (Halliday 1998). Lower rank syndrome is defined as a structure consisting of nominalizing metaphors as controlling metaphor, with type 6 or/and type 13 metaphors as secondary metaphors. Grammatically speaking, a lower rank syndrome can be realized in the form of a nominal group as in

The driver's	rapid	downhill	driving	of the bus
13	6	6	2	13

where the instance of '*driving*' is type 2 metaphor, '*driver's*' and '*of the bus*' are type 13 metaphors and '*rapid*' and '*downhill*' are type 6 metaphors.

Higher rank syndrome is defined as a structure consisting of two lower rank syndromes joined by a verbalized relator. It is typically realized in grammar as a clause of relational type.

The driver's rapid downhill driving of the bus caused the brake failure.
13   6   6   2   13   9   13   2

Lower rank syndrome and higher rank syndrome structures can be formulated as $1/2 + [6]/[13]$ for lower rank syndrome and as 1st $\{1/2 + [6]/[13]\} + 9 + 2^{nd}$ $\{1/2 + [6]/[13]\}$ for higher rank syndrome.

Lower rank syndrome and higher rank syndrome structures have different functions in discourse. 'the lower rank syndrome is directly associated with taxonomic categorizing of the activities in a particular field and the higher rank syndrome is directly associated with realizing logical reasoning with the ranking clause' (Halliday 1998: 218). Higher rank syndrome structure is an important linguistic resource whereby the buried reasoning can be achieved. Since this mode of meaning is typical of written language, higher rank syndrome is also called 'favourite clause type' by Halliday (1998).

5 Token and value are functional labels in systemic functional grammar for the elements that are involved in identifying relational clauses. Halliday (1994: 124) explains the two terms and their differences as follows:

> In any identifying clause, the two halves refer to the same thing; but the clause is not a tautology, so there must be some difference between them. This difference is one of form and function; or in terms of their generalized labels in the grammar, of TOKEN and VALUE – and either can be used to identify the other. If we say *Tom is the treasurer*, we are identifying 'Tom' by assigning him to a Value; if we say *Tom is the tall one*, we are identifying 'Tom' by assigning a Token to him. Every identifying clause faces either one way or the other.

References

Chen, Youping (2001) 'The use of grammatical metaphor by EFL students and their language proficiency – exploring the language maturity of Chinese university students'. PhD thesis, National University of Singapore.

Ellis, R. (1986) *Understanding Second Language Acquisition*. Oxford: Oxford University Press.

Ellis, R. (1994) *The Study of Second Language Acquisition*. Oxford: Oxford University Press.

Foley, J. (1994) 'Moving from "common-sense knowledge" to "Educational Knowledge" ', in S. Gopinathan, Anne Pakir, Ho Wah Kam and Vanithamani Saravanan (eds), *Language, Society and Education in Singapore: Issues and Trends*. Singapore: Times Academic Press.

Halliday, M.A.K. (1994) *An Introduction to Functional Grammar 2nd edn*. London: Edward Arnold.

Halliday, M.A.K. (1995) 'Language and the reshaping of human experience', in B. Dendrinos (ed.), *Proceedings of the Fourth International Symposium on Critical Analysis*. Athens: University of Athens.

Halliday, M.A.K. (1998) 'Things and relations: regrammaticising experience as technical knowledge', in J.R. Martin and Robert Veel (eds), *Reading Science*. London: Routledge.

Halliday, M.A.K. and Martin, J.R. (1993) *Writing Science: Literacy and Discursive Power*. London and Washington, DC: Falmer.

Halliday, M.A.K. and Matthiessen, C.M.I.M. (1999) *Construing Experience through Meaning: A Language-based Approach to Cognition*. London and New York: Cassell.

Martin, J.R. (1985) *Factual Writing: Exploring and Challenging Social Reality*. Geelong, Vic: Deakin University Press.

Martin, J.R. (1997) 'Analysing genre: functional parameters', in F. Christie and J.R. Martin (eds), *Genre and Institutions: Social Processes in the Workplace and School*. London and New York: Cassell.

Ravelli, L. (1998) 'Grammatical metaphor: an initial analysis', in E.H. Steiner and R. Veltman (eds), *Pragmatics, Discourse and Text: Some Systemically Inspired Approaches*. London: Pinter.

Appendix: sample texts

Decline of smallpox (report)

Smallpox, an *infectious* disease, ever resulted in great disaster in history even today someone felt terrible when mentioning it. Thanks to the development of modern science, the disease, which ever was impossible to cure, had become curable and been controled by mankind along with the decline of numbers who had it. The left graph show this situation.

From the graph, we can see from 1964 to 1977 the number of countries reporting cases of smallpox decreased from 30 to 2. Until to 1980, there is no one country. The speed of the decline was inspiring. From it, I think the factors which contributed to that decline, beside the promotion of medical, also should include the stability of the world. It means there is no war, full of peace and most countries' dedicating to development of society. So the governor placed an important on the health of civilization.

In spite of any causes, we should congratulate on the accomplishment. I also hope the allover development of mankind, among other things, including the health of people.

Why do some couples prefer having boys to girls? (explanation)

The status of man was different from that of women in old days, which affects us the point of having boys or having girls. Most people, especially in country, think boys are more important than girls, because they think only boys can proceed their family.

Then, why do some couples prefer having boys to having girls. First, with the development of society, people have been aware that boys and girls are same important. Second, for the reason of economy, to the family that isn't rich enough, girls means to save much money in the future. Of course, each has his reason. Nowadays, many facts have indicated that women are also important. For example, some women do better than man in some work. So we shouldn't have different point in having boys and having girls.

Is 'one couple one child' policy necessary in China? (exposition)

I agree with the point.

Now, there are more than 1.3 billion people in China. Though our country is very wide, too many people will cause our living environment bad. If one couple have not only one child, they will feel very busy and tired especially in cities. People often say, many people are easy to do sth. But I think it too many to do sth well. Another side, we are rich in total resource. But we are still very poor in average. Great population is the main reason.

If we can control the increase of population and try to develop the economy, we will have a high level of living condition. In order to realize that point, we think 'one couple one child policy' is very necessary in China.

Do 'lucky numbers' really bring good luck? (discussion)

Some of us may believe that some 'lucky numbers' can bring good luck. For example, they may think that the number 'eight' is connected with luck. Therefore, in everyday lives, they deliberately pursue these numbers, such as doing business on 'lucky' dates, installing telephone with 'lucky' code.

However, there are also many of us who think that luck has nothing to do with 'lucky numbers'. In their opinion, the 'lucky numbers' don't **exist** at all. So, one should have common-sense to these numbers.

As for me, I agree with the latter. Because I stick to the point that success is the result of diligence and believing the **existence** of 'lucky numbers' is only one kind of superstitional opinions. Hence, please allow me to persuade those who believe the **existence** of 'lucky numbers' to give up credulous ideas and make effort to success.

12 Supporting genre-based literacy pedagogy with technology – the implications for the framing and classification of the pedagogy

Robert A. Ellis

1 Introduction

Genre-based literacy pedagogy has had a significant influence on both the practice of, and research into, student literacy in primary and secondary educational contexts. Since the 1970s, its model of the literacy teaching and learning cycle and its theoretical foundation, systemic functional linguistics (SFL) (Halliday 1994), have been the basis of three main projects; the Writing Project at the University of Sydney, and the Language and Social Power Project and the Write It Right Project, both taking place in the Metropolitan East Disadvantaged Schools Programme in Sydney (Martin 1999).

The success of the approach to literacy education in these pre-tertiary educational contexts has also influenced approaches to literacy in higher education. Over the last 15 years in higher education, aspects of genre-based literacy pedagogy have been adapted to help tertiary students address their academic literacy needs, including understanding the purpose and register of academic texts, what it means to act as an academic writer and what sort of knowledge is necessary to be part of an academic community. These approaches have seen many SFL-based literacy research initiatives, including the adoption of SFL text analysis to reveal the genre of academic texts to students and inform feedback processes (Drury and Webb 1989, 1991; Taylor and Drury 1996; Hewings 2000), using SFL text analysis to reveal the genre of research articles (Mirahayuni 2001) and to identify elemental genres (Drury 2001), and using SFL as the basis of a literacy assessment system (Bonanno and Jones 1997). Despite this activity occurring across many institutions and in many different educational contexts, there is coherence to the work brought about through its common theoretical basis. If we search for the relationship between the focus of this research and the previous pre-tertiary projects, it is useful, and meaningful because of its coherence, to conceive of it as a Systemic Functional Linguistics Academic Literacy Project.

Within the SFL Academic Literacy Project, some attention has been paid towards the integration of technology into literacy tuition. Studies have used it as a means of integrating literacy instruction as a way of learning the discipline of curricula (Ellis 2000), they have used it to provide comprehensive analyses of texts across many disciplines (Woodward-Kron and Thomson 2000), and they have focused on modelling the genre and purpose of scientific reports for students (Drury, this volume).

While technology has been integrated into modified versions of genre-based literacy pedagogy, the way it relates to the pedagogy is yet to be investigated. Consequently, an important question remains: what is the relationship between genre-based literacy pedagogy and the sorts of technologies that are being used to support it? Furthermore, what is the significance of this relationship?

To understand the relationship between technology and genre-based literacy pedagogy, this study draws on Bernstein's tools for situating the modality of pedagogic discourse, framing and classification (Bernstein 1996). These tools can be used to identify what counts as acceptable pedagogic discourse in the classroom and who controls the learning.

The following begins with a discussion of the theoretical foundation of genre-based literacy pedagogy, and how it can be understood in terms of framing and classification. The influence of technology on the framing and classification of genre-based literacy pedagogy is then discussed using an undergraduate science subject as a case study, which draws on data gathered from discourse analyses and student access logs of the technologies used.

2 Genre-based literacy pedagogy

Genre-based literacy pedagogy has produced a number of teaching and learning models since it became the focus of research beginning in the late 1970s. One of its teaching and learning models, taken from the Write it Right Project in the Metropolitan East Region of Sydney's Disadvantaged Schools Programme, is depicted in Figure 12.1.

The teaching and learning process represented by the model in Figure 12.1 is divided into three stages: deconstruction, joint construction and independent construction. Learning within the process can begin at any point dependent on the students' needs. At all stages of this cycle, the social context of the genre and field knowledge required for the writing task are considered and made explicit (Martin 1999: 130). The deconstruction stage of the cycle is a critical analysis of models of the genre under focus. These models can be analysed for content, structure and language features to provide insight about the genre and register to the students. The joint construction stage foregrounds collaboration between the participants of the learning process in preparation of the text, and the individual construction stage focuses on the production of a text by each student.

During the life of the pre-tertiary projects, the genre-based literacy pedagogy model of teaching and learning underwent a number of pedagogical renovations. One of the main pedagogical renovations was to introduce waves of weak and strong framing and classification as appropriate to different stages of the learning cycle (Martin 1999: 143). The tools of

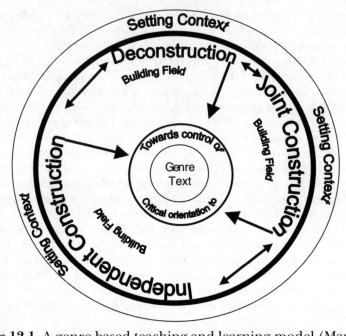

Figure 12.1 A genre-based teaching and learning model (Martin 1999: 131)

framing and classification were adopted from Basil Bernstein's discourse on social class and education (Berstein 1971, 1975, 1996). Bernstein argues that biases within education, biases in the form, content, access and opportunities of education, can eat away at the fundamental aspects of affirmation, motivation and imagination, which are essential resources for successful learning (Bernstein 1996: 5). In terms of literacy, access to the necessary genres and registers required for successful learning is one way to redress biases that may exist in education. Varying the framing and classification of the pedagogy surrounding the introduction of genres to students can be used to ameliorate any biases that may exist in the learning cycle as a result of differing student needs.

Framing refers to the degree of control teacher and pupil possess over the selection, organization, pacing and timing of knowledge transmitted and received in the pedagogical relationship (Bernstein 1975: 88–89; Atkinson 1985: 136). Weak framing means that there are more options available to the learners during learning and strong framing means less options/control are available.

Classification refers to the degree of boundary maintenance between contents. It does not refer to what is classified but to the relationships between contents. Strong classification insulates the contents by strong boundaries. Weak classification blurs the boundaries between the contents (Bernstein 1975).

These tools can be used to identify the modality of pedagogic discourse. For example, by placing framing on a continuum that represents weak and strong framing, its relationship to student and teacher control is clarified. Consider Figure 12.2 below.

In terms of control over learning processes, when framing weakens, students exercise more control, and when framing strengthens, the teacher is more in control. Similarly, with strong classification, the boundaries of the pedagogic discourse are strongly controlled, while weak classification would see other discourses enter into the substantive discourse. Within the genre-based teaching and learning cycle, both double framing and double classification can be identified. Double framing and double classification refers to the use of both weak and strong framing and weak and strong classification as deemed appropriate by the participants during the teaching and learning process (Martin and Rothery 1988). Table 12.1 maps double framing and classification onto a generalized version of the genre-based literacy pedagogy teaching and learning model.

The robust nature of genre-based literacy pedagogy is identified in Table 12.1 as its ability to adapt according to student and contextual needs. If students demonstrate good control of the genre they need to master, then the framing and classification can be weakened. If they require more guidance, then the framing and classification in the learning cycle can be strengthened.

3 Supporting genre-based literacy pedagogy with learning technologies

When learning technologies are used to support genre-based literacy pedagogy, significant changes to the framing and classification of the pedagogy occur. The classification of the pedagogical discourse, that is what counts as appropriate pedagogical discourse, becomes more complex as technological instruction enters the substantive discourse. Furthermore, the framing of the pedagogical discourse becomes more delicate, as the level of control over learning resources and activities available to the students increases. The following case study discusses how three technologies – a database, bulletin board and word-processor – influenced a tertiary application of genre-based literacy pedagogy, within a first-year undergraduate science subject.

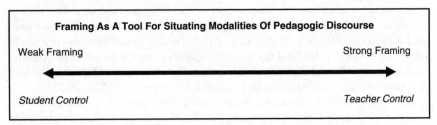

Figure 12.2 A continuum of weak and strong framing

Table 12.1 The double classification and framing potential of genre-based literacy pedagogy

Stage of the model	The nature of framing and classification at each stage
Deconstruction/modelling	• weak framing and classification occurs as teachers find ways of starting where students are at in order to open up the field and context of the genre • framing and classification values strengthen when a model text is introduced
Joint Construction	• weak framing and classification occur as students open up a new field • framing and classification values strengthen when teacher guides the students into organizing the material • framing values split according to field (content offered by students) and genre (structure guided by teacher)
Individual Construction	• weak framing and classification occur as students open up a new field • weak framing but relatively strong classification since students are aiming for a specific genre as they write a text on their own

Source: adapted from Martin 1999

4 Case study – undergraduate plant science and physiology

Plant science and physiology (PSP) is a core subject in the first year of an undergraduate horticultural science degree at a regional Sydney university. By the end of their enrolment, students were expected to sufficiently understand the knowledge they had studied in PSP so that they would be able to relate and apply it to new contexts. This meant understanding such topics as cell biology genetics, photosynthesis and plant growth regulators in sufficient depth to see a relationship between their principles and the related topics they would come across in the ensuing years of their study.

To assess the extent to which the students had achieved these outcomes, the lecturers designed the assessment framework shown in Table 12.2.

There were three main components in the PSP assessment framework: a scientific writing portfolio worth 30 per cent, minor tests worth 25 per cent and a final examination worth 45 per cent. While the writing portfolio was only 30 per cent of the final mark, its scientific content related directly to the minor texts and final examination. For a fuller discussion of the assessment and other features of the learning context, see elsewhere (Ellis 2000).

The assessment components were structurally related to maximize the support they could provide to help students develop sufficient scientific understanding and literacy to perform well. This meant that the writing tasks

Table 12.2 The assessment framework of plant science and physiology

No.	Assessment Component	Description	Weighting
1	Writing portfolio	A collection of eight written tasks varying in word length from 300–1200 words Submission of some preparation for the tasks, e.g. outlines, drafts Completion and submission of text analysis exercises in the scientific literacy database	20% + 10%
2	Minor tests 1–4	Four short tests drawing together key aspects of the science raised in the portfolio tasks as well as some relevant numeracy issues	25%
3	Final examination	Completion of three short essays in two hours dealing with topics raised in the portfolio tasks and the minor tests	45%
		Total	100%

supported the students' preparation for the minor tests and the minor tests supported the students' preparation for the final exam. The final exam was two hours long, during which the students were expected to complete three short essays on important areas of the science they studied throughout the semester. The minor tests were on the topics of water, mineral nutrition of plants, mitosis and meiosis, genetic traits, photosynthesis and plant growth regulators. The tasks of the scientific writing portfolio were designed to help the students develop their understanding of both the science and its written expression. The lecturers' intentions were that the students would draw on the formative learning provided by the writing tasks to perform well in their other assessment components.

5 The scientific writing portfolio

The scientific writing portfolio in the PSP curriculum is a collection of eight writing tasks between 300 and 1200 words, text analysis exercises, task out-lines and drafts that students completed at regular intervals throughout the semester. The writing tasks drew together the science the students studied in lectures, laboratories and the tutorial. Table 12.3 shows examples of the writing tasks.

A scientific writing portfolio was chosen for a number of reasons. First, by completing writing tasks every week or so, such as those shown in Table 12.3, and by receiving regular feedback, the lecturers felt that the students would be able to formatively develop and display their understanding of the science

Table 12.3 Examples of the writing tasks in the scientific writing portfolio

---

Task instructions

---

1. Discuss the three reasons for the development of agriculture (population growth, climate change or systemic risk minimization models) and decide which one is the most likely.

2. Discuss the causes of the variations seen in plant and animal species.

3. Describe the processes of light harvesting and energy conversion during the light reactions of photosynthesis. Describe the operation of each of these components and the total process of light harvesting, photolysis or water, electron transport, the production of NADPH, the role of thylakoid membrane and cyclic and non-cyclic photophosphorylation.

---

and their ability to write about it throughout the semester. This belief was consistent with the literature of previous research into the value of portfolios (McLeod 1992). Second, the variety of feedback processes that accompany portfolios makes them feasible for assessing large numbers of students (Lieber 1997). At the time of designing the PSP curriculum, the predicted cohort was to be around 70 students. Third, research has demonstrated that portfolios increase interest in students in the subject and improves their commitment (Raines 1996), an attractive outcome for the PSP lecturers and students. Given this, it was thought that a scientific writing portfolio would provide suitable opportunities for the formative development of the students' scientific understanding and writing.

6 Text deconstruction in plant science and physiology

The first stage of genre-based literacy pedagogy involves the deconstruction of the scientific text models. In plant science and physiology, students would normally engage in text deconstruction in the tutorials, after they had been to the related lectures and laboratory sessions. The lectures and laboratory sessions helped to prepare the students for this stage by beginning to build the Field with them. Lectures provided much of the background and references for further investigation of the topics, and the laboratory sessions allowed the students to engage in scientific experiments and processes about which they would write.

The tutorials were designed to support the students as they wrote about the science they had been studying. In the tutorials, students were assisted in building their understanding of the Field of the texts, that is, the scientific content of the texts. This was done through the use of exercises about the model texts that deconstructed them for their purpose and register. An important part of this process was the use of the scientific writing database. Students were provided with the scientific writing database so that they could access exercises that would help them to understand the purpose of the scientific texts (the genre), how the language was written (the register), answers to the exercises and feedback items.

All the contents of the database supported the writing portfolio tasks and its structure paralleled the scientific curriculum of the students. The structure of the database and how its scientific content is related is shown in Figure 12.3.

Figure 12.3 shows the contents and structure of the scientific writing database. Its structure is divided into three levels: model texts; exercises and answers to the exercises; and feedback items. The model texts and feedback items were created in html pages and the exercises were in word-processor files that allowed the students to analyse the texts by colour-coding sections according to features of the science and language.

The model texts were adapted from written texts addressing the same tasks provided by first-year undergraduate science students from previous cohorts. The texts were chosen on the basis of their potential to be used to reveal features of good scientific writing and poor scientific writing on each of the portfolio tasks.

The deconstruction phase of the learning cycle began with various tasks, such as those shown in Figure 12.4. The tasks deal with a range of scientific topics such as cell biology, plant nutrition, the domestication of plants, the structure of genomes, DNA and plant growth and development. A well-written paragraph of the task under scrutiny was modelled for genre and register. During the modelling process, it was contrasted with a poorly written paragraph. The modelling phase can use up to six tasks, each task focusing on one aspect of the genre or register of the good and poor paragraphs. Each of these tasks is an individual file within the scientific writing database of around 300 files that deal with the genre and register of the scientific language. The database was a flatfile database, using the functionality provided by the e-learning platform used, WebCT. Students were required to submit exercises that draw out the distinctions of the genre and register under investigation to a private forum on the bulletin board.

Figure 12.4 shows one of the database model paragraphs. It discusses some of the features of the genre of a paragraph under the topic of genetics. Students received background for this topic during their lecture and workshop, and the writing task for genetics expects them to produce paragraphs similar to this. The purpose of the model is to give students insight into the structure of a well-written paragraph that was produced by one of their peers. Figure 12.5 shows one of the exercises on register.

Figure 12.5 deals with thematic development of the paragraph in Figure 12.4. Models such as this are used to indicate the register of the language expected from the students. In the topic of genetics, students have other models to choose from which deal with issues of content, text development (Theme/Rheme), text cohesion (reference), and modality in writing (tenor). The exercise attached to this model is to compare its focus with the focus of a poorly written paragraph that the students have analysed.

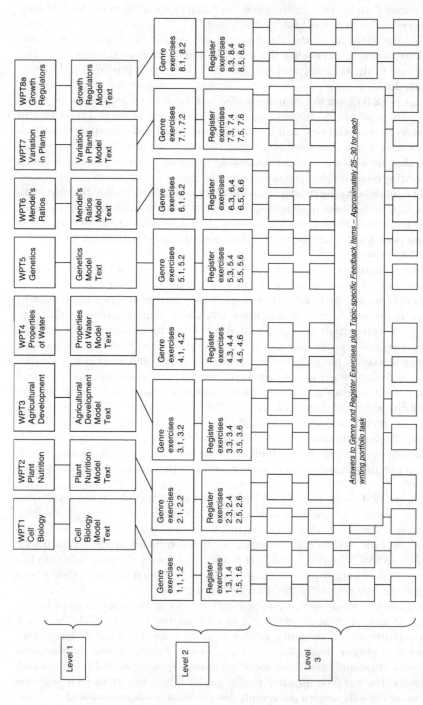

Figure 12.3 The structure of the scientific writing database

Model 6a	Commentary
(1)The relationship between chromosomes and genes can be revealed through the explanation of a number of facts and propositions. *(2)Firstly, chromosomes can be divided along their length into regions called genes and the areas between the genes are called intergenic regions. Genes are linear sequences of nucleotide pairs situated at points along a chromosome. The points are called loci (singluar. locus).* (3)Secondly, the chromosome theory of heredity proposes that chromosomes are the containers of genes. It suggests the reason certain traits are inherited together is that the genes controlling these traits are on the same chromosome. (4)Finally, genes occur in pairs, as do chromosomes. Genes separate equally into gametes, as do chromosomes. This parallel behaviour of genes and chromosomes led to the suggestion that specific genes reside on specific chromosomes. Proof of this relationship came from experiments with eye colour in Dropsophila carried out by Thomas Morgan in 1910 and Calvin Bridges in 1916. They proved that eye colour was on the X chromosome.	*The Structure of the Paragraph:* *The structure of the paragraphs in this writing task should generally contain at least the following stages sequenced as:* **1. Identify the main idea of the paragraph.** *2. Explain how a chromosome is divided into genes* 3. Explain the propositions of the chromosome theory of heredity. 4. Discuss the significance of the parallel behaviour of genes and chromosomes.

Figure 12.4 Database item 06ex.02: structure of a paragraph on the topic of genetics

Model 6a	Commentary
The relationship between chromosomes and genes can be revealed through the explanation of a number of facts and propositions. **Firstly, chromosomes** can be divided along their length into regions called genes and the areas between the genes are called intergenic regions. **Genes** are linear sequences of nucleotide pairs situated at points along a chromosome. **These points** are called loci (singluar. locus). **Secondly, the chromosome theory of heredity proposes** that chromosomes are the containers of genes. It suggests the reason certain traits are inherited together is that the genes controlling these traits are on the same chromosome. **Finally, genes** occur in pairs, as do chromosomes. **Genes** separate equally into gametes, as do chromosomes. **This parallel behaviour of genes and chromosomes** led to the suggestion that specific genes reside on specific chromosomes. **Proof of this relationship** came from experiments with eye colour in Dropsophila carried out by Thomas Morgan in 1910 and Calvin Bridges in 1916. They proved that eye colour was on the X chromosome.	*The information at the beginning of the sentences focuses the reader on the important knowledge in the paragraph.* *The **words highlighted** focus the information on the relationship between chromosomes and genes which is the purpose of the paragraph (see your writing task).*

Figure 12.5 Database item 06ex.03: focus a paragraph under the topic of genetics

Having the texts available to the students and lecturer in the database provides a range of unique strategies for control over the learning process for both the learners and the lecturers. Ideally, this control, or framing of the pedagogy, was negotiated between the students and lecturer, depending on the needs of the students. Using the topic of genetics as an example, with six model paragraphs dealing with the genre and register of the language, the entire class could do the tasks together during the tutorial or they could proceed through them at their own pace: they could complete all the tasks or they could choose which ones they felt would be beneficial to them; they could complete them in class or they could complete them before class; and they could choose the order in which they did them or they could follow a sequence determined by the teacher. These choices begin to identify the delicacy the database adds to the framing of the pedagogy.

The database also provided other unique methods of control over learning that can be used by both the students and the lecturer. The software supporting the database provides evidence of the learning pathway and processes that the students have chosen. For each student, the software provides a log of the pages that they have accessed. This information is available to the lecturer who can use it to ascertain which pages and exercises have been accessed by the students and the time spent on them. In addition, with the agreement of the students, group work using the bulletin board provides a log of the learning pathway. This evidence can be used reflectively to identify difficulties in the learning process. Figures 12.6 and 12.7 show examples of the access logs of two students.

Access number	Database Items	Date of Access
113	09ex.02	Wed Nov 1 10:45:03 2000
112	09a.01	Wed Nov 1 10:44:37 2000
111	09wpt – The Causes of Variation in Plant and Animal Species	Wed Nov 1 10:44:29 2000
110	06a.01	Wed Nov 1 10:43:23 2000
109	06wpt – Genetics	Wed Nov 1 10:43:16 2000
108	01ex.02	Wed Nov 1 10:35:21 2000
107	01ex.01	Wed Nov 1 10:32:28 2000
106	01a.01	Wed Nov 1 10:31:49 2000
105	01wpt – Cell Biology	Wed Nov 1 10:31:44 2000
104	10wpt – Photosynthesis	Wed Oct 25 10:29:06 2000
103	10ex.02	Wed Oct 25 10:25:54 2000
102	10a.01	Wed Oct 25 10:24:09 2000
101	10wpt – Photosynthesis	Wed Oct 25 10:24:00 2000
100	10ex.01	Wed Oct 25 10:13:18 2000
99	10a.01	Wed Oct 25 10:06:39 2000
98	10wpt – Photosynthesis	Wed Oct 25 10:05:05 2000
97	09ex.01	Wed Oct 11 10:35:07 2000
96	09a.01	Wed Oct 11 10:33:42 2000
95	09wpt – The Causes of Variation in Plant and Animal Species	Wed Oct 11 10:33:37 2000
94	09a.01	Wed Oct 11 10:27:12 2000
93	09wpt – The Causes of Variation in Plant and Animal Species	Wed Oct 11 10:26:58 2000
92	09a.01	Wed Oct 11 10:09:35 2000
91	09wpt – The Causes of Variation in Plant and Animal Species	Wed Oct 11 10:09:28 2000
90	07wpt – Mendelian Ratios	Wed Sep 6 10:04:16 2000
89	07ex.04	Wed Aug 30 10:40:41 2000
88	07a.01	Wed Aug 30 10:37:21 2000
87	07wpt – Mendelian Ratios	Wed Aug 30 10:37:12 2000
86	07a.01	Wed Aug 30 10:31:08 2000
85	07wpt – Mendelian Ratios	Wed Aug 30 10:30:58 2000
84	07ex.02	Wed Aug 30 10:26:57 2000

Figure 12.6 Plant science and physiology web site – history of use by student X

Access number	Database Items	Date of Access
107	10wpt – Photosynthesis	Tue Nov 14 22:03:38 2000
106	10wpt – Photosynthesis	Wed Nov 8 12:22:52 2000
105	10wpt – Photosynthesis	Sun Nov 5 10:31:43 2000
104	10a.01	Sun Nov 5 10:31:37 2000
103	10ex.04	Sun Nov 5 10:30:06 2000
102	10a.01	Sun Nov 5 10:29:09 2000
101	10ex.01	Sun Nov 5 10:27:22 2000
100	10a.01	Sun Nov 5 10:26:37 2000
99	10wpt – Photosynthesis	Sun Nov 5 10:26:22 2000
98	09a.01	Wed Oct 11 12:32:08 2000
97	09wpt – The Causes of Variation in Plant and Animal Species	Wed Oct 11 12:32:06 2000
96	09a.01	Wed Oct 11 12:18:44 2000
95	09wpt – The Causes of Variation in Plant and Animal Species	Wed Oct 11 12:18:41 2000
94	09a.01	Wed Oct 11 12:13:57 2000
93	09wpt – The Causes of Variation in Plant and Animal Species	Wed Oct 11 12:13:53 2000
92	09a.01	Fri Oct 6 22:31:58 2000
91	09wpt – The Causes of Variation in Plant and Animal Species	Fri Oct 6 22:29:06 2000
90	09a.01	Mon Oct 2 15:31:19 2000
89	09wpt – The Causes of Variation in Plant and Animal Species	Mon Oct 2 15:17:58 2000
88	09wpt – The Causes of Variation in Plant and Animal Species	Fri Sep 29 21:46:30 2000
87	07wpt – Mendelian Ratios	Wed Sep 6 15:19:32 2000
86	07a.01	Wed Sep 6 15:19:21 2000
85	07a.01	Wed Sep 6 15:15:46 2000
84	07wpt – Mendelian Ratios	Wed Sep 6 15:15:24 2000
83	07wpt – Mendelian Ratios	Wed Sep 6 13:51:46 2000
82	07wpt – Mendelian Ratios	Sun Sep 3 19:58:18 2000
81	07a.01	Sun Sep 3 19:58:14 2000
80	07ex.06	Sun Sep 3 19:55:38 2000
79	07a.01	Sun Sep 3 19:55:17 2000
78	07ex.03	Sun Sep 3 19:52:06 2000

Figure 12.7 Plant science and physiology web site – history of use by student Y

Figures 12.6 and 12.7 show the history of use of the PSP web site by student X and student Y. In Figure 12.6, the information is in three columns. The first column gives the number of times student X accessed pages in the web site (113), starting with the last access in the first row. The second column identifies the database items that were accessed. Those with titles are the instructions and exercises and those with numerical coding, such as no. 113, 09ex.02, are answers to exercises.

To compare how students X and Y used the web site, consider Figure 12.7 and look at access no. 93. We can see that on Wednesday Oct 11 at 12:13:53, the student accessed the instructions for wpt9 (which was the seventh writing portfolio). Taken by itself, this does not tell us much more than that the student clicked on this page. If, however, we look at the third column, we can begin to get a feeling for the pacing of the student. For example, within a period of 19 minutes, the student accessed the model paragraph and the written instructions a number of times. If we then look at the second column, we can begin to understand the selection and organization of the student. Student Y revisited the instructions a number of times within accesses 93 to 98. If we then contextualize this information with our knowledge of the subject, we can see that the student did this on a Wednesday, which we know was during the tutorial. If we look up and down column 3, we begin to understand when this student used to access the materials on the web site, and whether she was outside of the tutorial when she did this.

If we now compare the third column of student Y in Figure 12.7, with the third column of student X in Figure 12.6, we can see that Y made relatively significant use of the materials outside of the tutorial, while X used them only in the tutorial.

Using the database to support the deconstruction stage of genre-based literacy pedagogy makes elements of the framing more explicit and contributes to a more delicate understanding on the part of the teacher and the student of the control over the learning exerted by the student. Coupled with submissions by the students of completed exercises and tasks, this evidence may start to inform the teacher about the quality of the students' learning experience.

7 Joint construction activities in plant science and physiology

In plant science and physiology, the joint construction stage consisted of a variety of tasks. These included analysis of the question, brainstorming, and preparing outlines and the structure of the writing task. The framing of the activities depended on how much understanding the students had of the writing tasks they were engaging in. The following discusses one of the brainstorming exercises on the bulletin board.

One of the topics the students prepared dealt with plant growth regulators. A key aspect of this topic is the contribution of different types of regulators, Auxins, Gibberellins, Ethylene, Cytokinins and Absicic Acid, to plant growth. An initial activity for this topic was a brainstorm about the contribution of the different regulators to plant growth. Students were required to choose one regulator and post a short explanation of its role. Table 12.4 shows the postings records made by some of the students.

Table 12.4 can be read as 5 columns. Column 1 identifies the number of discussion fora on the bulletin board (4), column 2 identifies the number of postings. column 3 displays the topic, column 4 identifies who made the posting and column 5 identifies when the postings were made.

The framing of the exercise was weak in terms of selecting the regulator for discussion. Students were left to choose for themselves which plant growth regulator to write about. Of the 20 student postings in Table 12.4, 13 choose Auxins (65%), four chose Gibberellins (20%), one chose Ethylene (5%) and two chose Cytokinins (10%). Interestingly, no student made a posting on Abscisic Acid, a fifth plant growth regulator that was discussed in the related lecture. The choices made by the students suggested to the lecturer that a topic such as Abscisic Acid or Ethlyene was

Table 12.4 Records of postings made by students on the topic of plant growth regulators

Thread	No	Discussion Topic	Who	When
▼	0/14	🔍Auxins		
	✉	Auxins	Lecturer (bi104a_t)	October 31, 2000 5:27pm
	✉	⇨Re: Auxins	Scott (78723818)	November 8, 2000 10:26am
	✉	⇨Re: Auxins	Jonathan (12084087)	November 8, 2000 10:46am
	✉	⇨ Re: Auxins	Louise (77802820)	November 8, 2000 12:48pm
	✉	⇨Re: Auxins	Dominic (12023174)	November 8, 2000 10:55am
	✉	⇨Re: Auxins	Peter (12070567)	November 8, 2000 10:58am
	✉	⇨Re: Auxins	Naomi (78742770)	November 8, 2000 12:33pm
	✉	⇨Re: Auxins	Naomi (78742770)	November 8, 2000 12:38pm
	✉	⇨Re: Auxins	Matthew (12073775)	November 8, 2000 12:37pm
	✉	Re Auxins	Gregory (12073768)	November 8, 2000 12:38pm
	✉	Re Auxins	Matthew (12032703)	November 10, 2000 10:18am
	✉	Re Auxins	Ryan (12050143)	November 10, 2000 10:25am
	✉	Re Auxins	Taylor (76737767)	November 16, 2000 11:41am
	✉	Re Auxins	Christopher (12042702)	November 17, 2000 4:24pm
▼	0/5	Gibberellins		
	✉	🔍Gibberellins	Lecturer (bi104a_t)	October 31, 2000 5:27pm
	✉	⇨Re: Gibberellins	Merewyn (12072707)	November 8, 2000 11:46am
	✉	⇨Re: Gibberellins	Simon (77734187)	November 8, 2000 12:01pm
	✉	Re Gibberellins	Matthew (12063143)	November 8, 2000 10:43am
	✉	Re Gibberellins	Michael (12020748)	November 8, 2000 10:47am
▼	0/2	🔍 Ethylene		
	✉	Re Ethylene	Lecturer (bi104a_t)	October 31, 2000 5:28pm
	✉	⇨Re: Ethylene	Amanda (77725246)	November 8, 2000 12:36pm
▼	0/2	🔍Cytokinins		
	✉	Re Cytokinins	Amanda	November 8, 2000 10:46am
	✉	Re Cytokinins	Regina (12008054)	November 8, 2000 10:47am

comparatively less well understood by the students than the topic of Auxins. This proved to be the case in the discussion immediately following this exercise.

The framing of the exercise was weak in terms of pacing and timing. Students were able to spend as little or as much time as they liked on the exercise and they were able to complete the exercise in the tutorial, November 8, or afterwards. Table 12.4 shows that four students made a posting on the topic of Auxins after the tutorial.

The framing of the exercise was relatively strong in terms of organization. Students were expected to make their posting before they wrote about plant growth regulators as a writing task.

The different aspects of the framing (selection, organization, pacing, timing) can apply to more than just one feature of the learning process. For example, selection can apply not only to the topic being written about, but also to the partners with whom students were able to work with in the joint construction stage. The organizational features and asynchronous nature of the bulletin board can influence the selection of the partners in the joint construction stage in interesting ways.

Discussions using the bulletin board can be public, which means that all students in the tutorial can see the postings being made, or private, which means that only students selected by the lecturer as part of the private discussion forum can see the postings. In addition, the postings made to the bulletin board facilitate asynchronous communication. In other words, people can access the postings and contribute to the discussion at different times. These features of the bulletin board enhance the ability of the lecturer to double-frame the pedagogy. For example, if students are asked to write summary notes of a lecture relevant to one of the writing exercises, then the students could post these summaries to a public forum. In this case, the framing of the selection of asynchronous joint collaborators would be relatively weak. Alternatively, if the lecturer chooses to restrict the postings to a private forum, then control over the framing of the asynchronous collaborators strengthens. In both cases, the networked text-based nature of the bulletin board means that the timing of the collaborations is weak.

8 Individual construction in plant science and physiology

In plant science and physiology, the activities of the individual construction phase usually begin with each writer collecting and categorizing the writing preparation and resources that have been considered and developed in the previous stages. These included the text deconstruction exercises and any joint construction activities that were relevant. Once a first draft prepared by the writer has been produced, feedback and editing are important features of this stage of the writing process. In plant science and physiology, there were three types of feedback: from the lecturer, from peers and through the database. The following discusses the framing surrounding feedback through the database.

When students are at the individual construction stage, control over the depth and breadth of the feedback processes that they use can be framed by the database. Control over the feedback processes can be achieved through choice in the learning pathways provided by the database and choice in the extent of feedback sought using the bulletin board. If the student displays successful writing and editing during this stage of learning, they can use as many of the resources in the database as they choose in order to augment the feedback they receive. For students to do this successfully, they would need to be able to distil linguistic knowledge from examples whose content dealt with tangential scientific concepts. For students who required more support during this stage of learning, they can be directed to specific items in the database that dealt specifically with the linguistic issue with which they required help and whose content dealt with the same science as the task. If such an item does not exist in the database, the student and the lecturer can collaborate to create it and it could become part of the shared knowledge of the class. Consider the following database item.

Figure 12.8 is an example of one of the writing resources. It has been produced from student writing. The first row contains the labels for the contents underneath. The first cell in the second row is an example of student writing and the first cell in the third row is the correction. The right-hand column explains the contents of the left-hand column. The topic of this example is genetics.

The bottom row of Figure 12.8 identifies one of the methods used to promote student choice and control over learning. If a student's needs in terms of passive constructions are met by this single item, a simple reminder of passive constructions, then the feedback accessed from the database on this point can end here. If, however, the student wishes slightly more information about the passive, they can access other items identified in the bottom row. Figure 12.9 reveals one of the pathways.

9 Summarizing the influence of technology on the framing of genre-based literacy pedagogy

The generalized version of genre-based literacy pedagogy in Table 12.1 at the beginning of this chapter could have possibly glossed the above learning context had the technologies not been included. However, once the technologies are introduced into the teaching and learning cycle, there is the potential to examine its impact on the framing of the pedagogy in more delicate ways. Table 12.5 indicates the type of double framing that can be achieved within the model supported by technology.

Table 12.5 is a generative framework that can be used to better understand the relationship between technology and student control over learning in genre-based literacy pedagogy. The generative property of the table can be identified by the relationship between the third column, the qualities of

06.01 **Incomplete passive construction - "called" versus "are called".**	Explanation
Sentence 1 Chromosomes can be divided along their length into regions called genes. The areas between the genes **called** intergenic regions.	The highlighted verb in sentence 1 is incorrectly constructed.
Correction Chromosomes can be divided along their length into regions called genes. The areas between the genes **are called** intergenic regions.	This sentence has the correct passive construction of the verb.
Click here if you want to see how the passive voice is formed. Click 1, 2 for other examples using the passive voice	If you want more information on the passive, use these links.

Figure 12.8 Database item 06.01: passive constructions under the topic of 'genetics'

02.27	
The form of the passive – "to be" + "(root verb)-ed"	Explanation
Sentence 1 Knop and von Sachs grew plants in solutions and expanded the range of essential elements which **are need** by plants.	In sentence 1 'need' is incorrect. It is part of a passive verb and should have an '-ed' ending.
Correction Knop and von Sachs grew plants in solutions and expanded the range of essential elements which **are needed** by plants.	In the correction the full form of the passive verb has been provided.
are +need +-ed the verb "to be" +root of the verb "need" + past participle ending	The formation of the highlighted verb in the correction is displayed left.

Figure 12.9 Database item 02.27: passive voice use under the topic of 'plant nutrition'

framing, to any stage of the teaching and learning cycle, which are identified in terms of weak and strong framing in columns two and four. The four qualities of framing are repeated in this column to indicate that they can come into play at any stage of the learning process should either the lecturer or student decide to negotiate them. For example, learning during the modelling phase can require a choice of text models to be used as an entry into the desired genre. This can be framed weakly, by giving students choice, and/or strongly, by the lecturer emphasizing particular models. However, control over this stage of the learning process is not simply dichotomized into weak or strong framing (that is, more student control or more teacher guidance) but it is possible to negotiate which aspect of framing would benefit the students if they had control over it. Using technologies such as those discussed, negotiation can focus on how much control over each of the qualities of framing is to be given to the students. For example, lecturers may wish to restrict control over the selection of the model texts by the students, but may wish to give them flexibility in the pacing of the amount of time they spend on each model. If the students each have the potential to access the modelling process and any exercises and answers at their own pace using the database, then they can control their pacing and timing. This is an example of how Table 12.5 can be used to generate insight into the relationship between technology and double framing in genre-based literacy pedagogy. By teasing out each stage of the learning process, modelling, joint construction, and individual construction in relation to the qualities of framing identified in column 3, the potential contribution of the technologies discussed to framing are revealed.

The discussion of the case study so far has considered the relationship between framing and genre-based literacy pedagogy. Its significance is that

Table 12.5 A framework indicating the potential impact of technology on genre-based literacy pedagogy

Stage	Weak Framing	Aspects of Framing	Strong Framing
Modelling/ deconstruction using the database, face-to-face and asynchronous discussion	choice of models during modelling stage as students search for entry into genre	*selection* *organizing* *pacing* *timing*	foreground specific models as entry point
		selection organizing pacing timing	strengthen framing when specific genre is modelled
Joint Construction using the database, face-to-face and asynchronous discussion	choice of collaborative processes and partners	*selection* *organizing* *pacing* *timing*	foreground particular collaborative processes or identify partners
	choice of learning pathways in the database	selection organizing pacing timing	foreground particular pathways in the database
Individual Construction using the database, face-to-face and asynchronous discussion	choices of editing resources	*selection* *organizing* *pacing* *timing*	foreground particular editing resources
	choices of sources of feedback	selection organizing pacing timing	foreground particular sources of feedback

the technology increases the level of negotiable control over learning, or, in other words, technology can be used to enhance the extent of double framing. The discussion now turns to how technology influenced the classification of the pedagogical discourse.

10 Classification, discourses, recontextualization and PSP

Discourses can be divided into singulars and regions (Bernstein 1996: 23). A singular is one that maintains its boundaries intact, that is, it does not allow other discourses to dilute it. A discourse that is a region contains a number of discourses.

Within the institution of a university, the working relationships of staff can be thought of in these terms. If we look at the establishment of learning centres as exemplars, which offer some sort of central support to staff and students, and we conceive of a department as a singular, then those departments who do not choose to avail themselves of the central support in their curricula can still be thought of as singulars. Equally, those departments who choose to collaborate at the level of curriculum design with staff from learning centres have allowed other discourses to enter their disciplined-based knowledge area. The team-based approach to the design of curricula in those departments indicates the existence of regions.

Since its first delivery, the plant science and physiology subject discussed in the case study has never completely been a singular, as the lecturers have always introduced a discourse of pedagogy in some form or other. In two key collaborations since that time, the first focusing on literacy in science, and the second focusing on literacy and technology, then the classification of the pedagogical discourse has grown. In the first instance of collaboration between science lecturers and the learning and literacy lecturer, semester 1, 1999, the discourse in the tutorials recontextualized from two to three: from the science and pedagogy discourses, to science, pedagogy and linguistic. This occurred because the lecturers decided to adopt genre-based literacy pedagogy to facilitate learning for the students in PSP. This movement also crystallized the nature of the pedagogical discourse in the tutorials: from an eclectic approach to one that foregrounded decontextualization, joint construction and individual construction. The pedagogical discourse of PSP was recontextualized once again with the decision to support the pedagogy with technology. The region was recontextualized from three to four discourses, the additional discourse being a technical discourse.

Recontextualization of the region in PSP as a result of decisions to integrate a technical discourse into the pedagogy has serious implications for the classroom. The dominant discourse, the science discourse, could, if not properly managed, be overcome by the technical discourse. Since the learning outcomes are expressed in terms of scientific understanding, such a result would be disastrous. Thus the lecturers adopting regions need to have sufficient understanding of the potential of subservient discourses to assist learning and to understand their supporting role. In PSP, if the supporting discourses were not subordinated to the science discourse, then this could have led to a poor quality learning experience.

The relationship between the different discourses in the region of PSP can be identified through the following illustrative analysis. In order to get an indication of the role of the discourses during the semester, three tutorials were recorded and transcribed: one tutorial from the beginning of the semester, one from the middle, and one from the end. The transcripts capture only the main classroom level discourse of the tutorial, that between the lecturer and students. Table 12.6 shows extracts of the discourses and percentages of the different discourses.

In order to understand what was happening in the PSP tutorial discourse, the transcripts from the tutorials were analysed for the discourses used in the pedagogy. It became clear with the analysis that there were four discourses working together. The four discourses were the scientific discourse, the

Table 12.6 Distribution of the classroom level discourse region of PSP over three tutorials – substantive and technical discourses

Weeks	Week 2	Week 7	Week 12
No. of words	3700	3356	3663
Substantive discourses	58%	83%	96%
Illustrative example	S: . . . talks about the cell as a unit and that unit shows basic characteristics of life. Explains what they are and then goes on. That's one section – the introduction. [L: Okay.] Then explains how the cell is a component that is used to build up an organism and the organism contains the same characteristics as the cell. [L: And then?] Then it talks about those characteristics example of those characteristics being reproduction and the fact that it occurs in the nucleus of the cell.	S: We did calculations on a statistical thing. [L: What's the statistical thing? The Chi square? Why did you do that?] To see if the ratios were in an acceptable range. [L: Okay, but what was the whole point of the workshop?] The probability of certain traits.	S: Break up the bits . . . the scientific knowledge into areas which are related to each other . . . [L: So if you look at that . . . at that . . . paragraph . . . can you see any patterns or divisions in the science . . .]. Kind of the first sentence . . . tells you when and how . . . photosynthesis first occurs . . .
Technical discourse	42%	17%	4%
Illustrative example	L: So, if you can log into your web site you will see a number of tools on your homepage. One of them is the writing portfolio tasks Just click on that. There you will see the subjects or the name, just go back using the back button back to your homepage. Just click on the bulletin board. This is another tool we will be getting to today as well. Go to the top of your screen and click on back the same way that I am doing it on my screen. We might begin by going back to . . [muffled noise] . . . and finding out tasks, click it like this and go to cell biology.	L: So just save it to your desktop. Make sure you put your initials there, submit it, check the answer in the database first, do that by going back to your database and clicking on answers to exercise 7.1. Once you've done that go onto 7.2. How do you get back to the database? You've got a screen with a block, so click on the grey area like that. Is anybody stuck on how to save to the desktop or submit it?	S: How do I get to the question? L: To get to the question . . . you go . . . once you're there you go back. Scroll up.

pedagogical discourse, which dealt with the Genre-based literacy cycle, a linguistic discourse, which was most evident in the deconstruction phase, and a technical instruction discourse.

The analysis of the transcripts was designed to foreground what was happening to the technical instruction discourse. For this reason, and because at times one phrase could be part of two or more discourses, the discourses were grouped into two: with the scientific, pedagogical and linguistic discourse grouped and called the substantive discourses as one group, and the technical instruction discourse as the other. Table 12.6 shows quotations from the substantive discourse. For example, the second column shows:

> *S: We did calculations on a statistical thing. [L: What's the statistical thing? The Chi square? Why did you do that?] To see if the ratios were in an acceptable range. [L: Okay, but what was the whole point of the workshop?] The probability of certain traits.*

In this example, 'S' is the student discussing the Chi square and 'L' is the lecturer responding.

The last row in Table 12.6 shows extracts of the technical discourse in the three tutorials. For example, the bottom cell in column three shows a simple discussion on web site navigation.

> *S: How do I get to the question?*
>
> *L: To get to the question . . . you go . . . once you're there you go back. Scroll up.*

By analysing the discourses in this way, an interesting trend became evident. At the beginning of the semester, 42 per cent of the tutorial pedagogy was devoted to helping students develop their technological literacy sufficient to access the genre-based materials. As the semester progressed, the percentage of the PSP discourse devoted to technical instruction decreased significantly. The amount of tutorial time devoted to technical instruction went from 42 per cent in week 2, to 17 per cent in week 7 and to 4 per cent in week 12. There are many possible reasons for this, but it is likely that as the level of technical literacy of the students increased, then the need to strongly frame the technical instruction reduced.

11 Conclusion

When technologies, such as those discussed in this study, are used to support genre-based literacy pedagogy, the classification of the pedagogy is likely to become more complex and the delicacy of the framing of the pedagogy increases.

The introduction of genre-based literacy pedagogy into tertiary literacy contexts, in which the pedagogy is a way of helping the students come to terms with the genre of the discipline they are studying, increases the complexity of the substantive discourse. It adds a literacy discourse, which typically increases the number of discourses from two to three. When technology is used to support genre-based literacy pedagogy, the complexity of the substantive discourse increases yet again, moving from three to four discourses as a technical discourse is added. Lecturers using technology to support their pedagogy need to be aware of the potential for subordinate discourses to dominate the substantive discourse. If attention is not paid to this potential, the learning outcomes of the subject may be difficult to attain because of the misalignment among the subordinate and substantive discourses.

When genre-based literacy pedagogy is supported by technologies such as databases and bulletin boards, the framing of the pedagogy becomes more explicit and delicate. The technology provides control over aspects of framing (selection, organization, pacing and timing) so that the needs of the students can be met through more delicate control: one or more aspects of framing can be weakened or strengthened during the teaching and learning cycle depending on the control of the genre displayed by the student.

The use of genre-based literacy pedagogy in tertiary settings is helping students engage with their disciplinary knowledge as they start to become aware of the genres and register that they need to control to be successful students. When genre-based literacy pedagogy is supported by technology, the potential for student control over learning increases. While the technology increases the potential for control, it is not the technology per se that motivates its design. The motivation comes from a well-understood model of learning and teaching, genre-based literacy pedagogy. In all applications of technology in the learning process, the driver should be the learning, rather than the technology. The significance of this for the use of technology in this model of teaching and learning is that the technology should remain subordinate to the substantive discourse and learning outcomes of the learning experience.

References

Atkinson, P.A. (1985) *Language, Structure and Reproduction: An Introduction to the Sociology of Basil Bernstein*. London: Methuen.

Bernstein, B. (1971) *Class, Codes and Control 1: Theoretical Studies towards a Sociology of Language*. London: Routledge & Kegan Paul (Primary Socialisation, Language and Education).

Bernstein, B. (1975) *Class, Codes and Control 3: Towards a Theory of Educational Transmissions*. London: Routledge & Kegan Paul (Primary Socialisation, Language and Education).

Bernstein, B. (1996) *Pedagogy, Symbolic Control and Identity: Theory, Research, Critique*. London and Bristol, PA: Taylor & Francis (Critical Perspectives on Literacy and Education).

Bonanno, H. and Jones, J. (1997) *Measuring the Academic Skills of University Students (MASUS)*. Sydney: University of Sydney Learning Centre.

Drury, H. (2001) 'Short answers in first year undergraduate science writing – what kind of genres are they?', in M. Hewings (ed.), *Academic Writing in Context:*

Implications and Applications. Birmingham: University of Birmingham Press, pp. 104–21.

Drury, H. and Webb, C. (1989) 'Using text analysis strategies to improve student writing', *Research and Development in Higher Education*, 11, 92–9.

Drury, H. and Webb. C. (1991) 'Literacy at tertiary level: making explicit the writing requirements of a new culture', in F. Christie (ed.), *Literacy in Social Processes*. Geelong, Victoria: Centre for Studies of Language in Education, Deakin University.

Ellis, R.A. (2000) 'Writing to learn: designing interactive learning environments to promote engagement in learning through writing', in R. Sims, M. O'Reilly and S. Sawkins (eds), *Learning to Choose, Choosing to Learn*. Refereed Proceedings of the 17th Annual Conference of the Australian Society for Computers in Learning in Tertiary Education Conference. Lismore, NSW: Southern Cross University Press, pp. 155–66.

Halliday, M.A.K. (1994) *An Introduction to Functional Grammar* 2nd edn. London, Edward Arnold.

Hewings, A. (2000) 'Disciplinary engagement in undergraduate writing: An investigation of clause-initial elements in geography essays'. Unpublished thesis, University of Birmingham.

Lieber, T. (1997) 'Portfolio-based exit assessment: A progress report', *ADE Bulletin*, 116, 23–32.

Martin, J.R. (1999) 'Mentoring semogenesis: "genre-based" literacy pedagogy', in F. Christie (ed.), *Pedagogy and the Shaping of Consciousness: Linguistic and Social Processes*. London: Cassell (Open Linguistics Series), pp 123–55.

Martin, J.R. and Rothery, R. (1988) 'Framing and classification: double dealing in pedagogic discourse'. Paper presented at Post World Reading Congress Symposium on Language and Learning, Mt Gravatt College, Brisbane.

McLeod, S.H. (1992) 'Writing across the curriculum: an introduction', in S.H. McLeod and M. Soven (eds), *Writing Across the Curriculum*. Newbury Park: Sage Publications, pp. 1–11.

Mirahayuni, N.K. (2001) 'Investigating textual structure in native and non-native English research articles: strategy differences between English and Indonesian writers'. Unpublished thesis, University of New South Wales, Sydney.

Raines, P.A. (1996) 'Writing portfolios: turning the house into a home'. *English Journal*, 85(1), 41–5.

Taylor, C. and Drury, H. (1996) 'Teaching writing skills in the Science curriculum', in S. Leong and D. Kirkpatrick (eds), *Different Approaches*. Refereed Proceedings of the 19th Annual Conference of Higher Education Research and Development Society of Australasia (HERDSA) ACT, pp. 864–9.

Woodward-Kron, R. and Thomson, E. (2000) *Academic Writing: A Language-based Approach (CD-Rom)*. Wollongong: Gonichi Languages Services.

13 Teaching academic writing on screen: a search for best practice

Helen Drury

1 Abstract

Over the last 20 years, the teaching of academic writing at university has blossomed with research and practice focusing on both the product and the processes. One of the more influential approaches has been genre-based literacy pedagogy within the systemic functional linguistics (SFL) tradition. This pedagogy engages students in an interactive teaching/learning cycle where they acquire knowledge, understanding, practice in and feedback on the target genres and apply this in producing their own texts for particular purposes. With the movement towards delivery of teaching/learning experiences on screen, the challenge for teachers is, first, how to use the technology to adapt and redesign effective classroom practices such as genre-based literacy pedagogy for an online environment and, second, how to integrate this online environment with other learning contexts. The challenge for students is to create their own learning pathway through the network by choosing meaningful links and in so doing to teach themselves what they need to know, largely by reading, interpreting and interacting with the multimodal meanings on screen. This chapter will attempt to identify key principles for moving genre-based literacy pedagogy to an on-screen environment to teach academic writing in a multimodal context.

2 Introduction

The teaching of academic writing at university has been informed by a number of research traditions which have focused on both the product and the process. Ethnographic and linguistic research into writing and writing practices in many disciplines has accompanied developments in the language theories of rhetoric, discourse analysis, genre theory and systemic functional linguistics (SFL) which underpin much of the teaching of academic writing. Pedagogical practice has also been influenced by movements such as communicative language teaching, student-centred learning, the writing across the curriculum movement and genre-centred pedagogical approaches in both the discourse analysis and the SFL traditions. However, possibly the most recent influence has been afforded by technological advances which can deliver teaching and learning experiences on computer screen. This can either be seen as a largely negative influence prompted by changes in the student population such as increasing class sizes, a more diversified student population and a demand for more flexible course delivery, or as a positive opportunity offering new and possibly more effective ways of teaching and learning. What experts agree on, however, is that this new model for teaching and learning cannot be ignored.

> computers will reshape not just how we read and write and, by extension, how we teach these skills but our understanding of basic terms such as *reading, writing* and *text.* (Tuman 1992: 8; author's emphasis)

Although this new teaching and learning environment is flexible in that students can access it in their own time and at their own pace, it places more responsibility on students to structure their own learning by using the medium and in so doing to teach themselves what they perceive they need to know to fulfil their learning goals. For many students, especially those new to the university or from disadvantaged or non-English-speaking backgrounds, this can be a huge challenge. For students already struggling with academic literacy, this way of learning necessitates the negotiation of other literacies which have been termed 'multiliteracies' (Cope and Kalantzis 2000: 5) involving multilayered grammars (Selfe 1989). Overall, although many online learning environments have been developed, there is still much controversy about what and how and even whether students learn online (Alexander and McKenzie 1998). As teachers move into this new medium of instruction, they not only need to learn how to use the new technology to create learning materials and experiences online but also to decide how, and to what extent, they will integrate these online materials with their current curriculum and assessment practices. Lastly, and most importantly, they will need to assess students' multiliteracy proficiencies on entry to their online or integrated online/face-to-face courses so that appropriate teaching/learning activities can take place to allow students to critically negotiate this new learning environment.

This chapter will attempt to identify key principles for designing an on-screen environment to teach academic writing in a multimodal context. To do this, it will primarily draw on the pedagogical practices based on the theoretical framework of SFL, namely genre-based literacy pedagogy, and explore some of the ways this framework has been or could be adapted to teaching academic writing on screen in university contexts.

3 Moving genre-based literacy pedagogy on screen

Genre-based literacy pedagogy in SFL (Martin 1999) has provided a number of curriculum models for the classroom situation (see Ellis this volume for an example of one such model) which engage students in an interactive teaching and learning cycle where they acquire knowledge and understanding of the target genre and how to apply this in producing their own individual text. The teaching/learning cycle is typically divided into three phases: the modelling or deconstruction phase, joint construction and independent construction. The cycle can be entered at any point according to students' needs and can be accessed at different levels in that teachers can move back and forth between phases as appropriate. The modelling phase allows for all aspects of the genre to be made explicit from social context to lexico or visual grammatical features; joint construction makes the process of genre writing clear by engaging students, with the teacher as guide, in creating an example of the genre; and, finally, individual construction moves students on to writing/designing a draft of their own text for peer and teacher conferencing before the final version is written/designed. After this stage, students and teacher can engage in a critical analysis of the target genre, questioning the cultural values behind its structure and purpose and re-writing/re-designing it as a different genre (see Martin 1999; Cope and Kalantzis 1993 for more information on the genre-based teaching and learning cycle).

The genre-based literacy curriculum model described briefly above was initially developed to meet the literacy needs of the primary and secondary school. Within the university context this approach has been adapted in a number of ways (see Jones this volume) for face-to-face teaching of academic genres in a variety of disciplinary contexts. These contexts vary considerably and hence the 'curriculum' for teaching academic writing can be described along a continuum from a field-rich teaching/learning situation to a genre-rich situation as illustrated in Figure 13.1.

For example, a field-rich curriculum context for teaching academic writing can be seen within the core curriculum for first-year undergraduate study in the biological sciences at Sydney University, a one-semester course. The teaching/learning cycle primarily for the laboratory report genre in this field at this level is illustrated in Figure 13.2.

As with other on-screen teaching and learning environments, it is these tried and tested face-to-face classroom approaches to teaching and learning that largely form the basis for the on-screen design (New London Group 2000; Snyder 1999; Young 1999).

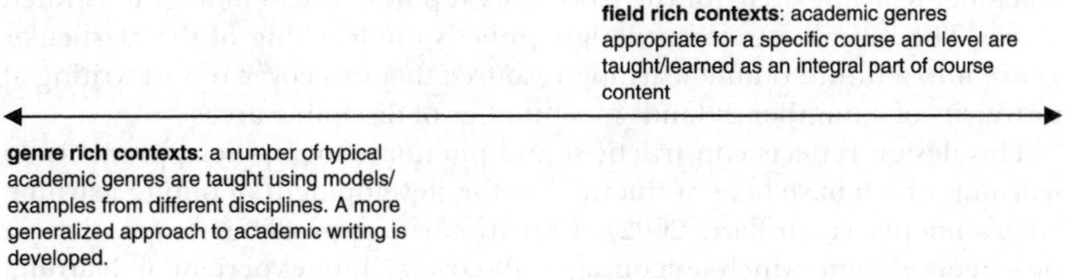

field rich contexts: academic genres appropriate for a specific course and level are taught/learned as an integral part of course content

genre rich contexts: a number of typical academic genres are taught using models/examples from different disciplines. A more generalized approach to academic writing is developed.

Figure 13.1 Continuum of contexts for teaching academic writing at university

THE TEACHING/LEARNING CYCLE

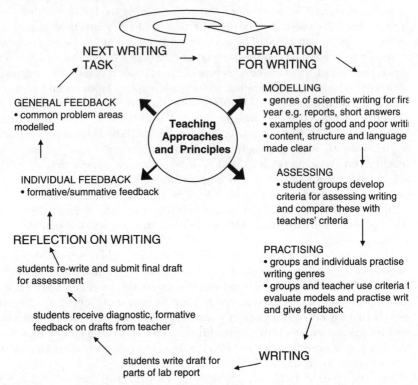

Figure 13.2 The teaching/learning cycle in first-year biology at Sydney University (Taylor and Drury 2002)

Moving most if not all genre-based literacy pedagogy on screen means that some, or even all, the instructional framework and discourse must also be on screen, whether integrated into an on-screen program, or through audio accompanying a program, or as part of online interaction through discussion, chat room, bulletin board, email, etc. Figure 13.3 illustrates one of the forms this pedagogy has taken in an on-screen adaptation of the teaching/learning cycle for the laboratory report genre in biology illustrated above. The overall on-screen design embeds the teaching of this particular genre into a future online learning resource that can cover report writing at university of a number of kinds in a number of discipline areas.

This design reflects constructivist and phenomenographic approaches to learning which have been influential in the development of online learning environments (Laurillard 2002). Constructivist approaches emphasize an on-screen design which encourages discovery and experiential learning while phenomenographic approaches focus on learners' conceptions of the subject matter as the basis for learning through interaction with on-screen

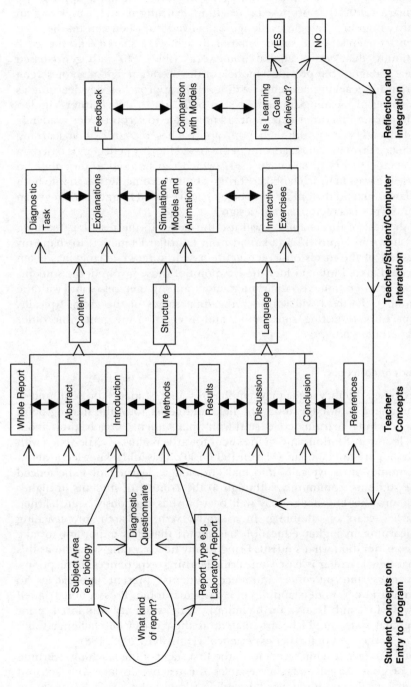

Figure 13.3 Flow-chart illustrating the teaching/learning cycle behind the on-screen Writing Reports at University program (Drury and O'Carroll 1999)

teacher designs or concepts. Drawing on phenomenographic approaches, Laurillard (2002) has proposed a teaching/learning model comprising an iterative, ongoing dialogic exchange or conversation between teacher and student concepts of the subject matter to achieve a shared learning goal. Combining this 'conversational framework' (ibid.: 86) with genre-based literacy pedagogy can provide a model for the overall design of an on-screen program for teaching academic writing. Both approaches view learning as the sharing of meanings in context and both aim to shift learners' under-standing from first-order experiential knowledge to second-order academic knowledge. However, although both approaches recognize that learning takes place through language, only genre-based literacy pedagogy is based on a systematic theory of language (SFL) which can be used to describe and analyse the ways in which language brings about learning. Research into both the classroom and the online discourse of genre-based literacy pedagogy can then inform on-screen program design.

In the rest of this chapter, I will use the stages in the teaching/learning cycle shown in Figure 13.3 (adapted from Laurillard's model) to shape my discussion of the forms on-screen genre-based literacy pedagogy has taken and could take. I will consider the viewpoint of those involved, the students and the teachers, and also their interactions among themselves and with the technology. Lastly, I will consider the final stages of the cycle, typically, the space for reflecting, questioning and integrating the genre into other domains of learning.

4 Student concepts

Genre-based literacy pedagogy emphasizes that students present under-standing and knowledge about the field and genre form the starting point of the teaching/learning cycle 'start with what students already know about the relevant institutions and guide them towards realms of experience with which they are not familiar' (Martin 1999: 130). This initial knowledge about a phenomenon is typically informal knowledge, learned or experienced in the students' community, although in the context of students in higher education, this knowledge may well be what has previously been learned in earlier years of schooling. In a similar vein, research into teaching and learning in higher education has shown that it is important to take into consideration what students bring to any new learning situation as this is what new learning is based on. Prior learning experiences, perceptions, approaches and outcomes influence students' present approaches to learning and new understandings of a particular topic (Prosser and Trigwell 1999; Taylor and Drury, forthcoming): 'The students' supposed prior conceptual state should be articulated, as then it can be challenged and refined in the light of further experience' (Laurrilard 2002: 188)

In face-to-face teaching situations, the first stage of the teaching/learning cycle of genre-based pedagogy enables the teacher to take into account learners' starting positions, what disciplinary knowledge and skills they bring to the classroom situation and their conceptions of the genre and the writing process. As well as these knowledge-sharing interactions between teacher and student, these initial teaching/learning situations may also involve students in a diagnostic reading and writing task integrated into their course of study (Bonnano and Jones 1997). Feedback on this task informs both teachers and students about student levels of control of one of the target genres of their course and both students and teachers can then build on this base level knowledge (Taylor and Drury 1996).

In contrast to the classroom situation, online programs are unlikely to have a fixed beginning point after the entry screen, even if they recommend a staged approach to the learning situation. Students typically create their own learning pathway as they move through the program: 'The reader of a hypertext not only chooses the way she reads but her choices in fact become what it is'. (Joyce 1997: 179) Also, in the classroom situation, all students generally work through the same content despite different entry levels, whereas an on-screen program offers students a choice in learning so that they can begin the program according to their present knowledge and needs. This is particularly useful in the case of teaching academic writing where students' needs vary considerably given their diverse backgrounds in terms of both language and education. However, this approach assumes that students already have some knowledge of their starting positions in terms of the genre they are learning which is not necessarily the case for all students. Programs can help students to reflect on what they already know by setting them diagnostic tasks. For example, the diagnostic questionnaire (see Figure 13.3) for the laboratory report writing program in biology has been influenced by phenomenographic research and adapted from the Approaches to Study Inventory (Entwistle and Ramsden 1983) which itself was adapted for online delivery in 1994 as the PASS package (Personalized Advice on Study Skills) (Tait and Entwistle 1996). Questions invite students to identify with a particular understanding of writing the report or parts of the report, an understanding shaped by their past experiences and approaches. Students' responses can be used to guide them to the parts of the program where their conceptions differ markedly from those required in the context.

5 Teacher concepts

Genre-based pedagogy emphasizes the importance of a 'visible and interventionist' role for the teacher (Martin 1999: 124). In any academic writing program, this means that both the pedagogical context of the learning space and the social context of the materials within that space need to be made explicit so that students understand what the purpose of the learning program is and the role of academic writing and genres in the discourse communities they are joining. In this sociocultural approach, new students to the 'community' are 'apprenticed' into the academic culture. Apprenticing begins in the initial stages of genre-based pedagogy as teachers and students share their understandings of the genre and its discipline purpose and context. However, the extent to which a 'thick' description (Swales 1990) of generic context is provided depends on the overall purpose of the program, the particular needs of the target audience and the specific knowledge about academic writing and genres designers/teachers wish students to understand. Typically information about the pedagogical context (the learning goals of the program, why it is important, how to learn from the program, how it links to the curriculum and to assessment practices) and the sociocultural context (the purpose of the genre, the importance of the genre within the discipline, how this genre relates to others) is provided explicitly on entry to the program, although this information is also provided through the examples, explanations and interactions of the program itself. This orientation information can also be provided off screen through face-to-face interaction with the teacher. In fact, even if the on-screen program provides a rich contextualization of the genre, it is still important, if possible, for teachers to introduce the program, its goals, characteristics, importance and place in the curriculum and assessment procedures in the face-to-face situation.

Teacher concepts are presented at every stage of the teaching/learning cycle but most intensively and authoritatively at the deconstruction stage, when the teacher explicitly uses example or model texts to present information on the characteristics of the genre within its discipline context. The teacher moves from the macro-level to the micro-level, linking the macro-characteristics of purpose and context to choices in the lexico or visual grammar of the text examples. At the same time as students learn the typical features of the genre they also learn a metalanguage to be able to talk about these features in the examples they are exploring and in their own writing and images and that of their peers. In the same way, an on-screen design needs to deconstruct the genre by using the available technology to allow students to move between the macro- and micro-levels of description and analysis of the text examples on display while at the same time making the linkages between the different levels and their realizations explicit. Instead of print-based teaching materials, the teacher/designer needs to create a hypertext learning environment which consists of an on-screen network composed of blocks or modules of linked multimodal texts through which learners will navigate in different ways.

When students enter an on-screen hypertext environment, they are presented with an overview or menu of the parts of the program in the form of a choice of hyperlinks – 'devices to orient navigation: graphic overviews, concept maps, directions, web views' (Snyder 1996: 18). This overview creates meaning in terms of its textual and visual content and also in terms of its network and layout design, although, as with printed materials, students will 'read' the meaning in a number of ways

> links change the way in which material is read and understood . . . though it is far from inevitable that the connection a designer/author intends is the one that readers will necessarily draw. (Burbules 1997: 105)

When creating a program to teach academic writing, it makes sense to draw on a theory of language to inform the design of such a program. SFL can provide a useful framework for the teacher/designer to create a meaningful network choice system for a particular purpose within a particular context. In the SFL model, meaning-making systems are described in terms of strata or levels where higher level or more generalized abstract descriptions of meaning-making, for example, choices among genres, are realized by choices in lower-level strata such as choices of stages in the schematic structure of a genre or, at a lower level, choices of patterns of wordings or representations in the lexicogrammar or visuals of a particular stage. These interconnected systems of visual and/or verbal meaning-making can be used to create a network of hyperlink menus and sub-menus which are not only a means of interacting with and navigating through the program but also an overview of the knowledge about language that the program aims to teach: 'Overviews organize efficiently a body of complex ideas whose centre will vary in the opinion of different readers and writers' (Snyder 1996: 18).

For example, the navigation system of the laboratory report writing program in Figure 13.4 is designed to allow students to learn about the elemental genres (Martin 1994) that make up the report, the schematic structure within each genre and the language choices that realize this struc-

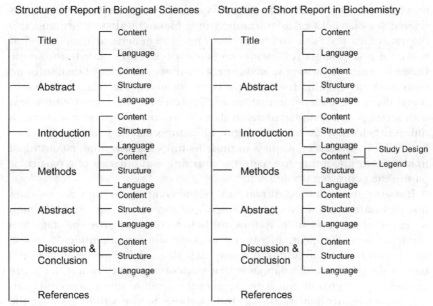

Figure 13.4 Navigation design for the Laboratory Report Writing Program in Biological Sciences and Biochemistry (Drury 2001)

ture. The menu design itself shows students the macro- and micro-level structure of a report. The macro-menu was created using headings which reflect the different parts of the report, typically, abstract, title, introduction, methods, etc. Each macro-menu item in turn has its own sub-menu, generally consisting of three parts which are related to learning about the schematic structure and lexico/representational grammar of each elemental genre, namely, content, structure and language (see Figure 13.3 and Figure 13.4). In general, this two-level hierarchy and the repetition of the sub-menu items within each part create a simple but effective navigation framework. Where there are genre variations in the schematic structure, as in the short report for biochemistry which has two different macro-stages, namely, Study Design and Legend, these are identified in a further sub-level in the hierarchical structure within the Methods part of the report. This short report genre, in fact, has no Methods section since it is largely replaced by the two new sub-parts. However, the more traditional and familiar report design has been retained so as to guide students from the more familiar structure they have met in first-year courses in biology to this new structure required for their report in the second-year course in biochemistry. In this way, the different purposes of the two kinds of reports and hence their structures are made clear.

To some extent, a computer-based mode of delivery lends itself to learning about generic structure as the schematic structure of the genre can be used to create hyperlinks as we have seen above in the laboratory report genre and each link takes the student to a chunk or block of text which has its own internal cohesion and meaning. On screen, the genre becomes an interrelated set of blocks of text arranged in a hierarchical structure and this diagram of the text can enhance understanding of generic structure and how blocks of text (sub-genres, elemental genres) build up to create the whole (macro-genre or hybrid or mixed genre). Within each block of text, software tools such as highlighting, roll-overs, animations, etc. can be used to reveal discourse, lexicogrammatical and representational aspects of the text with accompanying explanations so that the way meanings operate through different selections and combinations of features can be made explicit (see Figure 13.5). On-screen displays of these features enhance understanding of how they work together to create the meaning and purpose of a particular part of the genre as a whole.

However, the structural display unit of the computer – the screen – does not necessarily contain the visual display of a generic stage, and although screen scrolling is possible, it does not help to conceptualize the stage as a whole, as text disappears off screen, making connections difficult among and between parts. In addition, since each stage in the genre makes up a part of the program, the danger is that students may understand the genre as made up of separate unrelated segments instead of interconnected parts which each contribute meaning and purpose to the whole text. At the moment, the only way students gain an overview of how the parts make up the whole is through a print copy. In the laboratory report programs, a

CONCLUSION: Language: Information Structure

 Conclusion
Cost assessment of purchasing a new tower or repacking an existing one shows that the two options do not differ too greatly in price. The main discrepancy between the costs arises from the difference in down time of the plant. Purchase is more expensive in the short term, but the 'down time' factor makes it cheaper in the long run. Considering that in the next few years the tower will need to be replaced anyway, it is recommended that a new tower is purchased.

 Previous   Next

The preferred option, already introduced in the first sentence, becomes the focus of the sentence beginnings in the last 2 sentences.

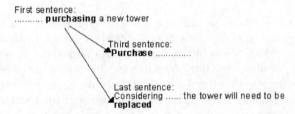

Figure 13.5 Part of the screen display making explicit the information structure of the conclusion of the chemical engineering laboratory report. The feedback is in the lower half of the screen.

menu item 'Whole Report' does attempt to provide some linkage between the different parts of the report mainly through the role of the aim, as macro- theme in the report. Rolling the cursor over the participants in this macro-Theme highlights the linked participants in the results and discussion sections.

In the joint construction phase of the cycle, teachers and students model and practise the process of writing the genre, drafting and re-drafting, deleting irrelevant material, synthesizing and integrating material. In the classroom situation, this is an interactive process and the extent to which it can be an interaction on screen is discussed below.

6 Interaction

In the face-to-face situation, student learning is facilitated by interactions with the teacher and with peers. It is these interactions that bring about learning. Genre-based literacy pedagogy uses the term 'scaffolding' to describe student/teacher interactions as the teacher's modelling, questioning, prompting and commenting guides learners to slowly and systematically articulate their knowledge and understanding of the genre until a shared conception is reached. In a similar vein, teaching approaches influenced by phenomenographic research highlight the importance of teachers engaging with students in an adaptive and iterative 'dialogue' or 'conversation' to make explicit and share their understandings of topics or concepts in their discipline and this interaction brings about learning (Ramsden 1992; Prosser and Trigwell 1999; Laurillard 2002). This practice of 'guidance through interaction in the context of shared experience' (Martin 1999: 126) is a feature of all stages of the learning cycle but it is most prominent at the joint construction stage when students and the teacher jointly construct the genre. Interaction and scaffolding also enable students to learn and use the metalanguage associated with genre construction. The ability to use a language to talk about features of their own writing, use of visuals or other media is a powerful way of developing multiliteracies.

Studies of the classroom discourse of scaffolding have tracked the way spoken language accompanies and facilitates student learning (Christie 2000; Martin 1999). Shifts in the ways that students and teachers are using language to talk about the topic (field), their increasing use of technical and abstract language (mode) and the changes in the degree of control of the interaction by teacher and students (tenor) have been analysed to display the gradual development of a shared understanding brought about through spoken interactional language. Shifts in field knowledge occur as students' initial or informal understandings of the world (first-order knowledge) are moved through teacher guidance towards the formal discipline-based knowledge of the world (second-order knowledge). This shift involves changes in mode as teachers and students move from the mode of speaking about disciplinary knowledge in everyday, common-sense ways to the more abstract formal language used to write or represent how disciplines view the world. Shifts in tenor between teachers and students occur as teachers move from explicit modelling of the genre through interaction to student control of the production of the genre.

It is certainly difficult if not impossible for an on-screen program to create the discourse of scaffolding recorded in face-to-face interactions which studies suggest is essential for learning to take place. However, interaction does take place with on-screen displays whether they are in the form of programs, discussion lists, chat rooms, or emails, etc. and whether the interaction is solely with the computer or among students and teacher mediated by the computer. The question is how and to what extent these interactions bring about learning.

7 Interaction with the computer

The shifts in learners' understanding of the genre brought about by scaffolding in the face-to-face situation rely on learners navigating through the on-screen program according to their changing interests and needs and integrating their growing understandings of each screen display to build up a concept of the whole. Although learners have more control of this process than in the classroom, scaffolding on screen relies on students' constant awareness of what they are learning; essentially, scaffolding is a cognitive exercise, a dialogue with one's self. Typically, learners will attempt to create a coherent pathway through the learning program and draw on familiar 'reading' strategies. A hypertext structure and labelling system that provides a coherent overview can in itself aid learning in this environment. For example, the structure of an on-screen academic writing program can present an authoritative hierarchy of knowledge about the genre – the teacher's concept – which shapes learners' own understandings. However, research suggests that learning will not necessarily be any different or better than learning from and interacting with materials presented in print form (Foltz 1996) and, in some cases, particular kinds of structural overviews may even inhibit a deeper understanding of the content especially for less knowledgeable learners (Hofman and van Oostendorp 1999). In addition, it must be remembered that hypertext designs give a biased view since they 'exclude other knowledge options' (Luke 2000: 71): 'The use and placement of links is one of the vital ways in which the tacit assumptions and values of the designer/author are manifested in a hypertext – yet they are rarely considered as such' (Burbules 1997: 105).

Unlike print-based teaching materials, on-screen materials for deconstructing genres, such as model and example texts or visuals, allow students to actively follow hyperlinks or highlighted hot spots which immediately reveal aspects of their discourse and lexicogrammatical or representational structure. This interaction, both a physical and a mental interaction, it is claimed, is the basis for a deeper engagement with the learning materials, since students have to reflect and think critically to make the connections between the different modules of information for themselves (Snyder 1996; Bolter 1998) Certainly, a network of hyperlinks can reinforce the ways in which the genre is understood as a series of stages realized through choices at the discourse and lexicogrammatical or representational levels. In addition, an on-screen program can offer a database of different kinds of examples of a genre than would be possible in a typical classroom situation and students can access and interact with these according to their learning goals and needs (Ellis 2000). As in the classroom situation, students will need to test their understandings as they build up their knowledge of the genre and they can do this through interaction with the exercises or tasks in the program and the feedback generated through this interaction.

Although on-screen interactive exercises or tasks have been adapted from classroom exercises developed to enhance genre understandings or genre writing, the types of exercise or tasks on screen are constrained by the technology, many of them adapted to a multiple choice or yes/no format. It is difficult to design these tasks, similar to drill and practice exercises, to address more complex rhetorical concepts and even if this can be achieved, students are not given the opportunity to articulate their own understandings but are simply asked to interact by clicking to show their agreement or disagreement with a computer/teacher articulation. More open-ended exercises can only invite students to mentally 'articulate' their own understandings, for example, whether a genre example meets the evaluation criteria for an assignment task, and use their own judgement to see if this is close to the computer/teacher feedback. Even when typing, text boxes are given for students to articulate their own understandings in writing and compare these to standardized feedback, it is up to the students to judge to what extent their understandings match those of the computer/teacher. Although these kinds of exercises certainly allow students to take more responsibility for their learning, they are a challenge for weaker and less motivated students, who may well be unable or unwilling to make the necessary articulations and comparisons.

Providing appropriate, concise computer/teacher feedback is also a challenge for the teacher/designer. Unlike the dynamic classroom situation, where the possibility exists for teachers to gauge student understanding and continue with scaffolding when appropriate, this is not possible on screen within the confines of typical learning program tasks. Students' individual needs are unlikely to be met through computer feedback, even though experienced teachers will attempt to address typical student problem areas in the program design. In particular, it appears that the needs of poorer performing students fail to be met by computer-based feedback despite their longer engagement with the program (Peat and Franklin 2003)

Hyperlink and interactive exercise design can be made sensitive or adaptive to students' interactions so that the student learner shapes the environment to their own needs. For example, diagnostic exercises as discussed earlier can help students to assess their background knowledge and abilities, and in this way guide them to parts of the program that suit their particular needs. Student responses to exercises can also be programmed to take students on different pathways through a program or provide more or less information according to learners' abilities. However, these types of design are not only technically challenging but also demanding in terms of their instructional design (see Figure 13.6 for the first stage of a prototype design for the introduction part of a laboratory report writing program for first-year chemistry where students' responses take them on different pathways through the program). It is also the case that these kinds of designs restrict student control over the level of engagement they wish to have with the program. Those students seeking information or checking their understandings in a particular area may well decide not to enter such a program, as finding the specific information they are seeking would not be possible without 'doing the program'. However, this kind of situated learning comes closest to scaffolding towards a shared understanding of the genre which is found in the face-to-face situation as each student response is linked to knowledge about the genre which is appropriate to their current level of understanding. Also 'learning-by-doing', it is claimed, is closer to students' prior experiences of interacting and learning from computers outside the university context, particularly in the context of computer games (Johnson-

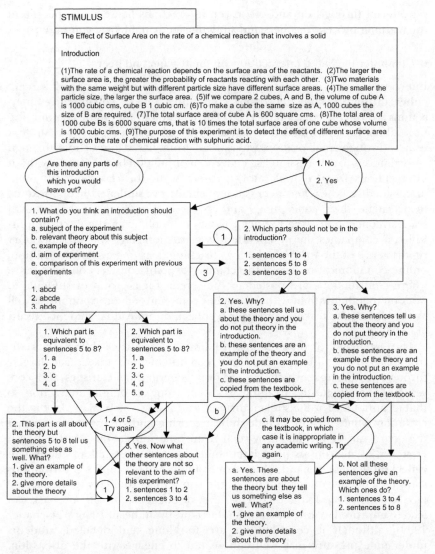

Figure 13.6 Adaptive hyperlink prototype design for laboratory report for chemistry

Eilola 1997; Smith and Curtin 1997). However, once again, students do not articulate their understandings, either in speech or writing, and the ways in which teacher concepts are expressed through feedback and program design are far removed from teacher scaffolding in the classroom. In addition, the sociocultural dimension of learning within a community is absent from mere interaction with an on-screen program, although these dimensions can be introduced through on and off screen interactions between the people in the learning process, teachers and students, mediated by the computer.

8 Computer-mediated interaction with the teacher and peers

Interaction with teachers and peers can take place either on or off screen, either through online networked communication or collaborative inter-actions around the computer screen. The technology for online communica-tion allows for individual interactions between teacher/peer and student usually through email or more widespread group-based interactions through contributions to a discussion list, chat room or bulletin board with or without interventions from a moderator/teacher. As in the classroom situation, discussion lists or teacher/peer–student emails give students the opportunity to articulate their conceptions and to receive feedback in the form of teacher conceptions (see Extract 1 for an example from the discussion list which accompanies the independent construction stage for the laboratory report genre of the writing in biology teaching/learning cycle). In addition, online communication offers the chance for joint construction of a genre where contributions are posted to the screen for a group of students to work on together with or without teacher comments or contributions, as well as the chance for teacher and peer feedback on individual students' drafts (Ellis 2000).

The 'language' of on-screen scaffolding and feedback differs markedly from face-to-face interactions. On-screen interactions take place largely through written text which has its own generic characteristics and con-ventions. Paralinguistic meaning is absent from an online interaction so that it cannot mirror the spoken form of scaffolding which takes place in the classroom where the often subtle shifts in moving students towards control of the genre can be facilitated by such features as intonation (Martin 1999). However, asynchronous or delayed time discussion lists allow students to reflect on the task at hand, which can result in more complex contributions showing a deeper understanding of the issues than are likely in the face-to-face situation (see Extract 1). This level of engagement with the task can lead to improved writing outcomes (Harris and Wambeam 1996; Warschauer 1999), although if contributions are too long and detailed, students under time pressure may well choose not to engage with the discussion. (Warschauer 1999).

Extract 1: Discussion list extract illustrating online scaffolding for the laboratory report genre

Student says: Aren't we trying to use reference material to improve the actual testing procedure. Isn't the aim of the discussion section to discuss not how to improve the actual quality of water, but the means to which its quality is known? ie the limitations and subsequent improvements which can be made. The reference materials don't really provide much info on this. Am I discussing the wrong thing, or ??? thanks.

Teacher says: Yes, you're correct and definitely on the right track – there are numerous limitations to the way, and rigour with which, we tested the water – as you can see by comparing our protocol with those in the refs eg NHMRC. Look at the detail in their testing procedures both in terms of qualitative tests and quantitative measures. (Sorry I can't go into more detail here- otherwise I'll have written the discussion for you!) Of course you can also mention ways to try improving the water quality so that it could be OK to drink – they are suggested in the refs too. You'll find you can't do everything without running out of words, choose a few relevant examples of improvements to discuss.

(Webteach: Hughes and Hewson 1998)

However, contributions can also be basic question and answer interactions requiring a 'quick fix' approach (see Extract 2).

Extract 2: Discussion list extract illustrating online scaffolding for the laboratory report genre

Student 1 says: I'm just wondering what the EPA site is? Never heard of it before.
Student 2 says: In reply to Student 1. Look at the required reference material which you should have purchased from the copy centre. It has the url for the epa (http://www.epa.gov/safewater/source/therule.html). If you were wondering, EPA stands for Environmental Protection Agency. Hope this helps.

(Webteach: Hughes and Hewson 1998)

Although all students have the opportunity to contribute as in the classroom situation, many students remain 'listeners' or lurkers and do not go through the process of actually articulating their own understandings. However, student evaluations of the biology laboratory report discussion list site point to the benefit that lurkers (90 per cent of the cohort (780 students) also obtain from having common problems addressed (Taylor 2002). The teacher can respond to a particular student's conception and in this way give specific feedback pertinent to that particular student's understanding at that moment in time and since this response is available for all students to read, the teacher may well be providing scaffolding for a number of students. If the discussion list is closely linked with the context and purpose of assessment tasks, it will be extensively used (Lea 2001). For example, 95 per cent of students visiting the biology laboratory report discussion site reported that they used it in their report writing (Taylor 2002). However, students may still find it difficult to integrate the content of online discussions into the assignment task (Lea 2000) and may well need teacher modelling and guidance to do so (Lea 2001).

9 Reflection and integration

In the university context, successful learning of academic writing and genres (including multimodal genres) is evident if the student can independently complete assignment tasks across the disciplines they are studying to an acceptable level of competence: 'Becoming fully literate in today's society, at least in the industrialized world, means gaining competent control of representational forms in a variety of media and learning how those forms best combine in a variety of genres and discourses' (Warschauer 1999: 177). This level of competency shows a degree of reflection on and integration of knowledge about the typical genre conventions of the discipline and the process of writing in an academic context. Although genre-based literacy pedagogy includes spaces for integration and reflection at every stage of the cycle, these activities occur more towards the end of the cycle when students are constructing their own genre to fulfil the course requirements and moving towards a critical orientation towards the genre itself. In the face-to-face situation, reflection and integration at this stage are facilitated by feedback from teacher and peers. On screen, students are directing their own learning experience and creating their own curriculum through their choice of pathways through the program, an activity that requires both reflection as to where to go next and integration with what has gone before. Reflection on their own practices and knowledge can be encouraged through interaction with diagnostic and other tasks or through contributing to and responding to a discussion list, especially if this is linked to the joint and independent construction phases. However, the success of these activities depends on the teacher/moderator who designs the feedback or shapes the discussion. Integration of knowledge about genre product and processes learned on screen can be encouraged through linking on-screen programs and associated networked interactions with the goals and assessed assignments of a particular course.

Although university assignments will generally require an analytical, critical and persuasive approach to the topic, they do not usually require a critical orientation to the genre, that is, students are not required to question and critique the actual genre that is used to present their point of view. In addition, as yet, few academic assignments draw on the new genres associated with hypertext which are seen to be questioning or 'remediating' (Bolter 2001) the more traditional essay and report genres of the university (see Kairos 8.1 Spring 2003 Issues of New Media http://english.ttu.edu/kairos/ for examples of some of these new genres in an academic context). Thus, the critical orientation phase of genre-based literacy pedagogy, an extension of independent construction, is largely absent in most academic writing programs, whether on or off screen. The emphasis is more on controlling of rather than challenging of the genre and the main challenge is whether students can transfer and, if necessary, transform their on-screen learning to new contexts with similar purposes and make comparisons across and between genres; in other words, be able to effectively use the discourses of the communities they are joining. If, for example, students have access to a report writing resource where the genres for different disciplines and purposes are juxtaposed, they can begin to understand how effective communication involves a choice between and among a variety of meaning-making resources and that their choice will be shaped by the context and purpose of the task they are engaged in. Such a resource on screen situates the report genre among multiple perspectives and provides the basis for students to adopt a critical and transformative approach as it reveals the sociocultural practices behind the reporting of disciplinary knowledge.

10 Conclusion

In searching for key principles for moving genre-based literacy pedagogy for teaching academic writing and genres to an on-screen medium, we have considered aspects of the teaching/learning cycle that involve the participants – students and teachers, their interactions and the learning goal. For students, the chance to engage with a program according to their needs and interests combined with the integration of the program into their own curriculum and its assessment practices gives meaning to their pathways through the program. For teachers, the medium allows them to design new curricula to display on screen their insights and knowledge about academic writing and genres and the discourse communities in which they are used. These designs exploit the qualities of a hypertext and database environment to change the way students conceive the product and process of academic writing within different discourse communities. Interaction between teacher and students and among students is the key to learning both on and off screen. At the moment, on-screen tasks which rely on computer-based feedback cannot provide a rich scaffolding environment. However, electronic and around-screen interactions focusing on these tasks and the joint and independent construction of genres can go some way towards providing the scaffolding for students to gain mastery over the genre conventions they need for a particular purpose and audience. Although the design of on-screen programs may encourage deeper learning outcomes and reflection on and integration of knowledge, this will not occur unless there is a clear and meaningful purpose for engaging with the program. Ultimately, an on-screen program can only be successful in terms of the whole-learning context in which it is used.

References

Alexander, S. and McKenzie, J. (1998) *An Evaluation of Information Technology Projects for University Learning.* Canberra: Committee for University Teaching and Staff Development.

Bolter, J.D. (1998) 'Hypertext and the question of visual literacy', in D. Reinking, M.C. McKenna, L.D. Labbo and R.D. Kieffer (eds), *Handbook of Literacy and Technology Transformations in a Post-typographic World.* Mahwah, NJ: Lawrence Erlbaum Associates, pp. 3–13.

Bolter, J.D. (2001) *Writing Space Computers, Hypertext, and the Remediation of Print* 2nd edn. Mahwah, NJ: Lawrence Erlbaum Associates.

Bonnano, H. and Jones, J. (1997) *Measuring the Academic Skills of University Students: The MASUS Procedure, A Diagnostic Assessment.* Sydney: University of Sydney, Learning Centre Publication.

Burbules, N. (1997) 'Rhetorics of the web: hyperreading and critical literacy', in I. Snyder (ed.), *Page to Screen: Taking Literacy into the Electronic Era.* St Leonards, NSW: Allen & Unwin, pp. 102–22.

Christie, F. (2000) 'The language of classroom interaction and learning', in L. Unsworth (ed.), *Researching Language in Schools and Communities.* London and Washington: Cassell, pp. 184–203.

Cope, B. and Kalantzis, M. (1993) 'Introduction: how a genre approach to literacy can transform the way writing is taught', in B. Cope and M. Kalantzis (eds), *The Powers of Literacy: A Genre Approach to Teaching Writing.* London: Falmer Press.

Cope, B. and Kalantzis, M. (2000) *Multiliteracies Literacy Learning and the Design of Social Futures.* South Yarra, Vic.: Macmillan.

Drury, H. and O'Carroll, P. (1999) *How to Write a Report.* http://fybio.bio.usyd-.edu.au/vle/L1/ResourceCentre/CAL/WritingSkills/WritingSkills.html

Drury, H. (2001) 'Short answers in first year undergraduate science writing – what kind of genius are they?', in M. Herrings (ed.), *Academic Writing in Context: Implications and Applications.* Birmingham: University of Birmingham Press, pp. 104–21.

Ellis, R. (2000) 'Writing to learn: designing interactive learning environments to promote engagement in learning through writing', *ASCILITE 2000, Learning to Choose Choosing to Learn.* http://www.ascilite.org.au/conferences/coffs00/

Entwistle, N.J. and Ramsden, P. (1983) *Understanding Student Learning.* London: Croom Helm.

Foltz, P.W. (1996) 'Comprehension, coherence, and strategies in hypertext and linear text', in J.F. Rouet, J.J. Levonen, A. Dillon and R.J. Spiro (eds), *Hypertext and Cognition.* Mahwah, NJ: Lawrence Erlbaum Associates, pp. 109–36.

Harris, L. and Wambeam, C. (1996) 'The internet-based composition classroom: a study in pedagogy', *Computers and Composition,* 13, 353–71.

Hofman, R. and van Oostendorp, H. (1999) 'Cognitive effects of a structural overview in a hypertext', *British Journal of Educational Technology,* 30(2), 129–40.

Hughes, C. and Hewson, L. (1998) 'Online interactions: developing a neglected aspect of the virtual classroom', *Educational Technology,* 38(4), 48–55.

Johnson-Eilola, J. (1997) 'Living on the surface: learning in the age of global communication networks', in I. Snyder (ed.), *Page to Screen: Taking Literacy into the Electronic Era.* St Leonards, NSW: Allen & Unwin, pp. 185–210.

Joyce, M. (1997) 'New stories for new readers; contour, coherence and constructive hypertext', in I. Snyder (ed.), *Page to Screen: Taking Literacy into the Electronic Era.* St Leonards, NSW: Allen & Unwin, pp. 163–82.

Laurillard, D. (2002) *Rethinking University Teaching* 2nd edn. London and New York: Routledge/Falmer Press.

Lea, M. (2000) 'Computer conferencing: new possibilities for writing and learning in higher education', in M. Lea and B. Stierer (eds), *Students Writing in Higher Education: New Contexts.* Milton Keynes: Open University Press, pp. 69–85.

Lea, M. (2001) 'Computer conferencing and assessment: new ways of writing in higher education', *Studies in Higher Education,* 26(2), 163–81.

Luke, C. (2000) 'Cyber-schooling and technological change: multiliteracies for new times', in B. Cope and M. Kalantzis (eds), *Multiliteracies Literacy Learning and the Design of Social Futures.* South Yarra: Macmillan, pp. 69–91.

Martin, J.R. (1994) 'Macro-genres: the ecology of the page', *Network* 21 (Newsletter with news, views and reviews in systemic linguistics and related areas), pp. 29–52. http://minerva.ling.mq.edu.au/Resources/Network/Network.html.

Martin, J.R. (1999) 'Mentoring semogenesis: "genre-based" literacy pedagogy', in F. Christie (ed.), *Pedagogy and the Shaping of Consciousness: Linguistic and Social Processes.* London: Cassell, pp. 123–55.

New London Group (2000) 'A pedagogy of multiliteracies designing social futures', in B. Cope and M. Kalantzis (eds), *Multiliteracies Literacy Learning and the Design of Social Futures.* South Yarra: Macmillan, pp. 9–37.

Peat, M. and Franklin, S. (2003) 'Has student learning been improved by the use of online and offline formative assessment opportunities?', *Australian Journal of Educational Technology,* 19(1), 87–99.

Prosser, M. and Trigwell, K. (1999) *Understanding Learning and Teaching.* Buckingham: SRHE and Open University Press.

Ramsden, P. (1992) *Learning to Teach in Higher Education.* London: Routledge.

Selfe, C. (1989) 'Redefining literacy: the multilayered grammars of computers', in G. Hawisher and C. Selfe (eds), *Critical Perspectives on Computers and Composition Instruction.* New York: Teachers College, Columbia University.

Smith, R. and Curtin, P. (1997) 'Children, computers and life online: education in a cyber-world', in I. Snyder (ed.), *Page to Screen: Taking Literacy into the Electronic Era.* St Leonards, NSW: Allen & Unwin, pp. 211–33.

Snyder, I. (1996) *Hypertext: The Electronic Labyrinth.* Carlton South, Vic.: Melbourne University Press.

Snyder, I. (1999) 'Integrating computers into the literacy curriculum: more difficult than we first imagined', in J. Hancock (ed.), *Teaching Literacy Using Information Technology.* Carlton South, Vic.: Australian Literacy Educators' Association, pp. 11–30.

Swales, J. (1990) *Genre Analysis.* Cambridge: Cambridge University Press.

Tait, H. and Entwistle, N.J. (1996) 'Identifying students at risk through ineffective study strategies', *Higher Education,* 31, 97–116.

Taylor, C. (2002) 'Communicating to learn to write: unraveling the learning process in online discussion in scientific report writing'. Poster presentation at 8th International Conference of the European Association for Research on Learning and Instruction Writing Special Interest Group.

Taylor, C. and Drury, H. (1996) 'Teaching writing skills in the science curriculum', in S. Leong and D. Kirkpatrick (eds), *Proceedings of the Annual Conference of the Higher Education and Research and Development Society of Australasia (HERDSA) Different Approaches: Theory and Practice in Higher Education,* 19, 864–9.

Taylor, C. and Drury, H. (2002) 'Incorporating undergraduate students' prior writing experiences and expectations into an undergraduate science curriculum'. Poster presentation at the International Conference on The First-Year Experience, 1–5 July 2002, Bath, UK.

Taylor, C. and Drury, H. (forthcoming) 'The effect of prior student experience, attitudes and approaches on performance in an undergraduate science writing program', in G. Rijlaarsdam, H. van den Bergh, and M. Couzijn (eds), *Effective Teaching of Writing.* Dordrecht: Kluwer Academic Publishers.

Tuman, M.C. (1992) *Literacy Online: The Promise (and Peril) of Reading and Writing with Computers.* Pittsburgh and London: University of Pittsburgh Press.

Warschauer, M. (1999) *Electronic Literacies: Language, Culture and Power in Online Education.* Mahwah, NJ: Lawrence Erlbaum Associates.

Young, A. (1999) *Teaching Writing Across the Curriculum* 3rd edn. Upper Saddle River, NJ: Prentice Hall.

14   Learning to write in the disciplines: the application of systemic functional linguistic theory to the teaching and research of student writing

Janet Jones

1 Introduction

Over the last decade, discussion of the research and practices of academic writing in universities in Australia has taken place in a climate of rapid change in higher education. The changing face of universities reflects their various responses to pressures both external and internal to the institution. External factors include the expansion of universities as 'knowledge markets', the impact of new technologies and the push from the government and employment sectors to improve the quality of graduate outcomes. These factors can be viewed in a context of shrinking government funding for public universities and their increased accountability to government bodies. Within universities, factors such as the ever-increasing diversity of the student body, the push for more 'flexible' modes of course delivery and increased concern for quality assurance in teaching and learning have all helped to re-focus attention on the practices of academic writing research and pedagogy.

The current focus on student writing in Australia should also be seen in relation to the ongoing debate over the last decade about the falling standards of students' 'generic' skills and attributes. This debate has not been confined to Australia; indeed, the concept of a set of generic, core or key skills, qualities and attributes that support lifelong learning has been firmly placed on the global higher education agenda (Bennett *et al.* 1999; Gibbs *et al.* 1994). Within the concept of generic attributes is an acknow-ledgement, albeit often implicit, of the university's responsibility to develop students' writing. A wide range of views which provide much of the impetus for current research are encompassed by questions such as *whose responsibility is it to teach academic writing to students? why are the 'standards' of their writing declining? what is the nature and purpose of student writing within the academy?* and *what constitutes a 'critical approach' to academic writing pedagogy?*

Viewed through the global context of students learning to write in English at university, this chapter will be mainly concerned with student writing in the context of one Australian metropolitan university. In academic writing pedagogy, students' writing practices may be shaped by different models of language, by the social contexts of these practices and by research which analyses these practices and contexts. A particular focus in this chapter, then, will be on how one theory of language in context, systemic functional linguistics (SFL), has been recontextualized to shape the research and practice of the Learning Centre at the University of Sydney.

Although the teaching of writing in universities in Australia may take place within an academic department such as Linguistics or English, or be the focus of a credit bearing English for Academic Purposes (EAP) course, learning centres are typically charged with the role of assisting students to develop their writing and other 'generic' skills for academic purposes. Such centres are diverse in their location within the institution, the conditions of employment of their staff, their status and the type of work they perform.

In the last few years, however, there has been a shift from a 'marginalized' perception of these units towards a more empowered view of their role and academic standing within the institution. Moreover, as this chapter will show, a meaningful approach to teaching writing in a learning centre can be one which offers students in any discipline an insight into the purposes and contexts of their own writing.

There are two main sections to the chapter. Part 1 discusses academic writing pedagogy and research from an international perspective and concludes with an overview of Australian perspectives. The purpose of this discussion is twofold: first, to highlight aspects of the distinctive and yet complementary approaches to research and practice in the field; and second, to distil some of the key issues of these approaches, which will serve as a backdrop to critically examine the work of the Learning Centre in Part 2.

2 Part 1 Student writing in international contexts: research and practice

Today, those engaged in teaching students to write in English in universities around the world have recourse to a rich tapestry of perspectives on research and pedagogical practices, many of which are broadly framed within socio-cultural theories of language and learning. Contributions from fields of inquiry such as EAP and genre theories, from movements such as writing across the curriculum (WAC), and from studies within 'critical academic literacies' frameworks provide many of the current perspectives. Recent collections of these contributions (Candlin and Plum 1998; Clark and Ivanič 1997; Flowerdew and Peacock 2001; Hewings 2001; Johns 1997, 2002; Jones *et al.* 1999; McLeod *et al.* 2001) reveal many points of convergence. From both research and practitioner perspectives, the collections advocate a more critical awareness of the role of language in constructing texts, writer identities and disciplinary communities, and view writing as a socially and culturally embedded practice. The result is an encouraging acknowledgement that an interdisciplinary approach to research on student writing is a fruitful if challenging way forward for pedagogy (Candlin and Hyland 1999; Flowerdew and Peacock, 2001; Johns 2002; Lea and Stierer 2000).

It is beyond the scope of this chapter to analyse in depth all the issues raised in these collections. However, the following three sections will high-light some of the key issues foregrounded in these collections within the areas of EAP and genre analysis, the writing across the curriculum movement and the academic literacies frameworks.

3 EAP and genre analysis

In recent years, some researchers have expressed concern that broader and more critical approaches to research and practice within EAP and genre analysis are needed. This concern relates to the development of EAP as a discipline and its large scope as an international field of activity today.

3.1 Critical views of EAP

Within the disciplinary framework of EAP, the call for a 'critical view' of EAP (Benesch 1996, 1999; Pennycook 1997) has resulted in rethinking aspects of EAP teacher roles and practices within the university (Dudley-Evans 2001: 233). Benesch (1996, 1999) calls for a more critical role for EAP through redefining and challenging power relations between the EAP teacher, the subject teacher and the student. She argues that traditional collaborative and 'team teaching' approaches (e.g. Dudley-Evans 1984), in which the EAP teacher intervenes in the subject discourse to make it more 'transparent' for the non-native speaker (NNS) student, are not critical enough of how power is manifested in the classroom. She questions traditional approaches to needs analysis, in which students' needs are described in terms of the genres and skills they will need for their target courses, and which have been the foundation (and justification) of much EAP practice. She advocates a shift beyond 'the descriptive approach of needs analysis' to 'rights analysis', which 'examines how power is exercised and resisted in an academic setting, including the pedagogy and the curriculum' (Benesch 1999: 313–14). In addition to being criticized as too 'accommodationist' (Benesch 1993: 714; Pennycook 1994), the EAP enterprise has been characterized as being dom-inated by overly 'pragmatic' approaches, which reinforce the dominant ideology of the university, and aim to 'assimilate . . . students uncritically into academic life and US society' (Benesch 1993: 714). In a defence of pragma-tism, Allison argues that his view of pragmatism in EAP 'does not presuppose . . . a single coherent ideology or discourse' (1996: 86) and he does not assume that 'a discourse or an educational status quo seeks to maintain itself by suppressing dissenting voices' (ibid.: 86). Allison's views, however, are challenged by the 'critical pragmatism' of Pennycook (1997), which attempts to deconstruct the 'discourses of neutrality' he claims are inherent in much of EAP. These discourses, he argues, can be found in claims for the 'univer-sality' of subject-specific discourses, in the neutrality of 'content' and genres for EAP courses and in views of the universities as 'neutral sites' in relation to knowledge and culture (ibid.: 257–63). Pennycook's 'critical *praxis*' of EAP is characterized by a socio-political view of language and knowledge which recognizes that 'language, knowledge culture form a complex tangle that cannot be avoided' (ibid.: 266).

3.2 Broadening the scope of genre analysis

Genre analysis, as conceived by Swales (1990) and elaborated by Bhatia (1993), was based on three key and interlocking elements: the concepts of *discourse community, genre*, and language and learning *task*, driven by communicative purpose. According to Flowerdew and Peacock, the scope of genre analysis has now become broadened to include a more 'dynamic' notion of genre in which 'members of the discourse community (along with their physical situation) now become a primary focus of the analysis, equal to if not more important than the text' (2001: 16). Recent accounts of the different approaches to genre analysis as both research and pedagogy (Hyon 1996; Paltridge 2001; Swales 2001) have also reinforced the shift from detached 'text-bound' analyses of genres to research which provides a much richer account of the contexts in which they occur. This has also resulted in research-led evidence of the disciplinary variation of genres and discourse and a shift away from the view of academic discourse as 'monolithic' and homogeneous and of genres as 'independent' of other related texts. Despite this evidence, however, Swales maintains that 'beliefs about the transparency, the neutrality and the universality of scientific language continue to be widely held within academic and research communities' (2001: 42), and these beliefs remain a source of tension for those engaged in teaching students to write.

This section has provided a selective discussion of some of the key issues within EAP and genre analysis as they pertain to academic writing pedagogy and research. They can be summarized as: the call for more critical approaches to research and pedagogy; debate about the concept of pragmatism and the 'service' orientation of EAP; and a growing recognition of the need to broaden the scope of the language description of genres to include a more critical and ethnographically informed account of the contexts in which students are writing. This latter aspect has strengthened the role of linguistic theory, particularly of SFL theory, in EAP and genre analysis. Interestingly, Flowerdew classifies the approach to genre of those working within SFL in Australia as 'grounded in the linguistic, but with a theoretically and ethnographically informed account of context and discourse communities' (2002: 91).

4 Writing across the curriculum

In the USA, the writing across the curriculum (WAC) movement has become a significant force in the teaching of writing across the academy. Similar to the concern about the standard of students' generic skills in the 1980s and 1990s in Britain and in Australia, the WAC movement grew out of dissatisfaction from employers and universities with the standard of students' communication skills. Recent accounts of the growth of WAC programmes and practices claim that the strength of the movement derives from its adherence over the years to a number of basic principles:

• WAC programmes should incorporate both 'writing to learn' and 'learning to write' approaches
• the quality of student writing is a university-wide responsibility
• writing skills must be practised and reinforced within and across disciplines (McLeod and Maimon 2000; Young 1999).

Originally designed for a less linguistically diverse student population, WAC programmes have recently been challenged to broaden their scope to address the needs of English as a Second Language (ESL) students (Johns 2001). Although the disjunction between WAC programmes and EAP (ESL) programmes may still persist, there are common areas of concern (Bazerman 1998). Within the WAC movement, arguments for a more critical pedagogy in WAC (LeCourt 1996) and for a stronger focus on the socio-cultural and, indeed, socio-political nature of literacy (Villanueva 2001) echo some of the main issues in EAP outlined above. There is, however, a perception that WAC directors do act as 'change agents' in a 'quietly subversive' way (McLeod and Maimon 2000), yet there has been a call for WAC programmes to play a more strategic and proactive role within the academy, to counter the highly individualized and ad hoc responses of many institutions in the United States (Blumner *et al.* 2001).

5 Academic literacies frameworks

Many of the recent publications from the UK and the USA within academic literacies frameworks have points of comparison with the socio-cultural and critical framing of EAP and genre analysis discussed above. In this section I will discuss the major contributions to the field of student writing of academic literacies frameworks in the UK and the USA and conclude by reviewing some key Australian contributions. Each of these frameworks draws on SFL and related theories.

5.1 The UK

The academic literacies approach, based on the research of Lea and Street (1998), offers significant insights into the way in which academic writing is perceived by students and staff in learning support units and faculties. The researchers used an integrated methodology which combined an 'ethnographic style approach' and linguistic analysis in order to interpret a range of interview and textual data. Several points of interest emerged from the research from the student perspective. Students perceived that disciplinary divides were in many cases irrelevant, but were aware of the need to 'unpack' the requirements of each writing task at a more complex level than a genre such as the 'essay' or 'report'. They admitted that their difficulties lay 'in trying to gauge the deeper levels of variation in knowledge' as they moved from subject to subject which went beyond 'using the correct terminology' or just learning to do 'academic writing' (ibid.: 163–4). Lea and Street claim that evidence such as this 'did not appear to support the notion of generic transferable writing skills across the university' (ibid.: 164).

One significant aspect of the research was the delineation of three models of student writing: 'study skills', 'academic socialization' and 'academic literacies'. The distinctions between the three perspectives provide an important conceptual map of the models of student writing and a useful framework for reflection on current practices of writing pedagogy. In the study skills model, which Lea and Street claim is informed by behavioural theories of learning, writing is seen as a set of technical skills which, once learned, can be transferred to other situations. The academic socialization model, informed by psychosocial theories of learning and framed within phenomenographic methodologies (Marton and Booth 1997; Marton *et al.* 1997), focuses more on how students are acculturated into the university context and on how they approach and perceive their learning and their academic tasks. This model conceptualizes student approaches to learning and to their academic tasks as 'surface', 'deep' or 'strategic' while the relationship between language and power is undertheorized (Lea 1999: 105–6; Lea and Street 1998: 159). There is also an assumption that the academic culture is homogeneous, resonating with views of the monolithic nature of academic discourse within EAP and that student writing is 'a transparent medium of representation' (Lea and Street 1998: 159).

The academic literacies model 'sees literacies as social practices . . . and views writing and learning at the level of epistemology and identities rather than skill or socialization' and 'the institutions in which academic practices take place as constituted in, and as sites of, discourse and power' (ibid.: 159). The social and ideological orientation underpinning this approach derives from 'New Literacy Studies' (Barton 1994; Street 1984) with allied fields of enquiry from critical discourse analysis (Fairclough 1992), critical language awareness and writer identity (Ivanič, 1998), SFL (Halliday 1985; Martin 1992) and the earlier work of Bazerman (1988) on the social construction of knowledge. While not outwardly condemning the first two approaches and claiming that the academic literacies model 'successfully encapsulates' the other two models, the authors clearly privilege the third model, since it reinforces the notion that writers' identities and practices are made meaningful within a social context.

5.2 The USA and the Socioliterate approach of Johns

The Socioliterate approach to academic writing pedagogy and research proposed by Johns (1997) in the USA also has at its core a pluralized definition of academic literacies. Her approach is closely related to other socially framed theories of literacy while 'the text and language elements' of the approach 'draw extensively' on SFL (ibid.: 14–15). One significant contribution is her empowered view of literacy teachers in universities. In reviewing the various approaches to collaborative teaching prevalent in the USA and elsewhere (e.g. Content-Based Instruction (CBI), Language-across-the Curriculum (LAC), Writing across the Curriculum (WAC) and team-teaching within EAP), Johns calls for literacy teachers to act as 'mediators' among students, faculty and administrators to collaboratively examine the interactions of the texts, roles and contexts in both research and practice (ibid.: 71–91).

5.3 Australia

Recent student writing research and pedagogy in Australia can also be viewed within academic literacies models and has points of convergence with the approaches outlined above. Baynham (2000) has provided a useful classification of approaches to academic writing pedagogy and their theoretical bases. He identifies three approaches: 'skills-based', 'text-based' (Freedman and Medway 1994; Halliday and Martin 1993; Swales 1990), and 'practice-based' (Bazerman 1988; Latour 1987; Myers 1990) and advocates a combination of the latter two perspectives, since they have 'a powerful potential' for both pedagogy and research (Baynham 2000: 20). Again, the notion that writing practices and pedagogy need to be linked to the context of their use is an underlying theme in his work. In its scope and depth, one of the most significant pieces of research in Australia into academic literacies is the project entitled *Framing Student Literacy: Cross-cultural Aspects of Communication Skills in Australian University Settings.* This four-part project (with teams from four universities) was governed by a view that academic literacies are 'situation-specific' and linked with cultural and disciplinary differences. The Macquarie University team, headed by Chris Candlin, focused on research into the cultures of academic literacies, especially in two major but distinctive disciplines: psychology and computing (Candlin and Plum 1998). Similar to the Lea and Street research, the project employed a multidisciplinary methodology, integrating SFL and Rhetorical Structure Theory (RST) analysis of texts and text structures, discourse analytical studies of writing, ethnomethodological interpretation of participants and processes, and ethnographic accounts of students, tutors and assessment practices.

The research and practices of student writing discussed above within EAP and genre analysis, WAC and academic literacies frameworks have many points of contact. Writing is seen as social practice and the analysis of contextual factors occupy a central position in the research which informs pedagogy. If the ultimate goal of research and pedagogy is to improve the experience of student writers by helping them to control the patterns of language valued by the disciplines, thereby providing a better understanding of the contexts and processes in which they are engaged, a multidisciplinary approach seems to be a productive way forward. The challenge is to keep alive those perspectives on research and practice which are mutually reinforcing and enriching and not to 'end up as pidgin speakers of a range of theories' (Martin 2000b: 123), which would preclude the possibility of a genuine dialectic between theory and practice.

In the discussion of the last three sections, several recurring issues emerge which provide the backdrop for Part 2. If writing is seen as social practice and context is seen as central to the practice, then unpacking the link between text and context is crucial in the push towards a more critical pedagogy. The student writers' choice of concepts and ideas within a discipline, their awareness of the audience for whom they are writing and of their own position in the text seem to demand an understanding of how language works in context and the application of a theory that will provide students with that understanding.

6 Part 2 SFL and student writing: the dialectic of theory and practice

This section is concerned with how SFL theory, as a theory of language in context, has been recontextualized to become the foundation of an approach which supports the research and teaching of student writing. The discussion will focus on how the theory has been engaged in the practice of the Learning Centre at the University of Sydney. To situate the Learning Centre in its Australian context, I will first elaborate on the distinctive role of learning centres in Australia and how they have become positioned to make a key contribution to the area of student writing. I will then illustrate the Centre's approach by discussing two examples of its work. In doing this, issues which have arisen from the discussion in Part 1 will be revisited, particularly in relation to how the 'service' orientation of a centralized learning support unit can be reconciled with a critical approach to practice and how a theory of text in context can be deployed to achieve this.

7 Learning centres in Australia, changing contexts, changing identities

Interestingly, in the academic literacies literature reviewed above, the role of learning units in the UK in teaching writing was described as 'marginal', catering 'largely for students deemed to be non-traditional (Lea and Stierer 2000: 3) and associated with the Study Skills model (Baynham 2000; Street 1999). Lea and Stierer mention the 'growing recognition of the importance of embedding support for student writing within the mainstream curriculum' (2000: 2). They describe this as a 'contrasting approach' to that which is offered within learning units. The approach implied in these comments also contrasts with Johns' (1997) empowered view of literacy teachers as 'campus mediators', with the 'critical' views of EAP practices of Benesch and Pennycook and with McLeod's view of WAC directors as agents of change, reviewed in Part 1.

In the introduction to this chapter, I alluded to the fact that there has been a positive shift in the perception of learning centres in Australia towards a more empowered view of their role and status. In addition, one consequence of the generic attributes agenda has been greater attention given to the role of learning centres in catering not only for the diversity of student writing needs but also in helping to raise faculty staff awareness of the complexities of student writing. The crucial role of learning centres in this process has been acknowledged in Australia for a number of years (Candy *et al.* 1994; Lee *et al.* 1995; Threadgold *et al.* 1997). The shift in perception of learning centre role and status, originating in part from within the units, has also occurred at an institutional and faculty level and has had a major impact on learning centre practice. Pedagogy has moved away from a study skills-based approach to one which has much in common with the academic literacies frameworks outlined in Part 1. Most units adopt an approach which is informed by processes of collaboration between students, staff in academic departments and other administrative units across the institution.

8 Student writing and SFL in Australia

The contributions of SFL to academic writing pedagogy and research in Australia have been acknowledged outside Australia. Within EAP, useful accounts of SFL genre theory and the genre-related pedagogies of the 'Sydney School' have been provided by Feez (2002), Hyon (1996), Johns (1997), Macken-Horarik (2002), with other recent references by Swales (2001: 47–8) and Paltridge (2001: 58). The term 'Sydney School' referred originally to a major intervention into writing pedagogy at the school level, based on the systemic functional linguistics of Halliday, Martin and others at the University of Sydney (Green and Lee 1994: 207–8). Martin (1998, 1999, 2000b) has since elaborated the description to refer more broadly to the work of Hallidayan educational linguists in Sydney in the area of literacy teaching at both school and adult levels. Outside Sydney there is a growing body of work on student writing which has drawn on SFL and other theories, some of which has been reported in conference proceedings such as Chanock (2000) and Golebiowski (1997). Much of the work, however, remains unreported or is difficult to find as it tends to be published not within educational linguistics or EAP journals but in those journals dedicated to teaching and learning within the disciplines or other more general higher education journals.

9 SFL and the work of the Learning Centre

The Learning Centre services a very large and diverse community at the University of Sydney, with over 40,000 students and 17 faculties. The Centre lies outside the college/faculty structure and is located within a central administrative portfolio as a unit of Student Services. The Centre's role is to provide learning and academic skills support for all students regardless of background. Since its inception in 1991, the Learning Centre has offered a programme of support for students in three modes encompassing a large complexity of teaching practice:

- *a Central Programme* of academic skills workshops, offered outside the students' degree courses
- *a Faculty Programme* comprising collaborative work with staff in academic departments to develop students' writing and other areas within their degree courses
- *an Independent Learning Programme* of learning resources designed for individual students and offered in consultation with a lecturer or as computer-based resources for independent study.

From the beginning, SFL theory has played a major role in the development of the Centre's teaching and research. Most of those working at the Centre (past and present) had a background in SFL in the 1980s and 1990s and studied in the Department of Linguistics at the University of Sydney under Michael Halliday and Jim Martin. Although we have been influenced by the work in genre-based literacy pedagogy at school and adult levels mentioned above, we have had to recontextualize the theory for our purposes. Most of us also had a background in EAP and, as 'teacher linguists' we sought a socially framed theory of language that could provide an explanatory account of student literacy practices at all levels of university study and of the contexts in which students have to operate.

Over the years we have continually grappled with issues of consistency, relevance, useability and transferability in the application of SFL. The theory has, however, provided us with a powerful model of language in context. Whether the writing tuition occurs within or outside the students' subject curriculum, the theory can be used as an explanatory tool to help make explicit to students the writing practices of their disciplines. In so doing, it can help build a metalanguage we can use in our interactions with students and subject staff about language and how it means in a given context. To illustrate the Centre's approach, the final section of this chapter uses two examples of our work which focus on student writing. I chose these examples with the intention of highlighting a number of points about SFL theory and its relationship to our work:

- how it has informed our research and teaching practice
- how it has been recontextualized for our students and for staff in the disciplines
- how it has facilitated a genuinely transdisciplinary approach to research and practice.

10 Example 1 Writing a Literature Review

The first example illustrates how aspects of SFL theory have been used in our teaching practice and how the theory has been recontextualized for postgraduate research students writing their thesis.

10.1 Theory informing practice

The example is from a six-hour course entitled *Writing a Literature Review*, which is offered to graduate students in the Central Programme and in the Faculty Programme. The course aims to help students understand the purpose of the literature review as a component of the thesis and reflect on their role as a writer of this component. It also aims to help them understand how language is used to shape the review and to apply these understandings to their own writing. The design of the course has been informed both by collaboration with staff in the disciplines to select valued and relevant texts and by SFL analysis of these texts. Figure 14.1 illustrates this two-way flow of information into the design of the course materials.

Figure 14.2 shows an extract from Part 2 of the course notes for the student. This version was offered to graduate research students from English and non-English speaking backgrounds in the Faculty of Agriculture. Students were at different stages of writing up their literature review. All were reasonably experienced writers but with varying levels of understanding about language. The extract shows the course objectives and course outline, a group exercise (𝕞) and an individual exercise (𝕚).

10.2 Recontextualizing the theory for students

Since the main focus of the course is on the organization and appraisal of the literature selected for the review, students are introduced to SFL concepts

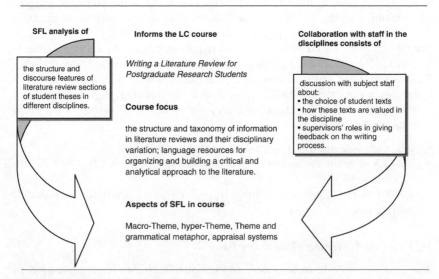

Figure 14.1 Teaching students to write a literature review: the role of SFL and collaboration with staff in the disciplines

WRITING A LITERATURE REVIEW

The objectives of this course are to help you understand your role as a writer in:

• examining the context, purpose and characteristics of the literature review as a component of your thesis
• managing and organizing the literature
• understanding the principles of developing an analytical approach to the literature
• using the language to compare and evaluate sources.

Course Outline:

Part 1:   Organizing the literature
Part 2:   Developing an analytical approach to the literature
Part 3:   Giving the review a focus
Part 4:   The language of evaluation and comparison

Part 2: Developing an analytical approach to the literature

The first step in developing an analytical approach to the literature involves deciding on how you are going to organize the literature. This involves key decisions about

▪   what topics and sub-topics you are going to use to divide up the literature
▪   how you will sequence the literature to fulfil the purpose of the review

2.1   Classifying the literature into topics

On Handout 1 are extracts from the Table of Contents (A) and the literature review (B) from a student thesis on <u>Fleece Rot and Bodystrike</u>.

Look at both extracts and discuss the following questions:
• How do the headings and subheadings in (A) and (B) indicate the organization of the literature?
• Which schema has the writer used to organize the information, e.g. time, importance, generality etc?
<u>Now...</u>
Highlight the first sentences (the hyper-Themes)of each paragraph of (B) and then look at the headings and sub-headings of (B).
• Does the text reflect the organizing schema used by the writer?
• Does this schema relate to the first paragraph (the macro-Theme) in (B)? If so how?

Look at your draft literature review.
• How do your headings and sub-headings reflect your method of organization?
• How have you classified and sequenced the information?
• Does your macro-Theme predict and reflect your hyper-Themes?

Figure 14.2 Extract from Part 2 of the LC course *Writing a Literature Review*

and analyses which help to make these aspects explicit, particularly those related to the textual and interpersonal metafunctions (Halliday and Hasan 1985; Martin 2000a; Rothery and Stenglin 2000). Part 2 of the course, for example, covers some of the language resources of texture (Halliday 1985: 313–18; Halliday and Hasan 1976: 324; Martin 1992: 406–17), which relate to the overall structure of the text. In the exercise shown in the extract in Figure 14.2, students work first in groups through text examples, tracking hyper-Themes. They discuss how these relate to the macro-Theme, headings and subheadings as depicted in the table of contents and in the text itself. They then work individually on their own literature review drafts, applying their understanding of these concepts, with the teacher facilitating the process. Through students' engagement with the text examples and through reflection on their own writing, aspects of the theory are used to make explicit to them how language works to achieve its purpose in a given context.

11 Example 2 The MASUS project

The second example discusses an institution-wide project which has drawn on SFL theory for research and practice. Compared with Example 1, the project has involved a different kind of recontextualization of the theory and has resulted in genuinely transdisciplinary research, bringing together distinct sets of expertise to solve a perceived problem: that of undergraduate student writing in the disciplines.

11.1 Theory informing practice

The Centre was commissioned to develop a diagnostic test instrument to assess students' academic writing skills. The instrument (Measuring the Academic Skills of University Students (MASUS), Bonanno and Jones 1997) was designed as a procedure to be used by faculties as an integral component of their courses and to provide, through the Learning Centre Programmes, a systematic framework for follow-up support for those students identified as needing it.

The MASUS procedure requires students to write a short essay or other genre based on some disciplinary content such as course readings or lectures. The instrument assesses students' ability to write about a given body of knowledge in a reasoned and critical way, together with their ability use the language resources appropriate for the required task. Their writing is rated from 4 (excellent) to 1 (inadequate) on each of four main criteria:

A   Use of the source material
B   Structure and development of the text
C   Academic writing style appropriate for the task
D   Grammatical correctness

Each of these criteria is further broken down into sub-criteria or descriptors, representing a complex spectrum of perspectives on the student's writing, from a macro-level (genre and discourse/register) to a micro-level (lexico-grammar). For example, Criterion C on the rating sheet used by Learning Centre lecturers is shown in Figure 14.3.

C. Academic writing style – does the language conform to the patterns of written academic English appropriate for the task?	4 3 2 1	
Appropriate use of: • grammatical metaphor and nominal group structure • interpersonal metaphor • modality and appraisal systems • taxonomic relations (Theme and hyper-Theme) • resources of cohesion (conjunction, lexical cohesion, reference) A = appropriate NA = not appropriate	A	NA

Figure 14.3 Criteria and sub-criteria for Area C (MASUS)

Earlier research involving SFL analysis of a large corpus of student writing from different disciplines formed the basis of the descriptors of the instrument (Drury 1991; Drury and Webb 1991; Jones 1991; Jones *et al.* 1989). Analysis of these texts took into account the context for which the students were writing; for example, their course, the year of study, the assessment question, the course lecturers' written feedback and the final mark. Results of the analysis led to the development of an SFL framework for the diagnostic instrument, which was then linked to the academic writing component of the Centre's curriculum.

11.2 Recontextualizing the theory for staff and students

Since the instrument was designed to be used by both subject lecturers and Learning Centre lecturers, while the four main criteria do not change, different versions of the rating sheet are used, depending on who is responsible for the marking of the students' texts. If the marking is carried out by the course lecturers, we work with them to 'translate' the SFL technicality of the sub-descriptors into a mutually agreed version. In order to ensure the validity of the criteria in this translation process, a training session prior to the marking is conducted. This involves Centre lecturers training subject lecturers on the use of the instrument and a cross-marking session of some student texts, the object of which is to achieve a shared understanding of the meaning of the criteria. After the marking is complete students receive four separate ratings on each of the four main criteria, enabling them to identify areas of strength and weakness in their writing. They are also given a feedback sheet with explanations and annotated text examples of what the ratings mean and advice on the appropriate follow-up support they can access through the Learning Centre programmes or through lectures and tutorials in their department.

11.3 Facilitating a transdisciplinary approach to research

Since its beginning, the MASUS procedure has been used across the university in a number of departments with over 10,000 students (mainly first years) participating. Earlier research aimed to validate the instrument and to analyse the relationship between MASUS results and other student variables, such as language background and matriculation or Higher School Certificate (HSC) English score (Webb and Bonanno 1995; Webb *et al.* 1995). The MASUS model used in one faculty, Pharmacy, has been an integral component of the first-year course since 1993. More recently, the Faculty has been interested to explore with us through research, the writing profile of their students and examine its relationship to a range of other variables. Three studies were conducted between 1995 and 1999, which examined the relationship of MASUS ratings to students' progression through the degree, to selection procedures, and to students' choice of school subjects in their final school year examination (for full reports see Holder *et al.* 1999; Jones *et al.* 2000a; Jones *et al.* 2000b).

The findings of these studies, together with the demands of the profession, have been powerful incentives for the Faculty of Pharmacy to retain a high focus on the communication skills of their students in their curriculum. The MASUS project in pharmacy and its related research and teaching out-comes have facilitated an ongoing dialogue about student writing between the key partners in the process – Pharmacy staff, Learning Centre staff and students. It has been critical to keep this dialogue open to enable productive negotiation across disciplinary boundaries.

Over the years the MASUS diagnostic procedure has played a key role in the Learning Centre's faculty partnerships and has been a crucial agent in changing perceptions about student writing. Across the institution, the project has helped raise awareness of the complexities of academic writing in the disciplines and of the need for an explicit focus on students' writing development within the context of their course. An important part of the Centre's role is to facilitate the integration of such a perspective into the students' curriculum, thereby demonstrating to lecturers and students that academic writing is not a neutral enterprise but is shaped by socially driven purposes and contexts.

12 Concluding comments

Although the curriculum of the Learning Centre has been designed to reflect institutional goals and policies which are related to the development of students' generic attributes, it is nevertheless predicated on a socially framed and theoretically driven approach to practice. Our perceptions of the Centre's institutional role and our responses to student needs have helped to shape a mutually reinforcing cycle of research and practice. As I have shown in this chapter, the SFL theory underpinning the research and practice of the Learning Centre has been recontextualized to serve as a powerful technology to help build students' and teachers' understanding of how and why language works in the way it does. The theory has been applied to give students the necessary tools to learn how a text is linked to its context and to reflect on their roles as writers in these contexts. The theory has also helped to facilitate dialogue about student writing with teachers in the disciplines and about how this writing should be assessed. Since students want a metalanguage they can use and we as teachers of writing need a metalanguage to talk to them and to their subject teachers about language, the 'consumability' of SFL theory (Martin 1998) for a Centre such as ours is eminently appealing. Part of this appeal derives from the fact that the theory 'is premised on the complete interconnectedness of the linguistic and the social' which provides a 'resource for developing students' awareness of both the fundamentally social nature of the literate practices they are engaged in and how they are socially positioned by these practices' (Unsworth 2000: 245).

Learning centres in universities in Australia provide an academic learning support service to a very diverse student body. This service orientation, as I have shown, can and should not preclude a critical and theoretically driven approach to practice. The central location of such units also provides the opportunity to move beyond highly individualized and ad hoc responses to requests for service towards an approach which is both strategic in its application and capable of shaping transdisciplinary perspectives on language and learning. This entails working collaboratively across disciplinary divides and engaging productively with various perceptions of language and learning, thereby creating potentially powerful partnerships across the institution. Whether we align ourselves with the more empowered conceptions of our role as change agents and as 'campus mediators' through these partnerships depends on us and our beliefs about how language functions in context.

References

Allison, D. (1996) 'Pragmatist discourse and English for academic purposes', *Pergamon*, 15(2), 85–103.

Barton, D. (1994) *Literacy: An Introduction to the Ecology of Written Language*. Oxford: Blackwell.

Baynham, M. (2000) 'Academic writing in new and emergent discipline areas', in M.R. Lea and B. Stierer (eds), *Student Writing in Higher Education: New Contexts*. Buckingham: The Society for Research into Higher Education and Open University Press, pp. 17–31.

Bazerman, C. (1988) *Shaping Written Knowledge: The Genre and Activity of the Experimental Article in Science*. Madison, WI: University of Wisconsin Press.

Bazerman, C. (1998) 'Charles Bazerman on John Swales: An interview with Tony Dudley-Evans', *English for Specific Purposes*, 17(1), 105–12.

Benesch, S. (1993) 'ESL, ideology, and the politics of pragmatism', *TESOL Quarterly*, 27(4), 705–16.

Benesch, S. (1996) 'Needs analysis and curriculum development in EAP', *TESOL Quarterly*, 23, 421–45.

Benesch, S. (1999) 'Rights analysis: studying power in an academic setting', *English for Specific Purposes*, 18(4), 313–27.

Bennett, N., Dunne, E. and Carre, C. (1999) 'Patterns of core and generic skill provision in higher education', *Higher Education*, 37(1), 71–93.

Bhatia, V.K. (1993) *Analysing Genres: Language Use of Professional Settings*. London: Longman.

Blumner, J., Eliason, J. and Fritz, F. (2001) 'Beyond the reactive: WAC programs and the steps ahead', *The WAC Journal*, 12, 21–36.

Bonanno, H. and Jones, J. (1997) *Measuring the Academic Skills of University Students: The MASUS Procedure: A Diagnostic Assessment*. Sydney: Learning Centre Publications, University of Sydney.

Candlin, C.N. and Hyland, K. (eds) (1999) *Writing: Texts, Processes and Practices*. New York: Addison Wesley Longman Limited.

Candlin, C.N. and Plum, G. (eds) (1998) *Researching Academic Literacies: Framing Student Literacy: Cross-cultural Aspects of Communication Skills in Australian University Settings*. Sydney: NCELTR, Macquarie University.

Candy, P., Crebert, G. and O'Leary, J. (1994) *Developing Lifelong Learners Through Undergraduate Education: Commissioned Report No. 28*. Canberra, ACT: National Board of Employment Education and Training (Australian Government Publishing Service).

Chanock, K. (2000) *Sources of Confusion: Refereed Proceedings of the National Language and Academic Skills Conference*. Melbourne: La Trobe University.

Clark, R. and Ivanič, R. (1997) *The Politics of Writing*. London: Routledge.

Drury, H. (1991) 'The use of systemic linguistics to describe student summaries at university level' in E. Ventola (ed.), *Functional and Systemic Linguistics: Approaches and Uses*. Berlin: Mouton de Gruyter, pp. 431–56.

Drury, H. and Webb, C. (1991) 'Teaching academic writing at the tertiary level', *Prospect*, 7(1), 7–21.

Dudley-Evans, T. (1984) 'The team-teaching of writing skills', in R. Williams, J.M. Swales and J. Kirkman (eds), *Common Ground: Shared Interests in ESP and Communication Studies. ELT Documents 117*. Oxford: Pergamon, pp. 127–34.

Dudley-Evans, T. (2001) 'Team-teaching in EAP: changes and adaptations in the Birmingham Approach', in J. Flowerdew and M. Peacock (eds), *Research Perspectives on English for Academic Purposes*. Cambridge: Cambridge University Press, pp. 225–39.

Fairclough, N. (1992) *Critical Language Awareness*. London: Longman.

Feez, S. (2002) 'Heritage and innovation in second language education', in A.M. Johns, (ed) *Genre in the Classroom: Multiple Perspectives*. Mahwah, NJ: Lawrence Erlbaum Associates, pp. 43–69.

Flowerdew, J. (ed.) (2002) *Academic discourse*. Harlow: Longman.

Flowerdew, J. and Peacock, M. (eds) (2001) *Research Perspectives on English for Academic Purposes*. Cambridge: Cambridge University Press.

Freedman, A. and Medway, P. (eds) (1994) *Learning and Teaching Genre*. Portsmouth, NH: Heinemann/Boynton Cook.

Gibbs, G., Rust, C., Jenkins, A. and Jacques, J. (1994) *Developing Students' Transferable Skills*. Oxford: Oxford Centre for Staff Development.

Golebiowski, Z. (1997) *Policy and Practice of Tertiary Literacy Volume 1: Proceedings of the First National Conference on Tertiary Literacy: Research and Practice March 1996*. Victoria University of Technology, Melbourne.

Green, B. and Lee, A. (1994) 'Writing geography lessons: literacy, identity and schooling', in A. Freedman and P. Medway (eds), *Learning and Teaching Genre*. Portsmouth, NH: Heinemann/Boynton Cook, pp. 207–24.

Halliday, M.A.K. (1985) *An Introduction to Functional Grammar*. London: Edward Arnold.

Halliday, M.A.K. and Hasan, R. (1976) *Cohesion in English* 9th edn. London: Longman.

Halliday, M.A.K. and Hasan, R. (1985) *Language, Context and Text: Aspects of Language in a Social-Semiotic Perspective.* Geelong, Victoria: Deakin University Press.

Halliday, M.A.K. and Martin, J.R. (1993) *Writing Science: Literacy and Discursive Power.* London: Falmer.

Hewings, M. (ed.) (2001) *Academic Writing in Context: Implications and Applications.* Birmingham: University of Birmingham Press.

Holder, G.M., Jones, J., Robinson, R. and Krass, I. (1999) 'Academic literacy skills and progression rates amongst pharmacy students', *Higher Education Research and Development,* 18(1), 19–30.

Hyon, S. (1996) 'Genre in three traditions: implications for ESL', *TESOL Quarterly,* 30, 693–722.

Ivanič, R. (1998) *Writing and Identity: The Discoursal Construction of Identity in Academic Writing.* Amsterdam: John Benjamins.

Johns, A.M. (1997) *Text, Role, and Context: Developing Academic Literacies.* New York: Cambridge University Press.

Johns, A.M. (2001) 'ESL students and WAC programs: varied populations and diverse needs', in S. McLeod, E. Miraglia, M. Soven and C. Thaiss (eds), *WAC for the New Millennium: Strategies for Continuing Writing-Across-The-Curriculum Programs.* Urbana, IL: National Council of Teachers of English, pp. 141–64.

Johns, A.M. (ed.) (2002) *Genre in the Classroom: Multiple Perspectives.* Mahwah, NJ: Lawrence Erlbaum Associates.

Jones, C., Turner, J. and Street, B. (eds) (1999) *Students Writing in the University: Cultural and Epistemological Issues.* Amsterdam: John Benjamins.

Jones, J. (1991) 'Grammatical metaphor and technicality in academic writing: An exploration of ESL (English as a Second Language) and NS (Native Speaker) student texts' in F. Christie, (ed.). *Literacy in Social Processes: proceedings of the Inaugural Systemic Linguistics Conference, 1990, Deakin University, Victoria January 1990.* Darwin: Centre for Studies of Language in Education, Northern Territory University.

Jones, J., Holder, G.M. and Robinson, R. (2000a) 'School subjects and academic literacy skills at university', *Australian Journal of Career Development,* 9(2), 27–31.

Jones, J., Gollin, S., Drury, H. and Economou, D. (1989) 'Systemic functional linguistics and its application to the TESOL curriculum', in R. Hasan and J.R. Martin (eds), *Language Development: Learning Language, Learning Culture: Meaning and Choice in Language: Studies for Michael Halliday* (Vol. 27). Norwood, NJ: Ablex, pp. 257–328.

Jones, J., Holder, G.M., Robinson, R. and Krass, I. (2000b) 'Selecting pharmacy students with appropriate communication skills', *American Journal of Pharmaceutical Education,* 64, 68–73.

Latour, B. (1987) *Science in Action: How to Follow Scientists and Engineers Through Society.* Cambridge, MA: Harvard University Press.

Lea, M.R. (1999) 'Academic literacies and learning in higher education: constructing knowledge through texts and experience', in C. Jones, J. Turner and B. Street (eds), *Students Writing in the University: Cultural and Epistemological Issues.* Amsterdam: John Benjamins, pp. 103–24.

Lea, M.R. and Stierer, B. (eds) (2000) *Student Writing in Higher Education: New Contexts.* Buckingham: The Society for Research into Higher Education and Open University Press.

Lea, R.A. and Street, B. (1998) 'Student writing in higher education: an academic literacies approach', *Studies in Higher Education*, 23(2), 157–72.

LeCourt, D. (1996) 'WAC as critical pedagogy: the third stage?', *A Journal of Composition Theory*, 16, 389–405.

Lee, A., Baynham, M., Beck, D., Gordon, K. and San Miguel, C. (1995) 'Researching discipline specific academic literacy practices: some methodological issues' in A. Zelmer, C. Lynn (eds). Proceedings of the 1995 Annual Conference of the Higher Education Research and Development Society of Australasia (HERDSA). Central Queensland University pp. 464–469.

Macken-Horarik, M. (2002) ' "Something to shoot for": a systemic functional approach to teaching genre in secondary school science', in A.M. Johns (ed.), *Genre in the Classroom: Multiple Perspectives.* Mahwah, NJ: Lawrence Erlbaum Associates, pp. 17–42.

Martin, J.R. (1992) *English Text: System and Structure.* Amsterdam: John Benjamins.

Martin, J.R. (1998) 'Linguistics and the consumer', *Linguistics and Education*, 9(4), 411–48.

Martin, J.R. (1999) 'Mentoring semogenesis: "Genre-based" literacy pedagogy', in F. Christie (ed.), *Pedagogy and the Shaping of Consciousness: Linguistic and Social Processes.* London: Cassell, pp. 123–55.

Martin, J.R. (2000a) 'Beyond exchange: appraisal resources in English', in S. Hunston and G. Thompson (eds), *Evaluation in Text: Authorial Stance and the Construction of Discourse.* Oxford: Oxford University Press, pp. 142–75.

Martin, J.R. (2000b) 'Design and practice: enacting functional linguistics', *Annual Review of Applied Linguistics*, 20, 116–26.

Marton, F. and Booth, S. (1997) *Learning and Awareness.* Mahwah, NJ: Lawrence Erlbaum Associates.

Marton, F., Hounsell, D. and Entwistle, N. (eds) (1997) *The Experience of Learning.* Edinburgh: Scottish Academic Press.

McLeod, S. and Maimon, E. (2000) 'Clearing the air: WAC myths and realities', *College English*, 62(5), 573–83.

McLeod, S., Miraglia, E., Soven, M. and Thaiss, C. (eds) (2001) *WAC for the New Millennium: Strategies for Continuing Writing-Across-The-Curriculum Programs.* Urbana, IL: National Council of Teachers of English.

Myers, G. (1990) *Writing Biology: Texts in the Social Construction of Scientific Knowledge.* Madison, WI: The University of Wisconsin Press.

Paltridge, B. (2001) 'Linguistic research and EAP pedagogy', in J. Flowerdew and M. Peacock (eds). *Research Perspectives on English for Academic Purposes.* Cambridge: Cambridge University Press, pp. 55–70.

Pennycook, A. (1994) *The Cultural Politics of English as an International Language.* London: Addison Wesley Longman.

Pennycook, A. (1997) 'Vulgar pragmatism, critical pragmatism, and EAP', *Pergamon*, 16(4), 253–69.

Rothery, J. and Stenglin, M. (2000) 'Interpreting literature: the role of appraisal', in L. Unsworth (ed.), *Researching Language in Schools and Communities: Functional Linguistic Perspectives.* London: Cassell, pp. 222–44.

Street, B. (1984) *Literacy in Theory and Practice.* Cambridge: Cambridge University Press.

Street, B. (1999) 'Academic literacies', in C. Jones, J. Turner and B. Street (eds), *Students Writing in the University: Cultural and Epistemological Issues.* Amsterdam: John Benjamins, pp. 193–228.

Swales, J.M. (1990) *Genre Analysis: English in Academic and Research Settings.* Cambridge: Cambridge University Press.

Swales, J.M. (2001) 'EAP-related linguistic research: an intellectual history', in J.A Flowerdew and M. Peacock (eds), *Research Perspectives on English for Academic Purposes.* Cambridge: Cambridge University Press, pp. 42–55.

Threadgold, T., Absalom, D. and Golebiowski, Z. (1997) 'Tertiary literacy conference summary: what will count as tertiary literacy in the year 2000?'. in Policy and Practice of Tertiary Literacy Volume 1, Proceedings of the First National Conference on Tertiary Literacy 1996, Victoria University of Technology, Melbourne.

Unsworth, L. (ed.) (2000) *Researching Language in Schools and Communities.* London: Cassell.

Villanueva, V. (2001) 'The politics of literacy across the curriculum', in S. McLeod and E. Miraglia, M. Soven and C. Thaiss (eds), *WAC for the New Millennium: Strategies for Continuing Writing-Across-The-Curriculum Programs.* Urbana, IL: National Council of Teachers of English, pp. 165–78.

Webb, C. and Bonanno, H. (1995) 'Assessing the literacy skills of an increasingly diverse student population', *Research and Development in Higher Education, Higher Education Research and Development Society of Australasia, 17,* electronic version.

Webb, C., Drury, H. and English, L. (1995) 'Collaboration in subject design: integration of the teaching and assessment of literacy skills into a first year accounting course', *Accounting Education,* 4(4), 335–50.

Young, A. (1999) *Teaching Writing Across the Curriculum* 3rd edn. New Jersey: Prentice Hall.

Index

academic literacies framework
  Australia 260
  United Kingdom 258–9
  United States 259–60
academic socialization 259
academic writing
  ethnography 88–9
  standards 254
  teaching on screen 233–53
advance labels 118, 119
AFFECT 26, 30, 31, 159–60
Allison, D 256
anonymity, writers' 74–7
appeals to readers 8
appeals to shared knowledge 20–1
APPRAISAL 7, 26, 28–9, 153, 156, 159–66
APPRECIATION 26, 30–1, 159–60
art and design masters degrees 90–101
assessment genre 9, 14, 66, 214–15
ATTITUDE
  categories 26, 27, 159
  evoked 32
  explicit 27, 29
  field analysis 32
  implicit 29
  inscribed 32
  managing 24–44
  means for evoking 26
  prosodies 32–7
attitudinal meanings 27
attributive relational process 199
audience 6, 85–6, 93–4
Austria, business studies 62
author roles, student writers 45–65
authority, textual 70–4, 78, 187
autobiography 74–7

Baynham, M 260
Bazerman, C 88
Becher, T 96
Benesch, S 256
Berkenkotter, C 86–7
Bernstein, B 211, 212
Berry, M 162
Bhatia, VK 257
bias
  in education 212
  marking 66
Biber, D 136, 157
boundaries, phase 40–2
Brookes, A 86
bulletin board 224
business studies, Austria 62
business writing, German 45–65
Butler, C 47

Canagarajah, S 86
Candlin, C 260
chains of reasoning 104, 107
challenge 67, 110
Chanock, K 262
Chinese EFL writing 190–209
Chinese language, grammatical features
  200
classification 212–13, 227–30
clause complexes, analysis 139–40
Cloran, C 137
Clyne, MG 47
Coffin, C 111, 166
colligational patterns 117–22
congruent realization 191
Conrad, S 136, 157
context analysis 88–9

Davies, F 138, 162
deconstruction 211, 214, 216–22, 235, 240
directives 15–19
disciplines, academic
    communities 131–3
    cultures 96
    differences in writing 105, 122–4
    discourse features 11
discourse communities 131, 132
discourses 227–30

EFL 7, 153, 174, 190–209
elaboration 107–8, 112
ENGAGEMENT 5–23, 160
    features 7–9, 10–11
    patterns 10–11
engineering students 173
English as a Foreign Language 7, 153, 174, 190–209
English as a Second Language 7, 153, 172–3, 174
    SFL perspective 187–8
English for Academic Purposes 131–2, 256–7
English language competence 153
enhancement 107–8, 110–11, 112
ESL 7, 153, 172–3, 174
    SFL perspective 187–8
essays
    argumentative 105–12, 154–69
    geography 134–49
    history 105, 110–12
    management 105, 107–10
    presentation 71
    socio-political perspective 67, 68
    structure 71, 105–12
    thematic structure 135–49
ethnographic research, South Africa 69
evaluation 24, 25, 36, 37–9, 136, 137, 185
examinations 78
exegesis
    audience 93–4
    as genre 84–103
    language 99–100
    purpose 92–3
    relationship with other texts 97–8
    structure 94–6, 98
expansion 104, 107–8

'expert' texts 9–10
exposition 190
extension 107–8, 112

Fairclough, N 71, 84
Feak, C 97
Feez, S 262
field 29, 32
Flowerdew, J 257
foreign language learning, mother-tongue interference 199–203, 205
framing 212–13, 222–3
Francis, G 118, 119

generic nouns 117
generic structure 242
genre 86–8, 97
genre analysis 256–7
genre-based literacy pedagogy
    computer, interaction with 244–8
    curriculum 235
    peer interaction 248–9
    student concepts 238–9
    student/teacher interactions 243–4, 248–9
    teacher concepts 239–43
    teacher interaction 243–4
    technology, integration of 210–32, 233–53
geography
    as a discipline 133–4
    essays 134–49
    undergraduate writing 134–49
German business writing 45–65
Golebiowski, Z 262
Grabe, W 88
GRADUATION 26–30, 160
grammar 190–1
    teaching 204–5
grammatical metaphor 117, 121–2, 174–87
    textual metaphors 180
Grundy, P 86

Halliday, MAK 46, 104, 107, 137, 144, 174, 183, 191, 195, 198, 262
Hamp-Lyons, L 67
harmonies of attitudinal value 39–40
HEARSAY 161–3, 165–6, 168–9

hedged performatives 47
Hewings, A 162, 167
Hewings, M 167
Hoey, M 118
Hogue, A 113
Hong Kong undergraduates 9
Huckin, TN 86–7
Hunston, S 136, 185
Hyland, K 47, 61, 96, 136, 141
Hyon, S 262
hyper-New 163
hyper-Themes 112–24
hyperlinks 240, 245
hypertext environment 240–3

identity, in academic writing 67–9, 78
IELTS 153–71
individual construction activities 211,
    214, 224–5, 235
interactional resources 6–7
International English Language Testing
    System 153–71
interpersonal grammatical metaphor
    183
interpersonal meanings 5, 25, 32, 36
intersubjective meaning 183–6
Ivanič, R 68

Johns, AM 85, 259–60, 261, 262
joint construction activities 211, 214,
    222–4, 235, 243–4
JUDGEMENT 26, 30, 159–60

Kamler, B 86
Kaplan, R 88
Kress, G 68

laboratory reports 175–86, 236, 241–3
    hyperlink design 246–7
Laurillard, D 238
Lea, M 84, 261
Lea, RA 258–9
Learning Centre, University of Sydney
    262–9
learning centres 255, 261–2, 269
literacy pedagogy, genre-based
    See genre-based literacy pedagogy
literacy practices 132–3
literature review, writing 263–6
logico-semantic relations 107, 108

Macken-Horarik, M 262
macro-New 163
macro-phenomena 195
Malinowski, B 132
marking
    anonymous 66
    bias 66
    objectivity 75
Martin, JR 7, 26, 27, 29, 112, 113, 162,
    163, 186, 193, 262
MASUS project 266–8
Matthiessen, C 135, 195
Mauranen, A 162
metacommunication 49
metadiscursive devices 47, 118
metafunctions 48
metalinguistic labels 118
metaphorical language, grammatical
    problems 194
metaphorical realization 191, 192
metaphors 196
modal responsibility 183–6
modal verbs
    English 47
    German 47
modality
    explicit 183–6
    function in language 46
    implicit 183–6
    objective 183–6
    subjective 183–6
modalization 46
modals
    academic texts 47
    deontic 47, 49–54, 57–9, 60, 61
    epistemic 47, 49–57, 60
    metacommunicative 51–4
    (non)-metacommunicative 54–9
modulation 46
mother-tongue interference, foreign
    language learning 199–203, 205

native speakers 176
nominalizations 196
non-native English speakers 7, 153, 174

online learning environments 234,
    236–8, 240–3, 245–6, 248
organizing vocabulary 117–18
Oshima, A 113

Paltridge, B 262
Panther, K-U 47
paragraphs, relations between 105–12
Peacock, M 257
Pennycook, A 256
persuasion 136
phase boundaries 40–2
plant science study 214–30
post-modification 119–20
power relations 68
pre-modification 120–1
Prior, P 87
prior knowledge 238
proficient writers 177–85
PRONOUNCE 161–5, 167–9
pronouns
    inclusive 13–15
    second person 12
proposals 46
prosodies of attitude 32–7
prospective connections 119
Prosser, M 71

questions 19–20

Ravelli, LJ 162
reaction 31
reader-in-the-text 6
reader participation 15–16
readers
    appeals to 8
    expectations of inclusion 8
    rhetorical position 8
    solidarity with 11–15
realization relationship 191
reasoning 177–8
recontextualization 228
register, academic 174, 176, 186
reports, final-year 9
retrospective labels 118, 119
Rheme 157
rhetorical strategy 166–9
Rose, D 27
Rothery, J 27, 29

scaffolding 243–5, 248
science students 13, 173
science study, assessment 214–15
scientific discourses 104, 132, 173, 185
scientific writing database 216–22

scientific writing portfolio 215–16
second language writers 173, 176–85
semiotic abstractions 117
Simpson, J 68
social science students 13
solidarity, with readers 11–15
South Africa
    ethnographic research 69
    student writing 66–83
Spack, R 100
stance 6–7
    ambiguities 37–9
    evaluative 24, 25, 36
    interpersonal 186–7
Stenglin, M 27, 29
Stierer, B 261
Street, B 132–3, 258–9
student writing, South Africa 66–83
students, educational background 71
study skills 259
Swales, JM 85, 97, 257, 262
'Sydney School' 262
systemic functional linguistics
    IELTS 153
    Learning Centre, University of Sydney
        262–3
    and student writing 174–5, 261, 262
    use in teaching 263–8
Systemic Functional Linguistics
        Academic Literacy Project 210

taxonomies 109, 195
teaching academic writing, on screen
        233–53
teaching/learning cycle 211–12, 235–8
    deconstruction phase 211, 214,
        216–22, 235, 240
    independent construction phase 211,
        214, 224–5, 235
    integration 249–51
    joint construction phase 211, 214,
        222–4, 235, 243–4
    modelling phase 235
    reflection 249–51
technical writing, in a second language
        172–89
technicality 177–8, 186
technology, integration into literacy
        pedagogy 210–11, 225–7, 233–53
text deconstruction 216–22

textual authority 70–4, 78
textual markers 120–1
textual metaphors 180
textual structuring 178–82, 187
thematic progression 135
Theme 112, 153, 156–7
    analysis 139–40, 158–9, 166–9
    classification 137–9, 157–8
    interpersonal 137, 146, 157, 162
    marked 158
    multiple 143–7, 158
    significance 135–9
    textual 157
    thematic structure of essays 135–49
    topical 157
    unmarked topical 140–3
theses
    structure 98
    writing 84–5
Thing 195
things
    conscious 196, 197
    taxonomy 195
Thompson, G 6, 136, 139, 156–7
Threadgold, T 86, 87
Tickoo, ML 88
Token 197, 198
topic sentences 113, 118–19, 163
Trowler, PR 96

University of Sydney, Learning Centre
    262–9

valuation 31
Value 197, 198
van Leeuwen, T 49

Webb, C 71
Webber, P 19
White, P 7
Whittaker, R 137, 162
Wignell, P 142
Winter, E 118
writer-reader relations 5–23, 94
writers
    anonymity 74–7
    authorial self 69
    autobiographical self 69, 74
    identity 67–9
    proficient 177–85
    representation of self 69
    roles 60, 61
writing, academic
    See academic writing
writing across the curriculum 257–8
writing skills, diagnostic test 266–8

Zamel, V 100
Zhou, J 136